Shakespeare without Fear
A User-Friendly Guide to Acting Shakespeare

Joseph Olivieri
University of California at Los Angeles

Harcourt College Publishers
Fort Worth   Philadelphia   San Diego   New York   Orlando   Austin   San Antonio
Toronto   Montreal   London   Sydney   Tokyo

Publisher	Earl McPeek
Executive Editor	David C. Tatom
Acquisitions Editor	John Swanson
Developmental Editor	Michelle Vardemann
Market Strategist	Adrienne Krysiuk
Project Editor	Claudia Gravier
Art Director	Burl Sloan
Production Manager	Serena Sipho

Cover credit: Kevin McIntyre

ISBN: 0-15-508038-5

Library of Congress Catalog Card Number: 00-134029

Copyright © 2001 by Harcourt, Inc.

All rights reserved. No part of this publication may be reproduced or transmitted in any form or by any means, electronic or mechanical, including photocopy, recording, or any information storage and retrieval system, without permission in writing from the publisher.

Requests for permission to make copies of any part of the work should be mailed to: Permissions Department, Harcourt Brace & Company, 6277 Sea Harbor Drive, Orlando, FL 32887–6777.

Address for Domestic Orders
Harcourt College Publishers, 6277 Sea Harbor Drive, Orlando, FL 32887-6777
800-782-4479

Address for International Orders
International Customer Service
Harcourt Inc., 6277 Sea Harbor Drive, Orlando, FL 32887-6777
407-345-3800
(fax) 407-345-4060
(e-mail) hbintl@harcourtbrace.com

Address for Editorial Correspondence
Harcourt College Publishers, 301 Commerce Street, Suite 3700, Fort Worth, TX 76102

Web Site Address
http://www.harcourtcollege.com

Harcourt College Publishers will provide complimentary supplements or supplement packages to those adopters qualified under our adoption policy. Please contact your sales representative to learn how you qualify. If as an adopter or potential user you receive supplements you do not need, please return them to your sales representative or send them to: Attn: Returns Department, Troy Warehouse, 465 South Lincoln Drive, Troy, MO 63379.

Printed in the United States of America

0 1 2 3 4 5 6 7 8 9   039   9 8 7 6 5 4 3 2 1

Harcourt College Publishers

For Catherine

 is

A Harcourt Higher Learning Company

Now you will find Harcourt Brace's distinguished innovation, leadership, and support under a different name... a new brand that continues our unsurpassed quality, service, and commitment to education.

We are combining the strengths of our college imprints into one worldwide brand: Harcourt

Our mission is to make learning accessible to anyone, anywhere, anytime—reinforcing our commitment to lifelong learning.

We are now Harcourt College Publishers. Ask for us by name.

One Company
"Where Learning Comes to Life."

www.harcourtcollege.com
www.harcourt.com

About the Author

Joe Olivieri is currently a Visiting Associate Professor in the Theater Department at UCLA where he directs and teaches Period Acting styles with a primary focus on acting Shakespeare. Prior to joining the faculty at UCLA he was head of the MFA and BFA Acting programs at West Virginia University for nine years. He has an MFA in Acting from the prestigious American Conservatory Theatre, renowned for its classical actor training and has acted in television and in regional theatre, including Denver Center Theatre, PCPA Theaterfest, San Jose Repertory Company, Pittsburgh's City Theater and eight seasons with the Carnegie Mellon Showcase of New Plays. He is a founding member of the highly regarded, multi-award winning Pacific Resident Theatre in Los Angeles where he acts and directs. He has acted in and directed many productions of Shakespeare in both professional and university settings. He and his wife, actress Catherine Telford, live with their three cats in the Silver Lake area of Los Angeles.

PREFACE

The desire to write this book came from years of teaching classes in acting Shakespeare and Renaissance Drama with the aid of a few select chapters from many different textbooks I found to be of value to my student actors. I could find no single book that met all of my needs. Some texts that I read on acting Shakespeare were incomplete, highbrow or patronizing. Others were solid, useful texts but only of true benefit to those actors who already had some knowledge and experience acting his plays. I wanted to write a thorough, step-by-step book on acting Shakespeare that was straightforward and accessible.

I must also admit that I was just plain sick and tired of reading and hearing about *how difficult it is to act Shakespeare!* Yes, it's true. Acting Shakespeare is difficult. So what? So is anything worth doing well— playing the violin, downhill skiing, baking a soufflé. I know this may sound blasphemous, but I believe the awe and reverence that surround the works of Shakespeare serve to frighten the creative artist rather than inspire him. The fact is that the skills required to act Shakespeare are for the most part clear, objective and eminently attainable. Another bit of good news is that these specialized acting skills can be seamlessly married to those basic skills the actor uses when performing the plays of say, Arthur Miller, David Mamet and Wendy Wasserstein. Further, I have found that after a semester or two of working on Shakespeare, the actor most often has a newfound understanding of how to act in the plays of twentieth and twenty-first century playwrights.

Shakespeare without Fear begins at the beginning by delving into the meaning of Shakespeare's dialogue. It then reminds the actor that, when acting Shakespeare, it is essential to use all of the skills acquired while learning to act the plays of modern playwrights; these include objectives, actions, obstacles, personalizations and motivations. This is the bedrock for all actors hoping to bring Shakespeare's dramas to life on stage. After exploring what the character is saying and why he is saying it, I spend a good deal of time breaking down speeches and scenes into their component parts. Only in this way can the actor truly understand his character's journey and communicate that journey to his fellow actors and his audience with clarity and theatricality. The second half of the book focuses primarily on acting skills specific to Elizabethan theatre and theatre of elevated language in general: verse, scansion, rhetoric and text work. These skills are technical in nature but serve to help the actor speak with clarity, specificity, dynamism and depth of meaning and intent. They also assist the actor in finding and expressing the emotional core of Shakespeare's words.

The chapters that deal with uncovering Shakespeare's meaning, verse, scansion, rhetoric and text may at first seem a little daunting. I believe that one must be exhaustively thorough when first working on these areas of Shakespeare's dramatic dialogue.

The work comes much more readily and easily with time. Further, the information in this book, especially the information contained in technical sections, is not meant to be grasped fully in one reading. The actor should use individual chapters as guides and may wish to continually refer to them when working on a speech, scene or play. The detailed chapter summaries and suggested exercises will go a long way in reinforcing this important information both cerebrally and viscerally. This is meant to be a workbook. Please dog-ear pages, highlight passages, write in the margins and put the book through its paces. It is not meant to sit on a shelf.

The book is written in dialogue form, as a series of conversations between two fictitious students and myself. I spent the better part of a year writing a first draft of this text. When I sat down to work on a second draft, what had been evident to me on an unconscious level for some time finally became indisputable: although I fought against it, the book had a somewhat didactic, preachy tone. This was neither the way I taught Shakespeare nor the way I learned to act Shakespeare at the American Conservatory Theatre. It was neither the way I communicated with actors when I directed Shakespeare nor the way I communicated with directors when I acted Shakespeare. Rather, my experiences with the plays of Shakespeare revolved around diligent homework and practical work in the rehearsal space combined with *conversations*—conversations that involved the exchange of information through questions and answers, misunderstandings and clarifications, edifications and discoveries. These conversations were invaluable to me in informing the practical workings of rehearsal and performance, regardless of whether I was playing the role of actor, director or teacher. I found that casting aside my first draft and rewriting the book as a series of conversations was the ideal way to help the actor's work at home, in the classroom, in the rehearsal room, and on stage. It also keeps the actors' concerns at the forefront. My fictitious students, while vehicles for the dissemination of information, are really a synthesis of the questions, concerns and needs of my students, cast members and myself, throughout my years of teaching, directing and acting Shakespeare.

No acting textbook, regardless of its merit, can or should be the sole focus in the classroom. No printed material can replace the sweat, hard work and human interaction of the rehearsal room. However, a text, a *good* text, must assist the actor before and between class and rehearsal work. That is the goal of *Shakespeare without Fear*. It is meant to be a companion, a guide to complement the work of the instructor or director and to help shepherd the artist toward becoming the most competent actor of Shakespeare possible. I hope that you find it useful.

Acknowledgements

I want to thank my wife, Catherine Telford, for being my first editor and for her advice and insight into acting Shakespeare; Judy Moreland, my friend and colleague, for writing the section on text diagramming; my development editor, the incomparable Michelle Vardeman, for her skill and patience; Barbara Rosenberg for her generosity and guidance and—oh yeah—for offering me a book contract; John Swanson, for seeing the project through to completion; my project editor, Claudia Gravier for her guidance and thoroughness; Travis Tyre for his advice; the rest of the Harcourt book team: Serena Sipho, production manager and Burl Sloan, art director; my copyeditor, Michele Gitlin, for her expertise; the Theater faculty, administration and staff at UCLA and the Theater faculty, administration and staff at West Virginia University for their support; Nancy Houfek, Charlotte Fleck and Crystal Brian for their insightful and constructive criticism of my first draft; Lynne Soffer for her suggestions on research material; Janet Morrison, Jim Schlatter, Donna Snow, Frank and Sandy Gagliano, Gene Terruso, Laura Henry, Bob Leigh, Cheryl Donchey and Mel Shapiro for their support; my family, particularly my parents; my friends; my teachers and peers at the American Conservatory Theatre; my students at WVU and UCLA; my peers at Pacific Resident Theatre; Kurt Shore, my first partner in the creative arts; Jerry McGonigle, Victor Pappas, and Phil Beck, with whom I share a long-time love of Shakespeare; and finally, my mentors Jim Stanton, Irene Baird, Les Muchmore, Dugald MacArthur and Allen Fletcher.

Joe Olivieri
October 2000

BRIEF CONTENTS

Preface   vii

Introduction   xix

Chapter 1
    Where Do I Begin?   1

Chapter 2
    What Is My Character Saying?   7

Chapter 3
    Overview of Basic Acting Skills Applied to Shakespeare   26

Chapter 4
    Speeches   39

Chapter 5
    Scenes—The First Steps   80

Chapter 6
    Introduction to Scansion   106

Chapter 7
    Exploring Iambic Pentameter   134

Chapter 8
    Exploring Shakespeare's Rhythms   191

Chapter 9
    Exploring Shakespeare's Prose   206

Chapter 10
    Exploring Shakespeare's Rhetorical Figures   217

Chapter 11
    Exploring the Text   237

Chapter 12
    Potpourri   281

Appendix
    Getting the Part, Finding the Scene, Getting Online   295

Glossary   305

Bibliography   311

Suggestions for Further Readings   313

Contents

Preface   vii

Introduction   xix

Chapter 1
Where Do I Begin?   1

    Essential Books for Acting Shakespeare   1
    Summary   4
    Exercises   5

Chapter 2
What Is My Character Saying?   7

    Understanding Romeo's Speech   7
    Understanding Juliet's Speech   16
    Analyzing Shakespeare's Sentence Structure   21
    Summary   22
    Exercises   23

Chapter 3
Overview of Basic Acting Skills Applied to Shakespeare   26

    Objectives, Obstacles, Actions, and Motivations   26
    Substitution, Personalization, and Instincts   30
    Given and Imaginary Circumstances   32
    Summary   35
    Exercises   36
    Notes   38

Chapter 4
Speeches   39

    Analyzing Soliloquies   39
        Analyzing Juliet's Speech   44
        Analyzing Romeo's Speech   46

Analyzing Other Soliloquies   47
  Edmund from *King Lear*   47
  Lady Macbeth from *Macbeth*   50
  Richard, Earl of Gloucester, from *Richard III*   53
  Brutus from *Julius Caesar*   57
  Viola from *Twelfth Night*   60
  Angelo from *Measure for Measure*   63
  Chorus from *Romeo and Juliet*   66
Analyzing Monologues   68
  Bullingbrook from *Richard II*   68
  Portia from *The Merchant of Venice*   71
Discovery in the Moment   74
  Concentrating Fully on the Other Person(s)   75
Summary   76
Exercises   77

Chapter 5
Scenes—The First Steps   80

Scene Work: How to Begin   80
  Paraphrase the Scene   84
  Consider Objectives   86
  Personalize   86
  Explore the Given and Imaginary Circumstances   87
  Be Specific about the Environment   88
  Consider the Fourth Wall   89
Scene Work: Breaking Down the Scene into Beats   90
  Analyze the Beats   90
  Discover the Flexibility of Acting Choices   93
Scene Work: Rehearsing the Scene   94
Summary   96
Exercises   97

Chapter 6
Introduction to Scansion   106

Elements of Written and Spoken English   107
Shakespeare's Dramatic Poetry   109
  Blank Verse   111
  Rhyming Verse   111
Scansion   114
Purposes of Iambic Pentameter   115
Compression and Expansion   116
  Compression   117
  Expansion   120
Levels of Stress in Iambic Pentameter   122
Pliancy of Iambic Pentameter   124
  Shared Lines   127
  The Prefix "Un"   128
  Accent Shifts   128
  Stress Not the Negative   129

Why Study Scansion?   130
Summary   131
Exercises   132
Notes   133

Chapter 7
Exploring Iambic Pentameter   134

Defining the Variations on Iambic Pentameter   134
   The Trochee   135
   The Feminine Foot   135
   The Spondee and the Pyrrhic   135
   The Anapaest   136
   Lines Longer and Shorter than Five Feet   136
   Initial and Medial Truncation   137
Reviewing the Iamb and the Iambic Line   137
Analyzing Details in Shakespeare's Verse   140
Exploring the Variations   141
   Exploring the Trochee   141
   Exploring the Feminine Foot   149
   Exploring the Spondee and the Pyrrhic   160
   Exploring the Anapaest   166
   Exploring Lines Longer and Shorter than Five Feet   170
   Exploring Truncation   180
Using the Caesura   184
   The Masculine Caesura   184
   The Epic Caesura   185
   The Lyric Caesura   185
   The Actor's Use of the Caesura   186
Summary   189
Exercises   189
Notes   190

Chapter 8
Exploring Shakespeare's Rhythms   191

Rhythmic Turbulence   192
Rhythmic Pacing   198
Phrasing   202
Summary   204
Exercises   204
Notes   205

Chapter 9
Exploring Shakespeare's Prose   206

The Purposes of Prose   206
The Actor's Use of Prose   215
Summary   216
Exercises   216
Notes   216

Chapter 10
Exploring Shakespeare's Rhetorical Figures   217

    Rhetoric Defined   217
    Rhetorical Figures   218
        Schemes   219
        Tropes   227
    The Actor's Use of Rhetorical Figures   233
    Summary   234
    Exercises   234
    Notes   236

Chapter 11
Exploring the Text   237

    Passion and Form   237
    Operative Words   238
        Identifying Operative Words   238
        Marking Operative Words   248
    Diagramming the Text   248
        Step 1: Place Braces ({ }) around Complete Sentences   249
        Step 2: Place Angle Brackets (< >) around Images Made of Two or More Words   250
        Step 3: Place Straight Brackets ([ ]) around the Predicate   251
        Step 4: Circle the Antithesis   253
        Step 5: Underline Alliteration and Assonance   253
        Step 6: Mark Run-On Lines with an Arrow   254
        Step 7: Mark Lists and Builds with Numbers   254
        Step 8: Put It All Together   255
    Speaking the Text   258
        The Three Ps: Punch, Pitch, and Pace   259
        Vocal Coloring   262
        Sound Texturing   263
        Vocalizing Antitheses   264
        Vocalizing Alliteration and Assonance   265
        Vocalizing Builds and Lists   266
        The Four Basic Inflections   267
        Vocalizing Parenthetical Words and Phrases   269
        Vocalizing Shared Builds and Shared Antitheses   270
        Modulating Shakespeare's Builds   272
        What Is Elevated Language?   273
    Summary   274
    Exercises   277
    Notes   280

Chapter 12
Potpourri   281

    Asides   281
    Stage Directions   283
    Language Peculiarities   284

"Thou" and "You"   284
The Royal "We"   284
Frequently Mispronounced Words   285
History of the Period   286
Elizabethan Philosophy   286
Great Chain of Being   286
The Four Elements and the Four Humors   287
Folios and Quartos   288
Shakespeare's Sonnets   288
Sound and Rhythm: A Reminder   289
Act on the Word   290
Subtext in Shakespeare   290
Summary   293

Appendix
Getting the Part, Finding the Scene, Getting Online   295

Auditioning   295
Choosing a Piece   296
Preparing Your Piece   297
The Audition Process   298
Acting Exercises: Recommended Scenes   299
Scenes for Two Women   300
Scenes for Two Men   300
Scenes for One Woman and One Man   301
Shakespeare on the Web   302
Summary   303
Exercises   304
Notes   304

Glossary   305

Bibliography   311

Suggestions for Further Reading   313

Introduction

Shakespeare—(Shak′spir), William 1564–1616; English poet and dramatist: also spelled Shakespere, Shakspere, etc.

without—1. Not with; lacking (a shirt without buttons) 2. Free from (without fear).

Fear—1. A feeling of anxiety or agitation caused by the presence or nearness of danger, evil, pain, etc.; timidity; dread; terror; fright; apprehension. 2. Respectful awe; reverence.

William Shakespeare. Two words that inspire either delight or dread.

This book is for the Theatre student and actor who is excited about learning to act Shakespeare's words but frightened that it will be a task equivalent to Quantum Physics. I hope to remove mystery and fear and replace them with clarity and confidence by exploring what we actors need to know in order to act Shakespeare *well* in a clear, step by step process, written in plain English.

In order to give this process a frame of reference, I will enlist the assistance of two fictitious college acting students—one female and one male.

Let's get started.

CHAPTER 1

Where Do I Begin?

Sam and Liz are theatre majors at their university. They have taken classes in acting, movement, voice, and speech, but they are new to Renaissance drama. Their upcoming acting class will focus solely on the works of Shakespeare. The class will culminate in a workshop production of *Romeo and Juliet,* in which Liz and Sam will play the title roles. Their teacher/director has allocated monologues to the entire class as the first assignment. Sam has been given a speech spoken by Romeo, and Liz has been given a speech spoken by Juliet. All of the actors (a term that can apply to both men and women) have picked up copies of their respective speeches from their instructor, and now Sam and Liz sit excitedly and nervously on the steps outside the theatre, reading their assigned speeches for the first time, when I approach them.

Essential Books for Acting Shakespeare

JOE: May I help you two?
SAM: Yes. We're working on speeches from—
LIZ: He knows, Sam. He wrote it at the top of the chapter.
SAM: Oh.
LIZ: Yes. How do we get started? Where do we begin?

JOE: By surrounding yourselves with a small, solid arsenal of books. If you are serious about acting Shakespeare, you'll need at least these four things:

1. A good edition of Shakespeare's complete works
2. A good individual edition of the play you are currently working on
3. A good Shakespeare dictionary
4. A good Shakespeare pronunciation guide

LIZ: What constitutes "good"?

JOE: A good edition of Shakespeare's complete works has reliable glosses on each page of the play's text. A **gloss,** in case you're not familiar with the term, is a note of comment or explanation accompanying a text—as in a footnote or marginal note. A not-so-good edition either will have no glosses or will place explanatory notes in the back of the book. Also, a good edition will include a well-written general introduction to Shakespeare's life, historical background, theatre in Shakespeare's London, his writing style, and sources, as well as a thorough, insightful introduction/commentary to each play. Some convenient "good" editions include *Shakespeare: The Complete Works,* edited by G. B. Harrison and published by Harcourt College Publishers; *The Complete Pelican Shakespeare,* published by Penguin Books; and the popular *Riverside Shakespeare,* published by Houghton Mifflin.

A good "individual" edition will have similar elements, but the glosses will tend to be more numerous and thorough. Also, I find it a plus to have an edition that supplies a short, clear introduction to each scene of the play. It's much easier to understand Shakespeare when you know the gist of the story beforehand. Some editions that fit the bill are the *New Swan Shakespeare;* the *Folger Library* editions, which include both the *General Reader's Shakespeare* and *The New Folger Library Shakespeare* (I prefer the latter because it is more thorough); and *The Everyman Shakespeare,* which places the plot summaries at the back of the text. *The Arden Shakespeare* is another highly respected individual edition. Its critical and textual information is superior to any other editions I've mentioned. However, it is more expensive and may not be worth the money until you become more experienced with Shakespeare's work.

There are only two choices of Shakespeare dictionaries. The first, *A Shakespeare Glossary,* by C. T. Onions and published by Oxford University Press, is a one-volume dictionary that defines both archaic and obsolete words and is a great resource for modern readers. The second is a two-volume set, the *Shakespeare Lexicon and Quotation Dictionary* by Alexander Schmidt, published by Dover Publications. It is more thorough and claims to define every word used by Shakespeare. A third option, *The Oxford English Dictionary,* has an even broader scope and is considered the Rolls Royce of dictionaries. Often referred to as the **OED,** it defines every word ever used in the English language. It also explains how definitions of individual words have changed over time. This multi-volume masterpiece is very expensive, but you can generally find a set in most libraries. In addition, a photographically reduced, two-volume set of the OED exists, called *The Compact Edition of the Oxford English Dictionary.* It is also pricey, but not exorbitant, and is now available on CD-ROM. Try accessing your university's OED online.

Shakespeare pronunciation dictionaries present a slight problem. Two excellent dictionaries that deal exclusively with Shakespeare are currently out of print: *Shakespeare's Names* and *Shakespeare's Pronunciation,* both written by Helge Kökeritz. There are two other pronunciation dictionaries that include many of Shakespeare's words, although they have a wider overall scope. They are *Everyman's English Pronouncing Dictionary,* by Daniel Jones and A. C. Gimson and published by Dent, and *A Pronouncing Dictionary of American English,* by John S. Kenyon and Thomas A. Knott and published by Merriam-Webster. The Kenyon and Knott dictionary is preferable for American actors. These dictionaries use the International Phonetic Alphabet as a means of explaining pronunciation. The **IPA**, as it is often called, is a set of symbols for every sound—vowels, consonants, and diphthongs—used in the English language. A key for the symbols and corresponding sounds is provided.

SAM: I would like to own all the books you mentioned, but I'm a student. My funds are limited. I simply can't afford them.

JOE: There are ways to ease the financial burden. The reference section of your university library will have many of these books, and if they don't, ask your instructor, chairperson, or even the dean to order them. Used copies are out there, too. You just have to shop for them. This is also a good way to find out-of-print books. Also, many of my suggestions, particularly the individual editions, are available in relatively inexpensive paperback form.

LIZ: How do we use these books in preparing our monologues?

JOE: Let's take a look at the speeches you need to prepare. Liz, you first.

(Liz hands me a sheet of paper, on which is written:)

> JULIET: O Romeo, Romeo, wherefore art thou Romeo?
> Deny thy father and refuse thy name;
> Or if thou wilt not, be but sworn my love
> And I'll no longer be a Capulet.
> ROMEO: *(Aside)* Shall I hear more, or shall I speak at this?
> JULIET: 'Tis but thy name that is my enemy.
> Thou art thyself, though not a Montague.
> What's Montague? It is nor hand, nor foot,
> Nor arm, nor face, nor any other part
> Belonging to a man. O, be some other name!
> What's in a name? That which we call a rose
> By any other word would smell as sweet.
> So Romeo would, were he not Romeo called,
> Retain that dear perfection which he owes
> Without that title. Romeo, doff thy name,
> And for thy name, which is no part of thee,
> Take all myself. *(Romeo and Juliet 2, 2, 33–49)*

JOE: It's a beautiful speech, isn't it?
LIZ: Yes, it is. But how do I begin to work on the speech as an actor?
JOE: Simple—but very important. For both of you, the very first step in acting Shakespeare is to read the play.
LIZ: Well, of course, I intend to read the play. But I want to work on my speech first.
JOE: Tell me something Liz . . . do you ever talk without knowing why you're speaking?
LIZ: No.
SAM: You could've fooled me.
LIZ: Oh, shut up, Sam.
JOE: Well, that's what you're doing when you work on a speech without reading the play first. Knowing *what* you are saying, although vital, is not as important as knowing *why* you are saying it. . . . So go home now, eat dinner, and unwind. And when you feel refreshed, crack open the play and start reading. Try not to think too much about the characters as roles you will portray. Just read for the enjoyment of the story. Think of yourselves as audience members rather than actors. Be sure to read the short scene synopses in your individual editions before you read each scene. *Cliffs Notes, Monarch Notes,* or similar publications can be useful resources, but only as long as you're reading them *in addition* to reading the play, not *instead* of reading the play. Taking shortcuts will only hinder the quality of your acting work. Also, don't worry about understanding every word or phrase. Trying to understand every nuance will take much more time than you have. Check the glosses when passages are troublesome, but otherwise just enjoy the story.
SAM: But everybody knows the story of *Romeo and Juliet*. We know the basic characters and what happens. Can't we just start working on our speeches?
JOE: Have you ever heard the expression "the devil is in the details"?
SAM: Yes.
JOE: There are many details of the story that affect the characters' behavior in the play, many of which you may have skipped over when you first read the play, or have forgotten, or never knew. Just seeing the film version of a play or knowing the play's general storyline is no substitute for reading it carefully from start to finish. Besides, reading it now will give you a fresh look at the play. Enjoy reading *Romeo and Juliet,* and we will continue this discussion tomorrow.

SUMMARY

This chapter introduces Sam and Liz, two students who are preparing for the roles of Romeo and Juliet in a workshop production of Shakespeare's play. Joe helps them get started.

- At least four books are necessary when acting Shakespeare: a good edition of Shakespeare's complete works, a good individual edition of the play on which you are working, a Shakespeare dictionary, and a Shakespeare pronunciation guide.

- The first step in the acting process of any play, including Shakespeare's, is to read the play. Enjoy the story as a member of the audience, without thinking of the characters as roles you will portray or for which you will be auditioning.
- The edition of the play you are reading should contain a brief synopsis of each scene.
- Your comprehension of the story and your enjoyment of the play's narrative will be enhanced when you know the general storyline of each scene before reading it.
- A study guide is also a good idea, but such a guide should be read *in addition* to the play, not *instead* of it.
- Don't try to understand every word and phrase. Consult glosses or footnotes when passages become troublesome, but otherwise just have fun reading.

EXERCISES

SOLO EXERCISE 1.1

Shakespeare wrote tragedies, comedies, histories, and romances. Read one of each of these types of plays. Recommendations are:

Macbeth—tragedy

Much Ado about Nothing—comedy

Henry IV, Part 1—history

The Tempest—romance

Consider also reading a fifth play that defies such strict categorization, such as *All's Well That Ends Well, Troilus and Cressida,* or *Measure for Measure.*

Reading one play from each category is an excellent introduction to the approximately thirty-seven plays that Shakespeare penned or helped pen. It will provide you with a good understanding of Shakespeare's breadth of expression and styles, as well as his versatility of characters and situations. Read the introduction to the play first. Then, read a synopsis of the entire play. After getting an idea of the story, read the synopsis of each scene before reading the scene itself. Consult glosses and footnotes as well as a Shakespeare dictionary for difficult passages.

GROUP EXERCISE 1.1

Have your acting class or cast act out a play as a "dumb show"—that is, without words. The class should begin by standing in a large circle. A narrator must be selected (perhaps the instructor or a member of the group). He or she will use the synopsis of an individual edition for the narrative. As the narrator begins to read, any actor who feels inclined steps into the circle, takes on a role, and acts it out using only movement. Note: The instructor may change the cast for each act to give all a chance to participate.

Have fun with this exercise. Self-consciousness and inhibition may rise up to tell you this is a silly exercise, but this approach is an excellent way to reinforce the story of the play. The arc of characters and events can be made more clear and will often be more memorable than if you simply read the play by itself.

GROUP EXERCISE 1.2
This exercise is closely related to Group Exercise 1.1 and is especially helpful during the first week of rehearsals on a production. The cast or class begins by standing in a large circle. A narrator uses the scene-by-scene synopsis as the text. If the group is a cast in rehearsal, then each actor should enter the circle when his or her character's name is mentioned by the narrator. In this exercise, the actors may speak. Characters should exchange dialogue in a concise, simple paraphrase that is based on the narrator's text.

GROUP EXERCISE 1.3
This exercise is a variation on Group Exercises 1.1 and 1.2. The same steps are followed, but this exercise should be done as a cliché of a genre of theatre, music, literature, or film. For example, your class might attempt *The Tempest* as:

1. A Verdi opera (with actors singing in gibberish while acting out the play)
2. A spaghetti western (as in, "This here island ain't big enough fer the two of us!")
3. A Dr. Seuss book ("I do not like this Caliban, I do not like him, Sam I am.")

Have fun and know that while you are surrendering to the ridiculousness of the exercise, there is a serious purpose to it. By telling and retelling the story in different ways, the cast will retain the order of scenes, as well as the causes and effects of events throughout the entire play. The exercise will also clarify each character's individual story and show how it fits into the arc of the play as a whole.

CHAPTER 2

What Is My Character Saying?

(I meet with Liz and Sam early the next morning at a coffee shop near the theatre department.)

JOE: How did you both get along with the play?
LIZ: I loved it. You were right—there is a lot more to the story than I remembered. The footnotes and the plot summaries helped a lot.
SAM: I liked it too. Though I didn't worry too much about understanding every single word, I still followed the story pretty well. After I finished reading the play, I went back and looked at my speech again. I understood a lot of it, but some of it is still unclear.
JOE: Let's take a look at the speech.

Understanding Romeo's Speech

O, she doth teach the torches to burn bright!
It seems she hangs upon the cheek of night

> As a rich jewel in an Ethiop's ear—
> Beauty too rich for use, for earth too dear.
> So shows a snowy dove trooping with crows
> As yonder lady o'er her fellows shows.
> The measure done, I'll watch her place of stand,
> And, touching hers, make blessed my rude hand.
> Did my heart love till now? Forswear it, sight;
> For I ne'er saw true beauty till this night.
>
> *(Romeo and Juliet, 1, 5, 44–53)*

JOE: The speech contains some beautiful imagery, don't you think?

SAM: Yes, it does. But I'm not sure what all of it means.

JOE: Let's take a little of it at a time and see if we can make sense of it. Did you bring any of your Shakespeare "bibles" with you?

SAM: Sure did. *(Sam pulls several books from his bag—including* The Riverside Shakespeare, The New Folger Library Shakespeare, *the* New Swan Shakespeare, *the* Shakespeare Lexicon and Quotation Dictionary, The Compact Edition of the Oxford English Dictionary *(OED), and* Webster's New World Dictionary.*)*

JOE: Before we begin to work on the speech, tell me a little about the story up until this point.

SAM: It all takes place in Verona, Italy. There are two families, the Capulets and the Montagues, who hate each other. At the beginning of the play, they get into a street fight that is broken up by the Prince, who's angry because it's the third time that it's happened. He tells the two heads of the families that if it happens again, he'll put whoever's fighting to death. Everybody leaves except for Mr. and Mrs. Montague and Romeo's friend and cousin, Benvolio. Romeo's parents ask Benvolio if he has seen their son recently and he tells them that he saw Romeo walking early that morning and that Romeo spotted him and walked into the woods to avoid him. Mr. Montague says that his son walks and cries every morning and then locks himself in his room and closes the curtains and mopes all day. They're concerned about him and ask their nephew if he'll try to find out what's going on. Benvolio says that he will. Just then Romeo comes along and his parents leave. Benvolio asks Romeo why he is so sad. Romeo tells him that he's very upset about breaking up with his girlfriend, Rosaline. Nothing that Benvolio says will cheer him up. Then a servant of the Capulets comes along with a list of people that are going to be invited to a party at Mr. and Mrs. Capulet's that night. Romeo sees that Rosaline's name is on the list because she's a Capulet. Benvolio says that he's going to crash the party and that Romeo should come along in order to see Rosaline. Benvolio thinks that if Romeo compares her with all the other girls at the party, he'll realize that Rosaline is not as irreplaceable as Romeo thinks. They go to the party that evening with another friend named Mercutio. They wear masks so nobody will recognize them. It turns out that all the young people at the party are wearing masks, so they fit right in. Romeo is looking for Rosaline when his eyes light on another girl dancing with a group of others. He falls head over heels for her and completely forgets about Rosaline. He asks a servant who the girl is and the servant says that he doesn't know. That's when Romeo speaks the words of the speech. It turns out to be Juliet but he doesn't know that at the time.

JOE: Now let's take the speech a little at a time.

SAM: Okay.

JOE: Let's start with the first line: "O, she doth teach the torches to burn bright!" What does that mean?

SAM: Well, I take it to mean that the torches that are in the room to light the place get even brighter because she's there.

JOE: That's a good guess. You're close but that's not quite it. Let's take it one word or phrase at a time. What does O mean?

SAM: Is it an expression of emotion?

JOE: Yes. It is also a favorite word or expression in Shakespeare's plays and appears many times, spoken by a wide variety of characters. Let's look it up in the *Shakespeare Lexicon and Quotation Dictionary*. Before we continue, I want to give you both some tips on using the Lexicon as well as most other dictionaries. First, when you locate a word in the Lexicon, be sure that it is the part of speech—noun, verb, adjective, and so forth—that you're looking for. For example, if you were to look up the word *sacrifice*, you would first read, "*Sacrifice*, subst.—1. the act of offering any thing to God." The abbreviation "subst." is short for "substantive," which is a fancy word for "noun." Two more definitions follow. Then you will find the word again, only this time it will read, "*Sacrifice*, vb.—1. to offer up to heaven." Here, "vb." is short for "verb." A second definition follows. Most words will have more than one definition. Once you find the appropriate part of speech for your word, search for the definition that seems to fit. Then look under that definition for the play, scene, and line in which the word appears. For example, we are looking for the definition of O in *Romeo and Juliet*, Act 1, scene 5, line 44. Line numbers will vary somewhat, depending on the edition. A key to abbreviations in the front of the Lexicon will reveal that our play is written as *"Rom."* Therefore, we are looking for the definition of O in *Rom. 1, 5, 44,* being aware that the line number may vary as much as twenty places in either direction. There are three definitions of O but the third seems to be the one we want. It reads, "Interjection expressive of pain, of surprise or of desire, or used to give the speech the character of earnestness." Okay Sam, do me a favor and look for our play, act, scene, and line under that definition.

SAM: Sure. *(Sam looks carefully and thoroughly.)* I can't find it.

JOE: Although the Lexicon claims to define and locate every word in the Shakespeare canon, this is simply not true. Don't despair. If the line that contains the word for which you are looking is not cited, it will usually be fairly obvious which definition is intended. The context of the sentence in which the word appears as well as the examples from other plays, poems, and sonnets that are cited will help you decide which definition is the correct one. For example, the first definition of O is, "Any thing circular: 'may we cram within this wooden O the very casques that did affright the air at Agincourt?' *H5 Prol., 13*" (abbreviation for *King Henry V*, Prologue, line 13). The second definition of O is, "The arithmetical cipher: 'thou art an O without a figure' *Lr. 1, 4, 212*" (abbreviation for *King Lear*, Act 1, scene 4, line 212). It is obvious from the context of our line from *Romeo and Juliet* that neither of these definitions is the correct one. However, let's suppose that we need more information on which to base our decision. We look at examples of the third definition of O defined earlier. The first example we find is "'O, how quick is love!' *Ven.* 38" (abbreviation for *Venus and Adonis*, line 38). This example is remarkably similar to our line, "O, she doth teach the torches to burn bright!" We can now proceed, confidant that we have found the correct definition of O in this particular instance.

SAM: This is a lot of work and we're only on the first word! And it's not even a word—it's a letter! I thought that your book is called *Shakespeare without Fear?*

JOE: It's called *Shakespeare without Fear,* not *Shakespeare without Work*. Anything worth doing is going to involve time and energy. You are both just starting out, so we are proceeding slowly and methodically. The process moves more quickly with experience, just like anything else. Let's continue working.

SAM: Okay.

JOE: The rest of the line is ". . . she doth teach the torches to burn bright!" The keyword for unlocking the exact meaning of the line seems to be the verb *teach*. By the way, do you know what the word *doth* means?

SAM: Yes. It's an old word for *does*.

JOE: That's right.

SAM: Why do I have to look up the word *teach?* Doesn't it mean the same thing as it does today?

JOE: You've raised an interesting point. It is much less of a problem when actors working on Shakespeare are presented with an unfamiliar word; one simply looks up the definition. However, when actors come across a word with which they are familiar, they often take for granted that they know the definition intended by Shakespeare. The problem is that they could be dead wrong. In this instance, the difference in meaning is a subtle one, but significant nonetheless. The definition of *teach* in the Lexicon is a familiar one: "*Teach*—to instruct, to inform, to communicate knowledge or skill." However, a little further on we find the definition that pertains to our line from *Romeo and Juliet:* "Sometimes not so much to instruct as to tell, to show: 'she doth t. the torches to burn bright,' *Rom. 1, 5, 46*" (i.e., she shows the torches, by her own radiance, what it is to burn bright).

SAM: Isn't that kind of what I thought it meant?

JOE: No. What Romeo is saying, in essence, is that Juliet is an example to the torches of what it *really* means to burn brightly, not that the torches burn more brightly because Juliet is in the room. When acting Shakespeare, it is vital to be precise, exact, and specific. Language is thought in action. Clarity of thought leads to clarity of action. But now let's move on to the next section of dialogue: "It seems she hangs upon the cheek of night / As a rich jewel in an Ethiop's ear." Any thoughts on this line?

LIZ: I know that this is your speech, Sam, but can I take a shot?

SAM: Sure, Liz.

LIZ: Does it mean that she illuminates the night, standing out from all others in the room, the way a sparkling, diamond earring would on the ear of a black woman or a black man?

JOE: That's a very good paraphrasing of the line. However, the full meaning of Shakespeare's words goes beyond paraphrasing. Although it doesn't specify a diamond, I agree with you that the jewel would have to be a light-hued, sparkling stone in order to contrast with the dark, ebony skin tone of an Ethiopian.

SAM: By **paraphrasing**, do you mean putting it in your own words?

JOE: Yes. The OED defines it: "*Paraphrase* (from a Greek word meaning 'to tell the same thing in other words')—1. An expression in other words, usually fuller and clearer, of the sense of any passage or text. 2. To express the meaning of a word, phrase, passage or work in other words, usually with the object of fuller and clearer exposition." Paraphrasing is a great way to help you understand what a passage means. But, at best, it can only be an *approximation* of the meaning. Now, I am going to take some time here, because there is so much meaning in this particular line of dialogue. Let's proceed slowly. The first half of the line is, "It seems she hangs upon the cheek of night." Now, what does the word *hangs* mean?

LIZ: Is this going to be another word that doesn't mean what we think it means?

JOE: No. The definition in the Lexicon is "to be suspended, to be supported by an object above." What do you think is meant by *the cheek of night*?

SAM: Isn't that a metaphor?

JOE: Yes, it is. Webster's dictionary defines **metaphor** as "a figure of speech containing an implied comparison, in which a word or phrase ordinarily and primarily used of one thing is applied to another." I should mention here that Shakespeare also uses **simile,** which is similar to metaphor except that it uses the words *like* or *as* in its comparison. Getting back to our example, however, "the cheek of night" is an archaic metaphor, and the Lexicon isn't much help as to its exact meaning. The OED is slightly more helpful: "*Cheek*—of the sea, the heavens, night, etc. personified, i.e. the cloudy cheeks of heaven, Ocean's cheek reflects the tint of many a peak." It seems that it is a metaphor for those elements of nature that are vast, magnificent, and awe inspiring. It also seems to refer to the essence or center of that element of nature.

LIZ: "The cheek of night" also makes me think of—I don't know how to put it—warm and affectionate things, like "rosy cheeks." It's sort of romantic, too.

JOE: I agree. Most good metaphors defy a complete, literal definition. They are meant to have an emotional effect on the listener, and that defies logic. Also, keep in mind that language constantly changes and evolves. I feel that even if the images and feelings evoked from a word or phrase are based on contemporary definitions, when they fit the circumstances of the scene, by all means, use them.

SAM: I'm not quite clear on what you mean.

JOE: Here's an example. An actor was working on a Shakespeare scene in which his character uses the word *front*. In this particular case Shakespeare intended the word to mean "forehead," "brow," or "face"—definitions that have since fallen out of use. The actor uses the word in reference to a woman whom his character dislikes and feels is "putting on a front."

SAM: You mean like a candy store might be a front for a bookie joint or something?

JOE: Exactly. Even though this definition of the word didn't exist in Shakespeare's time, it certainly fits the character's feeling that the woman is not what she pretends to be. So, the actor decided to use the word *front* to mean not only "face" but also "two-faced."

SAM: I understand now, but how can the word have two meanings? If *front* means "face," then that's all it's supposed to mean, right?
JOE: Not necessarily. *Shakespeare often intended more than one definition of a word or phrase.* This gives the word or phrase layers of meaning.
LIZ: Can you give us an example?
JOE: Sure. We've explored the first half of the line: "It seems she hangs upon the cheek of night." Now let's look at the second half of the line: "As a rich jewel in an Ethiop's ear." Romeo doesn't just compare Juliet to a jewel, but to a *rich* jewel. What do you think he means with this adjective?
SAM: Rich means expensive, high quality. It's not a cheap imitation.
JOE: Yes, and that is the primary meaning, but there are other meanings as well, the ones that Shakespeare cleverly layers under the primary meaning, making the word fuller. *Rich*, as defined in the Lexicon, also means "fruitful, precious, and delightful." "Precious" and "delightful" certainly apply to Romeo's infatuation with Juliet. It is even possible that Romeo is already fantasizing Juliet as a wife and mother, in which case "fruitful" may also apply. The OED provides this definition: "*Rich*, adj.—of persons: exalted, noble, great."
LIZ: So, incorporating some or all of the other definitions brings layers of meaning to the word *rich* and the actor playing Romeo will have a deeper and fuller infatuation with Juliet. It really would be love at first sight.
JOE: Yes, I think so. Let's continue. Someone define the word *jewel* for me.
LIZ: Isn't it any kind of stone that is rare and therefore valuable?
JOE: Yes. The Lexicon definition is, "Any personal ornament of gold or precious stones." The OED gives a similar definition. However, the OED also provides this definition of *jewel*: "Figuratively applied to a thing or person of great worth, or highly prized; a 'treasure,' 'gem.' " We still refer to individuals as "jewels" or "gems." So, as you can see, there are primary definitions of words and phrases but Shakespeare often layers other meanings beneath the primary ones.
SAM: Wait a second. I'm a little confused. On the one hand, you say to make sure that we find the right definitions of all the words in the speech. You also say that words that mean one thing today could have had a different definition hundreds of years ago. But then you turn around and say that we can use modern definitions and that just about any definition of a word is okay to use.
JOE: No, that is not what I said. Let me clarify. First of all, there is always only one primary definition intended by Shakespeare. All other definitions are either incorrect or secondary. We have already seen an example of this with the word O, which is the first word of your Romeo speech. Only one definition of O was intended by Shakespeare. All of the others are incorrect. This brings me to my second point: Not all of Shakespeare's words have secondary meanings. Many of Shakespeare's words have only one definition. Thirdly, there are no cut-and-dried rules regarding secondary definitions. Their function is to add depth and dimension to a passage. Therefore, it is sometimes an actor's personal choice as to which secondary meanings to incorporate. There are only two rules that apply: (1) The choice must stimulate the actor. (2) The choice must be consistent with your character and must serve the storyline. This brings me to my fourth and final point. Anything that stimulates the actor and serves the storyline is a valid acting choice. This includes

incorporating contemporary definitions. But remember that these definitions can only be secondary ones. Is that clearer?

SAM: Yes.

LIZ: So, what you are saying is always find and use the definition primarily intended by Shakespeare, the one we would use if we were paraphrasing. Then we should see if any other definitions apply. If they do, then we should incorporate any of the ones that help us make a stronger connection to the primary meaning.

JOE: Yes. Now, let's listen once more to the entire line: "It seems she hangs upon the cheek of night / As a rich jewel in an Ethiop's ear." An *Ethiop* is a citizen of the country of Ethiopia, which is on the continent of Africa. Any other ideas for layers of meaning?

SAM: Isn't there a comparison of "the cheek of night" to the Ethiop's cheek? Because the diamond earring would probably dangle from the person's ear at about the level of their cheek bone.

JOE: That's very possible. What else glitters and shines like a jewel and hangs or is suspended in the night sky?

SAM: A star.

JOE: Absolutely. A star. So Juliet is directly compared to a jewel and indirectly compared to a star. Such an indirect reference is called an **allusion.** In fact, throughout the play there are many allusions to stars as well as other "heavenly bodies," including angels. This imagery begins at the start of the play with the Chorus's reference to Romeo and Juliet as "star-crossed lovers." Let's move on. The next line is, "Beauty too rich for use, for earth too dear." Any ideas?

SAM: The words *use* and *dear* have me a little confused.

JOE: The Lexicon defines *use* in this instance as "practice customarily, to make a practice of." The OED definition is "the habitual, usual, or common practice." The Lexicon definition of *dear* is "precious, valuable, beloved, cherished." The OED adds "*Dear*—of persons: glorious, noble, honorable, worthy."

LIZ: Is Romeo still referring to Juliet as a jewel?

JOE: Yes, he is. Punctuation is a clue here. There is a dash (—) at the end of the previous line. It reads: "As a rich jewel in an Ethiop's ear— / Beauty too rich for use, for earth too dear." Romeo is saying that Juliet is not a common jewel; one to be worn every day. She is special and is a jewel that should only be worn on special occasions.

LIZ: But why does Romeo say "for earth too dear"?

SAM: Romeo also compares Juliet indirectly to a star. Is it a reference to that?

JOE: Yes, I think so. He is saying that she is too wonderful to stain herself with our common world and belongs in the heavens instead.

SAM: He really puts her on a pedestal. He doesn't even know her yet!

JOE: That's true. But you're looking at the situation with modern eyes. This brings me to an important point: When reading one of Shakespeare's plays, be sure to read the introduction and the afterword, in both your Complete Works and your individual edition. A solid introduction or afterword can give the reader a good deal of insight into the play. For example, the afterword in *The New Folger Library Shakespeare* addresses Romeo's infatuation with Juliet. Entitled "Romeo and Juliet: A Modern Perspective," Gail Kern Paster states that Romeo's view of women is based on "the idealizing view of the Petrarchan lover. In his melancholy, his desire for solitude, and his paradox-strewn language, Romeo identifies himself with the style of feeling and address that Renaissance culture named after the fourteenth-century Italian poet Francesco Petrarca or Petrarch" (p. 257). The Petrarchan lover sees "his beloved as perfect and perfectly chaste" (p. 257). This romantic view was very much in vogue in Shakespeare's time.

Liz: It's not that way at all today.

Joe: That's why it's very important to view Shakespeare's plays as works of a specific time and place. So much of Shakespeare's writing is universal and addresses the human condition regardless of time and place. But it is also a product of a sixteenth and seventeenth century English mind set. Part of our job as actors is to identify those differences between the Renaissance Englishman and the twenty-first century American and find a way to personalize them.

Sam: What do you mean by **personalize?**

Joe: The Webster's dictionary definition is, "*Personalize*—to apply to a particular person, especially to oneself." In other words, it means to understand on an intimate basis, not only with the head, but with the heart and soul as well. I will discuss personalization in greater detail at a later date. Let's get back to the line at hand: "Beauty too rich for use, for earth too dear." Any other ideas?

Sam: I assume that the word *rich* has the same multiple meanings that it does in the previous line.

Joe: Yes. In fact, it's a direct reference to the previous line. Romeo says that not only is Juliet a *rich* jewel, but she is *too rich* to be worn every day.

Liz: What about the word *beauty*? Does it have the same meaning that it does today?

Joe: Yes and no. I love the Lexicon definition, which is "*Beauty*—assemblage of graces to please the eye and mind." This definition goes beyond physical beauty. I don't mean to imply that we are concerned only with physical beauty today. However, I think that there was a wider definition of the word *beauty* in Shakespeare's day.

Liz: Next line?

Joe: Okay. "So shows a snowy dove trooping with crows / As yonder lady o'er her fellows shows."

Sam: Does it mean that Juliet stands out from all the other girls at the party the way that a white dove would stand out in the middle of a bunch of crows?

Joe: Very good. This line is an example of *simile,* which we touched on earlier, when we defined *metaphor*. Shakespeare has Romeo compare Juliet to a dove and her companions to crows. However, the comparison isn't direct. He uses the word *as* in order to make an indirect comparison.

Sam: If it were a metaphor, wouldn't Shakespeare have Romeo say something like, "She is a dove among a bunch of crows"?

Joe: Yes.

Liz: Shakespeare's sentence structure is different from how Sam "translated" it.

Joe: Yes. Although Sam's paraphrase is essentially correct, the order of imagery is not exact. Let's define some of the words and then attempt to paraphrase more precisely. The following definitions are from the Lexicon. "*So*—in such a manner, in the same manner, in such a degree, in the same degree." "*Shows*—to appear, to look." "*Snowy*—white like snow." "*Troop*—to march in company, to march in a body."

"*O'er*—higher in place, above." "*Fellow*—companion, comrade." Sam, would you like to try again?

SAM: Okay, give me a second. Um, let's see . . . "In the same manner appears a white dove marching with crows, as that young lady over there above her companions appears." How's that?

JOE: That's more exact.

LIZ: The sentence structure is strange.

JOE: Yes. You will encounter this unusual arrangement of words quite often in Shakespeare's writing.

LIZ: I think that I know what the next line means.

JOE: Go ahead.

LIZ: "The measure done, I'll watch her place of stand, / And, touching hers, make blessed my rude hand." Does it mean "When the dance is over, I'll watch where she stands and make my rough hand holy by touching her hand"?

JOE: Yes, very good.

LIZ: My edition of the play has footnotes for this line, so it was a little easier. In fact, they are the only footnotes for the entire passage in both my individual edition and my Complete Works.

JOE: That's why it is essential to own or to have access to a Shakespeare dictionary or the OED. Even the most thorough edition cannot provide the kind of in-depth definitions of words and passages that we actors need in order to bring Shakespeare to life onstage. But getting back to the line at hand, the words *blessed* and *rough* need further exploration. *Blessed* certainly has religious connotations. "Holy" is one of the definitions of the word as well as "consecrated" and "hallowed." However, it also means "blissful, fortunate, bestowing health and prosperity." *Rude* is defined as "harsh, rough, unpleasing to the sense." But, it also has a definition that goes a little further: "destitute of delicacy of feeling." Romeo implies that he is emotionally numb and can only become spiritually and emotionally alive by touching Juliet. Let's move on to the final lines in the passage: "Did my heart love till now? Forswear it, sight! / For I ne'er saw true beauty till this night."

SAM: The first line—"Did my heart love till now?"—is pretty clear, isn't it?

JOE: Yes, it is. But it is in the form of a question. Whom is he asking?

SAM: He seems to be asking himself.

LIZ: Isn't it called a rhetorical question?

JOE: Yes. The OED defines a **rhetorical question** as "questions that do not require an answer, but are only put in the form of a question in order to produce a greater effect." It is at this point in Romeo's infatuation with Juliet that he emphatically announces his undying love for her. Why doesn't he simply say "Did *I* love till now?"

SAM: I have a sneaking suspicion that it has something to do with the definition of the word *heart*.

JOE: Yes it does. The Lexicon gives the obvious definition of *heart* as "the seat of love and amorous desire." However, in Shakespeare's time, the heart was also synonymous with the soul and the mind, as well as the inmost and most vital part, the core, the very essence. So Romeo is stating emphatically, by way of a rhetorical question, that he loves Juliet with his heart, his mind, his soul, and his very core of being. Let's look at the next line: "Forswear it, sight!" What does *forswear* mean?

SAM: I looked this up. It means "to deny upon oath."

JOE: Right. He is speaking to his sense of sight. He is telling his eyes to admit that all of the women that they gazed on with love before seeing Juliet were actually only infatuations. And now for the final line: "For I ne'er saw true beauty till this night."

LIZ: Does *ne'er* mean "never"?

JOE: That's correct. *Ne'er* (pronounced "nare") is an antiquated contraction for the word *never*. So, Romeo is saying that the love that he felt for women in the past was not love at all, now that he can compare them with "true beauty." "True" means not only "genuine" and "real," but also "honest," "trustworthy," "to be depended on," and "not failing." Let's work on the Juliet speech now.

UNDERSTANDING JULIET'S SPEECH

> O Romeo, Romeo, wherefore art thou Romeo?
> Deny thy father and refuse thy name;
> Or if thou wilt not, be but sworn my love
> And I'll no longer be a Capulet.
> 'Tis but thy name that is my enemy.
> Thou art thyself, though not a Montague.
> What's Montague? It is nor hand, nor foot,
> Nor arm, nor face, nor any other part
> Belonging to a man. O, be some other name!
> What's in a name? That which we call a rose
> By any other word would smell as sweet.
> So Romeo would, were he not Romeo called,
> Retain that dear perfection which he owes
> Without that title. Romeo, doff thy name,
> And for thy name, which is no part of thee,
> Take all myself.   *(Romeo and Juliet, 2, 2, 33–36 and 38–49)*

JOE: As you can see, I've removed Romeo's "aside" line because Juliet doesn't hear it. Liz, why don't you fill us in on what happens in the story between Romeo's speech, which we just worked on, and this Juliet speech.

LIZ: Immediately after Romeo's speech, Tybalt says that he recognizes Romeo's voice and tells Mr. Capulet that a Montague has crashed the party. Tybalt is a Capulet and Juliet's cousin. Mr. Capulet tells him to leave the situation alone because Romeo has a good reputation in town and is behaving well at the party. Romeo goes up to Juliet and touches her hand. Then he kisses her, not once but twice! She seems to be as attracted to him as he is to her. Next, Juliet's nurse interrupts and says that her mother wants to talk to her. Juliet leaves temporarily and Romeo asks the nurse who Juliet is. He is surprised and upset that she is a Capulet. He leaves with his friends and Juliet calls the nurse over and asks who Romeo is. Just like Romeo, she seems surprised and upset that he is a Montague. A little while later, after all the guests have gone, she walks out on her balcony and speaks these lines. She doesn't know that Romeo is there and has seen her come out onto the balcony and will overhear everything she is about to say.

JOE: Let's proceed one line at a time, as we did with Sam's speech. The first line is "O Romeo, Romeo, wherefore art thou Romeo?" What is Juliet saying here?

LIZ: Well, at first I thought that it meant "Romeo, Romeo, where are you, Romeo?" I thought that the word *wherefore* meant "where."

JOE: And does it?

LIZ: No. It means "why." You were right about looking up words that we only think we know.

JOE: So, in essence, what is Juliet saying here?

LIZ: She's asking, "Why do you have to be named Romeo?" because his family is an enemy to her family.

JOE: Yes. Now let's get specific. What about the O that starts her line?

LIZ: Isn't it similar to the one in Sam's speech?

JOE: Yes. It is an emotional expression, this time of pain or frustration mixed with desire. She has most likely been thinking about the problem of loving a Montague ever since the party ended an hour or more ago. It becomes so overwhelming that she can't sleep and steps outside to collect herself. At this point the situation is so strong in her mind that she has to express it aloud. It only makes sense that she begins with such an emotional expression.

LIZ: How do you know that's what she did?

JOE: I don't. It's conjecture. However, as a great playwright, Shakespeare gives us enough clues to fill in the blanks. As an actor, it is our job to look for those clues in the play that help us fill in our character's ongoing life in between the scenes that the author gives us. Moving on, why do you think that she says his name three times in one sentence?

LIZ: It's all she can think about. She is fixated on him—not only her love for him but also, more importantly, the fact that he is a Montague. Saying his name twice immediately after the O shows how obsessed she is with him as well as the fact that it is his name that is their only problem. She states that openly with the second half of the line. She asks, "Why do you have to be named Romeo?"

JOE: How do you know she thinks all that?

LIZ: I don't. It's conjecture.

JOE: You're catching on. Next we have, "Deny thy father and refuse thy name." The two verbs seem to hold the key to the specific meaning of this line.

LIZ: *Deny* is a little tricky. The Lexicon's first definition is "to say no." That's the definition we're used to today but it didn't seem quite right for what Juliet is saying. I looked further on and found "to disown, to disavow." My line was cited under this definition so I knew it was the correct one.

JOE: What would you have done if your line wasn't cited?

LIZ: I would have chosen it anyway. There were five definitions listed but that one is the only one that made sense within the context of the line.

JOE: What about the word *refuse*?
LIZ: My line was cited under the correct definition of this word as well. *Refuse* is synonymous with *deny*. The Lexicon defines it "to disavow, to disown."
SAM: So she is asking Romeo to disown his father and his lineage, right?
JOE: Yes. But she doesn't see it as the only answer. This becomes apparent with the next line: "Or, if thou wilt not, be but sworn my love / And I'll no longer be a Capulet."
SAM: Right. Juliet says that she's willing to do the same thing because the hatred that her family has for the Montagues is just as stupid and wrong as the hatred that the Montagues have for the Capulets. The feud is so old that nobody even remembers what it was about.
JOE: Good observations. We're going a little quickly though. Let's back up a bit. What about the words *thou* and *thy*?
LIZ: *Thou* is an old word for "you" and *thy* is an old word for "your."
JOE: Right. There's more to it though. In Shakespeare's time, there were formal and informal forms of *you*. This continues to be true of many languages but has fallen by the wayside with English. *You* was formal and *thou* was informal. In other words, you would address someone that you knew very well as *thou* and someone you didn't know well as *you*. Even though Juliet has known Romeo all of five minutes, she feels that she already knows him intimately and addresses him in the informal. Let's look at the first half of the line: "Or, if thou wilt not, be but sworn my love."
LIZ: *Wilt* means "will." The word *but* had me a little confused at first.
JOE: Small, "linking" words such as *and, but, so,* and *if* can occasionally present problems because they can have many definitions, some of which are now obsolete. For example, the word *so* had nine definitions in the sixteenth and seventeenth centuries. This tiny two-letter word takes up three full pages in the Lexicon! What is the definition of *but* in this instance?
LIZ: There was a footnote in my individual edition. It means "only," as in "only be sworn my love." I had trouble with *sworn* though. It wasn't listed in the Lexicon.
JOE: Did you look under *swear*?
LIZ: No.
JOE: The Lexicon will often not list all forms of a word. For example, *sworn* is the past tense of *swear*, so it is listed under *swear*. The word *these* is listed under the word *this* because it is a plural form of that word. If you are unable to find a word in the Lexicon, see if it is a form of another word and look there instead. The definition of *sworn* will come as no surprise; it means "to have taken an oath." What about the word *love*?
LIZ: This line isn't cited under any definition but there is one that fits really well: "a person beloved; masculine, a lover, a paramour." Juliet wants Romeo to take an oath to be her one true love.
JOE: And if he agrees, then what?
LIZ: Then she will no longer be a Capulet. Juliet will disown her family and name.
JOE: Yes. Juliet is a very giving person, we are finding out. She first asks Romeo to make a great personal sacrifice, but then goes on to say that if he will be her love,

then she will make the sacrifice instead. Let's go on to the next line: "'Tis but thy name that is my enemy."

SAM: Does *'tis* mean "it is"?

LIZ: Yes, and *but* means "only," just like it did in the last line. Juliet is saying "It is only your name that is my enemy." Then she says, "Thou art thyself, though not a Montague." *Though* gave me some trouble. The line isn't cited in the Lexicon and the definitions are a little difficult to understand.

JOE: What did you come up with for the word *though*?

LIZ: There were footnotes in both of my editions that paraphrased the entire line, but I wanted to understand how all of the words interrelate. The footnote in the Folger edition says, "Thou art thyself, though not a Montague: i.e., you would still be yourself even if you were not called Montague." I sort of knew that already, because of the context of the speech up until this point. The Lexicon gives the definition of *though* as "notwithstanding that, however." That confused me, so I looked in the OED and found a definition that seemed to make sense: "Even if, even supposing that." But there still seemed to be missing words: "You are yourself, even if not a Montague" sounds incomplete.

JOE: That's because there *are* some words missing. It's called an **ellipsis.** The OED defines it as "the omission of one or more words in a sentence, which would be needed to complete the grammatical construction or fully to express the sense." We still do this today. For example, a cliché line in gangster movies is, "We know you're in there!" The line should be, "We know *that* you're in there!" If a friend walked up to you and said "Hungry?" you would know that he or she meant "*Are you* hungry?" Even ad campaigns use ellipses. We are all familiar with the slogan "Got milk?"—which combines an ellipsis with improper grammar. These modern ellipses are familiar and present few problems when used in contemporary plays. The same was true of Shakespeare's audiences. However, when we watch an Elizabethan play today, we are hearing ellipses that are over four hundred years old. This can sometimes be confusing. Anyway, the missing words in your paraphrase could be "You are yourself, even if *you were* not a Montague." Now let's move on.

LIZ: The next section is, "What's Montague? It is nor hand, nor foot, / Nor arm, nor face, nor any other part / Belonging to a man." It's pretty clear to me. Is the first line a rhetorical question?

JOE: Very good.

LIZ: The only word that I found a little strange is *nor*. Actually, it is the first *nor* that I found strange. The Lexicon was very helpful here. The line was cited under this subdefinition: "Nor . . . nor—for neither." The paraphrase would then be "It is neither hand, nor foot." . . . Next we have "O, be some other name!" You're right, Shakespeare sure loves the word O. In this case, I think that it's a combination of desire and emotional pain. She wishes something that can never be. The next section is pretty famous: "What's in a name? That which we call a rose / By any other word would smell as sweet." It starts out with another rhetorical question. It's pretty obvious that Juliet thinks names mean absolutely nothing even as she asks the question. There's a kind of ellipsis with the word *that* in the next line, it seems to me. I would say "that *thing* which we call a rose" or "that *object* which we call a rose" . . . Otherwise, the line is very clear. She is saying that the qualities of a rose remain unchanged, regardless of what we call it. With the next line she goes on to say that the same is true of Romeo: "So Romeo would, were he not Romeo called, / Retain that dear perfection which he owes / Without that title."

JOE: That's a pretty long sentence.

LIZ: Yes, it is. It took me a while to follow what was being said. The order of words in the sentence is strange. At first I thought that "So Romeo would, were he not Romeo called" was a complete sentence. Then I saw the comma.

JOE: Let's proceed slowly. What about the word *so*, keeping in mind what I said earlier about small, linking words.

LIZ: You were right. There are nine definitions of *so!* Although I couldn't find the line cited, the definitions that fit are the same as the definitions of *so* in Sam's speech: "in the same manner and in the same degree." Juliet is starting a comparison between a rose and Romeo. *Dear* has the same multiple meanings as it does in Sam's speech as well—"precious, valuable, beloved, cherished, noble, worthy," and so on. *Owes* means "possesses or owns." *Title* means "any appellation (label) or name." A paraphrase might be something like, "In the same way, Romeo would, even if he weren't called Romeo, keep that precious excellence he possesses, even without that label."

JOE: You're doing great. Let's work on the last line.

LIZ: Okay. The last line is, "Romeo, doff thy name, / And for thy name, which is no part of thee, / Take all myself." *Doff* is an interesting word. It means "to take off," as in to take off a piece of clothing. She's asking him to throw off his name, the way he would throw off his shirt. I think that's a great way to put it. It makes it seem like his name is no more important than a pair of socks, which is what she has been trying to say this whole time.

JOE: Yes. It is quite common for Shakespeare to use sensory or concrete imagery to deepen his meaning. This is a very important point. We have seen several examples in both of your speeches: "the cheek of night," "as a rich jewel in an Ethiop's ear," "that which we call a rose," and so on. Even dialogue that is not metaphor or simile often contains sensory imagery. By incorporating the image of Romeo throwing off his name as he would a scarf or coat, Shakespeare makes the image palpable. It is no longer only a concept, but a physical reality as well. You may also notice that the sounds comprising the word *doff* fit its imagery and meaning.

SAM: How do you mean?

JOE: Well, Juliet wants Romeo to cast off his name. We now know that the *conceptual* meaning of this phrase is underscored by *physical imagery,* derived from the verb *doff.* Does the phrase "cast off" or "throw off" seem slow and casual or quick and deliberate?

LIZ: Quick and deliberate. She wants Romeo to throw his name away without hesitation.

JOE: I agree. Therefore, Shakespeare chose a verb that not only contains concrete *visual* imagery, but also contains short, clipped *sounds*. The consonants "d" and "th" as well as the short vowel sound in between fit the imagery they mirror.

SAM: *Doff* is also a short, succinct one-syllable word.

JOE: Exactly. So, the *rhythm* of the word fits its quick, deliberate nature as well.

LIZ: So what you're saying is that Shakespeare not only uses primary and secondary definitions of words, but he also uses sensory definitions as well as words whose sounds and rhythms mirror their meaning and imagery.

JOE: Yes. That is why paraphrasing, although helpful to the actor, can only skirt the edges of a complete understanding of Shakespeare's dialogue. The compression of meaning and imagery of his language is impossible to duplicate with paraphrase. Please continue, Liz.

LIZ: The second part of Juliet's last line is, "And for thy name, which is no part of thee, / Take all myself." I have footnotes for the word *for*. It means "in exchange for." A paraphrase would go something like, "Romeo, throw off your name, and in exchange for your name, which has nothing to do with who you are, take all of me." I love that she says "Take all myself." She is saying that she will give her entire being—heart, mind, body, and soul—to him.

ANALYZING SHAKESPEARE'S SENTENCE STRUCTURE

JOE: You both did really well with this. Before we end for the day, I want to give you a small crash course on the differences between modern sentence structure and Shakespeare's sentence structure. The first difference is one we have already discussed—ellipses.... And by the way, note that *ellipsis* (pronounced "i-LIP-sis") is singular and *ellipses* (pronounced "i-LIP-seez") is the plural form.... Here are two examples of ellipses from the plays: "Do with your injuries as seems you best" (rather than "Do with your injuries as *it* seems *to* you best"), and "Me seemeth then it is no policy" (rather than "*To* me *it* seemeth then it is no policy"). Unfortunately, there are no hard-and-fast rules that apply to Shakespeare's ellipses. Frequent reading of his plays along with good ol' common sense and good footnotes will solve these problems ninety-nine percent of the time.

The second difference is word order. Shakespeare often scrambles "normal" English word order (subject—verb—object). For example, we would say, "I (subject) kissed (verb) her (object)." Shakespeare uses this order as well but not exclusively. He might phrase the sentence, "Her I kissed," or "Kissed I her." Here are a few examples of unusual word order from his plays: "This letter then to Friar Peter give" (rather than "Then give this letter to Friar Peter"), "Sorry am I his numbers are so few" (rather than "I am sorry his numbers are so few"), and "When devils will the blackest sins put on" (rather than "When devils will put on the blackest sins"). Unusual word order and ellipses are not mutually exclusive. You will often find both in a single sentence or phrase. For example, "Retire we to our chamber" (rather than "*Let* us retire to our chamber"), and "Urge it thou" (rather than "Thou *must* urge it"). The missing word *must* in the last example is known as an *auxiliary verb*.

This brings us to the third aspect of Shakespeare's sentence structure: Auxiliary verbs are often missing. My seventh grade English teacher often referred to these kinds of verbs as "helping verbs." Webster's dictionary defines *auxiliary verb* as "a verb that helps form tenses, aspects, moods, or voices of other verbs, as *have, be, may, can, must, do, shall, will*." Here are two more examples of missing auxiliary verbs that also contain unusual word order: "Revolt our subjects?" (rather than "*Do* our subjects revolt?"), and my personal favorite, "What heard you him say else?" (rather than "What else *did* you hear him say?").

A fourth difference is that negatives (such as the word *not*) in conjunction with a verb will often directly follow the verb. For example, we would say "don't go," but Shakespeare may say "go not." "I don't love you" might become "I love not you," and so on. Some examples from the plays include: "I tax not you" (rather than "I do not tax you"), "Seek not to know me" (rather than "Do not seek to know me"), and "I find not myself disposed" (rather than "I do not find myself disposed"). As you can see from these examples, auxiliary verbs are almost always absent as well.

The fifth and final major aspect of Shakespeare's sentence structure is incorrect grammar. This may seem surprising at first, but Shakespeare was more interested in *effective* language than *correct* language. This commitment to effective language is most often the reason for the other sentence structure variations cited. For example, Shakespeare didn't shift word order arbitrarily. It was usually because he wanted the imagery of a section of dialogue to be in a particular order or because he wanted the sentence or phrase to have a specific rhythm or even because he wished to give the character speaking the lines a unique way of talking. Here are some examples of grammatical irregularities from the plays: "Lord Angelo dukes it well in his absence." Lucio in *Measure for Measure* speaks this line. He transforms the noun *duke* into a verb in order to make a sarcastic comment on the cruel Angelo, who is temporarily filling in for the wise and noble Duke Vincentio. Another example is, "This was the most unkindest cut of all." Mark Antony in *Julius Caesar* speaks this line. He cleverly stirs the multitude to rise up against Caesar's assassins, led by Brutus, Caesar's former friend and ally. A larger section of this dialogue reads, "For Brutus, as you know, was Caesar's angel./Judge, O you gods, how dearly Caesar loved him!/This was the most unkindest cut of all." My seventh grade English teacher would have insisted on either "This was the most unkind cut of all" or "This was the unkindest cut of all." But Shakespeare knew that his *grammatically incorrect* choice was the most *dramatically correct* one. Shakespeare ends sentences with prepositions, uses dangling participles, split infinitives, double negatives and even, as we can see with this line—"nor no further in sport neither"—triple negatives! As we continue to read and act Shakespeare, these language peculiarities become familiar and present few problems. We've done a lot of work for one morning. Let's call it a day.

SUMMARY

In this chapter, Joe helps Liz and Sam understand what their characters are saying. They examine Shakespeare's words, his particular writing style, and his sentence structure.

- When working on a Shakespeare speech or scene, the actor must define every word and phrase. A Shakespeare dictionary is the primary source for defining unfamiliar

words. Glosses and footnotes in your Complete Works and individual edition are also helpful. Be sure to also define words that seem familiar but may have had a different definition in Shakespeare's day.
- Paraphrase words, phrases, and sentences. Putting the dialogue into your own words can help you to understand a passage more thoroughly.
- Shakespeare uses many metaphors and similes—which means that a word or phrase primarily used to mean one thing is applied to another. All metaphors and similes must be understood exactly.
- Shakespeare often intended more than one definition of a word or phrase, which deepens meaning. In addition, the actor can use contemporary definitions, not intended by Shakespeare, if they fit the circumstances of the scene and play. Contemporary definitions can only be secondary or tertiary.
- Be certain to read both the introduction and the afterword of the play on which you are working, in both your Complete Works and your individual edition. This can provide insight to your character's motivations and behavior. It can also help you to personalize the given circumstances of the play.
- There were two forms of the word *you* in Elizabethan England. "You" was formal and "thou" was informal.
- Shakespeare often uses physical imagery to deepen the meaning of his dialogue. In this way, conceptual language is married to language that contains sights, smells, sounds, textures, and even tastes.
- He also frequently uses words whose sounds and rhythms mirror their meaning and imagery.
- Shakespeare's sentence structure often varies from modern sentence structure, particularly in the following five ways:
  1. Ellipses—the omission of one or more words in a sentence—are frequent.
  2. Word order can be scrambled. The order of subject—verb—object is often altered.
  3. Auxiliary verbs, commonly called "helping verbs," are often missing.
  4. A negative that is in conjunction with a verb will often follow the verb; for instance, "don't go" can become "go not."
  5. In order to create effective language, Shakespeare often uses incorrect grammar.

EXERCISES

SOLO EXERCISE 2.1
Choose a short speech from a play in each of Shakespeare's four categories. For example:

Antony and Cleopatra—tragedy

The Comedy of Errors—comedy

Richard III—history

The Winter's Tale—romance

After reading the play, choose a speech that occurs early in the play. In this way, you will not need to remember in detail a plethora of information concerning plot, characters, and relationships. Here is an ideal speech for this exercise:

Antony and Cleopatra

Act 1, Scene 1

(Alexandria. A room in Cleopatra's palace. Enter Demetrius and Philo.)

PHILO: Nay, but this dotage of our general's
O'erflows the measure: those his goodly eyes,
That o'er the files and musters of the war
Have glowed like plated Mars, now bend, now turn,
The office and devotion of their view
Upon a tawny front: his captain's heart,
Which in the scuffles of great fights hath burst
The buckles on his breast, reneges all temper,
And is become the bellows and the fan
To cool a gipsy's lust.

(Flourish. Enter Antony, Cleopatra, her Ladies, the Train, with Eunuchs fanning her.)

Look, where they come:
Take but good note, and you shall see in him.
The triple pillar of the world transformed
Into a strumpet's fool: behold and see.
(Antony and Cleopatra, 1, 1, 1–13)

- Define every word in the speech, using a Shakespeare dictionary, such as the Lexicon and/or the OED. Consult footnotes and glosses as well.
- Paraphrase the primary meaning of all words, phrases, and sentences.
- Look for secondary and tertiary meanings of words and phrases. How do these layers of meaning affect the sense of the speech?

- Are there any words whose meaning has altered since Shakespeare's time?
- Locate all physical imagery in the passage. How does this concrete imagery strengthen and reinforce meaning, both intellectually and emotionally?
- Does Shakespeare shift the sentence structure anywhere in the speech? If so, how does an alteration of normal sentence structure affect the imagery of the line?
- Are there words and phrases whose sounds and rhythms underscore meaning and emotion?
- What does a detailed analysis of this *Antony and Cleopatra* speech tell the actor about the speaker? Philo is one of Antony's soldiers. He speaks the foregoing lines and never again appears in the play. What can you discern about his relationship with his silent companion Demetrius? What can you discern about his opinions of Antony? Of Cleopatra? Of Rome? Of Egypt? Of war?

SOLO EXERCISE 2.2
- Select a speech from any of Shakespeare's plays and paraphrase it, using only secondary and tertiary definitions.
- Now paraphrase the speech using only sensory imagery.
- Find all sounds and rhythms that mirror meaning. Exaggerate these sounds and rhythms. Give the sounds and rhythms the emotional life that you feel they contain.
- How does each of the above approaches to the speech affect the imagery, emotion, and sense of the speech?

CHAPTER 3

OVERVIEW OF BASIC ACTING SKILLS APPLIED TO SHAKESPEARE

OBJECTIVES, OBSTACLES, ACTIONS, AND MOTIVATIONS

(I meet Sam and Liz the following morning at the coffee shop.)

JOE: Are you two ready to continue to work on your monologues?
LIZ: Definitely.
SAM: I have almost all of my lines memorized. What else is there to do?
LIZ: We have to find an objective, for one thing, don't we? In other words, our characters must have a strong reason to speak the words.
SAM: Yes, I know. But what I mean is both of our speeches are not really addressed to anyone. Well, actually, Romeo's is addressed to Juliet and Juliet's to Romeo, but Juliet doesn't hear Romeo's speech. In fact, at that point in the play, she doesn't even know that Romeo exists, until he walks up to her later in the scene. And in

Juliet's monologue, she doesn't know that Romeo is there. In our acting classes, all of our scenes are with partners that are onstage with us, and who are aware that the other person is there.

JOE: I understand what you mean. I referred to your speeches as "monologues." Your speeches are actually a specific type of monologue called a "soliloquy." A **soliloquy** (pronounced "soe-LIL-o-kwee") is defined as "1. An act or instance of talking to oneself. 2. Lines in a drama in which a character reveals his thoughts to the audience, but not to the other characters, by speaking as if to himself."[1] Now that we are familiar with the story of the play as well as the exact meanings of your soliloquies, we must go about deciding how we wish to act the soliloquies. The logical place to begin is by reexamining the basic acting skills you learned in your acting classes and applying them to the speeches.[2] Let's return to something that Liz just mentioned, that all-important first commandment of acting: Your character must always have a strong, specific objective (also referred to as an intention). **Objective** is defined as "something aimed at or striven for." It can also be thought of as a "want, need, or desire." These are words we use every day. We say, "I really want her to like me," or "I really need this job,"—not "My objective is for her to like me," or "My objective is to get this job." The word *objective* is an "actor-speak" term. In order for your soliloquies to be effective, you must have an objective, a reason or need to speak the words.

SAM: Yes, that's true. But it's hard to want something from Juliet when I—meaning Romeo—know she can't even hear me. Also, if I were at a party and saw a woman that I was really attracted to, I wouldn't talk about it to myself. I would try to get up the courage to introduce myself and then wait for the right moment to do it.

JOE: Have you ever gone to a party and been stopped in your tracks, so to speak, by someone you found extremely attractive?

SAM: Yes. I was at a party last week and saw a girl—her name is Kate—who I couldn't take my eyes off of. I asked her out, but she had a boyfriend.

JOE: What were you thinking when you first saw Kate?

SAM: That she was incredible!

JOE: I'm sure that's true. But remember that objectives or desires must not only be strong, they must also be specific. What were you thinking specifically?

SAM: Well, she has really beautiful brown eyes. They glisten. And they're almond-shaped. She has a great smile too. And her laugh! It's infectious. I could tell by watching her that she really likes to laugh. And when she was listening to someone, I could sense that she was giving that person her full attention. I got close enough to hear her talking with her friends. She has a beautiful voice—I could listen to her for hours. And I could tell that she's smart and interesting and funny and—

JOE: Sorry to interrupt you, but you could probably go on and on about this young woman and her attributes. Do you see how much more specific you can be than "she's incredible"?

SAM: Yes, I guess you're right.

JOE: Was it scary to approach her and introduce yourself?

SAM: God, yes! I was shaking!

JOE: This brings me to the second commandment of acting: Every objective your character has should be fraught with obstacles. An **obstacle** is defined as "anything that gets in the way or hinders; impediment; obstruction; hindrance." Obstacles can be in us, in other people, or in the environment. The word *obstacle* is also an actor-speak term. Obstacles can be referred to as "problems." As actors, our characters must always have problems that hinder them from getting what they want.

LIZ: Why?

JOE: Because obstacles create conflict and conflict makes for good theatre. An audience wants to watch characters attempt to overcome sometimes insurmountable odds in order to attain their goal. Of course, sometimes we encounter obstacles in real life. In your case Sam, Kate's allure was not only exciting but scary as well. You were probably afraid of rejection, which would be an obstacle in you, or afraid of looking foolish in front of Kate, as well as your friends and peers, which would be an obstacle rooted in those around you.

SAM: Plus, the party was coming to a close and I was afraid that she was going to leave.

JOE: The time problem would be an obstacle in the environment. But you talked to her despite all of these impediments. Why?

SAM: I'm not sure. I guess it's because I knew that I would always regret it if I didn't at least try to get to know her.

JOE: So your need to make contact with her was greater than your fear of rejection, right?

SAM: Yes, I suppose that it was.

JOE: Good acting, good writing, and good theatre in general operate on the same principle. Not only should every objective be fraught with obstacles, but your character's motivation to achieve a want or need should be just slightly stronger than the problems that stand in the way of achieving that goal. Your character may or may not achieve his or her goals—that is determined by the playwright—but it should not be from lack of trying. As I stated earlier, obstacles create conflict and conflict makes for exciting theatre. A good play will weave obstacles into the plot, but it is also incumbent upon the actor to find and attempt to overcome as many valid obstacles as possible for his or her character. This brings me to the third commandment of acting: Always use strong, specific actions to achieve your character's objectives. An **action** is what you *do* in order to try to get what you want. This commandment is at the core of the craft of acting because acting is doing: To act is to do.

LIZ: So when Sam walked up to Kate, introduced himself, and asked her out—that was his action?

JOE: Yes. Sam wanted to date Kate—his objective. He had some problems though: He felt insecure, undeserving, and feared rejection and ridicule—his obstacles. Despite these problems, he decided to do something about his attraction to this young woman. He approached her, introduced himself, and asked for a date—his action. The most pressing problem for Sam was time. The party was about to end and Sam knew it was "now or never." This brings me to an important point: Obstacles often inform your actions.

SAM: What do you mean exactly?

JOE: Let me give you a simple example. Suppose that you are driving on a highway that has two lanes going in the same direction. You are in the left lane when you see a series of traffic cones that are placed to slowly but surely block access to the left lane. What do you do?

SAM: I would merge into the right lane.

JOE: Of course you would. The obstacles in your way—the road cones—informed your action—to steer the car into the right lane. Similarly, the "time" obstacle at the party informed you that you had to approach Kate at that moment, before she had a chance to leave.

SAM: Okay. I get what you mean.

JOE: I mentioned earlier that your character's motivation to achieve his needs should be slightly stronger than the obstacles that stand in his way. A character's motivation is not the same thing as his objective. The OED defines **motivation** as "that which 'moves' or induces a person to act in a certain way." Motivation incites your character to action. While an objective is *what* your character wants, his motivation is *why* he wants it. It is not enough for an actor to be clear only about *what* his character wants. His actions will not be honest, full, or exciting unless he is clear about *why* he wants it. In Sam's real-life scenario, when he first saw Kate, certain things about her attracted him. He then went about building a list of specific attributes about her that increased that attraction. In other words, Sam instinctively fueled his motivation to make contact. Eventually, his motivation was so strong that he overcame all problems that stood in his way. It was this motivation that "fired" him to action.

LIZ: You guys have been talking more about Sam's personal life than our soliloquies. Can we get back to *Romeo and Juliet?*

JOE: Of course. But I'm glad that you mentioned the party, Sam, because it has a number of parallels to the Romeo speech.

SAM: Yes, but I only *thought* all of those things about Kate. I didn't say them out loud, like Romeo. If I had done that, everyone at the party would have thought that I was a freak. Then I definitely wouldn't have stood a chance with her.

JOE: Have you ever acted in a musical?

SAM: Sure. Lots of them.

JOE: Did you ever play a character who sang to a woman or sang a song about a woman that he just met and flipped over?

SAM: Sure. In *Guys and Dolls* I played Sky Masterson and I sang to Sarah. In *West Side Story* I played Tony and I sang to and about Maria. In *Oklahoma*—

LIZ: Okay Sam, he doesn't want to hear your resumé.

JOE: Have you ever spontaneously burst into song in the presence of a woman?

SAM: No, of course not.

JOE: And yet you have no problems with singing to a woman in a musical. Why?

SAM: Because that's what you do in a musical.

JOE: Yes, and sometimes speaking your thoughts aloud is what you do in Shakespeare. It is a convention of the genre of Renaissance drama, just as bursting into song is a convention of the genre of the American musical. Webster's dictionary even cites soliloquies in its definition of **convention**: "*Convention*—a customary practice, rule, method, etc.; usage [the soliloquy was an Elizabethan dramatic 'convention']." Most Americans have grown up with musicals and are familiar and comfortable with its unique style. Most of us have *not* grown up watching Shakespeare, so its conventions seem strange and unfamiliar.

SAM: So, are you saying that I should treat Romeo's speech like the song "Maria" in *West Side Story?*

JOE: Yes, in a way. As I recall, the song "Maria" expresses Tony's feelings about his new love in a way similar to Romeo's soliloquy. Of course, you know that *West Side Story* is based on *Romeo and Juliet*.

SAM: Yes, I know. Okay, let me see if I have this straight. First, I have to find a reason for Romeo to say the words of the speech—

JOE: I have to interrupt you here. As an actor, you should always refer to your character in the first person rather than the third person. This helps you connect with the fictitious individual you will be portraying. Contrarily, speaking of your character in the third person can distance you from your character.

SAM: I understand. So, as Romeo, I have to discover a desire or need to say the words in the speech. That's my objective. I also have to ascertain *why* I want what I want. That is my motivation. Then I have to find all of the problems that stand in my way. Those are my obstacles. Finally, I have to figure out how to overcome those problems and do something to get what I want. That's my action. Am I right so far?

JOE: Absolutely.

SAM: So, as Romeo, my objective would be to meet Juliet.

JOE: That's on the right track, but it sounds a little mundane, don't you think?

SAM: What do you mean?

JOE: Always go for your fantasy when deciding on an objective. You should be able to phrase your objective in a way that excites you and makes you want to do something to achieve it. Does the sentence "I want to meet Juliet" excite you?

SAM: No.

JOE: What do you think Romeo's fantasy is at this point in the play?

SAM: I guess he wants Juliet to be as taken with him as he is with her. She would see him across the room and melt. He would find out by talking to her that he wants to live only for her and she wants to live only for him. They would get married, have lots of kids, and be blissful forever. But in order for all of this to happen, he has to meet her first.

JOE: That's much better. Perhaps a more immediate objective for Romeo at the top of the soliloquy would be to "fuel" himself with specifics about Juliet in order to summon up the courage to meet her, just as you went about building a list of particular attributes about Kate. It seems that you're a lot more romantic than you let on.

SAM: Hey, this is about what *Romeo* wants, not what *I* want!

JOE: But Romeo doesn't exist.

SAM: What do you mean?

SUBSTITUTION, PERSONALIZATION, AND INSTINCTS

JOE: This is something that actors often forget, particularly when it comes to famous characters like Romeo and Juliet. We seem to think that there is some ideal that must be achieved when portraying a well-known dramatic character. The simple fact is that if you are cast in the role, *you* are Romeo. The thousands of actors who have portrayed the role before you are irrelevant, although you may find it helpful to research former productions. In your university production, Romeo is Sam, as if you were born at a different time and place and lived under different circumstances. You must always use yourself in your acting.

SAM: But Romeo is different from me. For one thing I wouldn't mope around like he does in the beginning of the play, just because my girlfriend broke up with me.

JOE: We are all human and have experienced every emotion before the age of ten. Are you telling me that you have never been sad or depressed? You have never moped around, feeling sorry for yourself?

SAM: Sure I have, but not over a girlfriend.

JOE: Over what, then?

SAM: Well, there was a part that I was right for in a production last semester and I didn't get it. I was much better for it than the guy they cast and I gave a better audition, too. I know that it was childish, but I was depressed and moped around for a long time.

JOE: If you were cast as Romeo, you might use that time in your life as a *substitution* for Romeo's behavior over his break up with Rosaline. **Substitute** is defined as "to put in stead of; a person or thing serving or used in place of another."

LIZ: But wouldn't that make Sam detach from the story of the play? He would be talking about one thing but thinking about another.

JOE: That is certainly a danger. First of all, an actor would only use a substitution if he or she could not make a personal connection with what the playwright has provided. Sam has just admitted that it is impossible for him to grieve over the loss of a girlfriend. However, that is precisely what Romeo does in the first act of the play. Sam must find a way to personalize Romeo's situation. Substitution is simply one method of personalization. I mentioned the term **personalize** yesterday. The OED definition is, "*Personalize*—to render personal; to represent as personal, personify; to embody in a person, impersonate." Of course, the ideal means of personalization is to instinctively connect with the persons, relationships, and events in the play. When this occurs, it is fortunate indeed.

And this brings us to another important point: Actors should always trust their instincts. However, as we actors are painfully aware, we are not always able to make this instinctive connection. In these cases, we must find others means of personalization, such as substitution. Liz just mentioned a possible pitfall when using a substitution: It can detach the actor from the circumstances of the play. This can be avoided if the actor transfers the *essence* of the substitution to the circumstance or person in the play. In other words, if Sam were cast as Romeo, he might say to himself, "I don't know what it feels like to be depressed about the loss of a girlfriend, but I bet it feels very much like how I felt about losing that role last semester. I would probably feel similarly and act in a similar manner." Sam would therefore transfer the essence of the substitution—how he felt and acted—and use it for his—Romeo's—feelings and behavior over his breakup with Rosaline. It is an *emotional* rather than a *literal* substitution. Sam would eventually be able to drop the substitution, once it became synonymous with the person, thing, or event in the play.

GIVEN AND IMAGINARY CIRCUMSTANCES

JOE: A second way to personalize is by fantasizing the given circumstances of the play in sensory detail. Your character's **given circumstances** are everything that the playwright has written about your character's past, present, and expected future. If Sam were to use this method, he would "run movies in his head" of Romeo's relationship and subsequent breakup with Rosaline. Because the given circumstances of the relationship between Romeo and Rosaline are sketchy, Sam would use imaginary circumstances to fill in the details of the relationship. **Imaginary circumstances** are those invented by the actor to help make a fuller connection with the written material. The Romeo/Rosaline story is a *prior circumstance*—that is, it occurs before the play begins. Shakespeare is not all that interested in this prior circumstance because it is merely a catalyst for what he *is* interested in—the story of Romeo and Juliet. However, the actor playing Romeo must be *very* interested in the details of the Romeo/Rosaline story because it so strongly affects his behavior at the top of the play. Sam would use his imagination to create details about what "his" Rosaline looks and sounds like, as well as how he and Rosaline met, what they did together, the fun they had, the misery they endured, the details of the breakup, and so on. Sam would run these movies in *sensory detail;* that is, he would focus on the sights, sounds, smells, tastes, and tactile elements of these imaginary circumstances in an attempt to create a belief in them. Sensory elements are nonintellectual and can provide a more immediate, emotional connection with the written material. This method can be used with the playwright's given circumstances as well as the actor's imaginary circumstances in each and every moment of the play.

LIZ: I would be afraid that if I did all of that work, I would lose myself in the role.

JOE: Of course you wouldn't have a *complete* belief in these circumstances; after all, you aren't psychotic. You're always fully aware that these "memories" are fictitious, but if you are willing to buy into it, this form of personalization can be quite effective. Let's face it, acting is really only playing make-believe. As children, how many times have we all come home from a Saturday matinee and acted out the film we just saw with our friends? We became superheroes, cowboys, cowgirls, princes, princesses, and soldiers—and we *believed* it. It was this unfaltering belief that made the playing so much fun. It is really no different when we act in a play. We must take that leap of faith and have fun trusting and living the make-believe. Does any of this make sense?

SAM: Yes, it does. I got really excited about playing Romeo after reading the play because I wanted to be in the story. I wanted to be able to pretend that it was happening to me. I guess that sounds kind of childish, but it's true.

JOE: Not "childish," but "childlike." Let's move on. There is a third method of personalization that is a combination of both substitution and fantasizing in sensory detail. Let's use the circumstances in Romeo's soliloquy to explore this method. Sam, do you have a "Juliet" in mind?

SAM: I'm not sure what you mean. Liz will be playing Juliet. She's a good friend and a good actress and we work well together.

LIZ: Thanks, Sam.
JOE: Is your relationship with Liz similar to Romeo's relationship with Juliet?
SAM: No, not at all. Liz is a friend. We don't think of one another in a romantic way at all.
JOE: You've got a problem then, don't you? Don't get me wrong. When you begin rehearsals for your workshop production, you will certainly use everything about Liz that attracts you, as well as all of the aspects that make up your friendship and that are applicable to Romeo's relationship with Juliet. Anything about your relationship that is unlike Romeo's relationship with Juliet, such as a romantic attraction, must be personalized in a manner that draws you closer to Liz, not distances you from her. But right now, we are not working on the production; we are working on an isolated speech that you will present in class. Also, if there were open auditions for your production, it is possible that Liz wouldn't be cast. If you had auditioned and were cast as Romeo, it may have been opposite someone that you don't know very well—or worse, someone you dislike. Then what?
SAM: I guess I would use a substitution or the "running movies in your head" thing.
JOE: Yes, you could. But let's explore one other possibility. Can you think of someone who could be your Juliet?
SAM: You want me to say Kate, the girl from the party.
JOE: Yes.
SAM: But she rejected me.
JOE: That's why she is the perfect example of the third method of personalization, which combines substitution and fantasy. Was your reaction to seeing Kate for the first time similar to Romeo's first encounter with Juliet?
SAM: Definitely. She took my breath away! But she turned me down. Juliet didn't do that to Romeo.
JOE: If you were to use Kate as a substitution for Juliet while using this speech for an audition, it wouldn't necessarily be a problem, as Romeo doesn't know if he will be accepted or rejected by Juliet at this point in the play. However, it could be problematic to use Kate as a substitution for Juliet throughout the entire play unless you used fantasy as well.
SAM: How would I do that?
JOE: You would use the substitution of your first encounter with Kate up until the point in the conversation that she turned you down.[3] At this point you would shift into fantasy. Instead of rejecting you by telling you about her boyfriend, she would instead say that she was unattached or had just broken up with a guy who was a complete jerk. She would tell you that she would be thrilled to go out with you and had seen you around campus and found you very attractive, and so on. This would remove any stumbling blocks to your personalization.
LIZ: Our acting teacher refers to it as an "as if."
JOE: Yes. An "as if" can be real or fictitious. Liz, what do you think about beauty contests?
LIZ: Excuse me?
JOE: You heard me.
LIZ: I hate them. They're demeaning and they treat women as sexual objects. They should be abolished.

JOE: Let's say you were cast as a woman who has just become Miss America, and is thrilled about it. Can you think of a substitution?
LIZ: Hmmm... I wrote a short story that won a literary prize. I was very excited about it.
JOE: So becoming Miss America would be "as if" you had just won the literary prize. Can you think of a fantasy that would work for you as well?
LIZ: Sure, winning the Tony for best actress!
JOE: So, in this case, becoming Miss America would be "as if" you had just won the Tony award for best actress. The first "as if" is based in reality, while the second "as if" is fantasy. However, it is a fantasy that you can relate to and have probably daydreamed about. The same is probably true of Sam's encounter with Kate. He can relate to the fantasy portion of the scenario. Regardless of which means of personalization Sam uses, it is essential that he find an *emotional life* that parallels that of Romeo. A strong emotional life is essential for a character's motivation.
LIZ: What do you mean by **emotional life?**
JOE: It's an honest connection to the primary emotion of your character at a particular point in a play. For example, Romeo's emotional life at the beginning of the play can be described as extreme melancholy. This melancholia drives his behavior—long walks before dawn, sitting alone in a dark room for hours at a time, avoiding contact with others. His emotional life on seeing Juliet for the first time is passionate infatuation. This emotional life causes him to make contact with her. Juliet's emotional life parallels that of Romeo on their first meeting. However, after the party her emotional life turns to fear and anxiety. This causes her to walk onto her balcony and speak the words of her soliloquy. Again, if the actor cannot make an instinctive emotional connection with her character, then she must use personalization. This brings me to an important point: Finding the emotional life of a character is only a means to an end, and that end is your character's behavior. Remember—acting is *doing,* not *feeling.* Acting is like a pendulum. You must avoid both extremes of the pendulum. Some actors can access their emotional life quite readily but then choose merely to indulge in those emotions rather than use them to spur their character to action. Actors at the other extreme are "technicians." They put their entire being into the "doing" but their actions are devoid of an emotional life. Such actors can be exciting to watch but their work lacks a "soul."
LIZ: I did a scene last year in which my character had to cry. I used something from my own life to help me find the tears. But it really caused me a lot of personal pain. After the scene was over I couldn't let my substitution go. I cried at totally inappropriate times for more than a month.
JOE: Was the event you used as a substitution something with which you had reached closure?
LIZ: If you mean, was it something I had come to terms with, I guess the answer would be no.
JOE: Then you should never have used it as a substitution. Tapping into your emotions is dangerous territory to traverse. Substitutions must always be personal, but should never be inviolable.
LIZ: What's the difference between "personal" and "inviolable"?

JOE: Webster's dictionary defines *inviolable* as "not to be violated; not to be profaned or injured." Let me give you an example of what I mean. I have used the death of my grandmother as a substitution for a character that experiences the death of a close friend. This was obviously a very personal substitution and it worked well for me. However, my grandmother lived a long, healthy, happy life and I feel fortunate to have spent a good deal of time in her company. Although I miss her terribly, I have dealt with that loss. On the other hand, I had a girlfriend who died in a car accident over twenty years ago. I have never come to closure concerning this tragedy. Hence, I would never entertain the thought of using it in my acting. Both events are personal, but the second event is inviolable. Is that clear?

LIZ: Yes.

JOE: It is also important to keep your substitutions to yourself. In other words, don't tell anyone, especially your fellow actors, that you are using a substitution or tell them any details about it. Doing so could cause the substitution to lose its effectiveness. Always remember that regardless of which means of personalization you use, you must always transfer the essence of it onto the places, objects, or events in the play and onto the actors in your particular production of it. For example, if Sam were to use aspects of Kate to personalize Romeo's strong romantic feelings for Juliet in your workshop production, he would transfer those aspects onto Liz during rehearsals and performances, hence eventually dropping Kate out of the picture altogether. Now that we have explored some of the acting tools necessary to begin work on your pieces, let's work on your speeches in more detail.

Summary

In this chapter, Joe provides Sam and Liz with a brief overview of basic acting skills and how they can be applied to the plays of Shakespeare.

- The Romeo and Juliet speeches are called soliloquies. A soliloquy is a speech in which a character reveals his thoughts to the audience, but not to the other characters, by speaking as if to himself.
- The actor's first job is to find a strong, specific objective or goal, a reason for the character to speak the words of the speech.
- A character should also have obstacles, which are problems that stand in the way of achieving his or her goal. A character's objective should always be slightly stronger than the obstacles.
- An actor must do something to achieve the goal. This is known as an action. Obstacles often inform the character's actions.
- The actor must then personalize the given circumstances of the play in order to connect with the character's motivation. The character's motivation is *why* she wants what she wants.
- There are four ways to personalize.
    1. Make an instinctive connection to the character, relationships, and/or events. This is the ideal means of personalization.

2. Find a substitution. A substitution is a person, thing, or event used in place of another.
3. Fantasize the given circumstances in sensory detail.
4. Use a combination of substitution and fantasy.

- Personalization helps the actor find the character's emotional life and motivations to action. It also permits the actor to behave truthfully and fully onstage. These personalizations must ultimately help the connection between the character and the other actors' characters—not distance the actor from them.
- An actor must always use himself and trust his or her instincts. They are always right.

Exercises

SOLO EXERCISE 3.1

Choose a soliloquy from a play in each of Shakespeare's categories. For example:

King Lear—tragedy

Twelfth Night—comedy

Henry V—history

Cymbeline—romance

Read the play and do all of the work on the speech that you did in the exercises in Chapter 2. Now decide the character's objective with this soliloquy. What is he trying to achieve? Make all of the decisions that are necessary for you to begin to work on the speech as an actor. Let's use a soliloquy from *Twelfth Night* as an example:

> SEBASTIAN: This is the air; that is the glorious sun;
> This pearl she gave me, I do feel't and see't;
> And though 'tis wonder that enwraps me thus,
> Yet 'tis not madness. Where's Antonio, then?
> I could not find him at the Elephant:
> Yet there he was; and there I found this credit,
> That he did range the town to seek me out.
> His counsel now might do me golden service;
> For though my soul disputes well with my sense,
> That this may be some error, but no madness,
> Yet doth this accident and flood of fortune
> So far exceed all instance, all discourse,
> That I am ready to distrust mine eyes
> And wrangle with my reason that persuades me

> To any other trust but that I am mad,
> Or else the lady's mad; yet, if 'twere so,
> She could not sway her house, command her followers,
> Take and give back affairs and their dispatch
> With such a smooth, discreet and stable bearing
> As I perceive she does: there's something in't
> That is deceivable. But here the lady comes.
> (*Twelfth Night*, 4, 3, 1–21)

Sebastian is the twin brother of Viola, who is in disguise as a man. Olivia, the "lady" mentioned in this speech, has fallen in love with the disguised Viola and has mistaken Sebastian for his twin sister. Viola and Sebastian were separated in a shipwreck and neither is aware that the other is alive. Both siblings have found themselves washed ashore in Illyria, a country foreign to them. A sea captain named Antonio, who told Sebastian to meet him at an inn called "The Elephant," has assisted Sebastian. Sebastian is flabbergasted that Olivia and her followers seem not only to know him, but also to have strong opinions about him. Sebastian walks into Olivia's garden in order to be alone and attempt to resolve his situation.

1. What does Sebastian expect to accomplish with this soliloquy? What does he want?
2. What are the problems standing in the way of Sebastian getting what he wants?
3. What is he "doing" with the words in this speech? How can this help him to achieve his goal?
4. From his words, what can you ascertain about Sebastian's opinion of and feelings about Olivia? About Antonio?
5. If you were playing the role of Sebastian, how would you motivate this speech?
6. If you were working on this speech in class, who would be your Olivia?
7. Who would be your Antonio?
8. How would you personalize the pearl given to Sebastian by Olivia?
9. How would you personalize Illyria?
10. How would you personalize the predicament in which Sebastian finds himself?

SOLO EXERCISE 3.2

Parallel Soliloquy. Choose a soliloquy from one of Shakespeare's plays. Do all of the work necessary to begin work on the speech as an actor. Now find a circumstance from your life that most closely resembles the situation in which the character finds himself during the soliloquy. *Find the emotional essence of the soliloquy in order to find a parallel.* For example, in the speech examined in the preceding exercise, above all else, Sebastian is confused and is trying to discern what is *really* going on around him.

JOE: I once received a phone call from an old friend who castigated me for betraying a confidence. I was innocent of this charge but she insisted that it was true, refused to supply me with any additional information, and hung up on me. I promptly called her back but she refused to answer the phone. Desperate, I spent a good deal of time in my living room trying to figure out what had happened. How did she receive this erroneous information? From *whom* did she receive this erroneous information? Did she misunderstand something that someone said? And on and on.

An inner monologue such as the one described above could be used as a parallel soliloquy.

First, in the privacy of your room, try to find words that would be a fair expression of your thoughts during your actual situation. Speak these words aloud. Do this several times. Now substitute the words of the soliloquy but keep the given circumstances of your real-life situation. Do this several times as well. Present the soliloquy in class, using your real-life situation but Shakespeare's words. Re-create your real-life environment as well. For example, someone using the example given above would set up a simple environment that resembled his or her living room and speak the soliloquy in that environment. This is an excellent way in which to personalize your character's emotional life. Don't worry if the sense of Shakespeare's words does not exactly match what you thought in your true-life scenario. Stay true instead to the emotional equivalent of the speech. When you feel that you are making a strong emotional connection, set the exercise aside and work in detail on the actual meaning and imagery of the speech. This exercise is also a great way to get in touch with speaking your thoughts aloud as well as using such vocalizations to achieve a goal.

Note: If your real-life situation is not inviolable, you may wish to begin the exercise in class with the words from your real scenario and then segue into Shakespeare's words.

NOTES

1. Unlike the soliloquy, most of Shakespeare's monologues are speeches directed to a person or persons who are in the environment with the speaker and who are aware that they are being spoken to.
2. This chapter is not meant as a replacement for in-depth acting classes or comprehensive textbooks on acting. It is instead a reminder of basic acting skills and how we can apply those skills specifically to the plays of Shakespeare.
3. I prefer to use the word *substitution* for people, things, and events that are reality based; that is, substitutions always entail people that you actually know, relationships that you actually experienced, and/or events that actually occurred.

CHAPTER 4

SPEECHES

ANALYZING SOLILOQUIES

(Liz, Sam, and I continue our conversation at the coffee shop.)

JOE: Liz, your speech is of a different ilk from Sam's. Whereas Romeo's speech is a spontaneous expression of adulation, Juliet's speech is an attempt at problem solving. Soliloquies that attempt to resolve a problem are very common in Elizabethan drama. A character faced with a dilemma will often speak to herself in an attempt to arrive at a solution. In this case, Juliet is desperately trying to solve the problem of loving a member of a family that is loathed by her own. Now that we've discussed objectives, actions, obstacles, emotional life, motivation, and personalization—do you have any ideas on how to proceed with your Juliet speech?

LIZ: I think it's interesting that you asked Sam what he thought Romeo's fantasy was. It seems to me that Juliet's objective is a *complete* fantasy. I'm not sure how seriously she entertains the notion of either of them actually renouncing their families. She must know that it is really not possible for either herself or Romeo to do.

JOE: First of all, we know from the dialogue between the Nurse and Lady Capulet in Act 1, scene 3, that Juliet is two weeks shy of her fourteenth birthday. Much of what she says and does reflects her age and lack of experience. Are you telling me that you have never wanted something so badly that you fantasized about how to overcome seemingly overwhelming odds in order to achieve it?

LIZ: When I was thirteen, my family planned a trip to Hawaii. I had an appendicitis attack shortly before we had to leave. It was decided that after my operation, I would recuperate at my grandparents' house while the rest of my family went to Hawaii. I came up with every harebrained plan you could think of that would allow me to go on the vacation. Even after my family left, I bent my grandparents' ears with plans to join my family. One idea I had was to hire a nurse to go to Hawaii with me. I was going to pay her by taking on extra baby-sitting jobs for a year.

JOE: Did you actually think that any of these ideas would work?

LIZ: Yes and no. Even though I knew deep down that I wasn't going to Hawaii, my constant brainstorming gave me hope and kept me from despairing.

JOE: Isn't it possible that Juliet is doing the same thing?

LIZ: Yes, I guess so.

JOE: There is also a parallel between this speech and Romeo's speech. Juliet confesses her love and devotion to Romeo just as Romeo confessed his love and devotion to Juliet earlier at the party.

LIZ: I think that Juliet's objective is—

JOE: You're speaking of your character in the third person.

LIZ: Oh, right. I think that *my* objective is to make Romeo confess his undying love for me and to find a way to live "happily ever after" with him. The major obstacle is obviously the hatred between our families. I also think that another obstacle may be my insecurity about Romeo's feelings for me because I say "be but sworn my love, and I'll no longer be a Capulet." This insecurity becomes more apparent during my subsequent scene with Romeo. I am willing to make great sacrifices for him, but I want to be sure that his feelings are mutual. My insecurities may stem from feeling unworthy to be loved or at least unsure about having the qualities to attract a boy like Romeo. After all, I have probably never had a boyfriend and am new to romantic love. It seems that my actions are to reason ways to overcome our bloodlines and live happily together, even if it means never seeing our families again.

JOE: Do you have a substitute for Romeo?

LIZ: Yes, but I would rather not say who it is.

JOE: That's a good idea.

SAM: You seem to dwell a lot on substitutions. Do we always have to have substitutions for everything?

JOE: No, of course not. As I said earlier, substitutions are only necessary when there is no other means of connecting with the written material. However, substitutions are almost always necessary when working on a new audition piece or when working on a speech in class. The reason for this is fairly obvious: The world of the play is absent. Of course, we begin to connect to the world of the play by reading it, but we use substitutions here as well. We plug people we know or have seen into the cast list. Friar Lawrence is Uncle Fred, Paris is the guy who sits next to you in chemistry class, the Prince is Harrison Ford, and so on. Because the play is in our imaginings at this point, substitutions are certainly a necessity. However, once you are cast in a production, it is essential that you make a connection with each and every actor in the play. Even if the actress playing Juliet is someone whom you dislike, your first step is to connect with the woman herself. Find the attributes about her that attract you and use those attributes first. In addition, she will be drawing on those aspects of her personality that are most Juliet-like, which could reduce your need for a substitution. Also, at the risk of sounding like Will Rogers, it may be very possible that if you spend some quality time with your Juliet, you will discover that she is a fairly decent person after all. But if you still find that you need to use a substitution, *endow* your partner with the elements of that substitution. The OED defines **endow** as "to enrich or furnish with any 'gift,' quality, or power of mind or body; to invest (imaginatively) with a quality." This keeps you connected to the person who is onstage with you.

But at this juncture we are working on your speeches for class presentation or as possible future audition pieces. Let's return to your speech, Liz. I think that we left off with you deciding—wisely, I may add—that you did not wish to reveal the source of your substitution for Romeo. We discussed your overall objective as well as the obstacles that stand in Juliet's way.

LIZ: Yes, but I'm a little unclear about my actions. I said earlier that it seems that my actions are to figure out a way to live together happily, despite the hatred our families have for one another. But that isn't really an action. I come up with a number of ideas, but they are only *possibilities* for action, not acts in themselves.

SAM: If Liz were to use the speech as if Romeo were present, she could play actions to her imaginary Romeo, couldn't she?

JOE: Of course. She would have to.

SAM: Our acting teachers tell us to use active verbs when considering actions to play.

JOE: Yes. That's a great way to begin to think of actions. Juliet could "flatter" Romeo, "entice" him, "plead" with him, "command" him, and so on. Juliet can play a number of different actions in this speech. Some actions are implied in the text, but each actress portraying the role will choose her own actions to play to Romeo.

LIZ: Yes, but Romeo, at least as far as Juliet knows at this moment—I mean, as far as *I* know at this moment—isn't there.

JOE: You're right. You also put it well by calling Juliet's ideas "possibilities" for action. That is precisely what they are. This is frequently the case with soliloquies. Shakespeare's characters are doers; they are constantly trying to achieve goals. When those goals become overwhelming, Shakespeare will often allow a character to remove herself from outside stimuli and turn inward in an attempt to reason through possible paths of action to solve the problem at hand. Shakespeare's heroes, heroines, and villains are usually fiercely independent. They often do not have a confidant in whom to confide and ask advice, or if they do, they sometimes reject the advice and turn to the only person they can truly trust to help solve their problem—themselves! This "reasoning through" or "processing" of possible solutions is in itself extremely active. It is focused, energetic brainpower at work.

Now, when I say that these characters turn inward, I don't mean that they brood or contemplate. Rather, they engage those aspects of their own personas that can best help them arrive at a solution. Even Sam's Romeo speech implicitly involves problem solving. As soon as he sees Juliet, a big problem is inherent in his attraction:

"I have to meet this woman but if I reveal myself to her she may reject me, she might scream, I could be killed by an irate Capulet . . ." and so on. Although it may seem paradoxical at first, this "self-debating" or "reasoning through" to discover a path of action is in itself an action. I said earlier that *language is thought in action*. Nowhere in Shakespeare is this truer than in the soliloquy. We actors must always understand Shakespeare's dialogue as our characters' *forward momentum of thought*. I also commented previously that *clarity of meaning leads to clarity of thought, and clarity of thought leads to clarity of action*. Similarly, *depth of meaning leads to depth of thought, and depth of thought leads to depth of action*. This helps to ensure our characters' "forward momentum." Shakespeare provides this depth through multiple definitions, concrete imagery, and specific sounds and rhythms—all of which create a concentrated imagery, emotional life, and intent for our characters.

Liz: But in the soliloquy, is Juliet talking to herself or to Romeo?

Joe: The speaker in a Shakespearean soliloquy is usually addressing one of the following:

1. Someone who is unaware of the speaker's presence
2. Someone or something not present in the environment
3. The gods, spirits, or nature
4. Oneself or the audience

Sam's Romeo soliloquy falls under the first category because Juliet is unaware of Romeo's presence. The second and third options fall under a category called an *apostrophe*. An **apostrophe** is a figure of speech, by which a speaker addresses people or things that are absent or dead. Liz, your Juliet speech falls under the first of these types of apostrophes—addressing someone or something that is not in the speaker's space. Although the audience is aware that Romeo is overhearing her speech, Juliet thinks that she is addressing someone who is absent from her environment. So to answer your question, I believe that Juliet is addressing Romeo—but, in a way, she is addressing herself as well. She talks to an imaginary Romeo in an attempt to discover his true feelings for her as well as to solve the problem of their lineage. It may be a "practice session" of what she will request of Romeo when she next sees him. The fine art of debate was much in vogue during Shakespeare's time, whether it meant debating with others or with oneself, in order to arrive at a solution to a problem or to convince others that a given solution is best. A widely held belief was that breaking it down into its component parts and analyzing them could solve a problem. Shakespeare usually presents the problem itself—the objective as well as the obstacles that surround it—in the body of the soliloquy, usually in the first few lines. Juliet's speech is a typical example of this. She begins by saying—and I'm paraphrasing here—"Why do you have to be called Romeo? Reject your name or, if you won't, just swear that you love me and I'll reject my name. It is only your name that is my enemy." The problem is laid out immediately. At this point she begins to act and think like a lawyer or the captain of a debating team. She goes about presenting solid arguments for why it is appropriate for

Romeo to reject his name. Let's look at the following section of the speech with this in mind:

> Thou art thyself, though not a Montague.
> What's Montague? It is nor hand, nor foot,
> Nor arm, nor face, nor any other part
> Belonging to a man. O, be some other name!
> What's in a name? That which we call a rose
> By any other word would smell as sweet.
> So Romeo would, were he not Romeo called,
> Retain that dear perfection which he owes
> Without that title. Romeo, doff thy name,
> And for thy name, which is no part of thee,
> Take all myself. *(Romeo and Juliet, 2, 2, 39–49)*

It is a very convincing argument. She puts "titles" on trial, as it were. She poses rhetorical questions ("What's Montague?" and "What's in a name?") along with solid reasoning and comparisons ("that which we call a rose by any other word would smell as sweet") to make a solid case. She ends by making a bargain with her imaginary Romeo. She says, in effect, "If you give up your name, which I have just proven means nothing anyway, I will give you my entire being in exchange." She makes him an "offer he can't refuse" or would be stupid to refuse.

SAM: Does Juliet know what she is going to say in her argument beforehand? I mean, has she been lying in bed formulating it and then goes to the balcony to hear what it sounds like out loud?

JOE: No. I think using that imaginary circumstance would be a big mistake. It would remove the spontaneity from the piece. It is important for actors to adhere to the *illusion of the first time.* In other words, even though you have been rehearsing a monologue for months or you are in your second year of performances of a production, it must seem to an audience as though all of your thoughts and actions are happening for the first time. The best way to do that is to convince *yourself* that everything is happening for the first time. A good actor convinces the audience that what she is doing is real. A *great* actor convinces *herself* that what she is doing is real. The stimulus for your character's words should come to her the millisecond before they are uttered.

LIZ: That's easier said than done.

JOE: Of course it is. That's why acting classes and stage experience are so vital. No book can take the place of practical experience. However, I can help guide you. We have discussed objectives, but not specific categories of objectives. As you have probably learned in your acting classes, actors always work from the general to the specific. The most general objective is often referred to as a *life objective.* This is what your character wants most in life—love, respect, and so forth. These kinds of wants are abstract and "unactable." Next on the list is your character's *play objective* or *super objective.* This type of objective is more specific—it may be to get love and respect from a specific person—but is still too large to be acted upon. Your character's *act objectives*—as in Act 1, Act 2, and so on—and *scene objectives* are more specific, and her *beat objectives* are the most specific. Scene and beat objectives are specific enough to be actable. A **beat** in acting is a specific unit of thought or action. Each time an idea or action shifts, this is called a "beat change."

All of your character's objectives should have a commonality. In other words, all beat objectives in a scene should be in pursuit of that particular scene objective, all scene objectives should serve the play objective, and so on. In order to help clarify what I'm talking about, let's construct possible objectives for the character of Iago from Shakespeare's masterpiece, *Othello*. Let's say Iago's life objective is "to achieve unlimited power." His play objective is "to get revenge on and power over Othello." An act objective is "to drive Othello to jealous madness." As we get more specific, we begin to formulate objectives that we can act upon, such as "to convince Othello that Desdemona is sleeping with Cassio." A more specific scene objective is "to alert and incense Desdemona's father about the recent marriage of his daughter to Othello." This objective is certainly specific enough to do something about. In fact, the play begins with Iago waking Brabantio, Desdemona's father, from a sound sleep, and taunting him with racist epithets and crude sexual language regarding the wedding of his young white daughter to a middle-aged black man. He does this in order to so enrage Brabantio that he will try to annul the marriage. Iago achieves this objective. All of these wants and desires have a commonality: Trying to destroy Othello's marriage by incensing his new father-in-law and convincing Othello that he is a cuckold are ways for Iago to take revenge on, and power over, Othello. These bring Iago a step closer to achieving ultimate power.

Speeches, particularly soliloquies, operate in the same manner. In fact, it helps to think of a speech as a tiny play in itself. It consists of an overall objective, beat objectives that serve the overall soliloquy objective, and transitions between the beat objectives. These transitions are unspoken stimuli that are the genesis of each beat change. Deciding your character's overall reason for speaking a speech and then breaking the speech into its component parts—paying close attention to how and why one part leads to another—will guarantee a clear, dynamic forward momentum of thought for your character.

Analyzing Juliet's Speech

JOE: Let's analyze the Juliet speech with all of this in mind. As I mentioned earlier, Juliet has probably been lying in bed, tossing and turning with thoughts of Romeo and the unfortunate fact that he is a Montague. It becomes too much for her and she rises, steps outside into the night air and begins to problem-solve. This may be the unspoken stimulus that motivates her to speak the words:

> O Romeo, Romeo, wherefore art thou Romeo?
> Deny thy father and refuse thy name:
> Or if thou wilt not, be but sworn my love
> And I'll no longer be a Capulet.

These first few lines contain the overall objective of the speech. She wants Romeo to disown his family and pledge his love and devotion to her. If he is unwilling to do so, all he has to do is swear his love for her and she will disown her family. Next she expresses the reason for her request, which is the main obstacle to her union with Romeo:

> 'Tis but thy name that is my enemy.

Juliet says in essence, "I love you, but must hate your name, as I am a Capulet." Big problem. The stimulus for this line may be the fact that her objective seems cruel and unusual unless one takes this major problem into account. However, the line is also an expression of hope because it is not Romeo himself that she must hate, but merely his appelation. Now Juliet begins to persuade her imaginary Romeo to accept her plan in a logical and systematic manner:

> Thou art thyself, though not a Montague.

The transition into this line is a reasonable one. She has just stated that it is only his name that stands in the way of their happiness, and it would only follow that a name—and here she speaks his surname for the first time—has absolutely nothing to do with the person to which it is attached. She makes this point more specifically with her next few lines, which begin with a rhetorical question:

> What's Montague? . . .

Next, she uses a comparison to further drive her point home, building more evidence on the journey to her conclusion:

> . . . It is nor hand, nor foot
> Nor arm, nor face, nor any other part
> Belonging to a man. O, be some other name!

I think that it is the emotionally laden last line—"O, be some other name!"—that triggers the transition to the following section of dialogue. Because she is not yet fourteen, Juliet's emotions may get the better of her for a brief moment on this line. She may then realize that in order to get what she wants from her imaginary Romeo she must persuade logically, not emotionally. In any case, the impassioned utterance of "name" at the end of this section certainly triggers Juliet's next beat, which once again begins with a rhetorical question:

> What's in a name? That which we call a rose
> By any other word would smell as sweet.
> So Romeo would, were he not Romeo called,
> Retain that dear perfection which he owes
> Without that title. . . .

Now that she has fully crafted her argument, she concludes by offering Romeo a bargain:

> . . . Romeo, doff thy name,
> And for thy name, which is no part of thee,
> Take all myself.

In a way, it is a rewording of the beginning of the speech, but is now backed up by a specific, well-crafted argument. As you can see, each beat seems to "fire" or "ignite" the next. Transitions from beat to beat often move from the general to the specific.

Analyzing Romeo's Speech

SAM: Does that formula apply to my speech as well?
JOE: Yes—but as I said earlier, your speech is of a different ilk. Romeo has not been preoccupied with a problem, as Juliet has. He is, instead, suddenly and unexpectedly swept off his feet and must process his attraction to Juliet. Let's analyze your speech as well:

> O, she doth teach the torches to burn bright!

This line, although not an objective, reflects Romeo's general impression of his first glimpse of Juliet. He then proceeds to be more specific:

> It seems she hangs upon the cheek of night
> As a rich jewel in an Ethiop's ear—
> Beauty too rich for use, for earth too dear.
> So shows a snowy dove trooping with crows
> As yonder lady o'er her fellows shows.

Romeo uses metaphor extensively as a means of clarifying his attraction to Juliet. Next, he makes a decision on how to proceed, based on the intensity of this attraction:

> The measure done, I'll watch her place of stand,
> And, touching hers, make blessed my rude hand.

The final two lines, which begin with a rhetorical question, are a revelation to Romeo of his former blindness. It has taken the "bright light" of Juliet to jolt Romeo out of his darkness. This hearkens back to his heartbreak over the breakup with Rosaline, whom he now realizes he did not truly love:

> Did my heart love till now? Forswear it, sight;
> For I ne'er saw true beauty till this night.

You both have enough information now to begin working on your speeches for class. However, before we quit for the day, I want to explore examples of the two types of soliloquies that we have yet to cover.

Analyzing Other Soliloquies

Joe: The third option of whom to address in a Shakespearean soliloquy is also an apostrophe: addressing the gods, spirits, or nature—things that can never be present in the environment with the speaker, as they are ethereal and conceptual.

Edmund from *King Lear*

Joe: Let's examine such a soliloquy, spoken by Edmund in *King Lear*:

> Thou, Nature, art my goddess, to thy law
> My services are bound. Wherefore should I
> Stand in the plague of custom, and permit
> The curiosity of nations to deprive me,
> For that I am some twelve or fourteen moonshines
> Lag of a brother? Why bastard? Wherefore base?
> When my dimensions are as well compact,
> My mind as generous, and my shape as true,
> As honest madam's issue? Why brand they us
> With base? With baseness? bastardy? base, base?
> Who, in the lusty stealth of nature, take
> More composition, and fierce quality,
> Than doth within a dull, stale, tired bed
> Go to th' creating a whole tribe of fops,
> Got 'tween asleep and wake? Well then,
> Legitimate Edgar, I must have your land.
> Our father's love is to the bastard Edmund
> As to th' legitimate. Fine word, "legitimate"!
> Well, my legitimate, if this letter speed
> And my invention thrive, Edmund the base
> Shall top th' legitimate. I grow, I prosper:
> Now gods, stand up for bastards!   *(King Lear, 1, 2, 1–22)*

Edmund the bastard is the illegitimate second son of the Earl of Gloucester. He is enraged that he will not inherit from his father as will his older, legitimate brother, Edgar. He calls on the goddess of Nature to validate a treacherous course of action that he is about to implement, which will falsely implicate Edgar in a plot to kill their father. He also calls on the goddess of Nature to give him the strength to carry out his scheme. This is also a problem-solving speech and displays the same formula as the Juliet speech. Edmund begins by flattering Nature, saying that he is her servant and bound to do her bidding:

> Thou, Nature, art my goddess, to thy law
> My services are bound. . . .

Praying to Nature is the opposite of praying to God. By praying to Nature, Edmund rejects the Christian world in which he finds himself, a world that denies him any inheritance from his father's estate. Even if he were legitimate, Edmund would lose out, as the eldest son inherits the father's entire estate. This custom was practiced in England during Shakespeare's time and was opposed by many for good reason. In fact, many of Shakespeare's fellow playwrights were younger sons from wealthy families. Many graduated from the foremost universities in the country, yet had to eke out a living by writing plays for six or seven pounds apiece. Nature, on the other hand, is not bound by such restrictions. Survival of the fittest is the rule instead. The goddess of Nature rewards those with the ambition and savvy to get ahead by any means possible. This "law" of Nature is what Edmund is committing himself to in the first line of the soliloquy. Next, he states his objective and obstacle with one rhetorical question:

> . . . Wherefore should I
> Stand in the plague of custom, and permit
> The curiosity of nations to deprive me,
> For that I am some twelve or fourteen moonshines
> Lag of a brother? . . .

Edmund asks, "Why should I be subjected to the curse of primogeniture and allow the scrupulousness of society to disinherit me simply because I was born some twelve or fourteen months after my brother, Edgar?" Edmund's objective is implicit: He wishes to have a substantial portion of his father's estate. The obstacle is explicit: He is a bastard second son and hence will inherit nothing.

Next he processes the problem with a continuing series of rhetorical questions:

> . . . Why bastard? Wherefore base?
> When my dimensions are as well compact,
> My mind as generous, and my shape as true,
> As honest madam's issue? . . .

To Edmund, the answers to his questions are obvious. There is absolutely no reason for him to be branded with the name of bastard; a title that implies that he is vile and base. He states the reasons for this: His bodily parts are as well put together, his mind as gallant and high born, and his figure as well proportioned as any son born to a faithful, married woman. The word *true* also means that Edmund is genuine, "the real article," and as such deserves to be compensated. The validity of his argument now begins to light a fire under him as he repeats the rhetorical questions with moral outrage:

> . . . Why brand they us
> With base? With baseness? bastardy? base, base?

The fact that he asks four rhetorical questions in rapid succession, repeating the word *base* three times, reveals that Edmund is outraged and is rapidly convincing himself of the justness of his cause. He is well on his way to receiving the validity he needs from the goddess of Nature. In the next section, he really begins to "feel his oats":

> Who, in the lusty stealth of nature, take
> More composition, and fierce quality,
> Than doth within a dull, stale, tired bed
> Go to th' creating a whole tribe of fops,
> Got 'tween asleep and wake? . . .

Again, he compares himself with the progeny of legitimately born males. In the previous section he used the word *as* to prove his equality with Edgar—"as well compact," "as generous," "as true"—but now he uses the word *more* in order to prove his superiority to Edgar. He asks, in essence, "Why am I called base, who, being conceived in the secret passion of nature, am superior both physically and constitutionally to all the dispassionate married couples who fornicate in a half-sleep and hence create a brood of fools?" Edmund uses the word *nature* again to help his argument that the natural world is preferable to societal artifice. Now that he has built up an impressive argument to justify the plan that he wishes to undertake, he comes to a decision:

> . . . Well then,
> Legitimate Edgar, I must have your land.
> Our father's love is to the bastard Edmund
> As to th' legitimate. . . .

Now that Edmund has proven that he is superior to Edgar, a portion of his father's estate isn't enough; he must instead have it all. After all, Edgar and he equally share their father's love. Uttering the word *legitimate,* which Edmund thinks is a ridiculous word, transitions Edmund into the next section:

> . . . Fine word, "legitimate"!
> Well, my legitimate, if this letter speed
> And my invention thrive, Edmund the base
> Shall top th' legitimate. . . .

Edmund ridicules the word *legitimate,* saying that it is a "fine word." Shakespeare gives us multiple meanings of *fine.* It means "pure," "elegant," and "beautiful." However, it also means "thin," "minute," and "fragile." In other words, legitimacy is a thin, weak reason for Edgar to inherit their father's estate. Because this is true, according to Edmund, he must do something about it. He makes reference to a letter that he wrote. It purports to be written to him from Edgar and calls for Edmund to join Edgar in a plot to kill their father, Gloucester. Edmund plans to have it fall into Gloucester's hands. What he says in essence is, "If this letter falls quickly into my father's hands and succeeds in ridding me of Edgar, then I shall triumph over him."

Having constructed a strong argument for his upcoming plan, he is now quite full of himself as he says:

> . . . I grow, I prosper:
> Now gods, stand up for bastards!

Now that he has committed himself to his plan, which after all is Nature's plan, he calls on all the gods to support and watch over him as he begins to set his scheme in motion. Calling on more than one god is the act of a pagan, which hearkens back to the first line of the soliloquy, in which he calls not on God, but on Nature, to be his patron.

As you can see in this speech, Edmund is arguing his case to the goddess of Nature as well as to himself. Each beat is an accumulation of evidence that supports his case. It is the cumulative nature of the evidence built with each beat that ignites each subsequent beat. Sometimes a word or image spoken by the character in one beat is the transition to the next beat. For example, Edmund says, "Our father's love is to the bastard Edmund / As to th' legitimate." His utterance of the word *legitimate* ignites his next beat, which begins, "Fine word, 'legitimate.'"

Lady Macbeth from *Macbeth*

JOE: Another example of an apostrophe to a higher power is in *Macbeth*. Lady Macbeth has just received a letter from her husband, Macbeth, which says that Duncan, the king of Scotland, has promoted him for his valor in battle. He also tells her that he was visited by three witches that prophesized that he would become king. Lady Macbeth embraces the prophecy but fears that her husband "is too full of the milk of human kindness" to make the prophesy a reality. In other words, she feels that the only way for Macbeth to become king is for the two of them to murder Duncan. A messenger enters and tells her that Duncan and the nobles of Scotland, including Macbeth, are on their way to spend the night and celebrate Macbeth's promotion as well as their victory over the Scottish rebels. Lady Macbeth tells the servant to make ready for their arrival. The servant leaves to do her bidding, whereupon Lady Macbeth speaks these words:

> The raven himself is hoarse
> That croaks the fatal entrance of Duncan
> Under my battlements. Come, you spirits
> That tend on mortal thoughts, unsex me here,
> And fill me from the crown to the toe, top-full
> Of direst cruelty! Make thick my blood;
> Stop up the access and passage to remorse,
> That no compunctious visitings of nature
> Shake my fell purpose, nor keep peace between
> The effect and it! Come to my woman's breasts,
> And take my milk for gall, you murdering ministers,
> Wherever in your sightless substances

> You wait on nature's mischief! Come, thick night,
> And pall thee in the dunnest smoke of hell,
> That my keen knife see not the wound it makes,
> Nor heaven peep through the blanket of the dark,
> To cry "Hold, hold!" *(Macbeth, 1, 5, 38–54)*

With the first line, Lady Macbeth commits herself to her objective—Duncan's murder:

> The raven himself is hoarse
> That croaks the fatal entrance of Duncan
> Under my battlements. . . .

The raven was considered an omen of death. It was thought that a raven croaking on a house meant that death was near. Lady Macbeth suggests that "Here the air is so full of death that the raven is hoarse with croaking" (Macbeth, *New Swan*, p. 34). Now that she has committed to her objective, Lady Macbeth uses the remainder of the soliloquy to overcome her obstacle—her humanity. First she calls on the spirits that watch over those who think of murder:

> . . . Come, you spirits
> That tend on mortal thoughts, unsex me here,
> And fill me from the crown to the toe, top-full
> Of direst cruelty! Make thick my blood;
> Stop up th' access and passage to remorse,
> That no compunctious visitings of nature
> Shake my fell purpose, nor keep peace between
> Th' effect and it! . . .

She asks the spirits to "unsex" her, to remove her womanhood. She knows that her femininity is composed of tenderness and compassion, enemies to her purpose. In place of her womanhood, she asks the spirits to fill her from head to foot with dreadful inhumanity. *Crown* in this case means not only "head" but also the crown of a queen, which will be her reward when her husband becomes king. Next she asks the spirits to make her blood so thick that pity will be unable to flow through her veins, and feelings of kindness will not be allowed to sabotage her savage plan or prevent the *plot* of Duncan's murder—the "fell purpose"—from joining with the *act* of Duncan's murder—the effect. Shakespeare uses secondary meanings to strengthen the tactile, corporal imagery of this passage. The word *fell* is not only an adjective meaning "fierce," "savage," and "pernicious" but is also a noun for "skin." Now she becomes more specific and bold:

> . . . Come to my woman's breasts,
> And take my milk for gall, you murdering ministers,
> Wherever in your sightless substances
> You wait on nature's mischief! . . .

She says, "Come to my breasts, remove my mother's milk, and replace it with bile, you spirits who champion both murders and murderers, wherever in your invisible forms you assist the evil forces of nature." Whereas in the first section Lady Macbeth prays to the spirits that *think* about murder, she now prays to the spirits that *commit* murder. She becomes bolder, moving thought to action. She also becomes more specific. She first asks to have her overall womanhood removed. Now she asks that her mother's milk, the symbol of motherhood and femininity, be removed and replaced with bile. Shakespeare's physical imagery here is concentrated and emotionally laden. Now that she has readied herself for the murder of Duncan with the help of evil spirits, she asks evening to come quickly, that she may enact her plan before she loses her courage:

> . . . Come, thick night,
> And pall thee in the dunnest smoke of hell,
> That my keen knife see not the wound it makes,
> Nor heaven peep through the blanket of the dark,
> To cry "Hold, hold!"

Lady Macbeth asks the "thick night" to come quickly. This is the second time that she uses the word *thick*. The obvious definition appears in the Lexicon: "Having a great circumference, not thin or slender." But *thick* can also mean "morally vulgar." Therefore, she speaks to the night as an accomplice in her task, calling it amoral, unlike the bright day. The black cloak of night will aid her in her mission to remove Duncan. Similarly, "make thick my blood" in the previous section means not only to make her blood dense and impenetrable, but also to make it corrupt. In this section Lady Macbeth is saying, "Come quickly dense, immoral night and wrap yourself in the blackest smoke from the fires of hell, so that my sharp knife doesn't see the wound it makes nor heaven peep through the blanket of the dark to cry 'stop, stop.'" The word *keen* in the phrase "keen knife" means not only "sharp," but also "bitter," "acrimonious," and "eager." The wound that her knife will make is in the body of Duncan. The phrase "Nor heaven peep through the blanket of the dark" needs no paraphrasing. The imagery of the bright, moral light of heaven being unable to even "peep" through the impenetrable darkness of the villainous night is a powerful one. The "blanket of the dark" also conjures up an image of protection for Lady Macbeth, guarding her not only from a heaven that would attempt to prevent her from performing such a nefarious deed, but also from a God who would punish her for it.

There are actually three apostrophes in this soliloquy. First, Lady Macbeth summons the "spirits that tend on mortal thoughts." Next, she becomes bolder and summons the "murdering ministers." And finally, she summons the "thick night" to aid her in her purpose and to protect her from the admonition of heaven. The disturbing imagery of figuratively exchanging blood and body parts for their baneful counterparts reveals that Lady Macbeth must transform herself into a "Frankenstein monster" of sorts, in order to carry out her scheme. The physical imagery in this speech is particularly dense and disturbing. Typical of Shakespeare's dramatic dialogue, he provides Lady Macbeth with words whose sounds and rhythm underscore their meaning and emotion—words like "croaks," "thick," "gall," and "peep," as well as phrases like "murdering ministers" and "sightless substances."

A common pitfall in these types of soliloquies is that actors often use them to demonstrate how "evil" their characters are. They strut about the stage "proclaiming" in a loud and strident voice. However, an examination of the text in these cases reveals that both Edmund and Lady Macbeth call on higher powers because they feel that they lack the ability to achieve their goals alone. This indicates *vulnerability* in both characters. Vulnerability should not be confused with weakness. All actors must find the vulnerability in their characters. It is the core of your character's humanity. This is particularly important with villainous characters and antiheroes like Macbeth. Even a character like Richard III can be—dare I say it—likable. It is far too easy—and, in my opinion, boring—to create a villain with no conscience or center of pain. How much more interesting to play a Lady Macbeth or an Edmund who instills ambivalent feelings in their audiences, perhaps of pity as well as hatred. Lady Macbeth admits that she is too human and too much a woman to murder and desperately needs the "spirits that tend on mortal thoughts" to "stop up the access and passage to remorse." It is in fact her humanity that causes her death. Similarly, although his father loves him and treats him well, Edmund feels betrayed that he is treated as an inferior. He needs the goddess of Nature to validate his convictions and help him acquire the strength with which to carry out his plans for revenge.

The fourth option, addressing oneself or addressing the audience, is the most frequently used by Shakespeare. It was an accepted convention in Shakespeare's time for actors to address the audience during a soliloquy. This convention is still accepted today.

Richard, Earl of Gloucester, from *Richard III*

JOE: Let's look at an example from *Richard III*. Richard opens the play with this soliloquy:

> Now is the winter of our discontent
> Made glorious summer by this sun of York;
> And all the clouds that lour'd upon our house
> In the deep bosom of the ocean buried.
> Now are our brows bound with victorious wreaths;
> Our bruised arms hung up for monuments;
> Our stern alarums chang'd to merry meetings,
> Our dreadful marches to delightful measures.
> Grim-visag'd war hath smooth'd his wrinkled front;
> And now, instead of mounting barded steeds
> To fright the souls of fearful adversaries,
> He capers nimbly in a lady's chamber
> To the lascivious pleasing of a lute.

> But I, that am not shap'd for sportive tricks,
> Nor made to court an amorous looking-glass;
> I, that am rudely stamp'd, and want love's majesty
> To strut before a wanton ambling nymph;
> I, that am curtail'd of this fair proportion,
> Cheated of feature by dissembling nature,
> Deform'd, unfinish'd, sent before my time
> Into this breathing world, scarce half made up,
> And that so lamely and unfashionable
> That dogs bark at me as I halt by them;
> Why, I, in this weak piping time of peace,
> Have no delight to pass away the time,
> Unless to spy my shadow in the sun
> And descant on mine own deformity:
> And therefore, since I cannot prove a lover,
> To entertain these fair well-spoken days,
> I am determined to prove a villain
> And hate the idle pleasures of these days.
> Plots have I laid, inductions dangerous,
> By drunken prophecies, libels and dreams,
> To set my brother Clarence and the king
> In deadly hate the one against the other:
> And if King Edward be as true and just
> As I am subtle, false and treacherous,
> This day should Clarence closely be mew'd up,
> About a prophecy, which says that "G"
> Of Edward's heirs the murderer shall be.
> Dive, thoughts, down to my soul: here Clarence comes.
>
> *(Richard III, 1, 1, 1–41)*

Although the actor has a choice of directing these types of soliloquies either to himself or to the audience, some of the speeches seem to lend themselves to one or the other. In my opinion, Richard's soliloquy is not to himself but is instead, outwardly directed. He is certain of the path he wishes to take. He says, "Plots have I laid, inductions dangerous." Rather than struggling with an issue, he has already begun to put his plans into action and is trying to get the audience on his side. He lets us in on his schemes throughout the play, treating the members of the audience like trusted confidants. Richard begins by letting the audience in on the events that have transpired before the start of the play:

> Now is the winter of our discontent
> Made glorious summer by this sun of York;

> And all the clouds that lour'd upon our house
> In the deep bosom of the ocean buried.

The house of York, of which Richard is a member, has just defeated the house of Lancaster after the most recent battle in the interminable War of the Roses, a civil war over the English monarchy. The "sun of York" refers to the emblem of the blazing sun adopted by King Edward IV, Richard's elder brother. "Sun" also implies that Edward is the "bright sun" of the victorious Yorkists. In addition, it is a pun because Edward is the "son" of the Duke of York. Although the language that Richard chooses at the top of this soliloquy seems to glorify the victory of the house of York, it soon becomes apparent that he is being sarcastic. Here Shakespeare gives us Richard's objective and obstacle in an implicit manner; peace has finally come to England but, as we will soon discover, Richard hates peace and wants turmoil to come again. The words *summer, winter,* and *clouds* are here used figuratively, as is the phrase "deep bosom of the ocean." The word "loured" or *lowered* (pronounced "LAU-erd") means "to sink low." *House* has a double meaning. It refers to the house of York, which is the family tree. But it also suggests an actual structure with dark clouds sitting low over its roof. In other words, Richard tells us through physical imagery that the "winter of war" has transformed into the "summer of peace"; that the low, dark, thunderclouds of conflict have been entombed at the bottom of the sea. Next Richard's imagery becomes more specific as he goes into a detailed list of the items of peace, which have replaced those of war:

> Now are our brows bound with victorious wreaths;
> Our bruised arms hung up for monuments;
> Our stern alarums chang'd to merry meetings,
> Our dreadful marches to delightful measures.

Richard begins this section by saying that the Yorkists now wear victory crowns, and the coat of arms of those killed in battle are now hung on their tombs. His sarcasm then becomes more evident in his choice of language. "Stern alarums"—fierce trumpet calls to battle—have given way to "merry meetings"—happy parties. Venerable processions into battle—"dreadful marches"—have given way to pleasurable dances—"delightful measures." His choice of words here reveals that Richard considers war to be a brave, responsible use of a man's time and energy, while peacetime activities are frivolous and indulgent. In the next section he increases the imagery of his veneration of war and disdain for peace:

> Grim-visag'd war hath smooth'd his wrinkled front;
> And now, instead of mounting barded steeds
> To fright the souls of fearful adversaries,
> He capers nimbly in a lady's chamber
> To the lascivious pleasing of a lute.

Richard now personifies war, allowing the audience to have a more personal look at the tragedy of the coming of peace. He gives war a face—"visage" and "front."

He says that the countenance of war that once struck terror into the hearts of its enemies has now relaxed its once furrowed brow. And now, instead of riding atop armored horses to strike fear into the souls of his enemies, he dances in a woman's bedroom to the licentious, pleasurable sounds of a lute. Here Richard equates peace with wantonness. Peace has caused England to become a kind of Sodom and Gomorrah. Richard uses the concept of transformation just as Lady Macbeth does in the soliloquy we just analyzed. Peace has not simply *replaced* war. Instead, we have something even more tragic—war has *transformed* himself into peace. Richard presents war as a once great and trusted friend who has suddenly changed his personality in a way so radical that he is unrecognizable. Many of Shakespeare's words in this speech are an excellent example of the need to look up even words whose meaning we *think* we know. For instance, *stern, dreadful,* and *grim* have negative connotations today. However, in this case, these words connote power and bravery. In the next section, Richard puts himself into the picture, informing us of his personal reaction to this new, unpleasant situation in which he finds himself:

> But I, that am not shap'd for sportive tricks,
> Nor made to court an amorous looking-glass;
> I, that am rudely stamp'd, and want love's majesty
> To strut before a wanton ambling nymph;
> I, that am curtail'd of this fair proportion,
> Cheated of feature by dissembling nature,
> Deform'd, unfinish'd, sent before my time
> Into this breathing world, scarce half made up,
> And that so lamely and unfashionable
> That dogs bark at me as I halt by them;
> Why, I, in this weak piping time of peace,
> Have no delight to pass away the time,
> Unless to spy my shadow in the sun
> And descant on mine own deformity:

This is a long segment but it is straightforward. Richard builds a self-portrait of sorts in this section. In fact, if the language that he uses to describe himself were removed, we would have a short sentence, "But I, in this time of peace, have no delight to pass away the time. . . ." Richard is lame as well as a "crook-back"—he possesses a misshapen spine that gives him a hunchback. He says that he does not have the physical appearance to enjoy pleasurable caprices or to look vainly into a mirror. He uses the image of being stamped from a faulty mold, thus lacking love's grandeur to show off before a graceful beauty. He says that he was cheated by "dissembling nature," which often "disguises the true worth of men by their outward appearance" (Richard III, *Folger Library Shakespeare*, p. 1). Richard was sent into the world prematurely, before he was "complete," and in such an offensive manner that dogs bark at him as he limps past them. He continues to deride the current concord by calling it a "weak piping time of peace." He ironically states that the only activity he is fit for now is to view his shadow and comment on his deformity. *Descant* means not only "to comment on" but also "to sing." This continues his view of peace as an indulgent party, filled with music—"piping peace"—and lechery. Now that Richard has hopefully convinced the audience that peace is anathema that must be removed and has swayed the audience to pity his unfortunate appearance, he can now be explicit about his plans:

> And therefore, since I cannot prove a lover,
> To entertain these fair well-spoken days,
> I am determined to prove a villain
> And hate the idle pleasures of these days.
> Plots have I laid, inductions dangerous,
> By drunken prophecies, libels and dreams,
> To set my brother Clarence and the king
> In deadly hate the one against the other:
> And if King Edward be as true and just
> As I am subtle, false and treacherous,
> This day should Clarence closely be mew'd up,
> About a prophecy, which says that "G"
> Of Edward's heirs the murderer shall be.
> Dive, thoughts, down to my soul: here Clarence comes.

Because he cannot enjoy the current peace, Richard is determined to rebel against it. He then reveals his plan to take advantage of a prophecy, which he may have manufactured, that says an heir to Edward's throne with the initial "G" will murder Edward. Edward and Richard's brother, the Duke of Clarence, is named George. Richard says that if all has gone as planned, Clarence will be imprisoned this very day. Ironically, the "G" of the prophecy stands for "Gloucester," as Richard is presently the Earl of Gloucester. Richard terminates his talk with the audience when he sees his brother Clarence approach. Once again, Shakespeare furnishes his character with rich physical imagery, this time in order to help Richard move his audience to empathy and support. In addition, phrases like "weak, piping time of peace" contain sounds that reinforce Richard's feelings about amity. The actor can use the "k" and "p" sounds to show his disdain for peace.

Brutus from *Julius Caesar*

JOE: This next soliloquy, spoken by Brutus in *Julius Caesar,* on the other hand, seems to be self-directed:

> It must be by his death: and for my part,
> I know no personal cause to spurn at him,
> But for the general. He would be crown'd:
> How that might change his nature, there's the question.
> It is the bright day that brings forth the adder,

And that craves wary walking. Crown him?—that;—
And then, I grant, we put a sting in him
That at his will he may do danger with.
Th' abuse of greatness is when it disjoins
Remorse from power: and, to speak truth of Caesar,
I have not known when his affections sway'd
More than his reason. But 'tis a common proof,
That lowliness is young ambition's ladder,
Whereto the climber-upward turns his face;
But when he once attains the upmost round,
He then unto the ladder turns his back,
Looks in the clouds, scorning the base degrees
By which he did ascend. So Caesar may.
Then, lest he may, prevent. And, since the quarrel
Will bear no color for the thing he is,
Fashion it thus; that what he is, augmented,
Would run to these and these extremities:
And therefore think him as a serpent's egg
Which, hatch'd, would, as his kind, grow mischievous,
And kill him in the shell.   *(Julius Caesar, 2, 1, 10–34)*

Brutus's friend, Cassius, is pressuring Brutus to join his band of conspirators, who wish to rid Rome of Caesar. They feel that Caesar is becoming too powerful and will transform the republic of Rome into a dictatorship. Brutus is informed that the councillors of Rome intend to offer Caesar the crown the following day. In the middle of the night, Brutus cloisters himself in his orchard in order to come to a decision on how he will proceed in the matter. Brutus states his problem in the first two lines:

It must be by his death: and for my part,
I know no personal cause to spurn at him,
But for the general. . . .

He says that Rome can only be free if Caesar is killed. However, he has no personal reason to want him dead, except for the good of the Roman people. *Spurn* means "to treat with contempt" but it also means "to strike." So Brutus is saying both that he has no personal reason to condemn Caesar or to strike at him with an assassin's dagger. This overwhelming dilemma motivates Brutus to question what changes may occur if Caesar is allowed to wear the crown:

. . . He would be crown'd:
How that might change his nature, there's the question.
It is the bright day that brings forth the adder,
And that craves wary walking. Crown him?—that;—

> And then, I grant, we put a sting in him
> That at his will he may do danger with.
> Th' abuse of greatness is when it disjoins
> Remorse from power: . . .

The first phrase in this section contains an ellipsis. "He would be crowned" means "He would *like to* be crowned." Brutus uses the metaphor of a poisonous snake as he speculates on how the crown may affect Caesar. He says that the brilliant, warm sun, a metaphor for the crown, brings the adder out of its hole—the possible "sleeping tyrant" within Caesar—and that necessitates stepping carefully. Continuing the metaphor of the poisonous adder, Brutus says that if Caesar is crowned, the people of Rome will provide him with a "sting" that he may use at will in a dangerous and irresponsible manner. He goes on to say that the high office of king or emperor is abused when the sense of power cuts itself off from a sense of tenderness and compassion. The accumulation of evidence in support of Caesar's assassination most likely frightens Brutus and reminds him of all of Caesar's good qualities. After all, he must weigh all sides of the equation, in fairness to both Caesar and the future of Rome. Therefore Brutus next gives Caesar the benefit of the doubt:

> . . . and, to speak truth of Caesar,
> I have not known when his affections sway'd
> More than his reason. . . .

Brutus has known Caesar for a long time and says that he has never known Caesar to be ruled more by his personal inclinations than by his rational mind. But because he is more concerned with the possible loss of the Roman republic, Brutus quickly returns to Caesar's potential abuse of power:

> . . . But 'tis a common proof,
> That lowliness is young ambition's ladder,
> Whereto the climber-upward turns his face;
> But when he once attains the upmost round,
> He then unto the ladder turns his back,
> Looks in the clouds, scorning the base degrees
> By which he did ascend. So Caesar may.

It is generally acknowledged that an ambitious young man will pretend to be humble as he climbs the ladder of success. But as soon as he reaches the top rung of the ladder, he turns his back on it, looking to greater things and disdaining the lowly rungs that he had to ascend in order to reach the top. The rungs of the ladder are the people and institutions of Rome. At first, Caesar considers the people to be more important than him: "Whereto the climber-upward turns his face." But if he becomes king, he may condemn the very people he served and look instead to the heavens, perhaps thinking himself divine. Now that Brutus has fully debated the issue, he comes to a decision:

> Then, lest he may, prevent. And, since the quarrel
> Will bear no color for the thing he is,
> Fashion it thus; that what he is, augmented,
> Would run to these and these extremities:
> And therefore think him as a serpent's egg
> Which, hatch'd, would, as his kind, grow mischievous,
> And kill him in the shell.

Brutus decides that, because Caesar may very well abuse absolute power, it is best to stop him before he attains it. He goes on to say, "Because our purpose will seem unjustified due to Caesar's current proper conduct, we must defend our actions in this way: That, given the power he already possesses, if it is allowed to increase, he will abuse it in the manner in which I have just mentioned. Therefore, we must think of him as a serpent's egg, which if allowed to hatch, will become dangerous, as is a snake's nature, and kill him while he is still in his shell." The word *quarrel* has two meanings—"cause, occasion, motive of dispute," as well as "combat for a public cause." His decision to join the conspirators is not only a just cause that will benefit the citizens of Rome, but also one that must involve violence. Brutus has convinced himself that misuse of power would be inevitable if Caesar is given unlimited power. Consequently, his love for Caesar is superseded by his love for Rome.

This soliloquy is very different from Richard's. Brutus is soul-searching in order to arrive at the correct decision. He is a proud and noble individual, who cherishes his privacy. In my opinion, it would be out of character for him to address the audience.

Viola from *Twelfth Night*

JOE: Some soliloquies seem to work equally well with either choice. Here is an example from *Twelfth Night*. Viola, the heroine of the play, disguised as a young man named Cesario, has just wooed the countess Olivia in the name of her master, Orsino, with whom Viola is in love. Olivia, thinking that Viola is a man, is enamored of her and sends Malvolio, her servant, to return a ring of Orsino's that Viola supposedly left behind. This is a ploy to get Viola to visit Olivia once more. When Viola refuses to take the ring, Malvolio throws it on the ground and departs. Alone now, Viola speaks these words:

> I left no ring with her: what means this lady?
> Fortune forbid my outside have not charm'd her!
> She made good view of me; indeed, so much,
> That sure methought her eyes had lost her tongue,
> For she did speak in starts distractedly.
> She loves me, sure; the cunning of her passion
> Invites me in this churlish messenger.

> None of my lord's ring! Why, he sent her none.
> I am the man: if it be so, as 'tis,
> Poor lady, she were better love a dream.
> Disguise, I see thou art a wickedness,
> Wherein the pregnant enemy does much.
> How easy is it for the proper-false
> In women's waxen hearts to set their forms!
> Alas, our frailty is the cause, not we!
> For such as we are made of, such we be.
> How will this fadge? My master loves her dearly,
> And I, poor monster, fond as much on him;
> And she, mistaken, seems to dote on me.
> What will become of this? As I am man,
> My state is desperate for my master's love;
> As I am woman,—now alas the day!—
> What thriftless sighs shall poor Olivia breathe!
> O time! Thou must untangle this, not I;
> It is too hard a knot for me to untie!   (*Twelfth Night*, 2, 2, 17–41)

The problem is apparent to Viola immediately:

> I left no ring with her: what means this lady?
> Fortune forbid my outside have not charm'd her!

Viola may speak the first words—"I left no ring with her"—to herself or she may shout them after the departing Malvolio. She then tries to discern the reason for Olivia's machination as she asks herself—"What means this lady?" The answer begins to dawn. Although she desperately wants it to be untrue, Viola strongly suspects that her "outside," her disguise as a man, has caused Olivia to fall in love with her, rather than with her master, Orsino. This fear causes Viola to recall Olivia's behavior during their meeting:

> She made good view of me; indeed, so much,
> That sure methought her eyes had lost her tongue,
> For she did speak in starts distractedly.

Olivia looked at her, Cesario, very intently; so intently in fact, that what she saw caused her tongue to malfunction, because she stuttered as she spoke. This confirms Viola's suspicions:

> She loves me, sure; the cunning of her passion
> Invites me in this churlish messenger.
> None of my lord's ring! Why, he sent her none.
> I am the man: . . .

Viola is convinced that Olivia loves her and Olivia's passion has caused her to cunningly invite Viola to return by means of her rude messenger, Malvolio. "None of my lord's ring" echoes Malvolio's words to her from his mistress, Olivia. Suspicion has now become certainty. Olivia's behavior combined with the fact that Orsino never sent Olivia a ring can mean only one thing; that Viola is "the man," Olivia's intended love. This realization triggers a simpatico reaction in Viola: Olivia loves in vain just as Viola loves in vain. This awareness makes Viola curse her disguise. She now sees how susceptible her sex is to the allures of men:

> . . . if it be so, as 'tis,
> Poor lady, she were better love a dream.
> Disguise, I see thou art a wickedness,
> Wherein the pregnant enemy does much.
> How easy is it for the proper-false
> In women's waxen hearts to set their forms!
> Alas, our frailty is the cause, not we!
> For such as we are made of, such we be.

In this section, Viola identifies with Olivia. Viola believes that Olivia has as good a chance of winning Cesario's love as Viola has in winning the love of Orsino—zero! Viola comprehends that she and Olivia have become kindred spirits. Disguise, Viola says, is a tool of the ever-scheming devil, which is creating much chaos. She goes on to say, "How easy it is for handsome, deceitful men—'the proper-false'—to leave their impressions in the waxen hearts of women." Here Shakespeare uses the metaphor of pressing a strong, solid figure into a soft, vulnerable substance. Womankind is not at fault for loving men unwisely and too well, but rather the culprit is the vulnerability that women possess. Viola says that females have no other choice because "such as we are made of, such we be." The enormity of her problem now looms large and Viola anxiously wonders at the outcome:

> How will this fadge? My master loves her dearly,
> And I, poor monster, fond as much on him;
> And she, mistaken, seems to dote on me.
> What will become of this? As I am man,
> My state is desperate for my master's love;
> As I am woman,—now alas the day!—
> What thriftless sighs shall poor Olivia breathe!

"How can this all turn out well?" Viola wonders. *Fadge* means "to succeed." Orsino loves Olivia, Olivia loves Viola, and Viola loves Orsino. *Monster,* in this case, means "an unnatural creature," because Viola is both woman and man, her disguise as Cesario. As Cesario, she can never hope to win Orsino—and as Viola, all of Olivia's sighs of love will be in vain. The word *desperate* in this instance means "hopeless." After viewing her situation in detail, her problems now seem so overwhelming that Viola decides to let fate decide the outcome:

> O time! Thou must untangle this, not I;
> It is too hard a knot for me to untie!

Here, as a metaphor for Viola's predicament, Shakespeare uses a knot that is too difficult to be untied by human hands.

This is clearly a problem-solving soliloquy. However, unlike the two previous speeches, it seems equally appropriate for Viola to speak aloud to herself or to try to enlist the help of the good people in the audience.

Regardless of which option the actor or director chooses, *it is crucial for soliloquies to be active and outwardly directed*. If the character chooses to speak to herself, it should be to a specific aspect of her consciousness, which she can place on the fourth wall, above the heads of the audience members. This gives her a "scene partner" of sorts. It can be her rational self, her scheming self, her retribution self, her spiritual self, her conscience, and so on.

Angelo from *Measure for Measure*

JOE: In fact, one aspect of a character can debate with another aspect of the same character. For example, Angelo in *Measure for Measure* has a reputation for being a pious, religious man. So much so, in fact, that he condemns young Claudio to death for fornication with his fiancée before marriage. Claudio's sister, Isabella, a novice nun, pleads with Angelo to spare her brother's life. On their first meeting, Angelo finds himself irresistibly drawn to her and tells her to return the following day to hear his decision regarding her brother's predicament. He plans to make her a bargain: If she will sleep with him, he will spare Claudio's life. While awaiting Isabella's arrival, Angelo speaks a soliloquy in which the *pious* Angelo debates with the *wanton* Angelo about whether or not to go through with his despicable plan:

> When I would pray and think, I think and pray
> To several subjects. Heaven hath my empty words;
> Whilst my invention, hearing not my tongue,
> Anchors on Isabel: Heaven in my mouth,
> As if I did but only chew his name;
> And in my heart the strong and swelling evil
> Of my conception. The state, whereon I studied,
> Is like a good thing, being often read,
> Grown sere and tedious; yea, my gravity,
> Wherein—let no man hear me—I take pride,
> Could I with boot change for an idle plume,
> Which the air beats for vain. O place, O form,
> How often dost thou with thy case, thy habit,
> Wrench awe from fools and tie the wiser souls
> To thy false seeming! Blood, thou art blood:
> Let's write "good angel" on the devil's horn:
> 'Tis not the devil's crest.   *(Measure for Measure, 2, 4, 1–17)*

The function of this soliloquy is for Angelo to decide on an objective:

> When I would pray and think, I think and pray
> To several subjects. Heaven hath my empty words;
> Whilst my invention, hearing not my tongue,
> Anchors on Isabel: Heaven in my mouth,
> As if I did but only chew his name;
> And in my heart the strong and swelling evil
> Of my conception. . . .

Angelo pronounces that his thoughts and prayers take different directions. He prays for deliverance, but his thoughts—which ignore his words of prayer—are occupied with his lust for Isabel. His words of God, heaven, and devotion are just so many empty vowels and consonants, while in his heart he harbors his sinful plan. He uses images of pregnancy—"swelling" and "conception"—in describing his immoral design. If Angelo's objective is to proceed with his plan to seduce Isabel, his obstacle is his piety and devotion to God. If his objective is to continue in his role of a moral, inflexible public official, doling out justice as he sees fit without outside influence, then his obstacle is his overwhelming attraction to Isabel. His imagery in this section reveals his desire to lean in the direction of his craving for Isabel rather than toward heavenly devotion. Motivated by his lust for Isabel, Angelo now admits to himself that he has grown tired of his pious reputation and public duties:

> . . . The state, whereon I studied,
> Is like a good thing, being often read,
> Grown sere and tedious; yea, my gravity,
> Wherein—let no man hear me—I take pride,
> Could I with boot change for an idle plume,
> Which the air beats for vain. . . .

"The body politic and my position as a public official, which I have been contemplating, is like a good book that has been read too often and becomes dry, withered, and tiresome," says Angelo. He goes on to say that his dignity, in which he takes pride, he could with advantage exchange for "an idle plume, / Which the air beats for vain." *Idle* is defined as "useless, lacking seriousness and purpose." A *plume* is "feathers which serve to adorn." The word *vain* has two meanings. It means "frivolous, empty" and also "vanity." Angelo wants to exchange his morality, duty, and selfless behavior for wanton, indulgent, and purposeless behavior. Because he wants to give himself permission to proceed with his nefarious plan, Angelo goes one step further, condemning his station and political position:

> . . . O place, O form,
> How often dost thou with thy case, thy habit,
> Wrench awe from fools and tie the wiser souls
> To thy false seeming! . . .

Place refers to his official station. *Form* means "external appearances, empty show." Angelo says that his high political position in the state and the external trappings of his office have often, with its ornaments and dress, put fear into fools and convinced wise men, erroneously, that this external show had substance. This is a continuation of the idea that Angelo has been living a lie. He feels that he is a hypocrite and must now begin to behave in a truthful, albeit despicable manner. He now openly declares his true self:

> . . . Blood, thou art blood:
> Let's write "good angel" on the devil's horn:
> 'Tis not the devil's crest.

In this last section, Angelo decides that his objective is to bribe Isabel into having sex with him. He has spent the majority of the speech overcoming what he has decided is his obstacle—his upright, moral behavior and devotion to public duty, which he has concluded is nothing but "seeming," a false and empty package, adornments without substance. He commits himself to his plan with the line, "Blood, thou art blood." He speaks to himself, using the informal *thou*. *Blood* refers to Angelo's passion. He admits to himself that he is composed of passion and lust. He continues the theme of "being versus seeming" with his last line, "Let's write good angel on the devil's horn: / 'Tis not the devil's crest." In other words, "Say that we write the words 'good angel' on the devil's horns; that doesn't change his true nature." Angelo will *appear* pious, his seeming—while actually *behaving* immorally, his being.

LIZ: It seems to me that Angelo wants to seduce Isabel from the start and is only looking for some sort of permission to act on it.

JOE: Yes, you have a point. The purpose of many soliloquies is to seek validation for an objective. This is true of Richard. On the other hand, Edmund, Brutus, and Angelo, although still undecided at the beginning of their speeches, seem to be leaning in a particular direction from the start. Through the body of their soliloquies, they build evidence to support the objectives to which they are leaning.

SAM: Is Richard seeking validation from the audience?

JOE: Yes, very possibly. This brings me to an important point: If the actor chooses to speak to the people in the audience, he or she should decide exactly who they are. The actor can transform the audience into anyone or anything that will help achieve the character's objective. The audience can become a best friend, a confessor, a jury, or just about anything else. For example, the actor portraying Richard III may transform the audience into a group of noblemen whom he is trying to convince to join him in his mission to become king. To increase the stakes, the noblemen could be "on the fence" about whether to aid Richard in his quest or to join forces to oppose him. No one need know your substitutions. The important thing is that it works for you, the actor. Your character must have a strong need and must direct his words and actions outwardly. Otherwise, these speeches can become self-centered and indulgent or unfocused and just plain boring. If Richard is not motivated and excited to speak the opening lines of the play, they will be merely exposition.

SAM: If an actor chooses to have his character talk to the audience, he doesn't actually expect them to respond, does he?

JOE: Yes. An actor may attempt to get the audience to be silently riveted on his character or to be leaning forward in their seats. He may try to get them to laugh at his humor or to applaud on his exit, which would signal approval of his character's actions.

A character appears in several of Shakespeare's plays who speaks only soliloquies and only to the audience, never to the other characters in the play. In *The Winter's Tale* he is called Time, in *Henry IV Part 2* he is called Rumor, in *Pericles* he is Gower and in both *Henry VIII* and *Troilus and Cressida* he is nameless. In *Romeo and Juliet* and *Henry V* he is known simply as Chorus, which is the most common title for this type of character. The soliloquies spoken by the Chorus are not problem-solving soliloquies. Rather, the Chorus's purpose is to inform the audience of what has occurred prior to the start of the play and/or what has transpired between scenes. He sometimes provides an epilogue as well. The Chorus must also excite the audience's imagination and whet its appetite for the scenes to come.

Chorus from *Romeo and Juliet*

JOE: The Chorus is the first character we hear and see in the play:

> Two households, both alike in dignity,
> In fair Verona, where we lay our scene,
> From ancient grudge break to new mutiny,
> Where civil blood makes civil hands unclean.
> From forth the fatal loins of these two foes
> A pair of star-cross'd lovers take their life,
> Whose misadventur'd piteous overthrows
> Do with their death bury their parents' strife.
> The fearful passage of their death-mark'd love,
> And the continuance of their parents' rage
> Which, but their children's end, naught could remove,
> Is now the two hours' traffic of our stage;
> The which if you with patient ears attend,
> What here shall miss, our toil shall strive to mend.
> *(Romeo and Juliet, Prologue, 1–14)*

Let's paraphrase the soliloquy:

> Two families, both identical in honor and social standing,
> In the city of Verona, where our play takes place,
> Because of an inciting incident that took place long ago, erupt into a new feud,

> Where the blood of one's fellow citizens makes the hands of citizens unclean.
> From the wombs of these two families, who are enemies in this fatal way,
> Two lovers, ill-fated by the stars, commit suicide;
> Whose unfortunate, lamentable ruin
> Do, with their death, end their parents' feud.
> The dreadful course of their doomed love
> And the permanence of their parents' violent hatred,
> Which nothing could eliminate except the death of their children,
> Is the story that we will be telling for the next two hours on our stage;
> The which, if you will listen patiently,
> Whatever is lacking here, our work in the performance will try to make clear.

The Chorus is an omniscient character. He knows what has happened and what will happen. The playwright uses the character to clarify plot, provide background information, and arouse the audience. As you can see in the above example, the Chorus gives away the ending of the play. At first glimpse, this may seem unwise. But actually, knowing that Romeo and Juliet will die does much to draw in the audience over the course of the play. As they get to know and like the main characters, their sense of pathos is heightened. They want the two to succeed but are cognizant of the fact that they will instead die tragically. Also, although the audience members know the ending, they don't know the details of the story or how and why Romeo and Juliet die. Therefore their interest will be piqued. The Chorus uses emotionally laden imagery that is sorely lacking in our paraphrasing. Phrases like "star-crossed lovers," "misadventured piteous overthrows," and "fearful passage of their death-marked love" are romantic and dramatic and are meant to have a strong impact on the audience. As a point of interest, this speech is written in "sonnet" form. Sonnets will be discussed in Chapter 12.

Because there was little to no scenery in Elizabethan theatre, the Chorus was sometimes employed to create scenery with words. For example, in the prologue to *Henry V*, the Chorus says:

> Suppose within the girdle of these walls
> Are now confin'd two mighty monarchies,
> Whose high, upreared, and abutting fronts
> The perilous narrow ocean parts asunder.
> Piece out our imperfections with your thoughts;
> Into a thousand parts divide one man,
> And make imaginary puissance;
> Think, when we talk of horses, that you see them
> Printing their proud hoofs i' th' receiving earth;
>
> *(Henry V, Prologue 19–27)*

The Chorus asks the audience to imaginatively supply armies and horses to what they actually see onstage and he does so with rich visual imagery. However, other of Shakespeare's characters also provide this "scene painting" (Matthews, 74). For example, Friar Lawrence opens Act 2, scene 3 of *Romeo and Juliet* with these lines:

> The grey-ey'd morn smiles on the frowning night,
> Check'ring the eastern clouds with streaks of light,
> And fleckled darkness like a drunkard reels
> From forth day's path and Titan's fiery wheels.
> *(Romeo and Juliet, 2, 3, 1–4)*

ANALYZING MONOLOGUES

JOE: There is one more type of speech that we have yet to explore and that is the **monologue**. For our purposes I would like to use the word *monologue* to refer to speeches that are directed to a character or characters who are onstage with the speaker and who are also listening intently to what is being said to them. Monologues are similar to soliloquies in that they usually involve problem solving. They also consist of an overall objective, beat objectives, and transitions. However, monologues are less problematic than soliloquies. With monologues our scene partners are no longer imaginary or endowed. They are characters onstage with us, with their own agendas and opinions. They respond, usually nonverbally, to what we are saying to them in our monologues, which alters the manner in which we address them. It may be helpful at first in these situations to think of your character as an extremely talented attorney presenting his case to a jury.

Bullingbrook from *Richard II*

JOE: Let's look at this example spoken by Henry Bullingbrook in *Richard II*:

> As I was banish'd, I was banish'd Hereford;
> But as I come, I come for Lancaster.
> And, noble uncle, I beseech your grace
> Look on my wrongs with an indifferent eye:
> You are my father, for methinks in you
> I see old Gaunt alive; O, then, my father,
> Will you permit that I shall stand condemn'd
> A wandering vagabond; my rights and royalties
> Pluck'd from my arms perforce and given away
> To upstart unthrifts? Wherefore was I born?
> If that my cousin king be King of England,
> It must be granted I am Duke of Lancaster.

> You have a son, Aumerle, my noble cousin;
> Had you first died, and he been thus trod down,
> He should have found his uncle Gaunt a father,
> To rouse his wrongs and chase them to the bay.
> I am denied to sue my livery here,
> And yet my letters-patents give me leave:
> My father's goods are all distrain'd and sold,
> And these and all are all amiss employ'd.
> What would you have me do? I am a subject,
> And I challenge law: attorneys are denied me;
> And therefore, personally I lay my claim
> To my inheritance of free descent. *(Richard II, 2, 3, 113–136)*

His cousin, King Richard II, has exiled Henry Bullingbrook, Duke of Hereford, from England for six years. Bullingbrook returns long before his allotted time has expired and attempts to convince his uncle, the Duke of York, his father's brother, that he is justified in doing so because he must claim the title of Duke of Lancaster, inherited from his recently deceased father, John of Gaunt. (In reality, Bullingbrook harbors a stronger objective—to become King—a goal that he eventually achieves.) First, Bullingbrook states his objective:

> As I was banish'd, I was banish'd Hereford;
> But as I come, I come for Lancaster.

Bullingbrook wants to return to England, legally. He says that he only wants what is rightfully his, his deceased father's land and title. Now he addresses his obstacle:

> And, noble uncle, I beseech your grace
> Look on my wrongs with an indifferent eye:

Richard has left his Uncle York in charge of the country while he is off fighting a war in Ireland. York has come with armed men to ensure that his nephew, Bullingbrook, leaves England. Bullingbrook begs his uncle to look at his situation impartially, "with an indifferent eye." Next, Bullingbrook begins to try to convince his uncle to join him in his quest:

> You are my father, for methinks in you
> I see old Gaunt alive; O, then, my father,
> Will you permit that I shall stand condemn'd
> A wandering vagabond; my rights and royalties
> Pluck'd from my arms perforce and given away
> To upstart unthrifts? Wherefore was I born?

He begins by playing on his uncle's affections, saying that York is in fact now his father. Now that York is hopefully looking at his situation with paternal eyes, far from the impartiality that Bullingbrook first requested, Bullingbrook asks York if he will tolerate the litany of wrongs that are heaped on his "son." "Will you," asks Bullingbrook, "allow me to wander the globe, aimlessly, while my rights and royal privileges as a Duke are snatched from me by force and given to spendthrifts who suddenly find themselves promoted to royalty? Why then was I born of royal blood?" *Upstart* does not mean what it does today. It means "someone who is suddenly raised to a position of honor." Next he brings his nemesis, King Richard, into the equation with one simple but meaningful sentence:

> If that my cousin king be King of England,
> It must be granted I am Duke of Lancaster.

"If that" simply means "if." He states that "if it is true that my cousin the king is King of England, then it logically follows that I am the Duke of Lancaster." The phrase "cousin king" is a contemptuous one. The king should be referred to as "His Majesty" or "His Royal Highness" or a similar title of respect, regardless of one's kinship to the king. At the very least, the monarch should be called "King Richard." Even if Bullingbrook were to say "my cousin *the* king," it would be disrespectful; "cousin king" goes a step further. It could almost be written "cousin-king" or even "cousinking." In addition, the noun *cousin* sounds very much like the verb *cozen* (pronounced "KAH-zin"), which means "to cheat." Richard is portrayed as a "cheating king" who has robbed Bullingbrook of his rightful inheritance. Now Bullingbrook plays on his uncle's affections in an even more effective manner:

> You have a son, Aumerle, my noble cousin;
> Had you first died, and he been thus trod down,
> He should have found his uncle Gaunt a father,
> To rouse his wrongs and chase them to the bay.

He cleverly asks his uncle what he would do if his son were in the same trouble and he, York, had died instead of John of Gaunt, York's brother. He comments, "If you had died first rather than my father, and your son had found himself trampled on as I have, my father would have treated him as his own son and rushed to alleviate his injustices." The phrase "roused his wrongs and chased them to the bay" is metaphoric language taken from hunting. *Rouse* means "to startle prey from its lair." *Bay* means "a last stand." Bullingbrook says that his father would have flushed Aumerle's wrongs out of their lair, hunted them down and destroyed them as a hunter would kill its prey. It is also significant that he uses the term "noble cousin" in referring to York's son, Aumerle. "Noble-cousin" is the antithesis of "cousin-king." An "exalted cousin" is the opposite of a "cheating cousin." By utilizing such strong imagery, Bullingbrook attempts to instill a sense of guilt and shame in his uncle if he were to refuse to help him. Moreover, Bullingbrook has identified himself with York's biological son, Aumerle. Now that Bullingbrook is optimistic that his uncle is "in his camp," he reiterates his injustices in a more specific and intense way:

> I am denied to sue my livery here,
> And yet my letters-patents give me leave:

> My father's goods are all distrain'd and sold,
> And these and all are all amiss employ'd.
> What would you have me do? . . .

"I am forbidden to petition for my inheritance here in Britain and yet the legal papers that I have state that I can," says Bullingbrook. "My father's property and possessions are all confiscated and sold and these and everything else belonging to my father are wrongfully entrusted. What do you expect me to do?" He uses clear, concise language in this section, simple and impassioned. Bullingbrook knows that he has a valid argument and he hopes that in his heart of hearts, his uncle knows it too. Bullingbrook continues in this succinct, straightforward manner as he informs his uncle of his plan to take what is rightfully his, hopefully with his uncle's help:

> . . . I am a subject,
> And I challenge law: attorneys are denied me;
> And therefore, personally I lay my claim
> To my inheritance of free descent.

He remarks, "I am an English subject and demand my legal rights. I am denied legal council, and therefore I must personally claim my inheritance through legitimate succession." The word *challenge* is misleading. Here it means "to embrace." This monologue is similar to Juliet's speech in that it puts forth an objective—"As I was banished, I was banished Hereford; / But as I come, I come for Lancaster"—and addresses an obstacle—"I beseech your grace / Look on my wrongs with an indifferent eye." It then presents solid arguments to lend credence to the objective in order to persuade the person(s) to whom the speech is directed—in this case, the Duke of York. Unlike the Juliet speech, Bullingbrook's address to his Uncle York is not an apostrophe, because Bullingbrook is aware that York is a present, living, breathing character with his own opinions and agenda, who is taking in and processing all that is being said to him by his nephew.

Portia from *The Merchant of Venice*

JOE: Let's examine another such speech spoken by Portia in *The Merchant of Venice*:

> I pray you, tarry: pause a day or two
> Before you hazard; for, in choosing wrong,
> I lose your company: therefore forbear awhile.
> There's something tells me, but it is not love,
> I would not lose you; and you know yourself,
> Hate counsels not in such a quality.
> But lest you should not understand me well—
> And yet a maiden hath no tongue but thought—
> I would detain you here some month or two
> Before you venture for me. I could teach you

> How to choose right, but I am then forsworn;
> So will I never be: so may you miss me;
> But if you do, you'll make me wish a sin,
> That I had been forsworn. Beshrew your eyes,
> They have o'erlook'd me and divided me;
> One half of me is yours, the other half yours,
> Mine own, I would say; but if mine, then yours,
> And so all yours. O, these naughty times
> Put bars between the owners and their rights!
> And so, though yours, not yours. Prove it so,
> Let fortune go to hell for it, not I.
> I speak too long; but 'tis to peize the time,
> To eche it and to draw it out in length,
> To stay you from election. *(The Merchant of Venice, 3, 2, 1–24)*

Portia's father has willed that she must secure a husband by having interested suitors choose between three caskets, one of gold, one of silver, and one of lead. Her picture is in one of the caskets and the young man that is fortunate enough to choose the correct one will win her hand in marriage. He who chooses wrongly, however, must vow never to marry. Portia is in love with Bassanio, and is afraid that he will choose the wrong casket. Unlike the Juliet speech that addresses an apparently absent Romeo, Portia speaks to a present Bassanio. Once again, Shakespeare is very consistent. First, we have the objective:

> I pray you, tarry: pause a day or two
> Before you hazard; . . .

As he is about to approach the caskets, Portia begs Bassanio to wait. She asks him to delay for one or two days before making a choice of caskets. Next she states her obstacle:

> . . . for, in choosing wrong,
> I lose your company: therefore forbear awhile.

If Bassanio chooses the wrong casket, Portia loses him forever. She would like a couple of extra days in his presence should he err in his mission. In order to give credence to her request, Portia wishes to let Bassanio know that she loves him. However, she also wishes to seem impartial to all her suitors, as her father commanded:

> There's something tells me, but it is not love,
> I would not lose you; and you know yourself,
> Hate counsels not in such a quality.

"There is something that persuades me," Portia declares, "that I don't want to lose you, but that something isn't love. But you know that hate would never give the advice that I'm giving you now." Because she must communicate her love for Bassanio indirectly, she gives it another shot:

> But lest you should not understand me well—
> And yet a maiden hath no tongue but thought—
> I would detain you here some month or two
> Before you venture for me. . . .

"Just in case you don't fully understand me—and yet the thoughts of a young woman shouldn't be uttered aloud—I want to keep you here for one or two months before you try your luck in making me your wife." Portia becomes more bold in her roundabout confession of love. Even though a maid shouldn't speak of her wishes, Portia does so anyway. Whereas she first requested that Bassanio wait one or two days, she now asks that he delay for one or two months. Now she begins to entertain the only certain way of guaranteeing that Bassanio will become her husband:

> . . . I could teach you
> How to choose right, but I am then forsworn;
> So will I never be: so may you miss me;
> But if you do, you'll make me wish a sin,
> That I had been forsworn. . . .

Portia says that she could easily inform Bassanio clandestinely of the correct casket but she immediately recognizes that in doing so she would break her promise to her late father—"but I am then forsworn"—and this, Portia says, she will never do. However, if she doesn't cheat, he may lose her forever. "But if you do lose me, you'll make me sin by wishing that I had told you which casket to pick," states Portia. She becomes more and more emotional in this section as she wavers back and forth about whether or not to deceive in order to win her beloved. This leads to an emotional declaration:

> . . . Beshrew your eyes,
> They have o'erlook'd me and divided me;
> One half of me is yours, the other half yours,
> Mine own, I would say; but if mine, then yours,
> And so all yours. . . .

Her earlier concern about not expressing her love overtly is now gone as Portia openly woos Bassanio. *Beshrew* means "to curse." However here it is used affectionately: "I curse your eyes because they have put a spell on me and divided me." Portia means that Bassanio has made Portia wish to both obey and defy her father's command. She plays on the word *divide* by saying that both her "halves" belong to Bassanio. This is done in both a dramatic and humorous way as she alters the pattern of speech on the phrase "one half of me is yours, the other half yours." Of course Bassanio, and we, expect her to say that the other half is hers. In this one sentence, Portia states "I am yours" four times. Now her overwhelming passion for Bassanio mixed with the fear that she may never see him again causes her to exclaim:

> . . . O, these naughty times
> Put bars between the owners and their rights!
> And so, though yours, not yours. Prove it so,
> Let fortune go to hell for it, not I.

Portia declares that these wicked times put a barrier between those that possess love for another—the owners—and their rightful claim to act on that love. "And because of this," says Portia, "although my heart is yours, I may not be yours in fact, in marriage. If that proves to be the case, let fate go to hell for it, not me." Portia now seemingly senses that all of her efforts to stall Bassanio are in vain as she remarks:

> I speak too long; but 'tis to peize the time,
> To eche it and to draw it out in length,
> To stay you from election.

Peize (pronounced "peeze") means "to weigh down" but in this instance it specifically means "to piece out, to draw out." *Eche* (pronounced "each") has a similar definition: "eke, extend, and increase." Portia says that she has been talking in order to put off the inevitable, Bassanio's act of choosing a casket.

While Bassanio is silent throughout this speech, he is obviously giving subtle, nonverbal signals in response to Portia's words. For example, she shifts thoughts suddenly—"But lest you should not understand me well— / And yet a maiden hath no tongue but thought—." It may simply be his presence that flusters her. It may be the manner in which he is looking at her when Portia exclaims, "Beshrew your eyes, / They have o'erlook'd me and divided me." Also, she may detect something in his demeanor that suggests he is determined to proceed immediately with choosing a casket. This may motivate her to speak the last lines of the speech, beginning with "I speak too long."

DISCOVERY IN THE MOMENT

JOE: In closing, I want to talk a little about being and staying in the moment. We have already touched on this when I briefly discussed the illusion of the first time. An essential element that is often lacking in Shakespearean speeches is a sense of discovery. We have discussed finding the stimulus, whatever it may be, that causes your character to move from beat to beat. Some stimuli are strong enough to be *discoveries in the moment*. There is an old television advertising campaign for the vegetable drink V-8, in which a man is seen having just finished a glass of "Beverage X." As he sets down the empty glass, he smacks a palm to his forehead and exclaims, "I could have had a V-8!" In other words, he had a "discovery in the moment." I use the term *V-8* in my acting classes when referring to such a discovery. I certainly don't mean that such "V-8s" involve head smacking or the snapping of fingers. These are cliché movements. However, when an actor truly allows these discoveries to occur as if for the first time, it can be exciting for an audience to watch and for an actor to experience. Here is an example of a discovery in the moment, taken from Bullingbrook's monologue that we explored earlier. I insert the V-8:

> If that my cousin king be King in England,
> It must be granted I am Duke of Lancaster.
> [V-8!] You have a son, Aumerle, my noble cousin;
> Had you first died, and he been thus trod down,
> He should have found his uncle Gaunt a father
> To rouse his wrongs and chase them to the bay.

Although Bullingbrook may know the basic outline of his argument to his uncle, he is "winging it" to a large extent. It is the word *cousin,* which he speaks in the first line—"if that my cousin king"—that gives him the idea to use the "if the situation were reversed" argument that begins with "You have a son, Aumerle, my noble cousin." It's almost as if the unspoken idea before the line is "and speaking of cousins . . ." If Bullingbrook had worded the first line "If that *Richard* be King in England" rather than "If that my *cousin king* be King in England," he may never have thought of using the argument entailing York's son, Aumerle.

SAM: But Shakespeare knew exactly how he wanted to construct the speech. If he wanted to write it differently, he would have.

JOE: Of course he would have. You the *actor* know that, but your *character* does not. Once you are in rehearsals and performance, the words that your character speaks are no longer Shakespeare's—they are yours. Romeo does not know that he is in a play entitled *Romeo and Juliet.* He is a living, breathing human being who finds himself in a particular set of circumstances, pursuing specific needs and reacting to people and events as they happen. Acting is difficult for many reasons, including the fact that actors are clairvoyant. They know exactly what their character will say at any given moment as well as what other characters will say in response. They know that they will die or marry or be imprisoned at the end of the play. Although the actor may be prescient, his character must not be.

Concentrating Fully on the Other Person(s)

JOE: We have discussed techniques to keep us in the moment but I have yet to mention the most obvious one—putting one hundred percent of your attention on the other person. We have focused on solo acting work to this point. At most, our scene partners have been silent observers of our speeches to them. Of course, true acting involves at least two people. In these cases we *react* as well as act. With soliloquies and audition pieces the actor must preplan his actions. Hopefully, the stimuli that trigger those actions will be spontaneous and organic, but in these situations we are acting alone and must plan the arc of our speeches beforehand. We may change or alter these actions as we continue to work on the speeches, but there is no one else onstage to react to. When we act with others, we cannot completely preplan our actions because we have no idea how others will respond to us. Sanford Meisner, the late, legendary actor and acting teacher, created an entire acting technique because he felt that actors did not fully listen and respond to one another. The first two commandments of his technique are:

1. Don't do anything until someone or something makes you do it.
2. Everything that you do depends on the other person.

A friend of mine, who teaches the Meisner technique, is fond of telling her students, "Let the other person be the captain of your ship." I like that image. When your attention and focus is off yourself and on the other person or persons onstage, you have no choice but to be in the moment.

Summary

In this chapter, Joe analyzes several soliloquies and monologues for Liz and Sam, explaining some of the figures of speech and other literary devices that Shakespeare employed.

- Like much of Shakespeare's dramatic dialogue, soliloquies often contain strong physical imagery, as well as words whose sounds and rhythms fit the images they describe.
- The actor must always find the vulnerability in her character. This is particularly true when portraying a villain or antihero.
- Soliloquies in which the character addresses himself can also be directed to the audience, a convention of Elizabethan Theatre.
- Regardless of which option the actor chooses, soliloquies must be outwardly directed. If the character chooses to speak to herself, it should be to a specific aspect of her consciousness. If the actor chooses to speak to the people in the audience, she should decide exactly who they are. The actor can transform the audience into anyone or anything that will help her character achieve her objective.
- There is a character that appears in several of Shakespeare's plays who speaks only soliloquies and only to the audience. This character is most often referred to as the Chorus.
- Because there was little to no scenery in the Elizabethan theatre, characters sometimes paint the scenery with words.
- Shakespeare's soliloquies are most often a character's attempt to solve a pressing problem.
- Substitutions, while usually necessary when working on a speech out of the context of the play, should only be used when absolutely necessary if you are cast in a production. In these cases, the actor must make a connection with every actor whose character he comes into contact with over the course of the play.
- Soliloquies involve our characters' *forward momentum of thought*. Because our characters speak their thoughts aloud, their *language is thought in action*.
- The speaker in a Shakespearean soliloquy is usually addressing one of the following:
  1. Someone who is unaware of the speaker's presence
  2. Someone or something not present in the environment

3. The gods, spirits, or nature
4. Oneself or the audience
- The second and third options above are called an *apostrophe*. An apostrophe is a figure of speech, by which a speaker addresses people or things that are absent or dead.
- Many soliloquies attempt to solve a problem by breaking down and analyzing its component parts.
- Shakespeare usually presents the objective and obstacle in the first few lines of a soliloquy.
- The actor must always adhere to the *illusion of the first time*. All of our thoughts and actions must occur as if for the first time.
- A soliloquy consists of an overall objective, beat objectives that serve the overall objective of the speech, and transitions between those beat objectives.
- In this chapter, we defined *monologues* as speeches that are directed at other on-stage characters (who are also listening intently to what is being said to them).
- Monologues are similar to soliloquies in all respects but one: Our scene partners are no longer imaginary or endowed. They are characters onstage with us, with their own agendas and opinions. They respond, usually nonverbally, to what we are saying to them.
- The nonverbal behavior of our partners affects the actions we play in a monologue as well as occasionally igniting beat changes.
- The actor must uncover and play all of her character's *discoveries in the moment*. A discovery in the moment is an image, idea, or revelation that occurs to your character the nanosecond before she utters it.
- The best way for the actor to remain in the moment is to put one hundred percent of his attention on his scene partner. This allows his character to *react* as well as to *act*.

EXERCISES

GROUP EXERCISE 4.1
Choose a soliloquy in which your character speaks to the audience. Use your classmates as your audience. Make a decision about the identity of your audience. For example, you may decide that they are a group of psychiatrists to whom you must prove your sanity. Now speak your soliloquy to them, pursuing your intended objective. The members of the class must raise their hands when and if they feel that they are being positively affected by your words. You must attempt to get all of your peers to raise their hands by the end of your speech.

GROUP EXERCISE 4.2
Choose a soliloquy spoken to an audience or to a higher power. This exercise is similar to Group Exercise 4.1 above. However, this time your peers are a jury and you are an attorney using the words of your soliloquy to convince them of the validity of your case. Again, jurists must raise their hands if they are being persuaded by your words. Attempt to convince all jurors by the end of your speech.

GROUP EXERCISE 4.3

Parallel Monologue. This exercise is similar to Solo Exercise 3.2 in the preceding chapter. Find a monologue from one of Shakespeare's plays. Do all of the work necessary to begin work on the speech as an actor. Now find a circumstance from your life that most closely resembles the situation of your character during the monologue. Once again, *find the emotional essence of the monologue in order to find a parallel.* This time, however, you will be speaking your words to someone. This exercise is particularly useful for speeches that may at first seem far from our realm of experience. For example, let's examine a speech spoken by King Richard in *Richard II*:

> HENRY BULLINGBROOK: Are you contented to resign the crown?
> KING RICHARD II: Ay, no; no, ay; for I must nothing be;
> Therefore no no, for I resign to thee.
> Now mark me, how I will undo myself;
> I give this heavy weight from off my head
> And this unwieldy sceptre from my hand,
> The pride of kingly sway from out my heart;
> With mine own tears I wash away my balm
> With mine own hands I give away my crown,
> With mine own tongue deny my sacred state,
> With mine own breath release all duty's rites:
> All pomp and majesty I do forswear;
> My manors, rents, revenues I forgo;
> My acts, decrees, and statutes I deny:
> God pardon all oaths that are broke to me!
> God keep all vows unbroke are made to thee!
> Make me, that nothing have, with nothing griev'd,
> And thou with all pleas'd, that hast all achiev'd!
> Long mayst thou live in Richard's seat to sit,
> And soon lie Richard in an earthly pit!
> God save King Harry, unking'd Richard says,
> And send him many years of sunshine days!
> *(Richard II, 4, 1, 200–221)*

In this speech, Richard resigns his crown and agrees to make his cousin, Henry Bullingbrook, king of England. Certainly, none of us has ever ruled a kingdom or been forced to give a kingdom away. However, we have all experienced betrayal. It is betrayal that is at the emotional core of this speech. Find a time in which you experienced a betrayal and faced your betrayers.

JOE: One of my former students used an experience from childhood. At the vulnerable age of eleven, he built a tree fort with some of his friends. Soon, the neighborhood bully decided that he wanted in on the fort and forced my student's buddies to join him in ousting my student from his own fort. My student confronted them and tried his best, while accepting his fate, to instill guilt in them for banishing him. He reminded them that the tree fort had been his idea, that he had found all of the wood to build the fort, and so on. Now, this may seem like a silly parallel. However, my student's feelings of betrayal at the time were extremely real and he was able to tap into the emotional life of the situation. That is all that matters—finding an emotional parallel that may still work for you.

In private, try to recall, as closely as possible, the words that you used in your actual situation. Speak these words aloud. Do this several times. Now substitute the words of the monologue but keep the given circumstances of your real-life situation. Do this several times as well.

Present the monologue in class, using your real-life situation, but Shakespeare's words. Re-create your actual life environment as well. In this exercise you must ask one or more of your peers to take the place of the person or persons that you addressed in your real-life monologue. Place them where you want them in your re-created environment. As in Solo Exercise 3.2, don't worry if the sense of Shakespeare's words does not match exactly what you said in your true-life scenario. Stay true instead to the emotional equivalent of the speech. When you feel that you are making a strong emotional connection, set the exercise aside and work in detail on the actual meaning and imagery of the speech.

Note: If your real-life situation is not inviolable, you may wish to begin the exercise in class with the words from your real scenario and then segue into Shakespeare's words.

SOLO EXERCISE 4.1
Song. Find a recording of a song (pop songs seem to work best) that you feel captures the essence of your speech. At home, play the song as you prepare to begin your speech. Feel free to move or dance around and sing along with the song. At the conclusion of the song or at a point in the song that you choose, stop the song and launch immediately into your speech. In class, play your selection or have a classmate play the song on a CD or cassette player for you, stopping the song at a point that you deem appropriate. Then, as you did at home, launch into your speech. This exercise is valuable in setting a mood for the speech as well as helping with the emotional life of your character at the time that it is spoken.

SOLO (OR GROUP OR COUPLE) EXERCISE 4.2
Offstage Scene. This exercise is for soliloquies that are spoken immediately after a character walks onstage. Decide what your character was doing offstage before your entrance. Rehearse and then reenact your offstage actions in class. Your exit from the exercise signals your entrance in the written scene. If you were alone, reenact what you did just prior to the scene; if you were with one or more people, invent a scenario and briefly rehearse it with your classmates before presenting it to the class. Choose a scenario that motivates your entrance into the scene as well as the speaking of your soliloquy. This exercise is also helpful with scene work.

Chapter 5

Scenes—The First Steps

Scene Work: How to Begin

(Liz, Sam, and I meet again, several days later at the coffee shop.)

JOE: How are you two getting along with your speeches?
SAM: They're going well. We've been working on them in class. We're going to continue to work on speeches periodically, but our instructor is now moving us on to scenes.
LIZ: Sam and I are doing our first scene together. Our instructor wanted us to do something very different from *Romeo and Juliet,* so she assigned us Act 1, scene 7, from *Macbeth.* It's a scene between Macbeth and Lady Macbeth.
SAM: Will you give us some advice on how to proceed?
JOE: Certainly. As we mentioned earlier, true acting involves at least two people. Let's briefly examine the actor's responsibilities when working on a Shakespearean scene. In many respects it is a task similar to that of any play. We have already refreshed our memories about reading the play for clues to character, intent, and relationships. Let's investigate your two-person scene, Act 1, scene 7, of *Macbeth:*

(Hautboys and torches. Enter a Sewer, and divers Servants with dishes and service, and pass over the stage. Then enter Macbeth.)

MACBETH: If it were done when 'tis done, then 'twere well
It were done quickly: if th' assassination
Could trammel up the consequence, and catch
With his surcease, success; that but this blow
Might be the be-all and the end-all here,
But here, upon this bank and shoal of time,
We'd jump the life to come. But in these cases
We still have judgment here; that we but teach
Bloody instructions, which, being taught, return
To plague th' inventor: this even-handed justice
Commends th' ingredients of our poison'd chalice
To our own lips. He's here in double trust;
First, as I am his kinsman and his subject,
Strong both against the deed; then, as his host,
Who should against his murderer shut the door,
Not bear the knife myself. Besides, this Duncan
Hath borne his faculties so meek, hath been
So clear in his great office, that his virtues
Will plead like angels, trumpet-tongu'd, against
The deep damnation of his taking-off;
And pity, like a naked new-born babe,
Striding the blast, or heaven's cherubim, hors'd
Upon the sightless couriers of the air,
Shall blow the horrid deed in every eye,
That tears shall drown the wind. I have no spur
To prick the sides of my intent, but only
Vaulting ambition, which o'erleaps itself
And falls on the other—

(Enter Lady Macbeth.)

How now! What news?
LADY M.: He has almost supp'd: why have you left the chamber?

MACBETH: Hath he ask'd for me?
LADY M.: Know you not he has?
MACBETH: We will proceed no further in this business:
He hath honor'd me of late; and I have bought
Golden opinions from all sorts of people,
Which would be worn now in their newest gloss,
Not cast aside so soon.
LADY M.: Was the hope drunk
Wherein you dress'd yourself? Hath it slept since?
And wakes it now, to look so green and pale
At what it did so freely? From this time
Such I account thy love. Art thou afeard
To be the same in thine own act and valor
As thou art in desire? Wouldst thou have that
Which thou esteem'st the ornament of life,
And live a coward in thine own esteem,
Letting "I dare not" wait upon "I would,"
Like the poor cat i' th' adage?
MACBETH: Prithee, peace!
I dare do all that may become a man;
Who dares do more is none.
LADY M.: What beast was't, then,
That made you break this enterprise to me?
When you durst do it, then you were a man;
And, to be more than what you were, you would
Be so much more the man. Nor time nor place
Did then adhere, and yet you would make both:
They have made themselves, and that their fitness now
Does unmake you. I have given suck, and know
How tender 'tis to love the babe that milks me:
I would, while it was smiling in my face,
Have pluck'd my nipple from his boneless gums,
And dash'd the brains out, had I so sworn as you
Have done to this.
MACBETH: If we should fail?
LADY M.: We fail!
But screw your courage to the sticking-place,
And we'll not fail. When Duncan is asleep—
Whereto the rather shall his day's hard journey
Soundly invite him—his two chamberlains

>   Will I with wine and wassail so convince
>   That memory, the warder of the brain,
>   Shall be a fume, and the receipt of reason
>   A limbeck only: when in swinish sleep
>   Their drenched natures lie as in a death,
>   What cannot you and I perform upon
>   Th' unguarded Duncan? What not put upon
>   His spongy officers, who shall bear the guilt
>   Of our great quell?
> MACBETH: Bring forth men-children only;
>   For thy undaunted mettle should compose
>   Nothing but males. Will it not be receiv'd,
>   When we have mark'd with blood those sleepy two
>   Of his own chamber and used their very daggers,
>   That they have done't?
> LADY M.:   Who dares receive it other,
>   As we shall make our griefs and clamor roar
>   Upon his death?
> MACBETH: I am settled, and bend up
>   Each corporal agent to this terrible feat.
>   Away, and mock the time with fairest show:
>   False face must hide what the false heart doth know.
>   *(Macbeth, 1, 7, 1–82)*

JOE: This scene occurs shortly after Lady Macbeth's soliloquy that we analyzed in the preceding chapter. You'll recall that Macbeth, a nobleman of Scotland, has just won an important battle, putting down a rebellion in his country. Three witches, who inform him that he will be king of Scotland, visit him on the battlefield. Duncan, the current king, promotes Macbeth for his bravery in battle. Duncan and other nobles will stay the night at the castle of Macbeth and his wife, Lady Macbeth, where they will celebrate their victory as well as Macbeth's promotion. Macbeth has written a letter to his wife, informing her of the witches' prophesy. Macbeth arrives home before Duncan and his entourage. Macbeth and his wife make a pact that Duncan will not leave the castle alive. They decide that they will drug his grooms, murder him in the middle of the night, and put the blame on the drugged guards. The above scene occurs in the middle of the celebratory dinner party in Macbeth's honor. Macbeth is having second thoughts and, as we now know is common with Shakespeare's characters, finds a place where he can be alone to reason through his problem by means of a soliloquy. But before he can truly come to a decision, his wife, who has noticed his absence, interrupts him.

SAM: Do we begin to work on scenes in the same way that we began work on our speeches?

JOE: Absolutely. Actors should always do all of the work that we have been talking about so far. After reading the play, actors should each investigate the meaning of their own words in depth, and then get together with their scene partners to exchange definitions, including multiple definitions. Actors should also identify physical imagery, rhythms, and sounds that may affect their characters in the scene.

Paraphrase the Scene

JOE: The next step is to come up with a paraphrasing of the scene, one that you will both feel comfortable using in rehearsal. Such a paraphrasing should entail the primary meaning of the scene. You should put the scene in words that feel comfortable coming from your mouths. Let's begin with a possible paraphrasing of the primary meaning of the soliloquy and scene:

MACBETH: If the murder were absolutely finished when we do it, then it would be best if it were done quickly. If the murder could prevent further consequences and secure with Duncan's death, success; if only this strike of the dagger were an event complete in itself, that would end completely here in this earthly life, I would take my chances with the afterlife. However, in cases of murder, like this, we always receive a sentence here on earth, in that we only teach others how to kill, and once they learn how, they practice their skill on us. This impartial justice gives us the cup of poison to drink that we prepared for someone else. The king is entrusted to me here in two ways. First, as I am his relative and subject, both strong reasons not to do him harm; then as I am his host, who should protect him from murderers, not be the murderer myself. Besides, Duncan has exercised his royal powers so kindly, has been so irreproachable as a ruler, that his virtues will speak on his behalf like angels with voices as loud as trumpets to all the world against the mortal sin of his murder; and pity, like a newborn infant, sitting astride that trumpet blast, or heaven's angelic children, mounted upon the invisible winds, will blow the knowledge of his murder into everyone's eyes, so that the tears of all mankind will drown the wind. I have nothing to propel my plan forward except leaping ambition, which, like a rider trying to mount his horse too strongly, misses the saddle and falls on the other—*(he is about to say "side" but is interrupted)*

(Enter Lady Macbeth. Macbeth is slightly startled.)

What?—Oh, what's going on back there?
LADY MACBETH: Duncan's almost finished supper. Why did you leave the dining room?
MACBETH: Has he asked for me?
LADY MACBETH: You know perfectly well that he has.

MACBETH: We are not going one step further with this plan. He's honored me recently and I've gained a shining reputation from all kinds of people, which want to be worn now like bright, new clothes, not discarded so soon.

LADY MACBETH: Were the clothes of ambition that you dressed in a lie that was only stimulated by booze? Has it slept since that time, and does it wake up now to look so sickly and fearfully at the promise that it made so openly? From this time forward I will think of your love in the same way—just a drunken promise. Are you afraid to be the same person in deeds of bravery as you are in your desires? Do you want to wear the crown of Scotland, that you judge to be the pinnacle of your successful career, and live a coward in your own estimation, letting "I don't dare" follow along with "I want to," like the poor cat in the proverb, that wanted to catch the fish in the pond, but was afraid to get her paws wet?

MACBETH: Please shut up! I have the courage to do everything that is fitting for a man to do; who has the courage to do more than that is no man at all.

LADY MACBETH: What beast was it then that made you propose this plan to me? When you did dare to do it, then you were a man. And to become greater than you are now, to become king, you would be an even more courageous man. Neither the time nor the place were suitable for the murder when you first thought of the plan and yet you were determined to arrange both. Both the time and the place have now presented themselves and their very suitability destroys your courage. I have nursed a child and know how wonderful it is to love the infant that nurses from my breast. I would, while it was smiling in my face, have pulled him violently from my nipple and dashed his brains out, if I had sworn to kill the baby in the same way that you have sworn to kill Duncan.

MACBETH: But what if our plan fails?

LADY MACBETH: Are you kidding? Fail? All you need to do is summon up every ounce of your noble courage, and there is no way that we can fail. When Duncan is asleep, which he will do deeply because of his long journey, I will so overpower his attendants with wine and partying that memory, the guardian of the brain, will be an alcoholic vapor and the receptacle of reason will be nothing more than a still. While they sleep like drunken pigs, what can we not do to the unguarded Duncan? What can we not blame his drunken guards for, who will take all of the guilt for our magnificent murder?

MACBETH: Give birth only to boys! Because your fearless spirit should create nothing but males. Won't it be believed, when we smear the guards in his bedroom with blood and use their daggers to kill Duncan, that they committed the murder?

LADY MACBETH: Who could possibly believe anything other than that, since we will make such an upheaval of grief over his death?

MACBETH: I have decided. And will summon up every power in my body in order to go through with the deed. Let's go back in, join our guests, and deceive the world by putting on a happy, loyal, and honest appearance. Our smiling faces have to hide the truth that is in our hearts.

JOE: Of course, this is my paraphrasing. You must come up with one that, while staying true to the meaning of the scene, is comfortable for you to speak. Once your paraphrase is complete, read it aloud to one another several times. This will give you an idea of what the scene is about so that you can form an objective for your character. It is possible that your character changes objectives during a scene. In this case, find the objective that starts the scene for you, and then make discoveries about how and why your objective may change during rehearsals with your partner. Be sure to do all of the detailed work on your scene that we did when working on your Romeo and Juliet speeches before you work on paraphrasing. Paraphrasing only gives you what Bertram Joseph, in his book *Acting Shakespeare*, refers to as Shakespeare's "surface sense." I like this term. In other words, paraphrasing only scratches the surface of Shakespeare's dialogue. However, this surface sense is what tells the basic story of a speech or scene.

Consider Objectives

SAM: I think that my objective with my soliloquy is to try to *decide* on an objective. As you said, I'm getting cold feet and need to come to a decision about whether to kill Duncan or let him live and enjoy my promotion and growing reputation. I come up with a lot of reasons why I should back out during the speech. By the end of the soliloquy, I come to the decision that I want out of the plan.

JOE: Yes, but Shakespeare cleverly has Lady Macbeth interrupt you before you can finish your soliloquy and be completely certain about breaking your vow to kill the king.

LIZ: I think that my first objective when I enter the scene is to discover my husband's state of mind and bring him back to the party and our plan. I think that I fear the worst, that he has become a coward, and hope for the best, that he simply needed to get away to focus and gather his strength for the task at hand. When he tells me that he wants out, I do everything in my power to "bring him back into the fold," so to speak, to make him want to be king so passionately that he will join me in committing murder for the greater glory of us both.

JOE: Very good.

SAM: I think that my scene objective is a little more complicated. It seems that the first part of the scene is to convince her that it is a terrible plan and that we should instead both bask in the light of my promotion and glowing reputation in the country. Then I seem to shift to the objective of making my wife allay all of my fears about killing Duncan in order for me to agree to proceed with the murder. But, it seems to me, that I must have wanted to be king for a long time in order to be influenced by my wife. So, it's possible that even at the beginning of the scene, deep down inside, although I'm telling her in no uncertain terms that I am aborting our plan, I really want her to convince me to go through with it.

JOE: That's a strong and valid option.

Personalize

SAM: But how can I want both things at the same time?

JOE: You need to personalize, not the motivation to kill Duncan, but the motivation to become king of Scotland. Your personalization has to make your character obsessive in his desire to wear the crown. However, the thought of the murder of Duncan in order to attain your goal is so abhorrent to you that you need to be alone to think things through. As the consequences inherent in such a plan grow stronger as you speak your thoughts aloud, the obstacle of the murder becomes so overwhelming that your objective, at least at the moment of your wife's arrival, is to persuade her to agree to abort the murder and live a comfortable life as the Thane of Glamis and of Cawdor.

LIZ: Our acting teachers tell us to be sure that we make a decision about our offstage life before our characters enter a scene.

JOE: Yes, that is vital. You must decide on a choice that stimulates you strongly to enter the environment of the scene. You must answer these questions concerning your character's entrance:

1. Where was I prior to my entrance?
2. What was I doing there?
3. Why did I leave?
4. Why have I come here?
5. Why have I come here right now?

Explore the Given and Imaginary Circumstances

JOE: Making strong sensory choices is invaluable. Let's start with Macbeth. What are the imaginary circumstances you have come up with before your soliloquy?

SAM: Duncan, his sons, my wife, and my fellow noblemen were having a great celebration. I was the center of attention and I was really enjoying it. Everyone flattered me, especially the king. As we were all about to sit down to dinner, Duncan quieted us and said that he wanted to make a toast. We all raised our glasses and the king said, "Here's to my friend and kinsman, Macbeth, without whom we would not be here tonight. I can never express my full gratitude to him. He is like a son to me, as beloved to me as Malcolm and Donalbain. I drink to your health and happiness!" I looked over at him and he had tears in his eyes as he looked at me with great affection. Everyone drank and applauded me. Then Duncan came over and hugged me and cried and kissed me on the cheek. I blushed and mumbled something, I don't remember what, because I was so flustered, and then he went to the other end of the table and hugged and kissed my wife. I found myself completely overwhelmed and confused. I was reminded that he is a great king, friend, and ally. I took the nearest opportunity to leave the chamber and find a place to be alone and solve my problem.

JOE: Good. Your imaginary circumstances are specific and loaded with sensory stimuli. By connecting to such a scenario, you will come onstage with a vital emotional life and intent. Now, what about you, Lady Macbeth?

LIZ: I was so proud of my husband during the banquet! After the toast, we sat down to eat and I was being the gracious hostess, talking to as many of the guests as I could, playing the loyal and grateful wife and subject. I was so taken with entertaining the entourage that it wasn't until I looked over to ask my husband a question that I saw his empty seat. Duncan noticed it at the same time. He asked, "Where is your husband? He is embarrassed by all this attention, I'm sure." I told him that I agreed and set off to find him. I could feel my heart beating loudly and strongly as I panicked about his absence. I was worried that all of Duncan's talk was making him sentimental and lily-livered. I got so panicked that I had to stop and take a deep breath and entertain the thought that Macbeth may have just needed to get some air and calm himself down. This allowed me to focus and I set out to continue my search until I found him standing alone.

JOE: Great.
SAM: Do our imaginary circumstances have to completely coincide?
JOE: If possible, that would be ideal. However, an imaginary circumstance that would "feed" you in the scene may do the opposite for Liz, and vice versa. In such cases, use what works best for you as long as it doesn't adversely affect you, your relationship in the scene, or the given circumstances of the scene and play.

Be Specific about the Environment

LIZ: Our teachers always tell us to be specific about the environment in which our scenes take place.
JOE: Yes. You must feel as if you are in a specific, detailed, complete environment that will stimulate your character and free you from tension.
SAM: Something that always gives me a problem with Shakespeare is locale. I know that we're supposed to be in our castle, but I've never been in a castle and I feel like I have a clichéd idea of one and wouldn't feel like I was in a real place during the scene.
JOE: Research is valuable in these cases. Find out as much about Scottish castles as possible, especially consulting publications with detailed photographs and ground plans. Also, it is common for Shakespeare productions to be updated. Especially with scene work, you can certainly use a place you are familiar with. Any large house that you know well would be better than a two-dimensional sketch of a castle.
SAM: But I think of Macbeth's castle as an eerie place. If I used a house that I know, I would feel too comfortable.
JOE: You're thinking in clichés. This is Macbeth and Lady Macbeth's home. They certainly would feel comfortable there. Obviously, if you set the scene in the time and place that was intended, there would not be the creature comforts that we have today, but there would probably be roaring fires in the many fireplaces to warm the castle. There would also be many burning sconces on the walls to give as much light as possible. I think that it can affect you powerfully to contemplate killing Duncan in the warmly decorated guest room where your family and friends usually stay when they visit. You must choose an environment that you feel is complete and real and that will free you to do your work in the scene. That doesn't mean you can't use physical conditions to help you in the scene and in the play. If you choose a castle for the environment of the scene, you have a frigid stone floor to walk on. Because of the size of the castle, you may have to find a remote area in which to be alone and such an area may not be as well lighted or warmed as the main rooms of your home. Scotland can be quite damp and cold and such a remote section in the

house or castle would be quite chilly. Environmental conditions can stimulate your character's actions.

LIZ: We use rehearsal furniture in our classes, but Shakespeare is very often played with very little furniture, or sometimes, no furniture at all. How can we feel like we are in a real place?

JOE: First of all, it is helpful to find a place to rehearse that is as similar to your idea of the environment as possible. Shakespeare usually gives you very little to go on—usually he will only indicate "an orchard" or "a street." In the case of your scene, it says "Inner court of Macbeth's castle." The ideal would be for Sam to choose a space that he has used as a place to be alone to think. Sam would describe such a place in detail to Liz and you would both recreate that space in your rehearsal room or classroom in detail.

SAM: The place that I always go to has only a bench in it.

JOE: That's fine. As Liz mentioned, Shakespeare is acted most often with a minimum of furniture. This is for a couple of reasons. One is that Elizabethan theatre traditionally used very little furniture due to the many scenes and scene changes in the plays of the day. Also, the plays of the time were about language and the dynamic between two or more characters. Furniture, other than the occasional chair or bench, was usually unnecessary. However, you must be very detailed about what is around you in your environment in your mind's eye, even though what is really around you are your instructor and classmates, who will be observing your scene.

Consider the Fourth Wall

SAM: Are you talking about our "fourth wall"?

JOE: Yes. The onstage environment often includes three "walls"—left, right, and rear. Actors should complete their environment by filling in the **fourth wall,** where the audience is located, with the remaining details of their environment. This frees actors to look out at the space occupied by the audience and, in their mind's eye, see what the characters would see if they were in that actual place. The concept of the fourth wall began with the use of the proscenium stage. In many theatre spaces today, however, three of the four walls, or all four walls, are filled with seats for the audience. This makes it even more essential for the actors to fill in those areas with the specificity of their environment.

LIZ: Why?

JOE: If you are motivated to move during your scene, you want to feel comfortable in doing so. For example, let's say that during a presentation of your scene, you—as Lady Macbeth—are motivated to move away from your husband because of your frustration at his "cowardice." I have seen many actors begin to act on such an impulse and then stop themselves because they do not believe in the reality of the space. Therefore, they stay in one area, refusing to ever break eye contact with their scene partners. Don't misunderstand me—I am not saying that actors should move about the stage gratuitously. However, denying a true character impulse for movement creates tension in the actor. Knowing and believing fully in the environment that you both create for the scene allows you to be truthful, spontaneous, and connected.

SAM: What is the next step?

Scene Work: Breaking Down the Scene into Beats

Joe: It is essential for actors to break the scene into beats. Just as we did with speeches, *you must understand each section of your scene as well as how and why one beat leads to another.* Unfortunately, actors all too often give lip service to this important step in the acting process. Understanding each beat as well as what "fires" the subsequent one can mean the difference between a clear, exciting scene and an opaque, static one. Let's do this with your scene:

> If it were done when 'tis done, then 'twere well
> It were done quickly: if th' assassination
> Could trammel up the consequence, and catch
> With his surcease, success; that but this blow
> Might be the be-all and the end-all here,
> But here, upon this bank and shoal of time,
> We'd jump the life to come. But in these cases
> We still have judgment here; that we but teach
> Bloody instructions, which, being taught, return
> To plague th' inventor: this even-handed justice
> Commends th' ingredients of our poison'd chalice
> To our own lips. . . .

Analyze the Beats

Joe: In this first section of Macbeth's soliloquy, he states his objective and obstacle immediately. He says that if the only consequence of Duncan's murder is his own succession to the throne, then he would want it to happen immediately. The obstacle follows. He says that he knows that this is untrue. Instead, there will be those who will be obsessed with avenging Duncan's death. Macbeth is examining the problems inherent in such a murder and this concern causes him to explore further difficulties that will occur if he enacts such a deed:

> . . . He's here in double trust;
> First, as I am his kinsman and his subject,
> Strong both against the deed; then, as his host,
> Who should against his murderer shut the door,
> Not bear the knife myself. Besides, this Duncan
> Hath borne his faculties so meek, hath been
> So clear in his great office, that his virtues
> Will plead like angels, trumpet-tongu'd, against
> The deep damnation of his taking-off;

> And pity, like a naked new-born babe,
> Striding the blast, or heaven's cherubim, hors'd
> Upon the sightless couriers of the air,
> Shall blow the horrid deed in every eye,
> That tears shall drown the wind. . . .

Problem begets problem in this section. Through strong physical imagery, Macbeth has built such a powerful argument against Duncan's murder that this obstacle causes him to change his objective from wanting to become king to contenting himself with a "lesser" but safer life as a respected and distinguished Thane:

> . . . I have no spur
> To prick the sides of my intent, but only
> Vaulting ambition, which o'erleaps itself
> And falls on the other—

Now the scene begins as Lady Macbeth enters:

(Enter Lady Macbeth.)

MACBETH: How now! What news?

LADY M.: He has almost supp'd: why have you left the chamber?

MACBETH: Hath he ask'd for me?

LADY M.:   Know you not he has?

MACBETH: We will proceed no further in this business:
He hath honor'd me of late; and I have bought
Golden opinions from all sorts of people,
Which would be worn now in their newest gloss,
Not cast aside so soon.

LADY M.:   Was the hope drunk
Wherein you dress'd yourself? Hath it slept since?
And wakes it now, to look so green and pale
At what it did so freely? From this time
Such I account thy love. Art thou afeard
To be the same in thine own act and valor
As thou art in desire? Wouldst thou have that
Which thou esteem'st the ornament of life,
And live a coward in thine own esteem,
Letting "I dare not" wait upon "I would,"
Like the poor cat i' th' adage?

MACBETH: Prithee, peace!
I dare do all that may become a man;
Who dares do more is none.

In this section, Lady Macbeth's worst fears are realized. Macbeth, in an attempt to put an end to the plan quickly and surely, comes on strong in no uncertain terms. He speaks as the head of the household, as the one who "wears the pants in the family." Lady Macbeth reacts instinctively and emotionally. She shames him for his cowardice and Macbeth responds defensively. Then Lady Macbeth seems to change tactics:

LADY M.:   What beast was't, then,
That made you break this enterprise to me?
When you durst do it, then you were a man;
And, to be more than what you were, you would
Be so much more the man. Nor time nor place
Did then adhere, and yet you would make both:
They have made themselves, and that their fitness now
Does unmake you. I have given suck, and know
How tender 'tis to love the babe that milks me:
I would, while it was smiling in my face,
Have pluck'd my nipple from his boneless gums,
And dash'd the brains out, had I so sworn as you
Have done to this.
MACBETH: If we should fail?

Because of Macbeth's defensive response to her words, it seems that Lady Macbeth takes a different approach. She seems to play on Macbeth's self-respect and manhood as well as his pride as a soldier, statesman, and man. She reminds him that true men never break their word and challenges his sense of responsibility. She also begins to play on his vanity with phrases like "you would be so much more the man." Macbeth is obviously affected by his wife's words because he responds with the question "If we should fail?" The fact that he responds with a question rather than a statement is a clear indication that he is open to his wife's persuasions. She has begun to allay his fears to a certain extent, but not to the extent that he is willing to murder Duncan. Lady Macbeth registers this openness on the part of her husband, the first in the scene, and seizes upon the opportunity to completely allay his fears and fill him with confidence:

LADY M.:   We fail!
But screw your courage to the sticking-place,
And we'll not fail. When Duncan is asleep—
Whereto the rather shall his day's hard journey
Soundly invite him—his two chamberlains

> Will I with wine and wassail so convince
> That memory, the warder of the brain,
> Shall be a fume, and the receipt of reason
> A limbeck only: when in swinish sleep
> Their drenched natures lie as in a death,
> What cannot you and I perform upon
> Th' unguarded Duncan? What not put upon
> His spongy officers, who shall bear the guilt
> Of our great quell?
> MACBETH: Bring forth men-children only;
> For thy undaunted mettle should compose
> Nothing but males. . . .

Lady Macbeth paints a strong, confident picture, making Duncan's murder seem as effortless as taking candy from a baby. Her imagery is seductive and sure. Macbeth responds positively, greatly impressed with his wife and her "undaunted mettle." He is being persuaded, but she must still do more to win him over:

> MACBETH: . . .Will it not be receiv'd,
> When we have mark'd with blood those sleepy two
> Of his own chamber and used their very daggers,
> That they have done't?
> LADY M.:   Who dares receive it other,
> As we shall make our griefs and clamor roar
> Upon his death?

This last question and Lady Macbeth's confident answer is finally enough to persuade Macbeth to continue on with their nefarious plan:

> MACBETH: I am settled, and bend up
> Each corporal agent to this terrible feat.
> Away, and mock the time with fairest show:
> False face must hide what the false heart doth know.

As you can see, it is essential to break the scene into its component parts, so that the arc of the scene is clear for both actors.

Discover the Flexibility of Acting Choices

SAM: The way that you've broken down the scene makes it seem like all actors must play the scene in the same way.

JOE: No, that isn't true. I have made observations about the tone and imagery of the dialogue of the characters. I have discussed possible objectives and tactics. However, the *actions* that the actors choose for their characters to play will vary from actor to actor. Actors can pursue the same objective by begging, threatening, seducing, and so on. Also, although I think that the objectives of this scene are fairly straightforward, there are many scenes in Shakespeare in which this is not true. In such cases, *actors playing the same role may choose different objectives for their characters to pursue in the same scene.* An actor should not ask himself whether an acting choice is right or wrong, but rather whether an acting choice is valid or invalid. An acting choice is valid if it is true to the character, the relationship(s) with the other character(s) onstage, and true to the story and given circumstances of the play.

LIZ: I have a question about your analysis of one of the sections of the scene. You said that Macbeth compliments his wife and her "undaunted mettle." But she has just told him that she would gladly kill her own baby if she had sworn to do so. How can he compliment her after she says something like that?

JOE: I think that you are not seeing the entire picture. First of all, Lady Macbeth does not say that she would *gladly* murder her own child. The point that she is emphatically making with this dialogue is that *a pledge is a pledge. Real* men, *noble* men are true to their word, regardless of the consequences. Such men do not honor their word only when it is convenient for them to do so. It is implied that if Lady Macbeth were to make a solemn oath to kill her infant, it would have to be for an extreme reason. For example, mythology contains stories of kings and queens sacrificing their children in order to prevent the gods from destroying their kingdoms. Such actions are exceptionally altruistic, because these rulers choose the well-being of their subjects over the lives of their own children. Such profound sacrifice makes these characters noble, not ignoble.

SAM: So, Lady Macbeth may be saying that, even though it would break her heart, she would kill her child if she made a solemn oath to do so?

JOE: Yes. This imagery helps remind Macbeth of what it means to be a man and a nobleman. That is why he tells his wife to "Bring forth men-children only." Macbeth is humbled and impressed that a woman has reminded him of what it means to be a man. We must keep in mind that the play takes place within an extremely patriarchal society.

LIZ: When I first read the scene, it seemed that Lady Macbeth could only speak the lines about murdering her baby in a violent and uncompromising way in order to shame Macbeth into submission, but that isn't necessarily true, is it?

JOE: No. It would certainly be a valid choice, but it is by no means the only choice. This is a good example of the fact that the same objective can be pursued in a myriad of ways. An actress playing Lady Macbeth can make it clear to her husband that such a despicable act would be abhorrent to her. But nevertheless, an oath is an oath. The lines may therefore be spoken with a great deal of vulnerability.

SCENE WORK: REHEARSING THE SCENE

LIZ: After we do all of this work, do we just keep rehearsing the scene as often as we can until we present it in class?

JOE: No, I think that could get predictable and boring. Once you have attained this stage of rehearsal, it is important to rehearse from beat to beat. In other words, don't simply run the entire scene from beginning to end over and over again. Put your attention on "the moment before" and then begin with Macbeth's entrance. Rehearse the soliloquy and the first beat of the scene. Do this several times, pausing to discuss the scene if you feel it necessary. Then move on to the second beat. You may have to take the scene from a point near the end of the first beat in order to register the transition that motivates the second beat. Do this until you feel that you are ready to move on to the third beat, and so on. You may find it helpful to always start from the beginning of the scene, adding beats each time. In other words, you can rehearse beat one, then move on to beats one and two, then one, two, and three, and so on.

LIZ: What about exercises?

JOE: Acting exercises are an important part of the rehearsal process. They can give you insight to the scene and provide you with variety during your scene rehearsals. You probably know of many acting exercises from your classes and reading assignments that you may find helpful. I will provide many more for your consideration.

SAM: Should we continue to use our paraphrasing of the scene in our rehearsals?

JOE: Yes, at least in the early stages of rehearsal. It will remind you of the basic story you are telling and help you to use Shakespeare's language as if it were your own. More importantly, repeated use of your paraphrasing will remind you of how woefully inadequate it is. In this way, rather than being intimidated by Shakespeare's words, you will embrace them because they alone can express the rich, sensuous, complex, and specific meaning of the scene.

LIZ: Can you give us some pointers for working on an undirected scene?

JOE: Yes. First and foremost, *do not direct one another.* In other words, don't say, something like, "You need to come on more strongly with your line in order for me to respond in the way my character is supposed to." *Your job as an actor is to respond in the moment to what you are getting from your partner,* based on your choice of objective, personalization of the given circumstances, and relationship. You may certainly suggest exercises or ideas that you may have about the scene. If you are respectful of one another and keep in mind that you are equals in this process, staying open to the give-and-take nature of scene work, you will find it rewarding.

Second, *don't "overtalk" the scene.* You are not in a drama literature class. Get the scene on its feet as often as possible and talk briefly between running beats or doing exercises, discussing what you feel worked and what you want to work on next. You will certainly want to talk about the scene in more depth, but save it for a phone conversation with your scene partner or for a meeting outside of the rehearsal space rather than wasting valuable rehearsal time.

Third, *get "off book" as soon as possible.* Getting off book, as you may know, means to memorize your lines. This allows you to focus on your partner and your environment rather than on a piece of paper. *Try to get off book in a neutral manner.* Don't learn your lines in a certain way. This leads to "line readings." The actor then speaks his lines in a preplanned fashion, rather than in a manner that is a truthful response to the actions of his scene partner.

Finally, during the last hours of scene rehearsals and during scene presentations, *let go of everything and put all of your attention on your scene partner.* Don't think about what you have worked on. Leave your homework at home where it belongs. Keep this important adage in mind: *During your solo preparation for the scene, all of the answers are in the text. During scene rehearsals, presentations, and performance, all of the answers are in your partner.* If you have worked diligently and efficiently, most of that work will be there for you if you simply listen and respond to your partner. Let him be the "captain of your ship." In this way, you will have fun. That final, all-important step of acting is often missed. If you have worked hard, you deserve to let go and have fun!

SAM: Is there any other work to do?

JOE: Yes. We will explore it in detail in our future meetings.

Summary

In this chapter, Joe outlines the steps necessary to prepare for a role, as Sam and Liz begin their scene work.

- True acting involves at least two people, and this can only happen during scene work.
- The actor must go through all of the steps described thus far (in the first four chapters). After reading the play, investigate the meaning of your words in depth, and then share and discuss with your scene partner all the definitions, including any multiple definitions.
- Identify physical imagery, rhythms, and sounds that may significantly affect your character in the scene.
- Create a paraphrase of the scene. It should be comfortable for both actors during rehearsals. Continue using the paraphrase periodically during rehearsals in order to reinforce the surface sense of the scene.
- Decide on a scene objective for your character. Occasionally an objective changes over the course of the scene. If this is the case, choose an objective to begin the scene and then discover how the objective changes during the rehearsal process.
- Actions and even objectives in the same scene may vary depending on each actor's interpretation of the characters, relationships, and given circumstances of the scene (and the play).
- Ask yourself whether an acting choice—such as an objective or action—is valid or invalid, not whether it is right or wrong. Acting choices are valid when they are true to the character, the onstage relationships, and the story (the given circumstances).
- Personalize all aspects of the given circumstances of the scene, including your relationships with all other characters in the scene.
- Make strong, sensory choices about where your character has come from before the scene. Ask the following questions:

1. Where was I (my character) prior to my entrance?
2. What was I doing there?
3. Why did I leave?
4. Why have I come here?
5. Why have I come here right now?

- Be specific about the environment in which your scenes take place. A specific space will stimulate the character to action, as well as free you from tension. Research any environments with which you are unfamiliar. Whenever possible and appropriate to the scene, substitute real and familiar places. Use your imagination (mind's eye) to fill in the details of your environment.
- Use environmental conditions to stimulate your character's actions. This allows you to move freely and instinctively within your chosen scene environment and permits a stronger and more specific connection to your scene partner.
- Break down the scene into beats. You must understand each section of your scene as well as how and why one beat leads to another. This is vital!
- Rehearse the scene from beat to beat before working the scene in its entirety.
- Acting exercises are an important part of the rehearsal process. Do not simply work on the scene itself. Do one or more exercises and then come back to the scene. This can provide insight into the scene and gives variety to your rehearsal process.
- Be certain not to direct each other during rehearsals. Make suggestions and give input, but do not try to control your partner or the process.
- Do not "overtalk" the scene. Analyze and discuss your scene, but when the conversation can be saved for the phone or meetings outside of the rehearsal space, do so. Set up your environment and get your scene on its feet.
- Learn your lines as quickly as possible so that you can give your full attention to your partner and your scene environment.
- Learn your lines in a neutral manner; otherwise, you may get stuck in "line readings," or vocal patterns that will be difficult to break. Learning your lines neutrally allows you to respond fully and truthfully to your partner.
- During your solo preparation for the scene, the answers are in the text. During scene rehearsals and performance, the answers are in your partner.
- During the final stages of your scene preparation and of course during your scene presentations, leave behind all of your homework, put your full attention on your scene partner, and listen, respond, and have fun!

EXERCISES

GROUP EXERCISE 5.1
Paraphrasing. We have discussed paraphrasing extensively. It is defined as "a rewording of the meaning expressed in something spoken or written." Paraphrasing Shakespeare's scenes during rehearsals is an exercise often used by actors and directors. It is especially useful if one or more of the actors is having difficulty making the language his own or infusing the words with intent and clarity.

JOE: I had to call someone a "guttersnipe" onstage (no, this was not a Shakespeare play) and I simply could not make it work. I temporarily replaced the word with one of the four-letter variety that would be more appropriate for a David Mamet play. The moment then came alive. I alternated between the two words until "guttersnipe" became emotionally synonymous with the substituted word.

This is an important point. Paraphrasing for too long a period may cause you to become dependent on the rewording. You must constantly return to the text until you feel that the replacement dialogue has served its purpose, at which point it must be discarded.

The paraphrasing should not be improvised. It is too difficult and imprecise a task. Script the paraphrased dialogue as closely as possible to Shakespeare's dialogue. Be specific in your substitutions. Your paraphrasing should concern itself with Shakespeare's primary meaning or surface sense. At best, this dialogue will only skirt the edges of the actual sense expressed by Shakespeare. Its purpose is to help you connect with material nearly a half-millennium old, to allow you to reach a place in which you can honestly say of Shakespeare's text, "This is simply the way that I talk." Of course, paraphrasing can also be useful for speeches and audition pieces.

Variation: After you have paraphrased the surface sense of your speech or scene, paraphrase the secondary meanings of your words. Rehearse with this paraphrasing to see how it affects your actions in the speech or scene.

COUPLE EXERCISE 5.1
Back-to-Back. Scene partners sit back-to-back on the floor with eyes closed. Each gives his weight over to the other so that neither is tense. Actors then speak their lines while their partners whisper any words that have an effect on them. Although uttering the partner's words, actors should whisper the words from their own point of view. For example, if your partner calls you a "cruel, ingrateful, savage and inhuman creature" *(Henry V, 2, 2, 94–95)*, it may cause you hurt, indignation, or amusement—and you would whisper your partner's words accordingly. This exercise can help you connect with your partner's imagery as well as your response to that imagery.

FOUR BASIC COMMUNICATION EXERCISES
The next four exercises (Couple Exercises 5.2a–5.2d) are about sending imagery and intent fully and clearly to your partner(s) with the dialogue of your scene. They help ensure that your actions are played completely and distinctly to the other person(s) onstage.

Keep in mind, however, that these exercises are not meant to produce line readings. How an actor communicates and images is up to him. The criteria for asking an actor to repeat a line is whether *he* is imaging and/or communicating—not whether the actor is imaging or communicating how and what *you* want him to.

These four exercises will use the following section of dialogue from *Troilus and Cressida* to illustrate the techniques:

> CRESSIDA: O, you shall be expos'd, my lord, to dangers
> As infinite as imminent! But I'll be true.
> TROILUS: And I'll grow friend with danger. Wear this sleeve.
> CRESSIDA: And you this glove. When shall I see you?

> TROILUS: I will corrupt the Grecian sentinels,
> To give thee nightly visitation.
> But yet be true.   *(Troilus and Cressida, 4, 4, 68–74)*

COUPLE EXERCISE 5.2A

Do You Know What I Mean? Select a section of dialogue that you would like to work on. After each line that is not in the form of a question (or after a phrase, if the line is unusually long), add a question such as one of the following: "Do you know what I mean?" "You know?" "Understand?" "Get me?" "See what I'm saying?" or "Okay?"

Using the *Troilus and Cressida* passage as an example, the exercise would go something like this:

> CRESSIDA: O, you shall be exposed, my lord, to dangers
> As infinite as imminent! *Do you know what I mean?* But I'll be true.
>   *You understand?*
> TROILUS: And I'll grow friend with danger. *You see?* Wear this sleeve.
>   *Okay?*
> CRESSIDA: And you this glove. *Understand me?* When shall I see you?
> TROILUS: I will corrupt the Grecian sentinels,
>   to give thee nightly visitation. *Get me?*
> But yet be true. *Do you know what I mean?*

Be sure to make the added questions a continuation of the line, not merely words that are tagged on. This exercise is meant to help eliminate "down endings." Down endings occur when an actor is not really asking for a response from the other character. (The response need not be a verbal one.) Lines that are in the form of a question are, of their nature, already asking for a response. Even lines that end with a period should imply that a response is desired. *Don't make statements. Ask for responses.*

COUPLE EXERCISE 5.2B

Talk to Me/Listen to Me. This variation begins in the same manner, with each actor saying his or her lines from a dialogue passage. However, in this exercise, if actor A feels that actor B is not communicating or is not asking for a response, actor A will say "Talk to me." Actor B will then repeat the line, trying to focus better, and prefacing it with "Listen to me." When actor A wishes the dialogue to proceed, he or she will simply nod.

Only say "Talk to me" when you feel it necessary. Otherwise, just nod your head after your partner's line and continue the dialogue. Do not abuse this exercise. I have seen actors angered at having to repeat a line one too many times. When it becomes obvious that your partner is doing the best that he or she can at that particular point in rehearsal, then nod and get on with the scene.

Again using the passage from *Troilus and Cressida*, the "Talk to Me/Listen to Me" exercise may go something like this:

CRESSIDA: O, you shall be exposed, my lord, to dangers as infinite as imminent! But I'll be true.
TROILUS: *(Nods his head)* And I'll grow friend with danger.
CRESSIDA: *Talk to me.*
TROILUS: *Listen to me.* And I'll grow friend with danger. Wear this sleeve.
CRESSIDA: *(Nods her head)* And you this glove. When shall I see you?
TROILUS: *Talk to me.*
CRESSIDA: *Listen to me.* And you this glove. When shall I see you?

And so on . . .

COUPLE EXERCISE 5.2C

Question. This exercise begins in the same manner as Couple Exercises 5.1a and 5.1b. Actor A says a line. If actor B wants it repeated, he or she says actor A's line in the form of a question, and actor A repeats the line attempting to more effectively communicate the line to actor B. You may do this with lines that are in the form of a question as well. As before, a nod of the head signals the continuation of the scene.

The "Question" exercise may go something like this:

TROILUS: And I'll grow friend with danger.
CRESSIDA: *And I'll grow friend with danger?*
TROILUS: And I'll grow friend with danger.
CRESSIDA: *(Nods her head)*
TROILUS: Wear this sleeve.
CRESSIDA: *(Nods her head)* And you this glove. When shall I see you?
TROILUS: *And you this glove? When shall I see you?*
CRESSIDA: And you this glove. When shall I see you?

And so on . . .

COUPLE EXERCISE 5.2D

What? As before, the actors say their lines. If either actor feels that a word spoken by his or her partner was not imaged or communicated, he or she repeats the partner's line as a question, inserting "what" for that word.

The "What?" exercise may go something like this:

TROILUS: And I'll grow friend with danger.
CRESSIDA: And I'll grow *what* with danger?
TROILUS: And I'll grow friend with danger.
CRESSIDA: *(Nods her head)*

And so on . . .

GROUP (OR COUPLE) EXERCISE 5.2
Scene in the Dark. This is a simple one to execute. Simply sit in a dark (completely dark if possible) space and go through the scene. Obviously, this is meant to isolate and heighten the sense of hearing. A well-acted Shakespearean scene can be just as exciting in the dark as on a stage.

COUPLE (OR SOLO) EXERCISE 5.3
Lifestyles of the Rich and Famous. This exercise helps the actor to create a strong, specific environment. The director or instructor acts as an interviewer who has been invited into the home of a Shakespearean character. For example, Hamlet, Richard III, Imogen, or the Macbeths give a guided tour of their abodes.

The space is actually an empty classroom or theatre, but the actors endow the space with furniture and objects and describe them as well as their history to the interviewer. I find it helpful to have the actors describe the floor and ceiling as well. Asking for a tour of the character's favorite room as well as his or her "private place" can further stimulate the actors' imaginations. If interviewing Falstaff or Caliban, the exercise can be called "Lifestyles of the Down and Out." Actors should supply their instructor or director with a diagram or ground plan of their palace or cottage. This exercise should be done before the "Letter" exercise and the "First Five Minutes of the Day" exercise, both of which follow.

SOLO EXERCISE 5.1
Letter. I find that this exercise works best at least halfway into the rehearsal process. The instructor or director should ask the actors to write a letter to someone that they truly wish to communicate with about any subject. The class or cast should write for approximately ten minutes and should not read or show their letters to anyone.

Next, the actors should each set up a simple environment where their characters would go to be alone and where they could write a letter undisturbed. The actors should now write a letter, as their character, to someone with whom they have a great desire to communicate—either someone from the play or someone from their imaginations. Their pen or pencil is to be endowed as a writing implement of the time in which the play (or production) takes place. Also (and this is most important) the actor cannot use his or her own handwriting style but should alter it to be the character's handwriting.

Do not think about it. Simply write and see what happens. Actors should write as their characters for at least ten minutes.

Do not expect any predictable results. This is a very freeing exercise and often reveals aspects of character, relationships, choices, and so on, that were lying dormant within the actor's creative consciousness. It is interesting for each actor to hold both letters up quickly to the group (upside down if necessary, to prevent nosiness) to show the differences in the handwriting styles.

SOLO (OR GROUP) EXERCISE 5.2
First Five Minutes of the Day. Many actors have a difficult time imaging Ophelia with a blemish problem or Macbeth sitting on a chamber pot. However, the actor must

embody a living, breathing human being. This exercise can help. It is simple: The actor "lives" the first five minutes of a typical day in the life of the character.

Rehearsal furniture is used to transform the classroom into a bedroom or other environment in which your character would usually awaken. The exercise begins with waking and proceeds with the activities of the first five minutes of the day. Nothing should be mimed. Bring in any objects needed to accomplish your morning tasks. (Obviously, certain objects will have to be endowed as period pieces.)

Because many of us engage in morning activities that we would not want observed by anyone, discretion should be observed. For example, if your character sleeps in the nude, wear enough clothing to be acceptable and endow yourself with a birthday suit. Any private bodily functions should occur after the fifth minute of the exercise (in other words, the exercise is over before these activities are acted out). Classmates can be enlisted to play servants, ladies-in-waiting, and so on.

SOLO EXERCISE 5.3

Daydreaming. This is a simple, fun exercise that can reap ample rewards. It can be done while shopping or walking, or in bed while waiting to fall asleep. (I do not suggest it while driving a car.) You simply run movies in your head, in sensory detail, about your character in various situations that are not written about. This can include your life between scenes and during the time before the play begins. Creating imaginary circumstances in conjunction with fleshing out the given circumstances can create a more three-dimensional character as well as widen your circle of acting choices and possibilities. If you are working on a scene rather than on the entire play, daydreaming the events of other scenes in which your character appears can be quite helpful.

COUPLE EXERCISE 5.4

Exchanging Lines. This one is simple to execute and should be done when the actors are familiar with the scene but are not quite off book (their lines are not yet fully memorized). Actors sit across from one another and go through the scene as if they were playing the role of their scene partner. Each actor should persue the objective of the character that he is reading. Actors should look at their scripts, take as many words from the page as they can, look their partner in the eye, and deliver the words with intent.

Do not expect any predictable results with this exercise. It is invaluable to "walk in your partner's shoes," so to speak. Wearing the skin of another character can reveal insight to your character and situation. Hearing and seeing your character's lines and intents being addressed to you can give you a deeper understanding of the scene.

COUPLE EXERCISE 5.5

Imaginary Circumstances. This is an excellent exercise for building a litany of imaginary circumstances between two scene partners, making for a fuller relationship between the two characters. The exercise only works when the two characters have a mutual past. Actors sit comfortably opposite one another. Actor A begins by saying something that his character did to actor B's character (in their imaginary past). Actor B then says what she did in response to actor A's action. For example, let's say that two actors are portraying Harry Percy, better known as Hotspur, and Lady Percy from

Henry IV, Part 1. They are a young married couple who are very much in love and have a healthy, happy relationship. One exchange of the exercise may go something like this:

ACTOR A (HOTSPUR): On our first meeting, I gave you a yellow rose.
ACTOR B (LADY PERCY): I pressed it within the pages of my bible.

Now actor B initiates an action:

LADY PERCY: I wrote you a love sonnet after our second meeting.
HOTSPUR: I keep it in a locket that I wear around my neck.

And so on:

HOTSPUR: The next day in the park I punched a man that was holding your hand.
LADY PERCY: I screamed at you, helped the man up, told you that he was my cousin, and made you leave, saying that I would never speak to you again.

It is important that each actor invent something that they *did*, not something that they *felt*. Do not be inhibited in speaking any ideas that come to you. You are not forced to incorporate all of the imaginary circumstances that are mentioned in the exercise. If something does not work for you, simply ignore it. This is a wonderful way to help build a full relationship in a short period of time. Try to choose imaginary circumstances that befit the character and relationship that Shakespeare suggests in the play. Imaginary circumstances must help you to more fully realize your objectives and actions in the scene and/or play.

COUPLE EXERCISE 5.6

Neutral Memorization. This exercise should be done in the early stages of rehearsal. Partners must choose a situation or scenario that is far removed from the circumstances of the scene and play. Now, run through your lines as if they befit the scenario. For example, do the scene as if:

1. You are chefs and cohosts of a cooking show on the Food Channel. The words are a recipe for crêpes suzette.
2. You are both calling a horse race.
3. You are candidates in a presidential debate.

The scenarios should be as silly as possible. The point is to repeat the lines until you learn them without developing "line readings," which are preplanned intonations of your lines that do not alter as rehearsal progresses.

COUPLE EXERCISE 5.7

Vocalizing Your Objective. This exercise is designed to keep the actor focused on his or her objective. As partners say their lines, each actor periodically vocalizes a brief phrase that concisely expresses his or her objective in the scene. The phrase needn't continue unaltered. If the objective changes over the course of the scene, the actor should change the words to express the new objective. For example, in Act 2, scene 4, from *Measure for Measure*, Angelo is trying to seduce Isabella and Isabella is trying to convince Angelo to release her condemned brother, Claudio. Here is a short section of that scene:

> ANGELO: Answer to this:
> I, now the voice of the recorded law,
> Pronounce a sentence on your brother's life:
> Might there not be a charity in sin
> To save this brother's life?
> ISABELLA: Please you to do't,
> I'll take it as a peril to my soul,
> It is no sin at all, but charity.
> ANGELO: Pleas'd you to do't at peril of your soul,
> Were equal poise of sin and charity.
> ISABELLA: That I do beg his life, if it be sin,
> Heaven let me bear it! You granting of my suit,
> If that be sin, I'll make it my morn prayer
> To have it added to the faults of mine,
> And nothing of your answer. *(Measure for Measure, 2, 4, 60–73)*

The "Vocalizing Your Objective" exercise, using this section of dialogue, may go something like this:

> ANGELO: Answer to this:
> I, now the voice of the recorded law,
> Pronounce a sentence on your brother's life:
> Might there not be a charity in sin
> To save this brother's life? *Love me!*
> ISABELLA: Please you to do't,
> I'll take it as a peril to my soul,
> It is no sin at all, but charity. *Spare my brother's life!*
> ANGELO: Pleas'd you to do't at peril of your soul,
> Were equal poise of sin and charity. *Make love with me.*
> ISABELLA: That I do beg his life, if it be sin,
> Heaven let me bear it! *Let him live!* You granting of my suit,
> If that be sin, I'll make it my morn prayer
> To have it added to the faults of mine,
> And nothing of your answer. *Release him now!*

This exercise does several things. First of all, it helps to ensure that the actor actually *has* an objective. Second, it is a good barometer as to whether or not the actor has chosen an intent that is simple and playable and that works for her and for the scene. Third, if the actor is not emotionally connected as she utters her improvised words, she knows that she needs a stronger personalization of the given circumstances. Finally, it keeps the actor cognizant of changes of objective as well as where and why such changes may occur.

This exercise works equally well with soliloquies and monologues.

COUPLE EXERCISE 5.8

Actions. Each actor in the scene sets two chairs side by side, about twelve inches apart, facing his or her partner's set of chairs, perhaps two feet away from the partner's chairs. Actors sit opposite one another and run through the scene. Every time either actor has a beat change or action change, he or she must switch chairs. Actors must be sure to finish the beat or action, switch chairs, and then begin the new beat or action. They should not bleed the movement and action together. This is a great way to understand the arc of a scene as well as help ensure that the actor plays different actions when appropriate. Actors can also stand opposite one another and change their position with each action or beat change.

Variation: Actors sit on the floor facing one another, three or four feet apart. With each beat change, the actor moves forward or backward slightly, depending on whether he or she is affecting the partner or being affected by his partner—forward if affecting or winning the beat, and backward if being affected or losing the beat.

CHAPTER 6

INTRODUCTION TO SCANSION

(Liz, Sam, and I meet a few weeks later at the coffee shop.)

JOE: How did your scenes go?
LIZ: Very well. We learned a lot from scene critiques and from working the scenes in class.
SAM: We're now focusing on our workshop production of *Romeo and Juliet*.
JOE: Have you begun rehearsals?
LIZ: Just one. We read through the play and the director talked about her ideas for the production.
SAM: It was a good rehearsal but the director began talking about *verse* and *prose* and *scansion* and *rhetorical figures*. It was a little confusing.
LIZ: She said that we didn't have to know any of that for the production. She told us about it in case we wanted to work on it on our own time.
JOE: The subject matter that your director mentioned is very worthwhile information for acting in Elizabethan drama. So far, we have been discussing many aspects of the craft of acting that would apply to any genre of theatre, not just Elizabethan drama.
SAM: What do you mean by **genre**?
JOE: The OED definition is short and to the point: "kind; sort; style." There are many genres or styles of theatre and each has its own particular demands. French farce,

the epic theatre of Bertolt Brecht, Restoration comedy—even the American musical—are each a theatrical style. Farce demands a facile body and excellent comic timing. The musical demands a fine singing voice and dancing ability. Elizabethan drama, also called Renaissance drama—the genre you're studying now—demands many of these abilities as well. There are numerous songs and dances in Shakespeare as well as slapstick comedy, swordplay, and much more. However, the primary demand of the genre of Elizabethan drama is an ability to deal with elevated language. Although there were many talented playwrights in Elizabethan England, we now recognize Shakespeare as the undisputed master. We have already made a good deal of progress in understanding and using Shakespeare's language, but there is much that we have yet to consider.

ELEMENTS OF WRITTEN AND SPOKEN ENGLISH

JOE: Let's begin by discussing some of the similarities and differences between written and spoken English. Structure and clarity of meaning in both written and spoken English are reliant on a set of conventions. As you may recall, we defined *convention* earlier. It means "a customary practice, rule, or method." The OED definition is more specific: "*Convention*—general agreement or consent, deliberate or implicit, as constituting the origin and foundation of any custom, institution, opinion, etc., or as embodied in any accepted usage, standard of behavior, method of artistic treatment, or the like."

Words are conventional in both written and spoken English. **Syntax,** defined as "the arrangement of words (in their appropriate forms) which shows their connection and relation in a sentence," is also conventional and is the same in both written and spoken English. Conventions of *written* English include punctuation, spelling, and spelling differences (for example, the American spelling of "practice" versus the British "practise"). Pronunciation and pronunciation differences (for example, "toe-MAY-toe" versus "toe-MAH-toe") are conventional in *spoken* English. Written and spoken English also differ in other ways. For instance, written English "strives to be clear and forceful through a range of techniques, extending from simple punctuation on the one hand, all the way up to careful phrasing and crafted structure on the other" (Matthews, *Shakespeare Spoken Here*, p. 13). Spoken English, on the other hand, relies on *sound patterns* for clarity and force. **Sound patterns** comprise "the whole complex of sound qualities—loud and soft, fast and slow, up and down, smooth and rough, strong and weak, pleasant and unpleasant—that inform spoken speech" (Matthews, p. 11). The most important of these sound patterns is stress.

LIZ: What do you mean by **stress?**

JOE: The OED defines it like this: "1. Noun—Relative loudness or force of vocal utterance; a greater degree of vocal force characterizing one syllable as compared with other syllables of the word, or one part of a syllable as compared with the rest; stress-accent. Also, superior loudness of voice as a means of emphasizing one or more of the words of a sentence more than the rest. 2. Verb—To lay the stress or emphasis on, emphasize (a word or phrase in speaking); to place a stress-accent upon (a syllable)." The OED definition mentions loudness as a means of achieving stress. This increase in volume is often accompanied by a change in inflection. The OED defines **inflection** as "a change in the pitch or tone of the voice." Although increases in volume as well as pitch variation are the most common means of producing stress, we can also stress a word or phrase through **pace**—speeding up or slowing down our rate of utterance—or can even frame it with *silence*.

LIZ: Why do we use stress?

JOE: Stress, in terms of the structure of our language in general, is used to differentiate word sounds and word groupings to more clearly convey meaning. The simplest kind of stress is called **accent**. The OED defines *accent* as "a prominence given to one syllable in a word or phrase, over the adjacent syllables." Many dictionaries use the acute accent to indicate primary stress (/). This accent mark is sometimes placed above the syllable receiving the most stress. The word *hello*, which is accented on the second syllable, would appear as *hel-ló*. Conversely, the word *apple*, which is accented on the first syllable, would appear as *áp-ple*.

Word accent allows us to clarify word meaning. It also permits us to differentiate between words that are spelled alike but differ in meaning—for example, the adjective *com-pléx,* meaning "not simple" and the noun *cóm-plex,* as in "an apartment complex."

We also use stress to clarify phrases. For example, there is a difference between *white hoúse,* meaning a house that happens to be white in color, and *White House,* meaning the residence of the U.S. president.

Stress is a relative rather than an absolute term. In other words, a stressed syllable simply has more stress than the unstressed syllables surrounding it. The human voice is capable of almost infinite shadings of stress. But most dictionaries recognize *primary stress,* as marked with an acute accent in the above examples; *secondary stress,* which is sometimes marked with a grave accent (\); and *tertiary stress* or lack of stress, which is unmarked.

In our computer age, it may be helpful to think of the marking for primary stress as a "forward slash" and the marking for secondary stress as a "back slash."[1] Using the forward slash and back slash markings together, our earlier example of "a house that is painted white" could be written *white hoúse,* and the building in Washington, D.C., could be written *Whìte Hoúse*. These markings can be used within a word as well—for example, *ò-ver-búr-den* and *àr-bi-tràr-y.*

Context also affects stress. Webster's dictionary defines **context** as "the parts of a sentence, paragraph, discourse, etc., immediately next to or surrounding a specified word or passage and determining its exact meaning." Let's look at a simple sentence:

John found the house.

If this sentence were to stand alone, it may be marked:

John found the house.

Now let's look at the sentence as if it were an answer to the following questions. First:

>Who found the house?

Here, the stress marks would be:

>／　　＼　　　＼
>John found the house.

Next, consider the response to this question:

>Did John lose the house?

The stress marks are now:

>＼　　／　　　＼
>John found the house.

We might pose the question this way:

>Did John find the apartment?

In this case the stress marks change to:

>＼　　＼　　　／
>John found the house.

Finally, the stress markings will change dramatically as a response to the following:

>John has been looking at hundreds of houses.
>Did he ever find one that he liked?
>
>＼　　＼　／　＼
>John found the house.

In this case, the context of the sentence calls for a word that would normally receive no stress whatever—the word *the*—to receive the primary stress in the sentence. As you can see, in these examples of how context affects stress, comparison and contrast are major factors in determining which syllables are stressed.

SHAKESPEARE'S DRAMATIC POETRY

JOE: So far, our examples of the nature of stress, ways of achieving stress, and levels of stress have been fairly mundane. However, stress is a vital aspect of speech—and speech is at the heart of human communication and interaction. When that interaction is heightened, as it is in a good or great play, language goes beyond simple clarity of meaning. And when a great play is written as poetry, as much of Shakespeare's plays are, that human interaction can reach heights of emotion, power, and beauty rarely found elsewhere.

LIZ: I know that Shakespeare wrote dramatic poetry but I'm unclear of exactly what that means. Specifically, what is *dramatic poetry?*

JOE: The word *dramatic* pertains to "drama." The OED defines **drama** as "a composition in prose or verse, adapted to be acted upon a stage, in which a story is related by means of dialogue and action: a play." **Poetry** is defined simply as "the art or work of the poet." The OED goes on to define the **function of poetry** as "the expression or embodiment of beautiful or elevated thought, imagination, or feeling, in language adapted to stir the imagination and emotions."

SAM: So **dramatic poetry** is language of a higher order that is in dialogue form and is used to tell the story of a play through the words of the characters in that play. Is that right?

JOE: Yes.

LIZ: All of the speeches that we have worked on so far seem to fit that definition.

JOE: Yes. All of the dialogue that we have explored is dramatic poetry.

SAM: Why have you waited so long to tell us that? We've been working on poetry all this time. Wouldn't it have helped to know specifics about this kind of writing while we were working on speeches and scenes?

JOE: Diving into an analysis of dramatic poetry at an earlier juncture would have been a mistake. We actors must keep in mind that all of Shakespeare's dialogue is, first and foremost, theatre. Therefore, we must always take first things first. Play, scene, and speech analyses—as well as finding and playing objectives, clarifying relationships, and personalizing the given circumstances in order to help tell the playwright's story clearly and dynamically—are the actor's primary job. In Shakespeare, the actor must always use poetic dialogue to help serve that purpose. Talking about the nature of dramatic poetry earlier would have complicated matters and distracted us from our principal goal.

SAM: In what way?

JOE: We would have been in danger of falling in love with the poetic language and playing it for its own sake. Bertram Joseph, in his book *Acting Shakespeare,* states, "No solution of the problem of acting Shakespeare today is to be found in giving what is often called a 'beautifully spoken,' but is in fact a comparatively undramatic, performance of a play" (p. 2). "If I were asked to choose between an 'unpoetical' performance which was at least good theatre, and one which was 'poetical' at the expense of the play's dramatic qualities, I would invariably choose good theatre" (p. 3). John Barton, in his book *Playing Shakespeare,* says, "To go for the heightened language is as dangerous as to [go] totally for naturalism" (p. 19). The good news is that we can have both well-spoken poetry and good theatre. After all, "No undramatic performance can really be beautifully spoken, for the sound of living emotion which comes from complete identification with the character in the imagined situation is an element essential to the real beauty of spoken Shakespeare" (Joseph, p. 2).

LIZ: But we *have* been working on some of the special concerns of Shakespeare's writing, haven't we? We've looked up words that we didn't understand or only *thought* we understood, we've discovered multiple definitions of words and phrases, we've discussed metaphors and apostrophes and some of the peculiarities of Shakespeare's sentence structure.

JOE: Yes, that's true. But we have only been skirting the edges of the demands of Shakespeare's writing. For instance, we have yet to talk about the *form* of Shakespeare's dramatic poetry. In addition to its definition of the *function of poetry,* mentioned earlier, the OED also defines poetry with special reference to its form. Thus, the **form of poetry** can be said to be "composition in verse or metrical language: usually also with choice of elevated words and figurative uses, and option of a syntactical order, differing more or less from those of ordinary speech or prose writing." Now we have a definition of both the *function* and the *form* of poetry.

Dramatic poetry is a composition in verse. Shakespeare wrote in two kinds of verse—blank verse and rhyming (or rhymed) verse. Simply put, **blank verse** is poetry that does *not* rhyme, and **rhyming verse** is poetry that *does* rhyme.

Blank Verse

JOE: Nearly seventy percent of Shakespeare's dramatic dialogue is written in blank verse. The Juliet speech that we worked on earlier is in blank verse:

> 'Tis but thy name that is my enemy.
> Thou art thyself, though not a Montague.
> What's Montague? It is nor hand, nor foot,
> Nor arm, nor face, nor any other part
> Belonging to a man. O, be some other name!
> What's in a name? That which we call a rose
> By any other word would smell as sweet.
> So Romeo would, were he not Romeo called,
> Retain that dear perfection which he owes
> Without that title. Romeo, doff thy name,
> And for thy name, which is no part of thee,
> Take all myself.   *(Romeo and Juliet, 2, 2, 38–49)*

As you can see by the underlined words at the end of each line, there is no rhyme pattern.

LIZ: Why did Shakespeare use blank verse?

JOE: The reason that over two-thirds of his dialogue is written in blank verse is that it more closely resembles human speech. After all, people seldom speak in rhyme. Blank verse permits the use of elevated language without the artificiality of a rhyme pattern.

Rhyming Verse

JOE: Almost ten percent of Shakespeare's dramatic dialogue is written in rhyming verse. The most common type of rhyming verse is the **rhyming couplet;** that is, line one rhymes with line two, line three with line four, and so on. The Romeo speech that we worked on earlier is written using rhyming couplets:

> O, she doth teach the torches to burn <u>bright</u>!
> It seems she hangs upon the cheek of <u>night</u>
> As a rich jewel in an Ethiop's <u>ear</u>—
> Beauty too rich for use, for earth too <u>dear</u>.
> So shows a snowy dove trooping with <u>crows</u>
> As yonder lady o'er her fellows <u>shows</u>.
> The measure done, I'll watch her place of <u>stand</u>,
> And, touching hers, make blessed my rude <u>hand</u>.
> Did my heart love till now? Forswear it, <u>sight</u>;
> For I ne'er saw true beauty till this <u>night</u>.
> *(Romeo and Juliet, 1, 5, 44–53)*

As you can see by the underlined words at the end of each line, there is a distinct rhyme pattern.

SAM: Why did Shakespeare use rhyming verse?

JOE: Rhyming is fun and energetic. He used rhyming verse primarily in his early romantic comedies. Plays like *A Midsummer Night's Dream* and *Love's Labor's Lost* revolve around naïve, earnest or calculating young lovers. Rhyming verse is the perfect form for this subject matter. Here is a section of rhyming verse from *A Midsummer Night's Dream*:

> How happy some o'er other some can <u>be</u>!
> Through Athens I am thought as fair as <u>she</u>
> But what of that? Demetrius thinks not <u>so</u>;
> He will not know what all but he do <u>know</u>;
> *(A Midsummer Night's Dream, 1, 1, 226–229)*

And here is a section of rhyming verse from *Love's Labor's Lost*. Like the earlier examples from *Romeo and Juliet* and *A Midsummer Night's Dream*, it utilizes rhyming couplets:

> PRINCESS: We are wise girls to mock our lovers so.
> ROSALINE: They are worse fools to purchase mocking <u>so</u>.
> That same Berowne I'll torture ere I <u>go</u>.
> O that I knew he were but in by th' week!
> How I would make him fawn, and beg, and <u>seek</u>,
> And wait the season, and observe the <u>times</u>,
> And spend his prodigal wits in bootless <u>rhymes</u>,
> And shape his service wholly to my <u>hests</u>,
> And make him proud to make me proud that <u>jests</u>!
> *(Love's Labor's Lost, 5, 2, 58–66)*

Rhyming couplets are also used when the subject of conversation is love. Our Romeo speech is a perfect example of this. Here is another example from *Romeo and Juliet*:

> FRIAR LAWRENCE: Be plain good son, and homely in thy <u>drift,</u>
>   Riddling confession finds but riddling <u>shrift.</u>
> ROMEO: Then plainly know my heart's dear love is <u>set</u>
>   On the fair daughter of rich <u>Capulet.</u>
>   *(Romeo and Juliet, 2, 3, 54–57)*

Occasionally, alternating rhymed couplets (often called **cross rhymes**) are used; that is, line one rhymes with line three, line two with line four, and so on. Here's an example from a soliloquy that we examined earlier from *Romeo and Juliet*:

> From forth the fatal loins of these two <u>foes</u>
> A pair of star-cross'd lovers take their <u>life;</u>
> Whose misadventur'd piteous <u>overthrows</u>
> Doth with their death bury their parents' <u>strife.</u>
>   *(Romeo and Juliet, 1, 1, 5–8)*

The limitations of rhyming verse caused Shakespeare to use it more sparingly and more specifically in his later plays. For example, he often uses isolated rhyming couplets to provide momentum from the end of one scene into the beginning of the next. Frequently the couplet is a wise, profound, or prophetic statement. At the end of Act 1, scene 1, of *Richard III*, Richard says:

> Clarence still breathes, Edward still lives and <u>reigns;</u>
> When they are gone, then must I count my <u>gains.</u>
>   *(Richard III, 1, 1, 160–161)*

Just as television programs leave us at a dramatic point in the story in order to keep our interest during the commercial break, dramatic use of rhyming couplets help to maintain the interest of the audience during scene transitions. Two sets of rhyming couplets are used in *Hamlet*, at the end of Act 3, scene 3. Hamlet comes upon his Uncle Claudius at prayer and contemplates killing him for murdering his father. He decides against it and speaks a rhyming couplet before his exit. Claudius then speaks a rhyming couplet before his exit, which ends the scene:

> HAMLET: My mother <u>stays,</u>
>   This physic but prolongs thy sickly <u>days.</u> *(Exits)*
> CLAUDIUS: My words fly up, my thoughts remain <u>below:</u>
>   Words without thoughts never to heaven <u>go.</u> *(Exits)*
>   *(Hamlet, 3, 3, 95–98)*

Occasionally these types of couplets are found *within* a scene. Again, from *Hamlet*:

> HAMLET: I must be cruel only to be <u>kind.</u>
>   This bad begins and worse remains <u>behind.</u>
>   *(Hamlet, 3, 4, 178–179)*

Scansion

LIZ: Okay. We now know that Shakespeare's dramatic poetry is dialogue that is written in verse. We also know that Shakespeare wrote in two types of verse—blank verse and rhyming verse. Can you tell us more about verse?

JOE: Yes. The OED defines **verse** as "language or literary work written or spoken in meter; poetry, especially with reference to metrical form." **Meter** is defined as "any specific form of poetic rhythm, its kind being determined by the character and number of syllables of which it consists."

LIZ: So one of the features of Shakespeare's dramatic poetry—which is also called verse—is its rhythm, or meter?

JOE: Yes. And a key feature of Shakespeare's meter is a pattern of syllables that follows an order of unstressed and stressed sounds. We also know that its specific meter or rhythm determines the type of verse. Shakespeare's verse, as well as the verse of all other Elizabethan playwrights, is known as **iambic pentameter** (pronounced "eye-AM-bic pen-TA-mi-ter"). An **iamb** (pronounced "EYE-am") is a two-syllable unit that consists of an unstressed syllable followed by a stressed syllable. It's easy to see that many words in the English language are natural iambs—for example, *intense, correct, today, alone,* and *polite.* Let's break down the word *pentameter. Penta* means "five" and *meter,* as we know, means "a specific rhythm." So Shakespeare's verse has the rhythm of five iambs. Each series of five iambs is known as a *line of verse* or a line of iambic pentameter. In his book, *Shakespeare's Metrical Art,* George T. Wright states that "the line is the indispensable unit of verse and the one by which we recognize its nature. . . . The meter of a line is its inner rhythmical structure, which in English we understand as a relationship between stressed and unstressed syllables" (p. ix).

SAM: Does a line of verse consist of five iambic words?

JOE: No. A verse line is determined by *syllables,* not words or phrases. Let's look at a line from the Juliet speech that we worked on earlier:

> Thou art thyself, though not a Montague.

This line is composed of five consecutive iambs. Let's use a vertical line to separate each iamb:

> Thou art | thyself, | though not | a Mon | tague.

Now let's put an acute accent (or forward slash) over each stressed syllable:

>   /   /   /   /   /
> Thou art | thyself | though not | a Mon | tague.

As you can see, the only *word* that is an iamb in this line is the word *thyself.* The first and third iambs each consist of two words, and the fourth and fifth iambs consist parts of words.

LIZ: Is each line of verse a complete sentence?

JOE: No. Let's look at a larger section of the Juliet speech:

Thou art thyself, though not a Montague.
What's Montague? It is nor hand, nor foot,
Nor arm, nor face, nor any other part
Belonging to a man. O, be some other name!
(Romeo and Juliet, 2, 1, 81–84)

You'll notice that the first letter of the first word of each line of verse is capitalized, whether or not it begins a sentence. These four lines of verse consist of four sentences. The first sentence is one complete line of verse. However, the second and fourth sentences are shorter than one line of verse, while the third sentence is much longer than one line of verse. By working on Shakespeare's verse in this way—separating iambs and deciding which syllables receive the primary stress—we are practicing what is known as scansion. **Scansion** is the identification and analysis of stress patterns in poetry. *Scansion* is a noun. The verb is "to scan."

PURPOSES OF IAMBIC PENTAMETER

LIZ: Why did Shakespeare and his contemporaries write in iambic pentameter?

JOE: The rhythm of iambic pentameter closely mirrors the natural rhythm of English speech. Its flowing rhythm helps clarify meaning and imagery and underscore emotion. Audiences become subconsciously aware of the alternating unstressed—stressed rhythm and expect words that carry meaning, imagery, and emotion to fall in stressed positions. Moreover, iambic pentameter can accommodate a good number of rhythmic variations.[2] In addition, the line length of pentameter is asymmetrical, which is more like everyday speech in nature. It tends to resist a balanced singsong rhythm that an even-numbered line length might invite. In Shakespeare's day, elaborate sets and lighting were nonexistent. There was nothing like *Cats* or *Les Miserables* in the sixteenth century. Instead, people went to "listen" to a play as well as to "watch" a play. The flowing rhythm of iambic pentameter makes the dialogue much easier to speak and to understand.

SAM: May I scan one of Romeo's lines?

JOE: Of course.

SAM: The line is, "But soft, what light through yonder window breaks?" I'll divide each iamb with a vertical line and place an accent mark above each stressed syllable:

$$\text{But soft,} \mid \overset{/}{\text{what light}} \mid \overset{/}{\text{through yon}} \mid \overset{/}{\text{der win}} \mid \overset{/}{\text{dow breaks?}}$$

JOE: Good job. Now let's move on. So far we have only been marking stressed syllables. In scansion, we mark unstressed syllables as well. A common symbol for an unstressed syllable looks like a lower case "u" ($\smile$).[3] A complete marking of your Romeo line would then be:

$$\overset{\smile\ \ /}{\text{But soft,}} \mid \overset{\smile\ \ /}{\text{what light}} \mid \overset{\smile\ \ /}{\text{through yon}} \mid \overset{\smile\ \ /}{\text{der win}} \mid \overset{\smile\ \ /}{\text{dow breaks?}}$$

In the jargon of scansion, an iamb is also known as a **foot** or a **measure**. A syllable is also known as a **beat**.

SAM: Scansion is kind of a no-brainer, isn't it? Every line of dialogue written in the verse Shakespeare used is going to have the rhythm of "da-DUM, da-DUM, da-DUM, da-DUM, da-DUM"—right?

JOE: Wrong. If it were that simple, there would be no reason to write at length about scansion. Try scanning the line that follows the one you just scanned. The line is:

> It is the East and Juliet is the sun.

SAM: Okay, here goes:

⏑ / ⏑ / ⏑ / ⏑/ ⏑ / /
It is | the East | and Jul | iet | is the | sun.

That's not right, is it?

COMPRESSION AND EXPANSION

JOE: No, it's not. This is an appropriate time to explain the practice of **compression** and **expansion**. Shakespeare and his contemporaries often elongated or shortened the pronunciation of certain words so that they fit an iambic rhythm.

SAM: How did he do that?

JOE: By removing an unstressed syllable from a word to compress it or by adding a syllable to expand it.

SAM: Do I need to either compress or expand one of the words to make the line scan properly?

JOE: Yes.

SAM: Which one? Compression or expansion?

JOE: You tell me.

SAM: The way that I scanned the line, there are five iambs plus an extra syllable. That means that I need to remove a syllable. So that would be compression, right?

JOE: You're catching on.

SAM: Which word should I compress?

JOE: You tell—

SAM: I know. "You tell me." The only word with more than one syllable is the word *Juliet*. Is that the word that I have to compress?

JOE: Yes.

SAM: The second syllable has the least amount of stress. If I remove it, her name would be pronounced "Jul-yet." Is that right?

JOE: Right as rain. Now scan the line.

SAM: Okay. Let's go again:

⏑ / ⏑ / ⏑ / ⏑ / ⏑ /
It is | the East | and Jul | iet is | the sun.

It scans.

Compression

JOE: Yes, it scans. Here are some examples of words that can be compressed by omitting an unstressed vowel sound:

accompany – a-cump-nee

innocent – in-sent

misery – miz-ree

romeo – rome-yo

virtuous – vir-chwus

The following line from *The Winter's Tale* compresses two words in order to fit the meter, but in my opinion the adjustments are fairly easy to make and the meaning of the words remains clear.

> Where 'tis | predom | inant; and | 'tis power | ful, think it[4]
> *(The Winter's Tale, 1, 2, 202)*

Predominant scans as "pre-dom-nant" and *powerful* as "pow'r-ful." Many two-syllable words with a medial (middle) "v" and/or ending with "l" or "n" are often compressed:

even – ev'n

heaven – heav'n

seven – sev'n

driven – driv'n

taken – ta'en (pronounded "tane")

fallen – fall'n

over – o'er (pronounced "or")

given – giv'n

never – ne'er (pronounced "nare")

devil – dev'l

evil – ev'l

loyal – loy'l

royal – roy'l

ever – e'er (pronounced "air")[5]

For example:

> And the | King's rouse | the <u>heaven</u> | shall bruit | again,
> *(Hamlet, 1, 2, 127)*

> Thou pois | onous slave, | got by | the <u>devil</u> | himself
> *(The Tempest, 1, 2, 319)*

Other two-syllable words that are often compressed include these:

whether – whe'er (pronounced "ware")

either – eith'r

power – pow'r

spirit – spir't

For example:

> That they | will guard | you, <u>whe'er</u> | you will | or no,
> *(Henry VI Part 2, 3, 2, 265)*

Words with "ing" endings are often compressed:

being – be'ng

going – go'ng

remembering – rememb'ring

For example:

> The in | terim, by | <u>remem</u> | <u>b'ring</u> you | 'tis past.
> *(Henry V, 5, Prol., 43)*

You'll notice the words "poisonous" and "interim" in the above examples are also compressed. Shakespeare also used elision (pronounced "i-LIZH-uhn") as a manner of compression. **Elision** involves slurring one word into the next by eliminating a vowel sound. This method often includes the words *in, it, of, the,* and *to*:

do it – do't

in it – in't

it is – 'tis

if it – if't
of it – of't
to it – to't
in faith – i'faith
of time – o'time
lose it – lose't
in the way – i'th'way
of the light – o'th'light

Here are some examples from *Macbeth,* with elisions underlined:

    Mine eyes | are made | the fools | <u>o' th'</u> oth | er senses,   *(2, 1, 44)*

    Let me | endure | your wrath, | <u>if't</u> be | not so.   *(5, 5, 35)*

"The" and "to" are often elided with a word beginning with a vowel:

the attempt – th'attempt
the end – th'end
the issue – th'issue
the orchard – th'orchard
the usurper – th'usurper
to allow – t'allow
to expose – t'expose
to illustrate – t'illustrate
to observe – t'observe
to understand – t'understand

Here are two examples from *Twelfth Night:*

    Like to | <u>th'Egyp</u> | tian thief | at point | of death,   *(5, 1, 118)*

    It is | too hard | a knot | for me | <u>t'untie</u>.   *(2, 2, 41)*

The words *his* and *her* can be compressed to *'s* and *'r*:

> A hal | ter par | don him: | and hell | gnaw's bones
>
> *(Othello, 4, 2, 136)*

The word *us* can also be represented as *'s*:

> Shall take | upon's | what else | remains | to do
>
> *(Macbeth, 5, 6, 5)*

Another form of compression still widely used today is *contraction*. By **contraction,** I mean making two words into one by eliminating certain sounds or letters:

we are – we're

they have – they've

she will – she'll

he is – he's

There are also contractions using archaic forms of *you* (the informal "thou") or *will* ("wilt"):

> Thou hadst (you had) – th'hadst:
>
> > Say if | th'hadst rath | er hear | it from | our mouths
> >
> > *(Macbeth, 5, 1, 26)*
>
> Thou wilt (you will) – thou'lt:
>
> > YOUNG SIWARD: What is | thy name? |
> >
> > MACBETH: Thou'lt be | afraid | to hear it.
> >
> > *(Macbeth, 5, 7, 1)*

Expansion

LIZ: Okay. Now can you give us an example of a line that uses *expansion*?
JOE: Sure. Let's look at a line spoken by Juliet:

> That "banished," that one word "banished"
>
> *(Romeo and Juliet, 3, 2, 113)*

In the sixteenth and early seventeenth centuries, the word ending "ed" could either be pronounced as a separate syllable or absorbed into the preceding syllable, as we do today. For example, we pronounce *beguiled, punished,* and *embroiled* as two-syllable words, whereas Elizabethans had the option of pronouncing them as three-syllable words: "be-guil-ed," "pun-ish-ed," and "em-broil-ed." Similarly *used* can be a one- or two-syllable word, *importuned* can be a three- or four-syllable word, and so on.

LIZ: Can I take a stab at scanning the Juliet line?
JOE: Go right ahead.
LIZ: How's this:

        ˇ   / ˇ/   ˇ   /   ˇ   /   ˇ/
That "ban | ished," | that one | word "ban | ished"

Is that right?

JOE: Excellently done. The following three lines spoken by Hotspur in *Henry IV Part 1,* show examples of both types of "ed" ending:

> Fresh as | a bride | groom and | his chin | new <u>reaped</u>
>
> <u>Showed</u> like | a stub | ble-land | at har | vest-home.
>
> He was | perfum | <u>ed</u> like | a mil | liner.
>
>   *(Henry IV Part 1, 1, 3, 34–36)*

The words *reaped* and *showed* in the first two lines have the "ed" ending absorbed (not voiced), whereas the "ed" ending of *perfumed* in the third line is pronounced in order to make the line scan. Many modern editors indicate when an "ed" ending is to be voiced. For example, *The Riverside Shakespeare* substitutes an apostrophe for the "e" when the "ed" ending is absorbed and spells the word fully when the "ed" is to be pronounced. In the above example, the three words in question would be spelled "reap'd," "show'd," and "perfumed." The G. B. Harrison edition places an accent mark (/) above the "ed" ending if it is to be pronounced. Be on the alert, however. Although most editors are competent, mistakes in notation do occasionally occur. These errors are by no means common but you should use your scanning skills to be sure.

There is another antiquated form of expansion that Shakespeare used. It involves words ending in the sounds "shun" and "shus." We pronounce the word *admission* using three syllables. The Elizabethan could also pronounce it "ad-mi-shee-un," making it a four-syllable word. Similarly, the word *delicious* could be pronounced "de-lish-ee-us." Here are two examples of this kind of expansion, from *Julius Caesar:*

> And say | you do't | by our | <u>permis</u> | <u>sion</u>   (3, 1, 247)
>
> Hath told | you Cae|sar was | <u>ambi</u> | <u>tious</u>   (3, 2, 78)

The word *permission* is pronounced "per-mish-shee-un" in the above example and the word *ambitious* is pronounced "am-bi-shee-us."

Words with similar suffix sounds (all involving a medial "ee" vowel sound) can also be expanded:

conscience – con-chee-unce

marriage – mar-ee-udge

million – mill-ee-un

ocean – o-shee-un

partial – par-shee-ul

patient – pay-shee-unt

Portia – Por-shee-uh

Let's look at a line from *King Henry V*:

> Swill'd with the wild and wasteful ocean. *(3, 1, 14)*

The line would scan:

> Swill'd with | the wild | and waste | ful o | cean.

LEVELS OF STRESS IN IAMBIC PENTAMETER

LIZ: Why are there only two levels of stress? Even dictionaries use three.

JOE: Remember that *stress* is relative. In iambic pentameter, a stressed syllable simply has more stress than the unstressed syllable in the same foot or measure. We stated earlier that the human voice is capable of almost infinite shadings of stress. Rather than recognizing three levels or degrees of stress, let's use five levels of stress for purposes of illustration:

1. No stress
2. Light stress
3. Medium stress
4. Medium-heavy stress
5. Heavy stress

Let's reexamine three lines we have scanned. I will place a number between 1 and 5 above each syllable, according to what degree of stress I think it should have. I will also provide a vertical bar between each iamb for easier identification:

> 2   4   2   5   2   3   1   5   1   5
> A. But soft, | what light | through yon | der win | dow breaks?

```
       1 2    1  5    1  5    1 2    1  5
```
B. It is | the East | and Jul | iet is | the sun

```
    1  2      2 4    1  3    1  5    1 2
```
C. He was | perfum | ed like | a mil | liner

Remember that there is a difference between *stress* and *emphasis*. If a syllable is given enough stress, it will be emphasized.

LIZ: Are you saying that not all iambs are created equal?

JOE: Yes, you could put it that way. In line B above, "and Jul" can be called a *heavy iamb* and "iet is" can be called a *light iamb*.

SAM: How did you know what stress levels to assign to each syllable?

JOE: My "sliding scale of stress" is arbitrary and only for purposes of illustration. Nevertheless, those syllables or words that communicate the strongest meaning, imagery, or emotion will get the strongest stress levels—words like *east, sun, Juliet,* and *light*. Iambs like "it is" from line B, or "he was" from line C, although they are lightly stressed, are important as well—not only because they provide linking words, but also because of their rhythm. The repetition of the flowing unstressed—stressed rhythm is easy on the tongue of the speaker as well as on the ears of the listener, whether the iambs are light, heavy, or in between. Words that often convey meaning, imagery, or emotion include nouns, verbs, adjectives, and occasionally adverbs. Words that rarely convey meaning, emotion, or imagery include articles (*a, an, the*), auxiliary verbs (*have, be, may, can*), possessive pronouns (*my, mine, your, his, hers, its, our*), prepositions (*by, for, from, in, with*), and conjunctions (*and, but, or, if, as*). But keep in mind that this is only a general rule of thumb. In verse particularly, small words often receive strong emphasis. This is true, for example, when the context demands it; remember our "John found the house" examples. Such words *must* be emphasized when involved in a comparison or a contrast. For instance, Liz, what would be your answer to this question: Is *Sam* playing Juliet?

LIZ: No, *I* am playing Juliet.

JOE: You stressed the word *I*. Why did you do that?

LIZ: Because it is compared and contrasted with the word *Sam* in your question.

JOE: Right. Here are some examples from Shakespeare's dramatic verse that use comparison and contrast of small words:

This <u>was</u> | your hus | band. Look | you now | what follows.

Here <u>is</u> | your hus | band, like | a mil | dewed ear

(Hamlet, 3, 4, 63–64)

<u>Your</u> cares | set up | do not | pluck <u>my</u> | cares down

(Richard II, 4, 1, 195)

In Shakespeare's verse, small words often carry strong emotion, and hence must be emphasized. For example, in this line from *Measure for Measure,* Lucio implores Isabella to return to Angelo to convince him to spare her brother's life:

> O, <u>to</u> | him, <u>to</u> | him wench! | He will | relent.
> *(Measure for Measure, 2, 2, 124)*

In the following selection, an outraged Archbishop of Canterbury speaks the following lines from *Henry IV Part 2* as he berates the masses for their fickleness in their choice of kings:

> <u>So, so,</u> | thou com | mon dog, | didst thou | disgorge
> Thy glut | ton bo | som of | the roy | al Richard,
> *(Henry IV Part 2, 1, 3, 96–97)*

The small word *so* here receives strong stress because it carries a good deal of emotion. In this instance, "so" means "in the same way."

PLIANCY OF IAMBIC PENTAMETER

SAM: You said that iambic pentameter mirrors the rhythms of English speech and that the line length of pentameter is more like everyday speech, but it still seems that the unstressed-stressed rhythm pattern can sound "singsongy."

JOE: There are two ways to give verse a singsong quality. One is by giving each foot equal *stress,* and the second is by giving each foot equal *time.* I think we are clear at this point that syllables and measures vary widely in levels of stress. This is also true of time. A syllable (beat) or measure (foot) can take any length of time to utter. For example, let's look at a section of dialogue from *King Lear.* King Lear is eighty years old. Wishing to retire, he unwisely gives away his kingdom to his two eldest but loveless daughters. When they refuse to care for him, castigating him instead, he angrily departs into a hostile night, where a storm is raging. Lear rages against the wind and the rain. Here is the first line of this famous speech:

> Blow winds and crack your cheeks! Rage! Blow!
> *(King Lear, 3, 2, 1)*

The line can be spoken:

> Blooooooow winds and crack your cheeks!
> Raaaaaaaaaaaaaaaaaaaaaaaaaaaaaaaaaaaaaaage!
> Bloooooooooooooooooooooooooooooooooooooooooooow!

I'm being a bit extreme to make a point. The fourth foot of the line—"Rage! Blow!"—may take ten seconds or more to utter, whereas the first three feet together may take half that time to speak. In other words, *a syllable or measure has nothing to do with real time.* Shakespeare takes advantage of this fact by providing the speaker with long-stressed vowel and diphthong sounds when he wants a word elongated and short-stressed vowel sounds when he wants a word to clip along at a more rapid pace. This gives the dialogue variety and dynamics. Shakespeare uses levels of stress in iambic pentameter to vary tempo as well. Light iambs can travel at greater speeds than heavy iambs. In this way, not only can a sound, syllable, or word be speeded up or slowed down, but longer phrases and even entire lines of dialogue can also increase or decrease in rate. Let's look at a longer section of Lear's speech:

> Blow winds and crack your cheeks! Rage! Blow!
> You cataracts and hurricanoes, spout
> Till you have drench'd our steeples, drown'd the cocks!
>
> *(King Lear, 3, 2, 1–3)*

Cataracts and hurricanoes are waterspouts or mighty falls of water. Lear calls for the winds to blow, the thunder to crack, and the rain to fall so strongly that it will drown the steeples of buildings as well as the weathercocks atop them. Let's scan the lines:

```
  (/)             /           (/)    /
 ˘  /   ˘ /    ˘  /    ˘  /   ˘   /
Blow winds | and crack | your cheeks! | Rage! Blow!
 ˘  /  ˘ /    ˘  /   ˘  /   ˘    /
You cat | aracts | and hur | rican | oes, spout
 ˘  /   ˘   /    ˘   /   ˘    /    ˘    /
Till you | have drench'd | our steep | les, drown'd | the cocks!
```

Now let's add levels of stress:

```
  (5)                       (5)
 4  5   1  5   2  5     4    5
Blow winds | and crack | your cheeks! | Rage! Blow!

 1 5   1 2    1  3    1 5    1    5
You cat | aracts | and hur | rican | oes, spout

 1  2   1    5    2   5   1    5    1   5
Till you | have drench'd | our steep | les, drown'd | the cocks!
```

Remember that these stress levels are arbitrary. Even so, it is clear that the second line is composed of slightly lighter iambs than is the first line. In addition, the stressed vowel sounds in the second line are short and clipped. Line three seems to lie somewhere in between the slower rate of line one and the quicker rate of line two. Modulating the length of sounds within words, as well as the stress levels of syllables, helps give iambic pentameter excitement and variety, while not betraying its overall alternating unstressed—stressed rhythm.

Another way that Shakespeare modifies the tempo of his verse is by using both monosyllabic and multisyllabic words. Lines of verse composed primarily of multiple-syllable words can be spoken more quickly than can those composed primarily of single-syllable words, particularly when those single-syllable words contain strong imagery. For example, the word *jail* and the word *penitentiary* are synonymous. Although *penitentiary* is a five-syllable word, it takes roughly the same amount of time to utter as the single-syllable word *jail*. However, *jail* occupies only a single beat in a line of verse, whereas *penitentiary* occupies two and a half feet. It would take ten such single-syllable words to form a line of verse, whereas it would take only two such five-syllable words to form a line of verse. We can see this technique put into practice with the first two lines of our *King Lear* speech:

> Blow winds | and crack | your cheeks! | Rage! Blow!
> You cat | aracts | and hur | rican | oes, spout

As you can see, the first line is composed entirely of single-syllable words that carry strong imagery, whereas the second line contains the three-syllable word *cataracts* as well as the four-syllable word *hurricanoes*. Hence, line two can be vocalized more quickly than line one.

LIZ: Is there anything else about iambic pentameter that prevents a singsong pattern to the dialogue while helping it sound like true human speech?

JOE: Yes. Unlike the meter of music, the meter of iambic pentameter permits *silence within a line*. A pause can set off one word, phrase, or sentence from another, which helps to clarify meaning. Of course this happens after strong punctuation, which separates one sentence from another. But it is also essential after weak punctuation, which separates one word or phrase from another. Even a phrase without punctuation may require a pause to clarify meaning. Take the following phrase, for example:

> The large flower shop.

A pause in two separate places can change the meaning of this phrase. First, consider this phrase (the symbol "^" indicates a pause):

> The large ^ flower shop.

The pause in this case suggests that the flower shop is large. Now consider the following:

> The large flower ^ shop.

The pause in this case suggests that the flowers within the shop are large.

Because a phrase or sentence can be shorter or longer than a line of verse, a pause can occur anywhere within a line of verse as well as at the end of a line of verse. Let's look once more at our section of dialogue from *King Lear*:

>   Blow winds | and crack | your cheeks! | ^ Rage! ^ Blow! ^
>
>   You cat | aracts | and hur | rican | oes, ^ spout
>
>   Till you | have drench'd | our steep | les, ^ drown'd | the cocks!

Pauses should never be overlong or indulgent. Often, a pause is only as long as is necessary for the actor to take in a lung full of air. These pauses separate one image, phrase, or sentence from another. But the iambic rhythm is never violated, merely temporarily interrupted. As we can see by the pauses before the word *spout* in the second line and the word *drowned* in the third line, a silence can even occur between the unstressed and stressed beats of an iamb. The strong stress levels of *spout* and *drowned* allow the two phrases to begin with a powerful, percussive punch. A pause within Shakespeare's dramatic dialogue is often referred to as a **caesura** (pronounced "si-ZHOO-ruh").

Before we close this discussion and move on to the rhythmic variations of iambic pentameter, there are a few more particulars about the verse form that I would like to discuss, as they can affect how a line will scan.

Shared Lines

JOE: Two or more characters sometimes share a line of verse. Most often these **shared lines** indicate that there is little or no pause between speakers. Cues are usually meant to be picked up immediately. This means that the characters are thinking quickly and responding in kind. Here are some examples:

>   BEROWNE: Did not | I dance | with you | in Brab | ant once?
>   KATHERINE: Did not | I dance | with you | in Barb | ant once?
>   BEROWNE: I know | you did. |
>   KATHERINE: How need | less was | it then
>   To ask | the question? |
>   BEROWNE: You must | not be | so quick.
>   *(Love's Labor's Lost, 2, 1, 114–117)*

The romantic verbal banter here is light and rapid. Now, here is an example from *Richard III*:

>   MARGARET: Thou rag | of hon | or! thou | detest | ed—
>   RICHARD: Marga | ret
>   MARGARET: Rich | ard!
>   RICHARD: Ha! |
>   MARGARET: I call | thee not.
>   *(Richard III, 1, 3, 232–233)*

Margaret and Richard are bitter enemies and are extremely competitive. They are always "on their toes" when in each other's company. Margaret was obviously going to end her line of verse with the name "Richard." However, Richard cleverly cuts her off and begins another line of verse by inserting Margaret's name. The shared line is intended to clip along. The following example is from *A Midsummer Night's Dream*:

TITANIA:	Peaseblos | som! Cob | web! Moth! | and Mus | tardseed!	
PEASEBLOSSOM:	Ready. |	
COBWEB:	And I. |	
MOTH:	And I. |	
MUSTARDSEED:	And I. |	
ALL:		Where shall | we go?

(A Midsummer Night's Dream, 3, 1, 162–163)

The excited fairies speak immediately after one another. You will notice that the formatting in cases of line sharing demands that each character's sentence begin to the right of the character speaking before him, until the verse line is complete.

The Prefix "Un"

JOE: Another feature of verse concerns words with the prefix "un." The first syllable of words like *unkind*, *unjust*, and *untimely* is often in a stressed position. Here are three examples:

$$\smile \quad / \quad \smile \quad /$$
To show \| an un \| felt sor \| row is \| an office

(Macbeth, 2, 3, 136)

$$\smile \quad / \quad \smile \quad /$$
I am \| surpris \| ed with \| an un \| couth fear

(Titus Andronicus, 2, 3, 211)

$$\smile \quad / \quad \smile \quad /$$
Than un \| swept stone, \| besmear'd \| with slut \| tish time.

(Sonnet 55, 4)

The following lines spoken by Hotspur in *Henry IV Part 1* show the prefix "un" in both stressed and unstressed positions:

$$\smile \quad / \quad \smile \quad / \quad \smile \quad /$$
He call'd \| them un \| taught knaves, \| unman \| nerly,

$$\smile \quad / \quad \smile \quad /$$
To bring \| a slov \| enly \| unhand \| some corse

(Henry IV Part 1, 1, 3, 43–44)

Accent Shifts

JOE: Another trait of verse concerns the pronunciation of certain words. We are familiar with some words whose accent can be shifted. We say both "into" and "into," "banal" and "ba<u>nal</u>," "<u>there</u>fore" and "the<u>re</u>fore." In Shakespeare's time however, the accent could be shifted for many words that we no longer alter. Here is a partial list:

as<u>pect</u>, bank<u>rupt</u>, <u>chas</u>tisement, de<u>mon</u>strate, envy, for<u>lorn</u>, hu<u>mane</u>, in<u>stinct</u>, <u>Ju</u>ly, la<u>men</u>table, <u>main</u>tain, op<u>por</u>tune, per<u>se</u>vere, <u>quin</u>tessence, re<u>venue</u>, se<u>cure</u>, tur<u>moil</u>, wel<u>come</u>

Scanning a line will usually inform the actor as to which syllables are accented. For example:

$$\text{(/)} \qquad \text{(⌣)} \qquad \text{(⌣)}$$
$$\breve{\text{Sound}}, \acute{\text{trum}} \mid \breve{\text{pets}}, \text{and} \mid \breve{\text{set}} \acute{\text{for}} \mid \breve{\text{ward}}, \underline{\text{com}} \mid \text{batants}.$$

(Richard II, 1, 3, 117)

Today, we would emphasize the second syllable of the word *combatants*, but scanning the line reveals that the first syllable is accented in this case.

LIZ: Wouldn't pronunciations like "wel<u>come</u>" or "tur<u>moil</u>" make the words unintelligible?

JOE: If pronouncing a word differently makes it difficult to understand or draws unnecessary attention to it, then by all means pronounce it in a way that will be familiar to modern ears. However, unusual pronunciations like "as<u>pect</u>" and "re<u>venue</u>," and even "am-bi-ti-on" and "ban-ish-ed," are common in modern Shakespeare productions and present few problems to the actor or the audience.

Stress Not the Negative

JOE: Shakespeare rarely places negatives in a stressed position, particularly when the negative immediately follows a verb. This is because it is the verb that carries meaning and imagery. For example:

This tempest <u>will</u> | <u>not</u> give | me leave | to ponder

(King Lear, 3, 4, 24)

They <u>were</u> | <u>not</u> with | Bassa | nio in | his ship

(The Merchant of Venice, 2, 8, 11)

Thou <u>com'st</u> | <u>not</u> to | be made | a scorn | in Rome

(Titus Andronicus, 1, 1, 265)

And if | I <u>do</u> | <u>not</u> by | thy hand, | thou art

(Cymbeline, 3, 4, 76)

          ˘   /   ˘   /
I am | amaz'd | and <u>know</u> | <u>not</u> what | to say.
(A Midsummer Night's Dream, 3, 2, 344)

However, a negative will occasionally be placed in a stressed position:

        ˘   /
And that | <u>you not</u> | delay | the pres | ent, but,
(Coriolanus, 1, 6, 60)

                                     ˘   /
And I | must know | it, else | he loves | <u>me not.</u>
(Henry IV Part 1, 2, 3, 64)

You will notice that in the above examples, *not* doesn't immediately follow a verb. Further, *not* is often stressed when it is part of a comparison:

If it | be so, | you have wound | a good | ly clew;
        ˘   /
If it | <u>be not,</u> | forswear't; | howe'er, | I charge thee,
(All's Well That Ends Well, 1, 3, 182–183)

KING JOHN: Acknowl | edge then | the king, | and let | me in.
                              ˘   /
HUBERT: That can | <u>we not;</u> | but he | that proves | the King,
(King John, 2, 1, 269–270)

But not always:

The words | of heaven: | on whom | it will, | it will;
             ˘   /   ˘   /
On whom | it will | <u>not, so;</u> | yet still | 'tis just.
(Measure for Measure, 1, 2, 122–123)

WHY STUDY SCANSION?

SAM: Why is it necessary for actors to learn all of the rules and regulations of scansion?

JOE: First of all, for clarity of meaning and imagery. As I stated earlier, the audience becomes subconsciously aware of the rhythm of the verse and expects syllables and words that carry meaning and imagery to fall in stressed positions. If an actor "misscans" his lines—stressing syllables that were not meant to be stressed or, conversely, passing over syllables that were intended to be stressed—the audience will be confused. The audience also expects syllables that have a strong emotional life to fall in stressed positions.

Scansion is similar to the musical score of a film. The music in a movie has an emotional effect on us by reinforcing the dramatic action. When it is done well, we are not consciously aware of its presence or its powerful effect. That's because music is received in a visceral manner rather than cerebrally. But its subconscious effect is very real. Take it away and the audience will feel cheated. Music and language have something in common, and that is *rhythm*. **Rhythm** is defined as follows: "1. The recurrence or repetition of stress, beat, sound, accent, motion, etc., usually occurring in a regular or harmonious pattern or manner. 2. Music; the relative duration and accent of musical sounds." It is not only the melody of music that affects us, but the rhythm as well. For example, what distinguishes a waltz from disco is not melody but rhythm. It is the rhythm of a waltz that gives it grace, the rhythm of swing that gives it excitement, the rhythm of a tango that gives it sensuality.

Shakespeare uses scansion to provide specific rhythms to reinforce and underscore his dramatic action. He was as brilliant with his choice of rhythms as he was with his choice of words. If we, as actors, will take the time to understand this simple system of rhythms, we will be amply rewarded. Conversely, if we ignore his rhythms, we may find ourselves playing hip-hop where Shakespeare intends a march. The result can be a confused and frustrated audience.

Liz: You keep talking about the actor's responsibility to the audience. What about the actor's responsibility to her fellow actors? Does knowledge of scansion help there too?

Joe: Of course you are right. The actor's primary concern is clarity of intent with fellow actors. Knowledge and practice of scansion helps the actor's character to communicate more clearly and dynamically with the other characters onstage. By doing this, the audience benefits as well. And now that we know something about the nature of Shakespeare's verse and of the rhythm and pliancy of iambic pentameter, in our next meeting we will explore the variations on the iamb and the iambic line that Shakespeare utilized to further the dramatic potential of his verse dialogue.

Summary

In this chapter, Joe introduces Liz and Sam to the elements of scansion. They learn how Shakespeare used stress patterns and rhythm to enrich the meaning of his words.

- Nearly seventy percent of Shakespeare's dialogue is written in blank verse. Blank verse is verse that does not rhyme.
- Nearly ten percent of Shakespeare's dialogue is written in rhyming (or rhymed) verse.
- Dramatic verse is dialogue that uses elevated words, figurative language, and an option of syntactical order.
- Syntax is the way words are arranged in a sentence.
- Shakespeare's verse also has a specific rhythm, or meter. The rhythm of his verse is based on iambic pentameter.

- An iamb is a two-syllable entity that consists of an unstressed syllable followed by a stressed syllable—as in the word *surprise*. An iamb is also called a "foot" or a "measure."
- A syllable can also be called a "beat."
- The term *pentameter* means that there are five iambs in a row. Each set of five iambs is called a "line" of verse or a line of iambic pentameter.
- Syllables—not words, phrases, or sentences—determine each iamb and each line of verse.
- A sentence can occupy one line of verse, can be shorter than one line of verse, or can be longer than one line of verse.
- Iambic pentameter came about because it is based on the natural rhythms of English speech.
- The ongoing rhythm of "da-DUM, da-DUM, da-DUM, da-DUM, da-DUM" could get monotonous if it weren't for several things:
  1. Each syllable can vary widely in levels of stress.
  2. A sound, syllable, word, phrase, or sentence can be speeded up or slowed down.
  3. Punctuation can be present, and pauses can occur within a line of verse.
- A pause in verse is known as a "caesura."
- Several factors can influence how a line will scan:
  1. Characters often share a line of verse.
  2. Words that begin with "un"—such as "unfair"—are often stressed on the first syllable.
  3. The accents of certain words can shift, as in re-ven-ue versus re-vén-ue.
  4. Negatives—like *not*—are rarely stressed, especially when they immediately follow a verb.
- It is important for actors to practice scansion because it helps provide clarity of meaning, imagery, and intent as well as underscoring the emotional life of the dialogue. This greatly aids communication between characters and with the audience.

EXERCISES

SOLO EXERCISE 6.1

Choose a short section of verse dialogue from one of Shakespeare's early plays—*Henry VI Parts 1, 2, and 3* or *The Comedy of Errors*, for example. Try to scan ten or twelve lines. Are most of the measures iambs? If you come across a measure that seems to be other than an iamb, what is its rhythmic nature?

Mark the measure with the unstressed and stressed marks that you think fit its rhythmic structure. How many words are there that contain long vowel sounds? How many contain short, clipped vowel sounds? Would you pause anywhere within a line of verse? Mark such pauses with the symbol "^" or some other marking of your choice. How would you rank the levels of stress for each syllable in your selection? Place a number between 1 and 5 above each beat.

GROUP EXERCISE 6.1
Iambic Fairy Tale. At least five or six actors are needed for this exercise. After explaining the iamb and the iambic line, the actors are asked to come to a consensus as to their favorite fairy tale. Actor 1 begins by telling the story with one line of iambic pentameter. Actor 2 picks up where actor 1 left off, and each actor continues the story with one line of verse until the fairy tale is completed. If time is limited, the story can be stopped after each actor has a chance to speak at least one line of iambic pentameter. The exercise may go something like this:

> ACTOR 1: Well, once | upon | a time | there was | a girl,
> ACTOR 2: and she | was told | to bring | some good|ies to
> ACTOR 3: her grand|mom, so | she set | off through | the woods.
> ACTOR 4: She hopped | and skipped | and had | a good | old time,
> ACTOR 5: until | a big | bad wolf | did come | along.
> And so on . . .

The purpose of the exercise is to make crystal clear the nature of the iambic line, as well as to illustrate how difficult it is to write dialogue in verse. Students often struggle to invent simple lines. Respect for Shakespeare's skill often escalates after this exercise.

NOTES

1. These markings are not the only ones used by dictionaries to indicate stress. Dictionaries vary in their markings and usually provide a key to all markings in the dictionary guide.
2. Shakespeare altered the iambic rhythm for specific reasons, especially in his later plays. These variations, as well as their functions, are explored in detail in Chapter 7.
3. A symbol that resembles a lowercase "x" is also acceptable to indicate an unstressed syllable, and a horizontal line (—) is also acceptable to indicate a stressed syllable.
4. This line and some that follow contain rhythmic variations that will be explained in Chapter 7.
5. This word should not be confused with the identically pronounced word *ere,* which means "before."

CHAPTER 7

Exploring Iambic Pentameter

(Sam, Liz, and I continue our discussion at the coffee shop.)

Defining the Variations on Iambic Pentameter

JOE: Iambic pentameter is more pliable and versatile than first appearances may indicate. But the limitations of an unaltering iambic rhythm became quickly apparent to Shakespeare and his fellow playwrights—and so specific variations on the iamb and the iambic line began to appear. These variations made the verse even more like human speech and underscored the dramatic action of the plays more effectively than the iamb and the iambic line alone. In Shakespeare, we see six basic variations on iambic pentameter:

1. The trochee
2. The feminine foot
3. The spondee and the pyrrhic
4. The anapaest

5. Lines that are longer or shorter than five feet
6. Initial truncation and medial truncation

The first four of these variations concern the types of feet (measures), and the remaining two have to do with the configuration of the entire line. We will begin with the first four variations, which are possible substitutions for the iamb. Like the iamb, each of these variations is also referred to as a *foot* or a *measure*. As we examine these variations, keep in mind that vertical bars are used to separate measures.

The Trochee

JOE: The **trochee** (pronounced "TROE-key") is the rhythmic opposite of the iamb. It is a two-syllable foot or measure that consists of *a stressed syllable followed by an unstressed syllable*. Words that have this rhythm include "table," "lettuce," and "paper." Here is a trochee in the first measure of a line of verse:

    / ˘
Murder | most foul, | as in | the best | it is,

(Hamlet, 1, 5, 27)

The Feminine Foot

JOE: The **feminine foot** contains three beats or syllables rather than two. It consists of *an unstressed syllable, followed by a stressed syllable, followed by another unstressed syllable*. Words that have this rhythm include "rehearsal," "involvement," and "seclusion." Here is a feminine foot in the last measure of a line of verse:

                            ˘ / ˘
Or I | should breathe | it so | into | thy body

(Henry VI Part 2, 3, 2, 398)

The Spondee and the Pyrrhic

JOE: Although the *spondee* (pronounced "SPAHN-DEE") and the *pyrrhic* (pronounced "PEER-ic") are separate types of measures, they often appear together. The **spondee** consists of *two strongly stressed syllables*. For example: "right now," "top gun," and "showoff." Here is a spondee in the first measure of a line of verse:

    / /
Fool, fool, | thou whet'st | a knife | to kill | thyself.

(Richard III, 1, 3, 243)

The pyrrhic foot is the rhythmic opposite of the spondee. The **pyrrhic** consists of *two weakly stressed syllables*. For example: "it is," "I am," and "in the." Here is a pyrrhic in the fourth measure of a line of verse:

                               ˘ ˘
Who al | most burst | to belch | it in | the sea.

(Richard III, 1, 4, 41)

I grouped the spondee and the pyrrhic under the same variation because they so often occur side by side. Such a configuration is known as an **ionic** (pronounced "eye-AHN-ic") or an **ionic phrase.** Here is a spondee and a pyrrhic in the second and third measures of a line of verse:

                 /   /   ˘   ˘
And take | deep trai | tors for | thy dear | est friends!
(Richard III, 1, 3, 224)

The Anapaest

JOE: The **anapaest** (pronounced "AN-uh-pest") consists of *two unstressed syllables followed by a stressed syllable.* The first two unstressed syllables are spoken more quickly than the final stressed syllable. For example: "it is gone," "I am mad," and "my intent." Here is an anapaest in the second measure of a line of verse:

                    ˘   ˘   /   (/)   /
You made | in a day, | my lord, | whole towns | to fly
(Henry IV Part 2, 2, 1, 160)

Whereas the foregoing variations pertain to *individual* feet, the final two variations concern the iambic *line.* Before we proceed, however, if you already know something about scansion you may be wondering why I didn't bring up a variant foot called a *dactyl* (pronounced "DACK-tuhl"). The **dactyl** is a *three-syllable measure that consists of a stressed syllable followed by two unstressed syllables.* Some words that have this rhythm are "universe," "argument," and "terminal." (The dactyl is the rhythmic opposite of the anapaest.) The dactyl is sometimes taught as a variant foot in iambic pentameter. However, in my extensive research, I have found no mention of the dactyl as a possible substitute for the iamb. This is a minor concern, as even if one admits the existence of the dactyl, it would affect perhaps only one or two percent of Shakespeare's verse dialogue. One possible explanation for this discrepancy is changes in pronunciation over time. For example, the word *gentleman,* which comprises a dactyl, could be pronounced as a two-syllable word in Elizabethan England. Other three-syllable words may have been similarly shortened. Further, because of the changes in English pronunciation, today we pronounce certain words as dactyls even if that was not originally intended.[1]

Lines Longer and Shorter than Five Feet

JOE: Now we'll introduce the variations on the iambic line itself. A line of verse can vary in length from one stressed syllable to seven feet. Here is a line of verse that is longer than five feet, in this case a six-foot line:

I leave | him to | your hand. | What muf | fled fel | low's that?
(Measure for Measure, 5, 1, 486)

And here is a line of verse that is shorter than five feet, in this case a three-foot line:

/ ᵕ
Hence with | thy stripes, | be gone!
(Antony and Cleopatra, 3, 13, 152)

Initial and Medial Truncation

Joe: **Initial truncation** means that *the first measure of a line of verse consists of only one stressed syllable.* Here is an example:

/
Ay, | what else? | And but | I be | deceiv'd
(The Taming of the Shrew, 4, 4, 2)

Medial truncation means that *the single stressed syllable occurs within a line, after punctuation.* Here is an example:

/
And so | all yours. | O, | these naugh | ty times
(The Merchant of Venice, 3, 2, 18)

Reviewing the Iamb and the Iambic Line

Liz: Before you describe the functions of these variations for us, can you discuss the function of the iamb and the iambic line in more detail?

Joe: Sure. Shakespeare chooses rhythms that fit the imagery and emotion of his dialogue. Because of the flexibility of iambic pentameter—the asymmetrical nature, the ability to accommodate a wide range of stress levels, the ability to move sounds, syllables, and words slowly or quickly, and the ability to pause within a line of verse—it is malleable enough to serve a wide range of imagery and emotion. And it manages to do all of this and still maintain a smooth flow. In fact, that's a good point to keep in mind: IAMBS FLOW. That is why they are the foundation and "norm" of the meter of Shakespeare's verse. Iambs keep things moving. They are self-propelling, like a line of dominoes. They link image to image in a fluid manner. Although he uses the variant feet when appropriate, Shakespeare returns again and again to an iambic pulse in order to establish it as the basis of his verse rhythm. Let's look again at three lines from *King Lear* in order to examine how the rhythms underscore the imagery and emotion of the dialogue:

```
      (5)                          (5)
  4   5   1   5   2   5        4       5
Blow winds | and crack | your cheeks ^ ! | Rage! ^ Blow!
```

```
      1   5   1 2   1   3   1 5   1     5
```
You cat | aracts | and hur | rican | oes ^ spout

```
      1 2   1     5     2 5   1     5     1   5
```
Till you | have drench'd | our steep | les, ^ drown'd | the cocks!

Recall that our stress levels move from 1 (no stress) to 5 (heavy stress), and the symbol "^" indicates a pause. Rate of utterance is not indicated but you'll remember that "Blow" at the top of the first line, as well as "Rage" and "Blow" at the end of the first line each have an elongated vowel sound while the second line moves sharply and quickly.

You'll recollect that old King Lear, abandoned by his eldest daughters, has bolted out into a turbulent storm. The tempest around him reflects the tempest within him as he rages against the storm, commanding that it punish him for foolishly giving away his kingdom. As we discussed earlier, the rhythm of these lines fluctuates from strong and sustained to quick and sharp. These rhythms reflect the tempo of the storm itself; strong, sustained wind and rain interspersed with sudden gusts and cracks of thunder and lightning. The turbulence within Lear is similarly expressed. The actor portraying Lear can express his rage with a strong, sustained tempo in the first line—especially the phrase "Rage! Blow!" which, with its long vowel sounds, is like a primal scream. His rage comes fast and crackling in the second line, like claps of thunder. Lear can further vent his anger by punching the word *spout* at the beginning of the phrase "spout / Till you have drenched our steeples" which occurs at the end of the second line, and by striking the word *drowned*, which begins the phrase "drowned the cocks!" in the middle of the third line. Utilizing not only language but rhythm as well creates a more exciting and enjoyable theatrical experience for the actor and the audience.

LIZ: Are there characters who are more inclined than others to speak using all iambs?

JOE: Because the iamb is the cornerstone of Shakespeare's verse, it is impossible to categorize why, when, and who uses iambic speech. The iamb is plentiful regardless of character, situation, or play. However, Shakespeare matured as a metrist. His early plays have a far more regular iambic rhythm than his later plays. *Henry IV Part 2* is one of Shakespeare's earliest plays, probably penned in 1591. Here is an example of verse dialogue from the play:

Thy lips | that kiss'd | the queen | shall sweep | the ground;

And thou | that smiledst | at good | Duke Hum | phrey's death,

Against | the sense | less winds | shalt grin | in vain,

Who in | contempt | shall hiss | at thee | again:

And wed | ded be | thou to | the hags | of hell,

For dar | ing to | affy | a might | y lord

Unto | the daugh | ter of | a worth | less king,

Having nei | ther sub | ject, wealth, | nor di | adem.

> By dev | ilish pol | icy | art thou | grown great,
>
> And, like | ambi | tious Syl | la, o | vergorg'd
>
> With gob | bets of | thy moth | er's bleed | ing heart.
>
> *(Henry IV Part 2, 4, 1, 75–85)*

As you can see, not only is most of the dialogue in strict iambic pentameter but also almost all phrases and sentences begin with the first syllable of a line of verse and end with the last syllable of a line of verse. The monotony and limitations of having characters only speak in ten-syllable iambic phrases and sentences prompted Shakespeare and his contemporaries to explore variations on the iamb and the iambic line and to break the strict link between phrase, sentence, and verse line. Shakespeare and his peers did use some variations, even in the earliest plays, but sparingly and still with mostly ten-syllable phrases and sentences. Here is an earlier section of dialogue from the same play, *Henry IV Part 2*:

> They say, | in him | they fear | your high | ness' death;
>
> And mere | instinct | of love | and loy | alty,
>
> Free from | a stub | born op | posite | intent,
>
> As be | ing thought | to con | tradict | your liking,
>
> Makes them | thus for | ward in | his ban | ishment.
>
> *(Henry IV Part 2, 3, 2, 249–253)*

The trochees in the first measure of the third and fifth lines and the feminine foot in the last measure of the fourth line make for some variety in rhythm, but the overall phrasing and tempo is still fairly regular.

Now, let's look at a short section of verse dialogue from one of Shakespeare's later plays. These are the first fourteen lines of the famous "To be or not to be" soliloquy from *Hamlet*, a play written in 1601, at the height of Shakespeare's genius:

> To be, | or not | to be: | that is | the question:
>
> Whether | 'tis no | bler in | the mind | to suffer
>
> The slings | and ar | rows of | outra | geous fortune,
>
> Or to | take arms | against | a sea | of troubles,
>
> And by | oppos | ing, end them? | To die: | to sleep—
>
> No more; | and by | a sleep | to say | we end
>
> The heart | -ache and | the thou | sand nat | ural shocks
>
> That flesh | is heir | to; 'tis | a con | summation

> Devout | ly to | be wish'd. | To die, | to sleep—
> To sleep: | perchance | to dream— | ay, there's | the rub;
> For in | that sleep | of death | what dreams | may come
> When we | have shuf | fled off | this mor | tal coil,
> Must give | us pause; | there's the | respect
> That makes | cala | mity | of so | long life: *(Hamlet, 3, 1, 55–68)*

Variations abound in this dialogue, in which Hamlet contemplates suicide. Trochees, feminine feet, spondees and pyrrhics, and even a four-foot line are all used to great effect. Many phrases and sentences start and end *within* lines of verse. Sentences vary in length from one measure to three and a half lines. The rhythms here are clearly more varied and dynamic than the dialogue we just looked at from Shakespeare's earlier play. Shakespeare matured not only as a metrist but also as a writer. The dialogue in *Henry IV Part 2* is declamatory, lacking spontaneity, whereas the dialogue in *Hamlet* is full of discoveries in the moment. Hamlet expresses his thoughts as they occur to him, which makes the dialogue much more exciting to speak and to listen to.

ANALYZING DETAILS IN SHAKESPEARE'S VERSE

JOE: Before we begin to explore each variation in depth, there are four specifics about Elizabethan verse that I must impart to you:

First, a line of verse that ends without punctuation or with weak punctuation (at most a comma) is called a **run-on line** or an *enjambed* (pronounced "in-JAMM'D") line. The noun is **enjambment** (pronounced "in-JAM-muhnt"). A line of verse that ends with strong punctuation is called an **end-stopped line**.[2] Let's look at four lines of verse from *Love's Labor's Lost*:

> Their several counsels they unbosom shall
> To loves mistook, and so be mock'd withal
> Upon the next occasion that we meet,
> With visages display'd, to talk and greet.
> *(Love's Labor's Lost, 5, 2, 141–144)*

The first three lines above are run-on lines but the fourth line is an end-stopped line.

Second, there is often more than one way to scan a line. Let's look at a line that we have already visited:

> Fresh as | a bride | groom and | his chin | new reap'd
> *(Henry IV Part 1, 1, 3, 34)*

In this case, I scanned the third foot—"groom and"—as an iamb. However, this foot can also be a trochee:

> Fresh as | a bride | gróom ănd | his chin | new reap'd

In addition, the fifth foot—"new reap'd"—can be either a heavy iamb or a spondee. Let's look at the first two lines of sonnet 18:

> Shall I | compare | *thee to* | a sum | mer's day?
> Thou art | *more love* | *ly and* | *more tem* | *perate*

The stress levels of the italicized measures are not obvious. "Shall I," "thee to," and "Thou art" can be either iambs or trochees; "more love" and "more tem" can be iambs or spondees; "ly and" and "perate" can be either pyrrhics or light iambs.

Third, there will often be more than one variation in a line. It is not unusual to find three or four of the variations in one line of verse.

Fourth, the rules and regulations that I am about to impart to you hold true more than ninety-five percent of the time. This means that on average, you may encounter four or five lines in every hundred that will not scan. Do not force these rules on such lines. Simply speak this dialogue as if it were prose.

As we explore the variations, I will continue to divide all measures with a vertical bar (|). However, for purposes of illustration and clarity, I will *not* mark iambs with stressed and unstressed symbols. Instead I will mark feet that are variations on iambic pentameter (like the trochee and the feminine foot) with stressed and unstressed symbols.

EXPLORING THE VARIATIONS

> For short passages in the theater, the ear can tolerate a series of regular verse lines. But, just as in every other aspect of theatrical performance the play must shift from one speed to another, break its tempo, change its characters, its mood, its pace, so the language of the play is required to change its nature from time to time—not only from prose to verse but from standard iambic pentameter to lines of more curious character. (Wright, *Shakespeare's Metrical Art*, p. 101)[3]

JOE: Shakespeare uses specific variations on iambic pentameter to make his verse more speechlike. Certain variations also permit rough rhythms to take over from the smooth rhythm of the iamb on occasion, usually at points where the dramatic action is also rough. Some variations allow quick, terse exchanges while others permit legato or lilting imagery. Let's explore each variation, as used by both the playwright and the actor.

Exploring the Trochee

JOE: As I stated earlier, a trochee is the rhythmic opposite of the iamb. The trochee consists of a stressed syllable followed by an unstressed syllable. Words that have this rhythm include "apple," "travel," and "courage." A trochee may be substituted for the iamb in any foot of the line, but it is unusual to find a trochee in the last foot of a line of verse or in the last foot of a sentence or phrase. Trochees are used frequently for beginnings, rarely for endings.

To add **punch**, or vocal force, to a syllable, word, or phrase, keep in mind that TROCHEES PUNCH. Their primary purpose is to begin a line, sentence, or phrase with a strong surge. Trochees often signify a new thought or resurgence within a thought. They rarely end verse lines, sentences, and phrases because *trochees have a falling inflection*. Hence, they are used sparingly. Their strength is in the percussive power of that first stressed syllable. As I mentioned earlier, iambs are "self-propelling," but trochees fall off. A series of iambs will almost always follow a single trochee for that reason, utilizing the strengths of both types of feet. This creates a punch-and-flow rhythm. The trochee "confers variety, grace, or energy on a line, relieving us from the continual tyranny of the same sound" (Wright, *Shakespeare's Metrical Art*, p. 186).

Now let's look at some examples. First, here is a trochee in the first foot of a line of verse:

> This nurse, this teeming womb of royal kings,
> / ˘
> Fear'd by | their breed, | and fam | ous by | their birth,
>
> *(Richard II, 2, 1, 51–52)*

As you can see from the above example, *because of the rhythmic inversion of the trochee, a slight pause is usually required before speaking it*. This small silence adds to the power of the trochee as well as lifting it out of the line. Next, we have a trochee in the first foot of a sentence within a line of verse:

> And I the matter will reword, which madness
>   / ˘
> Would gam | bol from. | Mother, | for love | of grace,
> Lay not that flattering unction to your soul,
>
> *(Hamlet, 3, 4, 143–145)*

Our next example illustrates a trochee in the first foot of a line that is also the first foot of a sentence:

>   (/   /)
> / ˘   ˘ /
> Cowards | die man | y times | before | their deaths,
> The valiant never taste of death but once.
>
> *(Julius Caesar, 2, 2, 32–33)*

You might also find a trochee in the first foot of a phrase:

>   (/)   / ˘
> ˘   /
> Friends, Ro | mans, coun | trymen, | lend me | your ears.
>
> *(Julius Caesar, 3, 2, 73)*

LIZ: How many trochees can there be in one line?
JOE: There is no rule concerning how many trochees can occur in a line of verse. But there will rarely be more than two in one line. Let's see some examples of two trochees in one line of verse:

/ ˘   / ˘
Make with | you by | due turn. | Only | we shall | retain
                                        (King Lear, 1, 1, 135)

/ ˘   / ˘
Come then, | and take | the last | warmth of | my lips.
                                        (Antony and Cleopatra, 5, 2, 291)

/ ˘   / ˘
Go to | their graves | like beds, | fight for | a plot
                                        (Hamlet, 3, 4, 144)

/ ˘   / ˘
Looks in | the clouds, | scorning | the base | degrees
                                        (Julius Caesar, 2, 1, 26)

Even out of context, it is evident in most of these lines that trochees provide rhythmic power to strong imagery. In *Richard III*, Lady Anne uses trochees to help launch her curses to Richard, the murderer of her husband, Edward, and her father-in-law, King Henry VI:

/ ˘   ˘ / ˘
Cursed | the heart | that had | the heart | to do it!
/ ˘
Cursed | the blood | that let | this blood | from hence!
                                        (Richard III, 1, 2, 15–16)

Because of this strength, soldiers in Shakespeare's plays are fond of trochees:

/ ˘
God and | our good | cause fight | upon | our side;
                                        (Richard III, 5, 3, 240)

/ ˘   / ˘
God and | Saint George! | Richmond | and vic | tory!
                                        (Richard III, 5, 3, 270)

/ ˘
Rome, I | have been | thy sol | dier for | ty years
                                        (Titus Andronicus, 1, 1, 193)

/ ˘
Look on | thy coun | try, look | on fer | tile France,
                                        (Henry VI Part 1, 3, 3, 44)

Cassius in *Julius Caesar*, an often flamboyant character, uses trochees in an almost overly dramatic way as he attempts to convince Brutus to join him in ridding Rome of Caesar:

Upon what meat doth this our Caesar feed

That he | is grown | so great? | /Age thou/ | art sham'd!

/Rome, thou/ | hast lost | the breed | of no | ble bloods!

(Julius Caesar, 1, 2, 149–151)

Trochees are used for a variety of imagery, however. The following line from *Romeo and Juliet* uses the trochee to help illustrate the impatience and energy of young love:

/Gallop/ | apace | you fie | ry-foot | ed steeds,

Toward Phoebus' lodging!   *Romeo and Juliet, 3, 2, 1–2)*

Juliet commands the horses that draw the chariot of the sun god to move quickly so that night may come immediately and she can be with Romeo.

But not all trochees are of this intensity. Sometimes the surge of a trochee is a gentle one:

There sleeps Titania sometime of the night,

/Lull'd in/ | these flowers | with dan | ces and | delight.

(A Midsummer Night's Dream, 2, 1, 253–254)

Full often hath she gossip'd by my side,

And sat with me on Neptune's yellow sands,

/Marking/ | th'embark | ed tra | ders on | the flood;

(A Midsummer Night's Dream, 2, 1, 125–127)

The barge she sat in, like a burnish'd throne,

/Burnt on/ | the water. | /The poop/ | was beat | en gold,

/Purple/ | the sails, | and so | perfum | ed that

The winds were love-sick with them;

(Antony and Cleopatra, 2, 2, 191–194)

The above three examples share a lyrical quality, in which trochees provide more of a soft push than a strong punch.

SAM: Does Shakespeare ever place trochees side by side?
JOE: Yes, occasionally he will put two trochees together in the first two measures of a line, sentence, or phrase.
LIZ: Is there a reason that Shakespeare puts two trochees together?

JOE: Yes. As I said earlier, trochees have a falling inflection. Iambs are self-propelling, but trochees fall off. Therefore, when Shakespeare puts two trochees together, he is purposely slowing the rate of utterance of those two feet.

Sometimes Shakespeare does this at the beginning of a line, sentence, or phrase. In the following example, Macbeth has just seen and railed at the ghost of Banquo. His wife reminds him that many people are present and have witnessed his strange behavior. He addresses his guests with this sudden realization and is slow to begin gathering his thoughts in inventing an excuse for his tirade:

> / ˘   / ˘
> Do not | muse at | me, my | most wor | thy friends,
>
> I have a strange infirmity, which is nothing
>
> To those that know me.
> *(Macbeth, 3, 4, 84–86)*

The two trochees are composed of one-syllable words and the word *muse* has a long vowel sound. This further slows the pace of the line. In the next example, the Earl of Gloucester, soon to be Richard III, woos Lady Anne, whose husband and father-in-law he recently murdered in battle. Anne spits in Richard's face for having the audacity to suggest that he would be a better husband than Edward, whom he killed:

> RICHARD: Why dost thou spit at me?
>
> LADY ANNE: Would it were mortal poison for thy sake!
> / ˘
> RICHARD: Never | came poi | son from | so sweet | a place.
> / ˘   / ˘
> LADY ANNE: Never | hung poi | son on | a foul | er toad.
> *(Richard III, 1, 2, 144–147)*

Anne takes the imagery of Richard's line and inverts it, using the verb *hung* instead of *came* and *fouler toad* instead of *sweeter place*. The two trochees at the top of Anne's line allow a strong, slower-paced rhythm to her scorn, giving special emphasis to the word *hung*.

Another example of side-by-side trochees at the beginning of a phrase is found in the next section of dialogue from *Julius Caesar*, in which Brutus tries to reassure his friend Cassius that once Caesar is killed, Mark Antony will be powerless to oppose them. We soon discover that he could not be more wrong. Cassius seems to sense the danger that Mark Antony holds in store for them:

> BRUTUS: And for Mark Antony, think not of him;
>
> For he can do no more than Caesar's arm
>
> When Cae | sar's head | is off. |
> / ˘   / ˘
> CASSIUS: Yet I | fear him,
> *(Julius Caesar, 2, 1, 181–183)*

The deliberate rhythms of successive trochees are appropriate for Cassius's prophetic dread. Once again, single-syllable words that carry strong imagery further slow the pace of the phrase.

In extremely rare instances Shakespeare will give a character a completely trochaic line. The following line from *King Lear,* with its trochaic repetition, reflects the agony of Lear's grief at the murder of his youngest daughter, Cordelia. He dies three lines later:

    LEAR: Thou'lt come no more,
    / ⌣   / ⌣   / ⌣   / ⌣   / ⌣
    <u>Never,</u> | <u>never,</u> | <u>never,</u> | <u>never,</u> | <u>never.</u>

                                                        (King Lear, 5, 3, 308–309)

Trochees have another important function. They occasionally occur in the middle of a line of verse with little or no punctuation (at most a comma). The trochee in this case acts like a "road bump." *It slows the line and, because the speaker must pause slightly before the trochee, special emphasis is given to the word or words constituting the trochee.* Here is an example from the Prologue to *Romeo and Juliet* that we looked at earlier:

    Two households, both alike in dignity,

    In fair Verona where we lay our scene,

                              / ⌣   /   / ⌣ ⌣
    From an | cient grudge | <u>break to</u> | new mu | tiny,

    Where civil blood makes civil hands unclean.

                                              (Romeo and Juliet, Prol., 1–4)

In the above example from *Romeo and Juliet,* the medial trochee in the third foot of the third line gives special attention to the word *break.* This is for thematic reasons. The story that we are about to witness is about things and people broken and divided. The primary definition of "break" in this instance is "to burst."

The following two examples use **alliteration** (words beginning with the same sound or spelling). *Alliteration helps to bind images together.* In the following example from *Henry V,* King Henry emboldens his troops for battle:

    In peace there's nothing so becomes a man

    As modest stillness and humility;

                                        / ⌣
    But when | the blast | of war | <u>blows in</u> | our ears

    Then imitate the action of the tiger;

                                                     (Henry V, 3, 1, 3–6)

The trochee in the fourth foot of the third line above gives renewed punch to the line as well as providing percussive power to the verb *blows,* pointing up the alliterative link with *blast.* The blast that Henry refers to is a trumpet blast summoning troops to battle. He wants to condition his troops to respond as warriors as soon as they hear the blast of war blow in their ears. Alliteration of the initial "b" sounds ties *but, blast* and *blows* together and makes for an exciting image. What if Shakespeare had instead written it this way:

> But when | we hear | the trum | pet call | of war
> Then imitate the action of the tiger:

I think you'll agree that the strict iambic rhythm and the choice of words of my rephrasing are not as emotionally charged as Shakespeare's dialogue.

In our final example, from *Richard II*, Sir Stephen Scroop tells King Richard that the rebel Bullingbrook is conquering England:

> So high above his limits swells the rage
> Of Bul | lingbrook, | covering | your fear | ful land
> With hard | bright steel, | and hearts | harder | than steel
> *(Richard II, 3, 2, 109–111)*

Here, Shakespeare uses two successive lines containing medial trochees, which rhythmically reinforces Bullingbrook's "swelling rage," of which Scroop speaks. As in our earlier example from *Henry V*, alliteration is used effectively in the last line above. Scroop says that not only are Bullingbrook's soldiers using steel weapons but their hearts are also made of steel, as they show no mercy in their conquests. The alliterative "h" sounds tie together *hard, hearts,* and *harder,* making for an emotionally stirring line.

Here are some additional examples of medial trochees:

> All souls | who would | be safe, | fly from | my side
> *(Richard II, 3, 2, 80)*

> For to | strange sores | strangely | they strain | the cure
> *(Much Ado about Nothing, 4, 1, 252)*

> Can cun | ning sin | cover | itself | withal
> *(Much Ado about Nothing, 4, 1, 36)*

> And to | the last | bended | their light | on me. *(Hamlet, 2, 1, 97)*

> Today | might I, | hanging | on Hot | spur's neck,
> *(Henry IV Part 2, 2, 3, 44)*

Shakespeare rarely ends a line of verse with a trochee because the unstressed beat of the trochee can cause the line to fade off. However, on occasion, contrast will cause him to employ a trochee at the end of a line. For example:

BULLINGBROOK: Mistake | not, un | cle, fur | ther than | you should.
YORK: Táke nŏt, | good cous | in, fur | ther than | yóu should.
(Richard II, 3, 3, 15–16)

There are also instances in which Shakespeare takes advantage of the falling inflection of a trochee to end a line. Let's examine a section of the opening soliloquy from *Richard III*:

I, that am curtail'd of this fair proportion,

Cheated of feature by dissembling nature,

Deform'd, unfinish'd, sent before my time

Into this breathing world scarce half made up,

And that so lamely and unfashionable

That dogs | bárk ăt | me as | I hált | bў them—
(Richard III, 1, 1, 18–23)

The last line in this excerpt contains two trochees, one in the second foot and one in the fifth foot. The imagery of this section is about Richard's physical deformities, which include his lameness. This last line, "That dogs bark at me as I halt by them," is itself lame. The rhythms are rough and halting. This is yet another example of how Shakespeare mirrors his dramatic action with rhythm.

SAM: The line is also made entirely of one-syllable words, many of which possess dense imagery.

JOE: Good point. As we now know, this gives the line a slower pace, which fits its "lame" nature.

Shakespeare also uses medial trochees to tie together two words that form a single image. He does this by tying together the stressed beat of the trochee with the stressed beat of the iamb preceding it. For example:

And mock'd | thĕ déad | bónes thăt | lay scat | ter'd by
(Richard III, 1, 4, 33)

He fires | thĕ próud | tóps ŏf | the east | ern pines
(Richard II, 3, 2, 42)

So shines | ă góod | déed ĭn | a naugh | ty world
(The Merchant of Venice, 5, 1, 91)

Okay. I think that a fitting close to this section is a passage from *Henry IV Part 1*. Hotspur gives voice to his hatred of poetry—that is to say, iambic pentameter. He ironically expresses his distaste in verse but chooses well-placed trochees to disturb the metric flow:

       ˘ ˘   /
I had rath | er hear | a bra | zen can | stick turn'd,
˘ ˘   /   /   /
Or a | dry wheel | grate on | the ax | le-tree,
                                / ˘
And that | would set | my teeth | nothing | on edge,
/ ˘
Nothing | so much | as minc | ing po | etry.
                     / ˘
'Tis like | the forc'd | gait of | a shuf | fling nag.

(Henry IV Part 1, 3, 1, 129–133)

The Actor's Use of the Trochee

LIZ: Won't trochees occur naturally as we speak Shakespeare's lines? Why do we have to know where and when they occur?

JOE: Yes, of course many trochees will occur naturally. But actors who are unfamiliar with the rules of scansion will misscan many lines, and some trochees intended by Shakespeare will be spoken with a different rhythm. Even so, most trochees may still occur naturally. But in order for the rhythm of Shakespeare's words to be most effective, they must be consciously utilized. Otherwise the rhythm can become gray, muddy, and sloppy. And when rhythm becomes muddy, so do meaning and clarity of action. We actors must intentionally utilize the trochee specifically and cleanly when acting Shakespeare's dramatic verse. The punch or surge of the trochee must always be married to the emotional life and intent of the dialogue. Because *trochees often signify a new thought or resurgence within a thought*, the actor must make such a shift cognitively and emotionally, and then marry the trochee to that new thought or resurgence within the thought. The actor must allow herself a pause, however brief, before uttering the trochee. Then she must strike it cleanly and strongly, employing its rhythm to help send the imagery and intent of the phrase or sentence dynamically, clearly, and efficiently to the other person onstage or possibly to the audience if speaking a soliloquy.

Exploring the Feminine Foot

JOE: A feminine foot can be substituted for the iamb only in the last foot of a line, sentence, or phrase. It is the only true three-syllable foot. As stated earlier, the feminine foot consists of an unstressed syllable, followed by a stressed syllable, followed by another unstressed syllable. Examples of words that have this rhythm are "ceramics," "removal," and "suspicion." *Whereas trochees are often for beginnings, feminine feet are always for endings.* In fact, this foot is often called a "feminine ending." (A measure that ends with an unstressed beat is considered feminine.) A feminine foot is also called an **amphibrach** (pronounced "AM-fi-BRAK").

    There are two types of feminine feet. Although they are rhythmically identical, they serve two distinctly different purposes. However, there is no terminology to distinguish between them. Therefore for our purposes, I will refer to the first type as a *run-on feminine foot* and the second type as an *epic feminine foot*.

The Run-On Feminine Foot

JOE: A run-on feminine foot occurs at the end of a line or phrase in which the thought, action, or through-line carries over into the following line or phrase. There is usually little or no punctuation at the end of the line in these cases. If the run-on feminine foot falls within the line, it will usually be followed by light punctuation (usually a comma or occasionally a semicolon). Such a line has eleven syllables instead of ten. Keep in mind that RUN-ON FEMININE FEET conTINue. The final unstressed beat gives the line an asymmetrical quality, rhythmically leaving the "ball in the air" as the thought continues to the next line or phrase. Here are some examples of a run-on feminine foot at the end of a line of verse:

By rea | son of | his ab | sence, there | is nothing
That you will feed on. But what is, come see,
(As You Like It, 2, 4, 85–86)

She loves | me sure, | the cun | ning of | her passion
Invites me in this churlish messenger.
(Twelfth Night, 2, 2, 22–23)

My rea | sons are | most strong, | and you | shall know them
When back again this ring shall be deliver'd;
(All's Well That Ends Well, 4, 2, 59–60)

And for | the love | he bear | eth to | your daughter,
And she to him, to stay him not too long,
(The Taming of the Shrew, 4, 4, 29)

And here we see the run-on feminine foot at the end of a phrase:

All but new things disdain; whose judgments are
Mere fa | thers of | their garments; | whose con | stancies
Expire before their fashions. This he wish'd.
(All's Well That Ends Well, 1, 2, 61–63)

That you protect this course and put it on
By your allowance; which if you should, the fault
Would not | scape censure, | nor the | redres | ses sleep,
(King Lear, 1, 4, 208–210)

> After the Danish sword, and thy free awe
> Pays hom | age to us— | thou mayst | not cold | ly set
> Our sovereign process, which imports at full,
>
> *(Hamlet, 4, 4, 61–63)*

As with the trochee, there can be two run-on feminine feet in one line, as shown in the following example:

> You were inspir'd to do those duties which
> You ten | der to her; | that you | in all | obey her,
> Save when command to your dismission tends,
>
> *(Cymbeline, 2, 3, 50–53)*

LIZ: What does it mean if a character uses a lot of run-on feminine feet?

JOE: It can mean a number of things. It depends on the character and the situation. Run-on feminine feet can be more effective than iambs in the last foot of run-on verse lines. *Because it breaks with the iambic convention, the extra unstressed syllable of the feminine foot is more speechlike and creates an expectation of more to come.* This is quite helpful for longer, more intricate sentences and phrases. The reasons that a character speaks using extended imagery are many. For example, Hamlet uses many run-on feminine feet (as well as spondees and ionics) in the following passage, in which he speaks excitedly and emotionally about his mother's second marriage to his father's brother:

> A lit | tle month, | or ere | those shoes | were old
> With which | she fol | low'd my | poor fa | ther's body,
> Like Ni | obe, | all tears— | why, she, | even she—
> O God, | a beast | that wants | discourse | of reason
> Would have | mourn'd long | er—mar | ried with | my uncle,
> My fa | ther's brother, | but no | more like | my father
> Than I | to Her | cules. | Within | a month,
>
> *(Hamlet, 1, 2, 147–153)*

In this case, an abundance of run-on feminine feet indicates Hamlet's anger and shame that his mother was so quick to marry his father's brother, which Hamlet considers incest. In sections of dialogue like this, where there is an abundance of run-on feminine feet (and run-on lines in general), the rhythms may be smooth, rough, or alternate between the two, as in this instance. But in all such cases the verse lines "overflow." The usual ten-syllable line is now eleven syllables long, or as with Hamlet's next-to-last line, which contains two run-on feminine feet, twelve syllables long. In this case, the overflow of the verse mirrors Hamlet's overflow of emotion.

Keep in mind that run-on lines needn't end with a feminine foot. An iamb (or any other type of foot) can also occur in the last foot of a run-on line. You'll recall that a *run-on line* (also known as *enjambment* or an *enjambed line*) is a line of verse that contains no strong punctuation. Two of the run-on lines in the above example from *Hamlet* end in iambs. An abundance of run-on lines that do *not* end in feminine feet can indicate the same traits as an abundance of run-on lines that *do* end in feminine feet. Shakespeare often combines the two.

For example, in the following section from *Othello*, Iago fans the spark of jealousy that he has planted in Othello's mind. He has intimated that Othello's wife, Desdemona, is unduly fond of Michael Cassio, Othello's lieutenant. When Othello asks Iago what he thinks of Cassio, Iago makes weak statements to the effect that Cassio is an honest man. But he does this in a hesitant manner, suggesting that he knows more than he is saying. This arouses Othello's suspicions and he insists that Iago express his thoughts about Cassio fully and honestly. In reality, there is nothing immoral at all in the relationship between Desdemona and Cassio but Iago hates Othello and is determined to deceive him. In the following section of dialogue, Iago continues to feign reluctance in speaking ill of Cassio or of Cassio's relationship with Desdemona. Of course, as Iago plans, this further suggests that Cassio and Desdemona are romantically involved. Shakespeare's use of multiple run-on lines, some ending with run-on feminine feet, helps prove to Othello that Iago is truly hesitant to relay information while at the same time suggesting that what he has to hide is indeed damning to both Cassio and Othello's wife:

OTHELLO: Thou dost conspire against thy friend, Iago,

If thou but think'st him wrong'd, and mak'st his ear

A stran | ger to | thy thoughts. |

IAGO: I do | beseech you,

Though I | perchance | am vi | cious in | my guess

(As I | confess | it is | my na | ture's plague

To spy | into | abuses, | and oft | my jea | lousy
 (/)   /
Shapes faults | that are | not), that | your wis | dom then,

From one | that so | imper | fectly | conjects,

Would take | no notice, | nor build | yourself | a trouble

Out of | his scat | tering and | unsur'd | observance.

It were | not for | your qui | et nor | your good,

Nor for | my man | hood, hon | esty, | and wisdom,

To let | you know | my thoughts.

OTHELLO: (Zounds), | what dŏst | thou mean?
(Othello, 3, 3, 142–154)

In the above dialogue, Othello, his jealous suspicions aroused by Iago, says to Iago in essence, "You are working against me if you think that I have been wronged and will not tell me about it." Iago replies, "I beseech you, though I for my own part am perhaps apt to see everything in the worst light, which is a fault in my nature that carries its own punishment with it, yet let me entreat you that my imperfect conjectures, with the loose and uncertain observations on which they are founded, may not be the means of raising disquiet in the breast of a person like yourself, whose wisdom is so much superior to mine" (Variorum Edition of *Othello*, p. 173). Iago further fans the fire of Othello's jealousy by adding, "It would not be good for your peace of mind nor for your welfare and it would be folly in me and would betray my manly qualities and sense of decency to express my thoughts to you."

Nine of the eleven lines spoken by Iago are run-on lines, five of which end in iambs. Iago uses one six-foot line (we will discuss six-foot lines later) and five run-on feminine feet. The entire section consists of only two sentences, the first of which is eight lines long. Shakespeare uses the run-on line and the run-on feminine foot to great effect in this section. Othello becomes more and more emotional during Iago's incessant talk until he can tolerate the suspense no longer and demands, "(Zounds,) what dost thou mean?"

The Epic Feminine Foot

JOE: An epic feminine foot is one that ends a sentence or occasionally a phrase. "Epic" is the term given to the strong punctuation, called an *epic caesura*, that follows this type of feminine foot. I am also using the name for the foot itself. (We'll discuss caesuras in detail later.) This type of feminine foot therefore is usually followed by strong punctuation (a period, exclamation point, question mark, colon, or occasionally a semicolon). The purpose of the epic feminine foot is the antithesis of the run-on feminine foot. The run-on feminine foot indicates that there is more to come, that the thought is not yet complete. Conversely, the epic feminine foot often indicates a strong break.[4]

Thus, we can say that EPIC FEMININE FEET end STRONGly. Let's take another look at Iago's speech from *Othello*:

IAGO: I do beseech you,

Though I perchance am vicious in my guess

(As I confess it is my nature's plague

To spy into abuses, and oft my jealousy

Shapes faults that are not), that your wisdom then,

From one that so imperfectly conjects,

>   Would take no notice, nor build yourself a trouble
>   Out of | his scat | tering and | unsur'd | observance.
>
>   It were not for your quiet nor your good,
>
>   Nor for my manhood, honesty, and wisdom,
>
>   To let you know my thoughts.

Iago's long first sentence ends with the word *observance*, which is the only epic feminine foot in his speech. Although his second shorter sentence is related to his first, there is a substantial break or shift after the epic feminine foot. The dialogue ending in the epic feminine foot is about Iago stating, "Don't listen to me, I'm probably wrong, I see infidelity even when it isn't there, pay no attention to me because you're so much more noble than I am." The dialogue after the epic feminine foot shifts to Iago saying, "And besides, it would really upset you if I told you what I know and I would feel like I betrayed my friend, Cassio, so please don't make me tell."

Now, in the following excerpt from *Hamlet*, Claudius has just eavesdropped on an encounter between Hamlet and Hamlet's beloved, Ophelia. Hamlet has been acting strangely and Claudius is desperate to know if Hamlet's behavior is truly madness or a ploy to reveal Claudius as the murderer of Hamlet's father. After witnessing Hamlet make veiled threats to him and rejecting Ophelia in a violent manner, Claudius is certain that Hamlet is not mad but instead plotting to trap him. Claudius comes out of hiding after Hamlet exits and says:

>   Love? His affections do not that way tend,
>
>   Nor what he spake, though it lack'd form a little,
>
>   Was not | like madness. | There's some | thing in | his soul
>
>   O'er which his melancholy sits on brood,
>
>   And I do doubt the hatch and the disclose
>
>   Will be some danger;   *(Hamlet, 3, 1, 162–167)*

Claudius says that Hamlet does not love, but is instead focused on hatred, not for Ophelia but for himself. He remarks that what Hamlet has spoken, although disjointed, was not madness. Hamlet made veiled threats to Claudius while talking to Ophelia. Claudius comes to the realization that Hamlet means him harm and must take steps to remove him. Claudius's first words state that he now believes that Hamlet is not mad. There is a shift after the epic feminine foot "like madness." The shift is Claudius's realization that Hamlet may seek revenge on him for his father's death and therefore must be removed.

LIZ: Are all such shifts preceded by an epic feminine foot?

JOE: No, certainly not. Any type of foot can precede such a shift. A helpful way to view the functions of the various types of measures is to think of them as "specialists." The epic feminine foot specializes in places where a substantial break or shift occurs in the dialogue—but it is not the only type of foot to do so. Trochees specialize in beginning lines and images with a strong punch—but again, it is not the only type of foot to do so. The iamb, on the other hand, is a "generalist." It often performs all of the functions of the other types of feet because it is the "norm" of the meter of verse and is therefore far more flexible and plentiful than the trochee, feminine foot, anapaest, spondee, or pyrrhic.

The epic feminine foot sometimes indicates a shift of focus from one character to another. In the following excerpt from *Othello,* Othello begins by addressing Iago. After the epic feminine foot "advantage," he addresses Desdemona:

> I prithee let thy wife attend on her,
>
> And bring | them af | ter in | the best | ad̆vắn̆tage.
>
> Come, Desdemona, I have but an hour *(Othello, 1, 3, 296–298)*

In the following selection from *Henry IV Part 1,* King Henry first addresses Hotspur. After the epic feminine foot "displease you," he addresses Hotspur's father, Northumberland:

> Art thou not asham'd? But, sirrah, henceforth
>
> Let me not hear you speak of Mortimer.
>
> Send me your prisoners with the speediest means,
>
> Or you shall hear in such a kind from me
>
> As will | dĭspléăse yŏu. | My lord | Northum | berland:
>
> We license your departure with your son.
>
> *(Henry IV Part 1, 1, 3, 118–123)*

SAM: Does the epic feminine foot indicate anything else?

JOE: Yes. Phrases and sentences that end in an epic feminine foot often carry strong emotion. That is certainly true of the above dialogue. Here are some more examples:

> To be | or not | to be, | that is | thĕ quéstĭon: *(Hamlet, 3, 1, 55)*

> Help me into some house, Benvolio,
>
> Or I | shall faint. | A plague | a' both | yŏur hóusĕs!
>
> *(Romeo and Juliet, 3, 1, 105–106)*

> The non | pareil | of this. | O ven | gĕánce, véngĕance!
>
> *(Cymbeline, 2, 5, 8)*

> To hell, | ăllégĭance! | vows to | the black | ĕst dévĭl!
>
> *(Hamlet, 4, 5, 132)*

Here I disclaim all my paternal care,

Propinquity and property of blood,

And as a stranger to my heart and me

Hold thee | from this | forever!   (*King Lear, 1, 1, 113–116*)

I should have fatted all the region kites

With this | slave's of | fal—blood | y, baw | dy villain!

Remorse | less, treach | erous, lech | erous, kind | less villain!

O, vengeance!   (*Hamlet, 2, 2, 553–556*)

You'll notice that these emotional passages also contain a number of trochees, spondees, and ionics. The strong emotion is not always anger or rage. An epic feminine foot can underscore passionate love and devotion. Cleopatra speaks the following words to Antony as he is about to leave her for a long journey to Rome:

Your honor calls you hence,

Therefore be deaf to my unpitied folly,

And all | the gods | go with you! | Upon | your sword

Sit laurel victory, and smooth success

Be strew'd before your feet!   (*Antony and Cleopatra, 1, 3, 97–101*)

Other Feminine Foot Examples

JOE: Some feminine feet that are followed by a comma or semicolon, especially those within the line, seem to possess traits of both epic and run-on feminine feet. Here is an example from *King Lear*. Lear has just banished his youngest daughter, Cordelia, for not exaggerating her declaration of love for him as her two older sisters have done. Cordelia defends her actions to her father:

No unchaste action, or dishonor'd step,

That hath depriv'd me of your grace and favor

But even for want of that for which I am richer—

A still-soliciting eye, and such a tongue

That I | am glad | I have not, | though not | to have it

Hath lost me in your liking.   (*King Lear, 1, 1, 228–233*)

The next-to-last line contains two feminine feet. The last foot of the line is a run-on feminine foot, but the third foot of the line has elements of an epic feminine foot even though a comma follows it. Cordelia is understandably upset at being verbally assaulted by her father for refusing to lie and exaggerate her love for him as her sisters Goneril and Regan have done. She defends her honesty. Her declaration of pride that she does not possess the deceitful "tongue" of her sisters is an emotional one.

Here are some additional examples:

Why, she should hang on him

As if increase of appetite had grown

By what | it fĕd ŏn, | and yet | within | a month—

(Hamlet, 1, 2, 143–145)

Yŏu, sírrăh, | that knew | me for | a fool, | ă cówărd,

One all | of lux | ury, | an ass, | a madman,

Wherein have I so deserv'd of you,

That you extol me thus? *(Measure for Measure, 5, 1, 500)*

O, if you raise this house against this house,

It will the woefullest division prove

That ever fell upon this cursed earth.

Prĕvént ĭt, | resist | it, let | it not | be so,

(Richard II, 4, 1, 145–148)

The first unstressed syllable of many epic feminine feet is fairly strong. For example, "You, sirrah" and "O, vengeance." Using our sliding scale of stress, these two epic feminine feet may look like this:

    4 5 1   4 5 3
You, sirrah and O, vengeance!

This is due to the strong emotional life or imagery that the epic feminine foot often contains. Sometimes the final unstressed syllable of the epic feminine foot is fairly strong. This is somewhat true with "O, vengeance!" Here is a better example:

                                      2   5   4
Ó thăt | I had | her here, | to tear | her limb-meal!

(Cymbeline, 2, 4, 147)

The Actor's Use of the Run-On Feminine Foot

JOE: Utilizing the run-on feminine foot should present few problems for the actor. Keeping the sense and intent of the entire phrase, clause, or sentence in mind as it is uttered should permit the final extra syllable to wrap around to the following line of verse effectively. For example, here is a line that we examined earlier, from a soliloquy from *Twelfth Night*:

                                               ᵕ ᵕ   ᵕ   / ᵕ

    She loves | me sure; | the cun | ning of | her passion

    Invites me in this churlish messenger.

                                                                 (*Twelfth Night*, 2, 2, 22–23)

The underlined portion of dialogue consists of a single clause (in this case, an independent clause):

    The cunning of her passion invites me in this churlish messenger.

Viola says here, "The craftiness that is derived from her (Olivia's) passion for me, invites me to visit her again by means of this rude messenger." Having a strong image of the meaning and intent of the clause as it is uttered, as well as paying attention to the scansion of the clause, should allow the rhythms to work for the actor. Because this particular clause is divided into two parts, the actor should take an extremely brief caesura (pause) between the first and second halves of the clause. I will again use the symbol "^" to indicate a pause:

    The cunning of her passion ^ invites me in this churlish messenger.

Many run-on feminine feet separate two related phrases or clauses. For example, later in the same soliloquy, we have:

    / ᵕ   ᵕ   / ᵕ

    How will | this fadge? | My mas | ter loves | her dearly, ^

    And I, poor monster, fond as much on him;

The underlined words above constitute two separate but related clauses. The caesura inserted at the end of the first line is necessary between the feminine foot "her dearly," which ends the first clause, and "And I," which begins the second clause. (The parenthetical phrase "poor monster" should also be framed on both sides with very brief pauses.)

    The actor's inflection should be somewhat lifted on a run-on feminine foot in order to indicate that the thought or through-line is ongoing. A sustained inflection may also be helpful in many cases. (Types of inflection will be discussed in Chapter 11.)

The Actor's Use of the Epic Feminine Foot

JOE: An epic feminine foot is followed by a more substantial caesura than the caesura that may follow a run-on feminine foot. It is essential that the actor connects with the appropriate emotional life of the character or makes the necessary cognitive or emotional shift that the epic feminine foot often indicates. For example, here is a section of Duke Orsino's famous speech that opens the play *Twelfth Night*:

> If mu | sic be | the food | of love, | play on,
> / ˘   ˘ ˘
> Give me | excess | of it; | that sur | feiting,
>   ˘ ˘
> The ap | petite | may sick | en and | so die.
> That strain | again, | it had | a dy | ing fall;
> / ˘   / ˘   ˘ ˘   /   /
> O, it | came o'er | my ear | like the | sweet sound
>   ˘ ˘
> That breathes | upon | a bank | of vi | olets,
> / ˘   ˘ / ˘
> Stealing | and giv | ing odor. | Enough, | no more,
>   (/   ˘)
>   ˘   /
> 'Tis not | so sweet | now as | it was | before.
>
> *(Twelfth Night, 1, 1, 1–8)*

Orsino is in love with the countess Olivia. His love is unrequited and he begins the play in a romantic melancholy. He says in effect, "If music is the nourishment that keeps love alive, give me too much of it, so that by consuming a surplus of it, I will lose my appetite for loving Olivia." Then Orsino commands his musicians to "Play that piece of music again. It had an ending that faded away. Oh, it fell on my ears like the beautiful whisper of the wind on a flowerbed of violets, both taking and giving fragrance." At this point Orsino makes a shift and commands his musicians, "Stop. Don't play anymore. The music has lost the sweetness that it had when I first heard it." The epic feminine foot (underlined) is both an emotional and a cognitive shift. The actor must personalize Orsino's predicament and discover for himself what it is about the music he has ordered that so strongly affects him. This triggers his command to his musicians to stop playing.

These shifts are not always profound. They are often subtle but important nonetheless. In the following exchange from *Richard III*, Richard (here called Gloucester) meets his brother George, the duke of Clarence, being led by armed guards to prison. You'll recall from our earlier analysis of Richard's opening soliloquy that Richard is responsible for Clarence's upcoming imprisonment, by spreading a rumor that someone with the initial "G" will murder their brother, King Edward. In this section, Richard feigns concern for his brother's plight:

> GLOUCESTER: Brother, farewell, I will unto the King,
>
> And whatsoe'er you will employ me in,
>
> Were it to call King Edward's widow sister,
>
> I will perform it to enfranchise you.
>
> Mean time, this deep disgrace in brotherhood
> / ˘   ˘ / ˘
> Touches | me deeper than | you can | imagine.
>
> CLARENCE: I know it pleaseth neither of us well.

GLOUCESTER: Well, your imprisonment shall not be long,

I will deliver you, or else lie for you.

               / ˘   ˘ / ˘

Meantime, | have patience. |

CLARENCE: I must | perforce. | Farewell.

(Richard III, 1, 1, 107–116)

Richard's first epic feminine foot (as well as the trochee that begins the line) underscores the irony of the situation. Not only has Richard no intention of helping Clarence, he promptly hires two hit men to murder him in prison. Richard's second epic feminine foot (and the trochee that precedes it) underscores his supposed "sincerity." Both epic feminine feet are particularly pointed.

     The actor's vocal inflection on speaking an epic feminine foot (that is followed by strong punctuation) is not lifted as it is with the run-on feminine foot. The actor's inflection must be pointed and indicate a completion of some sort. A *resolve inflection* (to be discussed later) is most often required when speaking an epic feminine foot. The epic caesura that follows the epic feminine foot is most often substantial.

SAM: Won't all of these caesuras slow the pace of the play? The audience will get bored if the actors are pausing all the time.

JOE: If the audience is bored, it's because the actors are being indulgent. Pauses should never be indulgent. A caesura can take a tenth of a second. Pauses should be only as long as necessary to clarify meaning or intent, or for your character to make a cognitive or emotional shift. When I say that an epic caesura is most often substantial, I don't necessarily mean that it will be substantial in duration. But, such pauses are often "weighty" because they frequently involve a transition or strong emotion. Such pauses must always be truthful to the character and the situation. *Any pause that exceeds its necessary length is done for a cheap effect or because the actor is more concerned with feeling than with doing.*

Exploring the Spondee and the Pyrrhic

JOE: A spondee or pyrrhic foot can be substituted for the iamb in any foot of the line. As we defined it earlier, recall that a spondee consists of two stressed heavily syllables. For example: "high five," "downtown," "time out." SPONDEES EXPLODE. Their purpose is to supply strong percussive power to the word or words that they contain. Spondees are often two words (or the accented syllables thereof) that form a single image. Here are some examples of spondees:

                /   /

Loud shouts | and sal | uta | tions from | their mouths,

(Henry IV Part 1, 3, 2, 53)

              / ˘   / /

Knavery's | <u>plain face</u> | is nev | er seen | till us'd.

(Othello, 2, 1, 312)

But this effusion of such manly drops,
This show'r, | blown up | by tem | pest of | the soul
(King John, 5, 2, 49–50)

Look, in | this place | ran Cas | sius' dag | ger through;
(Julius Caesar, 3, 2, 174)

And later in the same speech as our last example above, we have:

Kind souls, | what weep | you when | you but | behold
Our Caesar's vesture wounded?
(Julius Caesar, 3, 2, 195–196)

Also recall that a pyrrhic foot consists of two light, unstressed syllables. For example: "in the," "of a," "but he." PYRRHICS MINCE. Their purpose is to supply a quick, light rhythm to small, linking words or the unaccented syllables of words. For example:

Her char | iot is | an emp | ty ha | zel-nut,
(Romeo and Juliet, 1, 4, 59)

The thun | der-like | percus | sion of | the sounds,
(Coriolanus, 1, 4, 59)

Vouchsafe | to read | the pur | pose of | my coming
And sud | denly | resolve | me in | my suit.
(Love's Labor's Lost, 2, 1, 109–110)

Spondees and pyrrhic feet often occur side by side. As mentioned before, this two-measure configuration is called an *ionic* or an *ionic phrase*. Here are some examples of the various forms it can take. First we see ionics with the pyrrhic foot first:

And her | pale fire | she snatch | es from | the sun;
(Timon of Athens, 4, 3, 438)

And the | great Hec | tor's sword | had lack'd | a master
(Troilus and Cressida, 1, 3, 76)

In the two examples above, the ionic phrase falls in the first and second feet. In the examples below, it occurs in the second and third feet:

My fa | ther is | gone wild | into | his grave
(Henry IV Part 2, 5, 2, 123)

                    ˘   ˘   /   /
And melt | in her | own fire. | Proclaim | no shame
(Hamlet, 3, 4, 85)

Here are ionics in the third and fourth feet:

                       ˘   ˘ /   /
Which in | the scuf | fles of | great fights | hath burst
(Antony and Cleopatra, 1, 1, 7)

                     ˘ ˘ /   /
With half | their for | ces the | full pride | of France
(Henry V, 1, 2, 112)

And in the fourth and fifth feet:

                                       ˘   ˘ /   /
Who 'twas | that so | endur'd, | with his | strong arms
(King Lear, 5, 3, 212)

(/)
˘ /   ˘   ˘   /   /
Fret fet | lock deep | in gore, | and with | wild rage
(Henry V, 4, 8, 79)

The foregoing examples had the pyrrhic foot first, but ionics also appear with the spondee first:

    /   /   ˘   ˘
Great ri | vals in | our young | est daugh | ter's love
(King Lear, 1, 1, 46)

/   /   ˘   ˘   ˘   /   ˘
Wake Dun | can with | thy knocking! | I would | thou couldst.
(Macbeth, 2, 2, 71)

In each of the two examples above, the ionic phrase appeared in the first and second feet of the line. Below, we see the ionic in the second and third feet:

               /   /   ˘   ˘
And grow | big-bel | lied with | the wan | ton wind
(A Midsummer Night's Dream, 2, 1, 129)

/ ˘   /   /   ˘   ˘
O thou | fond ma | ny, with | what loud | applause
(Henry IV Part 2, 1, 3, 91)

Shakespeare also uses this variation in the third and fourth feet of a line, as shown in the following examples:

                    /   /   ˘   ˘   ˘ /   ˘
Exceed | ing wise, | fair-spok | en, and | persuading
(Henry VIII, 4, 2, 52)

$$\breve{\text{I am}} \mid \bar{\text{made}} \mid \text{of that} \mid \underline{\text{self met}} \mid \underline{\text{al as}} \mid \text{my sister}$$
(King Lear, 1, 1, 69)

And in the fourth and fifth feet:

$$\text{From an} \mid \text{cient grudge} \mid \text{break to} \mid \underline{\text{new mu}} \mid \underline{\text{tiny}}$$
(Romeo and Juliet, Prol., 3)

$$\text{To have} \mid \text{him kill} \mid \text{a king;} \mid \underline{\text{poor tres}} \mid \underline{\text{passes}}$$
(The Winter's Tale, 3, 2, 189)

Liz: Does Shakespeare ever put ionics in two succesive lines?
Joe: Of course. See these two examples:

$$\text{Is sick} \mid \text{lied o'er} \mid \underline{\text{with the}} \mid \underline{\text{pale cast}} \mid \text{of thought}$$
$$\text{And en} \mid \text{terpris} \mid \underline{\text{es of}} \mid \underline{\text{great pitch}} \mid \text{and moment}$$
(Hamlet, 3, 1, 84–85)

$$\text{Let Rome} \mid \text{in Ti} \mid \text{ber melt,} \mid \underline{\text{and the}} \mid \underline{\text{wide arch}}$$
$$\underline{\text{Of the}} \mid \underline{\text{rang'd em}} \mid \text{pire fall!} \mid \text{Here is} \mid \text{my space,}$$
(Antony and Cleopatra, 1, 1, 33–34)

Shakespeare also puts two ionics in the same line, as shown here:

$$\underline{\text{That her}} \mid \underline{\text{wide walks}} \mid \text{encom} \mid \underline{\text{pass'd but}} \mid \underline{\text{one man}}$$
(Julius Caesar, 1, 2, 155)

Sam: Are there any other variations of the ionic phrase?
Joe: Yes. For instance, we can have two pyrrhics serving one spondee:

$$\underline{\text{And that}} \mid \underline{\text{small mod}} \mid \underline{\text{el of}} \mid \text{the bar} \mid \text{ren earth}$$
(Richard II, 3, 2, 153)

Or there can be two spondees serving one pyrrhic:

$$\text{Disguise} \mid \underline{\text{fair na}} \mid \text{ture with} \mid \underline{\text{hard-fav}} \mid \text{or'd rage}$$
(Henry V, 3, 1, 8)

Finally, here is a line of all ionics:

$$\underline{\text{To my}} \mid \underline{\text{heart's hope!}} \mid \underline{\text{Gold, sil}} \mid \underline{\text{ver and}} \mid \underline{\text{base lead}}$$
(Merchant of Venice, 2, 9, 20)

I should point out that not everyone is in agreement about these two types of feet. Some feel that there is no such thing as a pyrrhic or a spondee because achieving equal stress is impossible. I think that this is too rigid an opinion. Fairly equal stress can be achieved and that's enough to be clearly discerned by the human ear.

I would say that any very light iamb is a candidate for a pyrrhic foot, and any heavy iamb with an unusually strong first syllable is a candidate for a spondee. Remember that the actor can always choose between a light iamb and a pyrrhic foot and between the type of heavy iamb mentioned above and a spondee. When acting Shakespeare, I tend to mark even light iambs as pyrrhic feet. Although such measures have a "pulse," marking them as pyrrhics reminds me that these feet must be spoken quickly and lightly. However, this is a personal choice. Always keep in mind that scansion is a tool for the actor. Whatever scansion markings help you to make a clearer, more dynamic connection to the text is right for you.[5]

I take a more conservative view when it comes to ionic phrases. Ionics dramatically interrupt the iambic flow of verse dialogue. Therefore, I believe that the pyrrhic feet in such cases should be equally light and the spondees should be equally heavy.

The spondee is a strong two-syllable image that is often paired with a pyrrhic foot for rhythmic balance. I liken the pyrrhic/spondee ionic to the high jump. The pyrrhic is the couple of catch steps the jumper takes to get ready for the vertical leap. The leap is the spondee. Stress levels may look like this:

                          1   1   5   5
The plough|man lost | his sweat, | and the | green corn
Hath rotted ere his youth attain'd a beard.
                  (*A Midsummer Night's Dream*, 2, 1, 94–95)

The spondee/pyrrhic ionic, on the other hand, is like the long jump. The spondee is the dramatic forward leap and the pyrrhic is the couple of steps the athlete needs to regain balance. Stress levels may look like this:

Now entertain conjecture of a time

When creeping murmur and the poring dark

/ ⌣   5   5   1   1
Fills the | wide ves | sel of | the un | iverse.   (*Henry V*, 4, Prol., 1–3)

Because of their theatrical potential, spondees and ionic phrases can be quite useful in rousing troops to battle. King Henry V uses them quite effectively in the famous "Once more unto the breach" speech (Act 3, scene 1, lines 1–34):

                                    (/)
       /   /   ⌣ ⌣   /   /   /
Once more | unto | the breach, | dear friends, | once more;   (1)

Disguise | fair na | ture with | hard fav | or'd rage;   (8)

Let it | pry through | the por | tage of | the head   (10)

Like the | brass can | non; let | the brow | oerwhelm it   (11)

Hold hard | the breath, | and bend | up ev | ery spirit   (16)

To his | full height. | On, on, | you nob | lest English, (17)

Whose blood | is let | from fa | thers of | war-proof!   (18)

Cry, "God | for Har | ry, Eng | land and | Saint George!   (34)

The Actor's Use of the Spondee and the Pyrrhic

The imagery contained in a spondee is vivid and must be allowed its full weight. The actor should never rush a spondee. Pyrrhics, on the other hand, are extremely light and quick. They link image to image as well as provide rhythmic balance to the spondee in an ionic phrase. The actor must touch on the pyrrhic foot lightly and swiftly, while striking the spondee strongly and deliberately. Articulation is essential when uttering the syllables or words in a pyrrhic foot. Because they lack imagery and can be uttered rapidly, it is easy for the actor to become sloppy in his articulation of pyrrhic feet. Similarly, the two strong syllables of the spondee must not be slurred together. I certainly don't mean that the actor should overarticulate or become pedantic—but clarity should never be sacrificed when speaking Shakespeare's dialogue. Again, as with all types of measures, *it is imperative that the actor marry imagery and intent to the percussive rhythms of the verse.* Like many epic feminine feet, the spondee often entails a strong emotional life. Making a vital connection to the emotional life of the character is essential because the spondee is often theatrical in nature and can seem technical and bombastic if not connected to imagery and motivation. Conversely, many actors who are not emotionally connected to their characters or the characters' situations become self-conscious and shy away from fully utilizing spondees. Even spondees that are not rooted in strong emotion are often pointed and must be given their due.

SAM: I'm confused about your numbering system. I'm worried that I might speak a "5–5" spondee as a "4–4" spondee or something like that. And to tell you the truth, I don't know if I could hear the difference.

JOE: My numbering system is arbitrary—and as I said earlier, is only for purposes of illustration. The human voice, as we now know, is capable of almost infinite shadings of stress. When we are onstage, our vocal shadings will not be conscious but will instead be inextricably tied to character, relationship, situation, emotion, and intent. The work that we actors do with scansion is homework. What we have been examining here—as well as much of what we'll take up later—is technical information that is essential in helping us bring Shakespeare's stories to life onstage. However, it is work that is *preparation for acting*. This is work that must be explored in rehearsals and during preparation outside of rehearsal. It must be consciously forgotten once we set foot onstage. *Homework must be left at home.* If we have prepared thoroughly, scansion will serve us in our acting without conscious effort on our part. We certainly can't be thinking about iambs and trochees while acting onstage. Our consciousness must be focused solely on our characters' wants as we listen and respond to those onstage with us.

Exploring the Anapaest

JOE: An anapaest can be substituted for the iamb in any foot of the line. Recall that an anapaest consists of two unstressed syllables followed by a stressed syllable. It is not truly a three-beat foot because the first two unstressed syllables are spoken in the time of one. For example: "in a rush," "to be sure," "on a roll." ANAPAESTS SKIP. They have a light, quick rhythm. Many anapaests involve words that can be compressed, including contraction and elision. Contraction, you may remember makes two words into one by eliminating certain sounds or letters. For example:

    I am made | of that | self met | al as | my sister
    (I'm made)   *(King Lear, 1, 1, 69)*

    And in | their ship | I am sure | Loren | zo is not.
                     (I'm sure)   *(The Merchant of Venice, 2, 7, 3)*

    I have done | the deed. | Dids't thou | not hear | a noise?
    (I've done)   *(Macbeth, 2, 2, 14)*

    She is young | and of | a no | ble mod | est nature
    (She's young)   *(Henry VIII, 5, 1, 135)*

Other anapaests involve words that are elided. Recall that *elision* involves slurring one word into the next by eliminating a vowel sound. For example:

    When he | the ambi | tious Nor | way com | bated
           (th'ambitious)   *(Hamlet, 1, 1, 61)*

    Awakes | me all | the enrol | led pen | alties
           (th'enrolled)   *(Measure for Measure, 1, 2, 166)*

    Would I | propose | to achieve | her whom | I love.
           (t'achieve)   *(Titus Andronicus, 2, 1, 80)*

        ˇ ˇ / ˇ ˇ   ˇ / ˇ
In the bot | tom of | a cow | slip. Here's | a voucher

(I'th' bottom)   (*Cymbeline*, 2, 3, 39)

    We can form other anapaests by joining two small words, or the unaccented syllables of words, with a strong single-syllable word, or the accented syllable of a word. For example:

                             (/)
            ˇ ˇ /   ˇ ˇ /
You made | in a day, | my lord, | whole towns | to fly
                                      (*Henry VI Part 2*, 2, 1, 160)

       ˇ ˇ /   ˇ / ˇ
And ma | ny an er | ror by | the same | example
                                (*The Merchant of Venice*, 4, 1, 221)

                ˇ ˇ /
Of rich | and ex | quisite form, | their val | ues great
                                   (*Cymbeline*, 1, 6, 190)

                          ˇ ˇ /
A poor | physi | cian's daugh | ter my wife! | Disdain
                                (*All's Well That Ends Well*, 2, 3, 115)

    Anapaests may be viewed as iambs that have fallen behind the pack and have to quickly "skip" forward in order to catch up. The result is a tendency toward rapid speech:

               ˇ ˇ   ˇ ˇ   ˇ /
Could make | him the | recei | ver of, | which he took,
           / ˇ   ˇ ˇ
As we | do air, | fast as | 'twas min | ist'red,
ˇ ˇ /
And in 's spring | became | a har | vest; liv'd | in court
                                      (*Cymbeline*, 1, 1, 44–46)

                                 (ˇ)
        ˇ ˇ /   ˇ ˇ   ˇ ˇ /
And for | I am rich | er than | to hang | by th' walls,
                         ˇ ˇ
I must | be ripp'd. | To pie | ces with | me! O!
                                    (*Cymbeline*, 3, 4, 52–53)

    You will notice that the measure "by th' walls" in the above example is not a true anapaest, but rather an iamb that utilizes elision. However, such iambs most often have the distinct skipping rhythm of the anapaest. Shakespeare often combines true anapaests with these "anapaestic" iambs. He also uses pyrrhic feet and light iambs in such sections of dialogue because, like anapaests, they help to create a quick pace. The anapaest's light, skipping rhythm can be fun and upbeat. The character of Time, who acts as the Chorus in *The Winter's Tale*, uses several anapaests, anapaestic iambs, and pyrrhics in his speech that opens Act 4 of the play:

(˘)
˘ ˘   /   ˘ ˘
To th' fresh | est things | now reign | ing, and | make stale
                                          (The Winter's Tale, 4, 1, 13)

(˘)
˘ ˘   /   ˘ ˘   /   /   ˘ ˘   ˘   /   ˘
Th' effects | of his | fond jeal | ousies | so grieving
                                       (The Winter's Tale, 4, 1, 18)

The first half of the play takes place in Sicilia. It is a country of turmoil, jealousy, and grief. The character of Time appears in the second half of the play to inform the audience that sixteen years have gone by and that the location has shifted to the country of Bohemia. Bohemia is the inverse of Sicilia. It is a pastoral, life-affirming land. It is spring, and a sheep-shearing festival is at hand. We are about to be introduced to two young lovers—Florizel and Perdita. Here is a longer passage from the same speech:

                              Imagine me,

                 (/ ˘)
/ ˘   ˘ /
Gentle | specta | tors, that | I now | may be

In fair | Bohem | ia, and | remem | ber well,

                 (˘)
      ˘ ˘ /   ˘ ˘ /   ˘ ˘
I men | tioned a son | o' th' King's, | which Flor | izel
            / ˘
I now | name to | you; and | with speed | so pace

                      ˘ ˘
To speak | of Per | dita, | now grown | in grace

Equal with wond'ring.   *(The Winter's Tale, 4, 1, 19–25)*

You can see from this passage that the speech is written in rhyming verse. This flowing rhymed verse and the imagery it contains—peppered with anapaests, pyrrhics, and light iambs—is an indication to the audience that the second half of the play is going to be about light, not darkness; about love, repentance, redemption, and rebirth.

    Anapaests are used effectively in the following romantic battle of wits between Petruchio and Kate in *The Taming of the Shrew*:

PETRUCHIO: Who knows not where a wasp does wear his sting?

˘ ˘   /
In his tail. |

                 ˘ ˘   /
KATHERINE: In his tongue. |

PETRUCHIO: Whose tongue?

KATHERINE: Yours, if you talk of tales, and so farewell.   (/)
                 /   ˘   ˘ ˘   /   /
PETRUCHIO: What, with | my tongue | in your tail? | Nay, come | again

Good Kate; I am a gentleman.
                                   (The Taming of the Shrew, 2, 1, 214–219)

Although they exchange insults, this is a love scene. Anapaests, with their skipping rhythm as well as line sharing, help with the quick-tongued quips that the lovers exchange.

The rhythm of the anapaest is also appropriate for scenes that are more serious in nature. In *Antony and Cleopatra*, Enobarbus, Antony's second in command, is angry and frustrated at Antony's stupidity in challenging Caesar to single combat:

> / /   / /
> Yes, like | enough! | High-bat | tled Cae | sar will
> ᵕ ᵕ   ᵕ ᵕ   /   (ᵕ) /
> Unstate | his hap | piness, | and be stag'd | to th' show
>   ᵕ / ᵕ
> Against | a sworder!
>
> *(Antony and Cleopatra, 3, 13, 29–31)*

Enobarbus sarcastically says in essence, "Oh, I'm sure he'll accept! Caesar, who commands the greatest armies in the world, will give up his winning position and come onstage to make an exhibition of himself against a professional swordsman!" Enobarbus is angry over Antony's behavior. The rough, strong rhythms of the first line reflect this. He is also impatient with Antony. The second line uses anapaests, a pyrrhic, and multiple-syllable words to ensure a quick iambic rhythm that underscores this impatience. The rapid, smooth rhythms come to an abrupt halt with the epic feminine foot and epic caesura that end the section.

In *Cymbeline*, Imogen gives a tongue lashing to the oafish Cloten, who tries to woo her for his wife:

> and learn now, for all,
> That I, | which know | my heart, | do here | pronounce
> (ᵕ) /
> ᵕᵕ /   ᵕᵕ   ᵕ / ᵕ
> By th' ve | ry truth | of it, | I care | not for you,
> ᵕᵕ
> And am | so near | the lack | of char | tity
> (ᵕ) /
> ᵕᵕ /   ᵕ / ᵕ   ᵕ / ᵕ
> To accuse | myself | I hate you; | which I | had rather
> You felt | than make't | my boast.   *(Cymbeline, 2, 3, 106–111)*

Once again, Shakespeare helps create a fast pace for Imogen's impatience with Cloten not only by using anapaests and a smooth iambic flow, but also by the use of several pyrrhic feet, which we now know are extremely light and swift moving. We also have an emotional epic feminine foot with "I hate you."

In the following dialogue, Iago has just implied that Desdemona has been deceiving her husband, Othello:

> IAGO: I see this hath a little dash'd your spirits.
>   ᵕ ᵕ /   ᵕ ᵕ /
> OTHELLO: Not a jot, | not a jot. |
>
> IAGO: I'faith, | I fear | it has.
>   *(Othello, 3, 3, 214–215)*

The words and rhythms of Othello's response belie his true feelings. He is very distraught at Iago's implications about Desdemona's alleged infidelity. The rhythm of two successive anapaests aids Othello in appearing nonchalant before Iago. But Iago sees through this façade, confident that his evil plan is working.

The Actor's Use of the Anapaest

JOE: The actor must *not* treat the three syllables of the anapaest in the same manner as the three syllables of a feminine foot. The first two unstressed beats of the anapaest are a unit that forms what would otherwise be the first unstressed beat of an iamb and hence must be spoken quickly. Conversely, the third stressed beat of the anapaest usually requires moderate to strong stress and should not be rushed.

Anapaests always move in the direction of an iambic flow. The first two unstressed syllables can often be slurred together, as long as doing so does not render the syllables incomprehensible. As with the pyrrhic foot, *articulation is important* when speaking the two unstressed beats of an anapaest. If a passage is seasoned with anapaests, there may also be a strongly regular, iambic flow, pyrrhics or light iambs, multiple syllable words, and compressed words ("Bo-heme-ya" rather than "Bo-he-me-uh," for example). Anapaests, especially when they are combined with these other elements, suggest that the character is "leaning into" the words with a certain fleetness. The reasons for this rapidity depend on the given circumstances of the character.

Exploring Lines Longer and Shorter than Five Feet

JOE: Lines of verse can vary in length from one stressed syllable to seven feet. Let's look at some examples.

Seven-Foot Lines

JOE: Seven-foot lines (iambic heptameter) are extremely rare in Shakespeare. There are only a handful in all of the plays. Here are a few of them:

A cher | ry lip, | a bon | ny eye, | a pas | sing pleas | ing tongue
(Richard III, 1, 1, 94)

Grace and | good dis | posi | tion | attend | your la | dyship
(Twelfth Night, 3, 1, 135)

In base | appli | ances. | This out | ward-saint | ed dep | uty
(Measure for Measure, 3, 1, 88)

Six-Foot Lines

JOE: The most common substitution for the five-foot line is the six-foot line (iambic hexameter), often called an **alexandrine** (pronounced "al-ix-ANN-drine"). For example:

> Whom I, | with this, | obe | dient steel, | three in | ches of it,
> *(The Tempest, 2, 1, 283)*

Shakespeare often chose alexandrines for the sake of convenience. In other words, if the dialogue he chose required six measures in a line, he took advantage of that accepted variation, similar to voicing or absorbing "ed" endings as needed:

> Sweeten | the bit | ter mock | you sent | his ma | jesty,
> *(Henry V, 2, 4, 122)*

> By fear | ing to | attempt. | Go to | lord An | gelo
> *(Measure for Measure, 1, 4, 79)*

> The cur | io | sity | of na | tions to | deprive me
> *(King Lear, 1, 2, 4)*

Alexandrines provide a symmetrical change from the asymmetrical pentameter line. Shakespeare sometimes takes advantage of this symmetry by splitting the six-foot line into two equal, related phrases:

> To have | what we | would have, | we speak | not what | we mean.
> *(Measure for Measure, 2, 4, 118)*

> Am I | not witch'd | like her? | Or thou | not false | like him?
> *(Henry VI Part 2, 3, 2, 119)*

> A thou | sand times | more fair, | ten thou | sand times | more rich,
> *(The Merchant of Venice, 3, 2, 155)*

or even *three* equal, related phrases:

> He hear | eth not, | he stir | reth not, | he mov | eth not,
> *(Romeo and Juliet, 2, 1, 15)*

Shakespeare will have two characters share a six-foot line on occasion. There seems to be a close connection between the characters in these cases. For example:

IAGO: I humbly do beseech you of your pardon

For too | much lov | ing you. |
˘ ˘   /   ˘ /˘
OTHELLO: I am bound | to thee | for ever.
(Othello, 3, 3, 212–213)

Sometimes these exchanges are printed as a series of three-foot lines. But they can also be viewed as shared alexandrines:

˘ / ˘
LEAR: So young | and so | untender?

CORDELIA: So young | my lord, | and true.
(King Lear, 1, 1, 106–107)

ANNE: I would | I knew | thy heart.

     ˘ ˘
RICHARD: 'Tis fig | ur'd in | my | tongue.

ANNE: I fear | me both | are false.

         ˘ ˘   /   /
RICHARD: Then nev | er was | man true.

     /   /
ANNE: Well, well, | put up | your sword.

       / ˘
RICHARD: Say then | my peace | is made.
        (˘   /)
       / ˘   ˘ /˘
ANNE: That shalt | thou know | hereafter.

RICHARD: But shall | I live | in hope?
        (/   ˘)
        /   /
ANNE: All men | I hope | live so.

RICHARD: Vouchsafe | to wear | this ring.

ANNE: To take | is not | to give.
(Richard III, 1, 2, 192–202)

BEROWNE: What time 'a day?

KATHERINE: The hour | that fools | should ask.

BEROWNE: Now fair | befall | your mask!
          (/   /)
           /   ˘ / ˘
KATHERINE: Fair fall | the face | it covers!

                      ˘ / ˘
BEROWNE: And send | you ma | ny lovers!

KATHERINE: Amen, | so you | be none.

         /   /
BEROWNE: Nay then | will I | be gone.
(Love's Labor's Lost, 2, 1, 121–127)

This is what George T. Wright says about the alexandrine: "The alexandrine often functions as a resting line, more roomy than most, but offering refuge only for a moment from the tenser, harder-working, less symmetrical pentameter" (*Shakespeare's Metrical Art*, p. 147). For example:

When that | the gen | eral is | not like | the hive

To whom | the for | agers | shall all | repair,

What hon | ey is | expected? | Degree | being viz | arded,

Th' unwor | thiest shows | as fair | ly in | the mask.

(*Troilus and Cressida*, 1, 3, 81–84)

The alexandrine (underlined) in the above example is definitely "roomier" than the pentameter lines that surround it. The line splits cleanly and symmetrically into two phrases. The possible ionic phrase, the epic feminine foot before the question mark, and the substantial pause of the epic caesura (signifying a shift for the speaker), as well as the possible ionic phrase that follows, help give the line a deliberate, unrushed nature.

Of course, six-foot lines are not always split into equal phrases. Especially in Shakespeare's later plays, punctuation can occur anywhere within an alexandrine. For example:

Some wine, | within | there, and | our vi | ands! For | tune knows
We scorn her most when most she offers blows.

(*Antony and Cleopatra*, 3, 11, 73–74)

When six-foot lines appear more frequently or in conjunction with a frequency of other variations, there is usually a dramatic reason for their appearance. They often appear in sections of verse that "overflow": in our discussion of run-on feminine feet, you'll recall that there was a six-foot line in the Iago speech that we examined.

Alexandrines, feminine feet, and run-on lines occur in the speeches by the Princes of Morocco and Aragon in *The Merchant of Venice* (Act 2, scenes 7 and 9) as they struggle to choose the casket containing the picture of Portia. Each casket contains an inscription written in iambic hexameter. On the gold casket is written:

"Who choos | eth me | shall gain | what ma | ny men | desire"

On the silver casket is written:

"Who choos | eth me | shall get | as much | as he | deserves"

On the lead casket is written:

"Who choos | eth me | must give | and haz | ard all | he hath"

The extra measure in these lines helps them to stand out in the dialogue as the princes repeat them. The pompous princes begin confidently but as they continue, they become insecure. Feminine feet, six-foot lines, and run-on lines pepper their speeches as they babble on to the wrong conclusions. The Prince of Aragon utters this six-foot line as he discovers the contents of the silver casket:

                               / ⌣   ⌣ ⌣

What's here? | The por | trait of | a blink | ing id | iot,
(The Merchant of Venice, 2, 9, 54)

Short Lines

JOE: The most common lengths of Shakespeare's short lines are three feet (iambic trimeter) and four feet (iambic tetrameter). Shakespeare uses short lines—lines between one syllable and four and a half feet in length—for several reasons. First of all, the use of occasional short lines is more like human speech. People don't always require ten or more syllables to say what they have to say. In this excerpt from *Julius Caesar*, Brutus summons his servant, Lucius:

> BRUTUS: What, Lu | cius, ho!
> I cannot, by the progress of the stars,
> Give guess how near to day. Lucius, I say!
> I would it were my fault to sleep so soundly.
> When, Lucius, when? awake, I say! what, Lucius!

(Enter Lucius.)

                                       /   ⌣

> LUCIUS: Call'd you, | my lord?
>
> BRUTUS: Get me a taper in my study, Lucius:
> When it is lighted, come and call me here.
>
> LUCIUS: I will, | my lord.

(Lucius exits.)

> BRUTUS: It must be by his death: and for my part,
> I know no personal cause to spurn at him,
(Julius Caesar, 2, 1, 1–11)

You may recognize that the last two lines that Brutus speaks in this excerpt are the first two lines of the soliloquy we analyzed earlier. *Shakespeare uses short lines here because lines of a longer duration are simply unnecessary.*

    Of course Shakespeare takes advantage of shared verse lines when he wants short, terse exchanges. Here is an example from the opening scene of *Hamlet*:

FRANCISCO: I think I hear them. Stand ho! Who is there?

HORATIO: Friends to | this ground. |

MARCELLUS: And liege | men to | the Dane.

FRANCISCO: Give you | good night. |

MARCELLUS: O, fare | well, hon | est soldier.

Who hath | reliev'd you? |

FRANCISCO: Barnar | do hath | my place.

Give you | good night. |

(Exit Francisco.)

MARCELLUS: Holla, | Barnar | do!

BARNARDO: Say—

What, is | Hora | tio there? |

HORATIO: A piece | of him.

BARNARDO: Welcome Horatio, welcome, good Marcellus.

(Hamlet, 1, 1, 14–20)

The verse lines shared by these four characters are not true short lines. However, it is a means of providing short exchanges between characters. Line sharing also allows little or no pause between speakers. In this case, the characters speak immediately after one another because they are "skittish" due to the expectation of a visit by the ghost of Hamlet's father.

From time to time Shakespeare combines shared verse lines with true short lines. Here is an example from *Julius Caesar*. Brutus and Cassius argue about their ongoing war with Mark Antony. The true short lines are underlined:

BRUTUS: I had rather be a dog, and bay the moon,

Than such | a Ro | man.

CASSIUS: Bru | tus, bait | not me,

I'll not endure it. You forget yourself

To hedge me in. I am a soldier, I,

Older in practice, abler than yourself

To make | conditions. |

BRUTUS: Go to; | you are | not, Cás|siŭs.

CASSIUS: I am.

BRUTUS: I say | yoŭ ăre nót.

CASSIUS: Urge me no more, I shall forget myself;

Have mind upon your health; tempt me no farther.

BRUTUS: Awáy, | slíght man!

CASSIUS: Is't pos | sible? |

BRUTUS: Héar mĕ, | for I | will speak.
(Julius Caesar, 4, 3, 27–38)

Shakespeare's combination of full verse lines, shared verse lines, and short lines gives the dialogue dynamism.

Short lines provide an interesting rhythmic alternative to the iambic line. The juxtaposition between the traditional flow of iambic pentameter and the intermittent short line can help the dramatic tension of a scene. Caesuras around short lines in these cases often seem appropriate. In the following example from *King Lear*, Lear addresses his youngest, favorite daughter, Cordelia. I will use the symbol "^" to indicate possible caesuras of a substantial duration:

LEAR: Now, our joy,
Although | our last | and least, | tŏ whóse | yŏung lóve
The vines | of France | and milk | of Bur | gundy
Strivĕ tó | be interess'd, | whăt cán | you say | to draw
A third | more op | ulĕnt thán | your sis | ters'? Speak.

CORDELIA: ^Nóthĭng, | My lórd.

LEAR: ^Nóthĭng?

CORDELIA: ^Nóthĭng. ^

LEAR: Nóthĭng | will come | of noth | ing, speak | again.
(King Lear, 1, 1, 82–90)

This section, particularly the three short lines, is the catalyst for the entire play. The rhythms underscore the dramatic action beautifully. Lear's lines flow for the most part, with occasional variations used to compliment his favorite daughter. The silences in the short lines are a dramatic contrast to the flowing verse that precedes it. Here is another example of the dramatic use of a short line, also from *King Lear*:

LEAR: The barbarous Scythian,

Or he that makes his generation messes

> To gorge his appetite, shall to my bosom
>
> Be as well neighbor'd, pitied, and reliev'd,
>
> As thou | my some | time daugh | ter.
>
> KENT: Good | my liege—
>
> LEAR: Peace, Kent! ^
>
> Come not between the dragon and his wrath;
>
>   *(King Lear, 1, 1, 116–122)*

The vain King Lear is enraged that his favorite daughter, Cordelia, will not express her love for him in an ingratiating manner. When Kent tries to intervene, he explodes with anger.

While the above examples can benefit from caesuras around short lines, *other short lines seem to specifically call for a pause or a physical action.*[6] I will place a "^" where a caesura or a physical action may be indicated. In this example from *Romeo and Juliet*, Romeo observes Juliet at her balcony:

> It is my lady, O, it is my love!
>
> O that | she knew | she were! ^
>
> She speaks, yet she says nothing; what of that?
>
>   *(Romeo and Juliet, 2, 2, 10–12)*

Romeo's pause indicates that he is observing Juliet's physical behavior. This short line indicates a pause for Romeo and a physical action for Juliet. In this case, the pause and physical action is indicated *after* the short line. A pause or physical action can also be indicated *before* the short line.

In the next example from *Othello*, Iago's wife, Emilia, has stolen Desdemona's handkerchief for her husband. An unsuspecting Desdemona asks her friend where it could be:

> DESDEMONA: Where should I lose the handkerchief, Emilia?
>
> EMILIA: ^ I know | not, madam.
>
> DESDEMONA: Believe me, I had rather have lost my purse
>
>   *(Othello, 3, 4, 23–25)*

Emilia knows full well what has happened to the handkerchief. I inserted a pause before Emilia's line to indicate that the usually honest Emilia may hesitate before lying to Desdemona.

A pause or physical action can also occur *within* a short line if strong punctuation is present. In such instances, the pause or physical action may occur immediately following the punctuation. The following is from Hamlet's "To be or not to be" soliloquy:

> For in that sleep of death what dreams may come,
>
> When we have shuffled off this mortal coil,
>
> Must give | us pause; ^ | there's the | respect
>
> (Hamlet, 3, 1, 65–67)

Shakespeare cleverly inserts a pause after Hamlet states that the fear of death causes him to pause before considering suicide as an alternative to his problem.

In *Timon of Athens* the generous Timon rails at his capitalistic guests for not supporting him in his time of need as he did for them:

> You fools of fortune, trencher-friends, time's flies,
>
> Cap-and-knee slaves, vapors, and minute-jacks!
>
> Of man | and beast | the in | finite mal | ady
>
> Crust you | quite o'er! | ^What, dost | thou go?
>
> Soft, take thy physic first—thou too—and thou;
>
> (Timon of Athens, 3, 6, 96–100)

In this case, Timon watches his guests leave during the missing foot after the exclamation point within the line.

Short lines also occur within speeches. Now and then such a short line signifies a transition of some sort. In this excerpt from *Julius Caesar,* Murellus rails at the Roman citizens for their fickleness:

> And when you saw his chariot but appear,
>
> Have you not made an universal shout,
>
> That Tiber trembl'd underneath her banks,
>
> To hear the replication of your sounds
>
> Made in | her con | cave shores?
>
> And do you now put on your best attire?
>
> And do you now cull out a holiday?
>
> And do you now strew flowers in his way
>
> That comes in triumph over Pompey's blood?
>
> Be gone!
>
> Run to your houses, fall upon your knees,
>
> Pray to the gods to intermit the plague
>
> That needs must light on this ingratitude.
>
> (Julius Caesar, 1, 1, 43–55)

Both short lines in the above speech indicate a transition. The second short line is quite an emotional one. But Shakespeare did not feel restricted with his use of short lines. At the beginning of a speech or within a speech we often find short lines that do not seem to signify a pause or a transition at all. Shakespeare also felt free to end a speech with a short line, without feeling compelled to have the line completed by another character. This happens often if the speech ends a scene. The short lines in these cases may signal the exit of a character. In *All's Well That Ends Well*, a short speech spoken by Helena ends Act 3, scene 7:

> Why then tonight
> Let us assay our plot, which if it speed,
> Is wicked meaning in a lawful deed,
> And lawful meaning in a lawful act,
> Where both not sin, and yet a sinful fact.
> But let's | about it.
>
> *(All's Well That Ends Well, 3, 7, 43–48)*

The Actor's Use of Long Lines

JOE: Most long lines, of which almost all are six feet in length, need no special attention. Six-foot lines (iambic hexameter), or alexandrines, tend to be more persistently iambic than five-foot lines. Many alexandrines have a "roomy," unrushed quality. These alexandrines should not be spoken quickly. The actor can take time in making his point. From time to time long lines are used in sections of text that "overflow." In these cases the character cannot express his thoughts concisely and may be overwhelmed emotionally. The reasons for this overflow vary from scene to scene and from play to play. The actor should be on alert for shared alexandrines as well as three-foot exchanges, which can also be viewed as shared alexandrines. In these situations, the connection between the two characters can be particularly close. Precise attention to the given circumstances in which the characters find themselves in these cases will help with the speaking of such lines.

The Actor's Use of Short Lines

JOE: Some short lines exist because ten syllable lines in these instances are unnecessary. These short lines—as well as extended dialogue written with short lines—are usually meant to clip along. However, some short lines indicate a pause or physical action. This can occur before or after the short line or within the short line if strong punctuation is present. Short lines that indicate a pause or physical action have nothing to do with real time. In other words, a line with three missing feet does not necessarily require a pause that is three times longer than a line with one missing foot. The pause or physical action should be determined by the reality of the moment. Short lines do not necessarily indicate a pause or physical action. If you cannot ascertain a reason for either, then get on with the play! Conversely, a pause or physical action can be indicated or inferred in a five-foot (or even six-foot) line. Short lines written in verse tend to follow the rules of verse. For example, a three-foot line might begin with a trochee or end with a feminine foot.

The actor should utilize these variant feet in the same way as with those that appear in pentameter lines. In other words: Use trochees to begin a new thought with a surge. Use spondees for a strongly emphasized two-syllable image. Use anapaests quickly and lightly, but give the stressed beat its due. Touch on pyrrhics lightly and rapidly. Use epic feminine feet for powerful emotion, a strong break, or focus change. Use run-on feminine feet for extended thoughts and imagery.

Exploring Truncation

JOE: As we've already mentioned, there are two types of truncation: *initial* truncation and *medial* truncation. Both types involve a measure that consists solely of one stressed syllable. In fact, the word *truncation* means "lopping off, shortening, or cutting the top or end from." Truncated lines "often occur at moments of tension and typically produce an effect of abruptness, anger, or astonishment" (Wright, *Shakespeare's Metrical Art*, p. 174).

Initial Truncation

JOE: The word *initial* means "first." In this variation, the first foot of the line consists of only one stressed syllable:

> /
> Twelve | year since, | Miran | da, twelve | year since
>
> Thy father was the Duke of Milan and
>
> A prince of power.   *(The Tempest, 1, 2, 53–55)*

>   Britain's a world
> /
> By | itself, | and we | will noth | ing pay
>
> For wearing our own noses.   *(Cymbeline, 3, 1, 12–14)*

> /   ᵕ ᵕ
> Jail | er, take | him to | thy cus | tody.
>   *(The Comedy of Errors, 1, 1, 155)*

> /
> Where | in have | I so | deserv'd | of you
>
> That you extol me thus? *(Measure for Measure, 5, 1, 502–503)*

The effect of this variation is that the first foot of the line has the rhythmic properties of a trochee. In other words, *the single strong syllable in the first foot of the line provides a punch or surge to the line,* much in the manner of a trochee. This gives the line an energetic start. In the following example, an impatient Olivia interrupts Cesario (Viola in disguise), who is trying to woo Olivia in the name of her master, Orsino:

> OLIVIA: I bade you never speak again of him;
> But would you undertake another suit,
> I had rather hear you to solicit that
> Than mu | sic from | the spheres. |
> VIOLA: Dear lǎdý—
> OLIVIA: Gíve | me leave, | beseech | you. I | did send,
> After the last enchantment you did here,
> A ring in chase of you;   *(Twelfth Night, 3, 1, 107–113)*

Olivia knows that "Cesario" is about to launch into a prepared speech on her master's behalf. Olivia will have none of it and uses the punch of the single beat (underlined) at the top of her line to demand that the subject be changed.

Medial Truncation

JOE: The word *medial* means "middle." In this type of truncation, the single strong syllable occurs immediately after punctuation within a line. Here are some examples:

> Is all the counsel that we two have shar'd,
> The sisters' vows, the hours that we have spent,
> When we have chid the hasty-footed time
> For part|ing us | — Ó, | is all | forgot?
>   *(A Midsummer Night's Dream, 3, 2, 198–201)*

> Nature seems dead, and wicked dreams abuse
> The cur | tain'd sleep; | wítch | craft cel | ebrates
> Pale Hecat's off'rings;   *(Macbeth, 2, 1, 50–52)*

> Whereon the numbers cannot try the cause,
> Which is not tomb enough and continent
> To hide | the slain? | Ó, | from this | time forth,
> My thoughts be bloody, or be nothing worth!
>   *(Hamlet, 4, 4, 63–66)*

Like its sister variation, medial truncation also has the rhythmic properties of a trochee. But rather than providing a surge at the beginning of a line of verse, *medial truncation gives a renewed surge within a line of verse.* Like initial truncation, the effect can be even stronger than a trochee, as there is no unstressed second syllable to deal with. Hotspur uses the strong punch of this single beat to help express his anger at a pompous lord in *Henry IV Part 1*:

                /   ᴗ   /
Came there | a cer | tain lord, | <u>neat</u> | and trim | ly dress'd
                                      (Henry IV Part 1, 1, 3, 33)

Medial truncation often signals a shift or a new beginning of some sort. Here is a section of Portia's soliloquy from *The Merchant of Venice* that we analyzed earlier:

    Beshrew your eyes,

They have o'erlook'd me and divided me:

One half of me is yours, the other half yours—

Mine own, I would say; but if mine, then yours,
        (/ ᴗ)
     /   /   /
And so | all yours. | <u>O,</u> | these naugh | ty times

Put bars between the owners and their rights!
                    /   ᴗ   /
And so | though yours, | not yours. | <u>Prove</u> | it so,

Let fortune go to hell for it, not I.
                     (The Merchant of Venice, 3, 2, 14–21)

There are two lines with medial truncation in this section. Each carries strong emotion and signals a transition of thought for Portia.

In the final act of *Richard III*, the Earl of Richmond prepares his troops for battle with the tyrant, King Richard:

More than I have said, loving countrymen,

The leisure and enforcement of the time
                      /
Forbids | to dwell | upon, | <u>yet</u> | remem | ber this:

God and our good cause fight upon our side;
                            (Richard III, 5, 3, 237–240)

Richmond states that he can no longer afford to use words to bolster his troops in their cause. However, he reminds them that God is on their side and therefore victory is certain. In this example and the excerpt from *The Merchant of Venice* as well as in may other instances, medial truncation has a quick, insistent quality.

Because it creates a short line, *medial truncation may indicate a pause or physical action between the punctuation and the single stressed syllable that follows it.* In this example, Othello checks to be sure that Desdemona has not given her strawberry-patterned handkerchief to Michael Cassio:

OTHELLO: Lend me | thy hand | kerchief. |

DESDEMONA: ^ Here | my lord.

(Othello, 3, 4, 52)

I inserted the pause. Because she is distressed by the loss of the handkerchief, which was a present from Othello, Desdemona may hesitate before handing him a different handkerchief. Several lines later, Othello drills his wife about the missing handkerchief:

Is't lost? | Is't gone? | ^ Speak, | is't out | o' th' way?

(Othello, 3, 4, 80)

Othello may pause briefly, waiting for Desdemona's reply. Now consider the following exchange:

POSTHUMUS: There lies | thy part! | *[Striking her; she falls.]*

PISANIO: O, | gentle | men help

(Cymbeline, 5, 5, 229)

In this case, the text indicates the physical action—Posthumus strikes Imogen.

The Actor's Use of Truncation

JOE: As I stated earlier, both initial and medial truncation can be used in much the same way as a trochee. The single stressed syllable is usually strongly stressed and must be attacked powerfully. With medial truncation, the actor should investigate whether a shift or transition is appropriate. Because truncation often occurs at moments of tension, the actor should (as always) marry the rhythm to the intent that arises from the given circumstances of the character.

Because it is a single-syllable measure, truncation tends to occur more suddenly and quickly than the trochee. For example, in the following excerpt from *Richard II*, Henry Bullingbrook (soon to become King Henry IV) and his accomplice, the Earl of Northumberland, plot with the Duke of York to overthrow King Richard. Northumberland makes a serious faux pas in front of York, King Richard's uncle, who is a new and tenuous ally against the king:

NORTHUMBERLAND: The news is very fair and good, my lord:

Richard not far from hence hath hid his head.

YORK: It would beseem the Lord Northumberland

To say *King* Richard. Alack the heavy day

When such a sacred king should hide his head!

NORTHUMBERLAND: Your Grace | mistakes; | on | ly to | be brief
(ᴜ /)
Left I | his ti | tle out. |

YORK: The time | hath been,
Would you have been so brief with him, he would
Have been so brief with you to shorten you,
For taking so the head, your whole head's length.
                              (Richard II, 3, 3, 5–14)

Northumberland is flustered by his mistake. Such a comment could cause York to withdraw his support for the rebellion. Northumberland speaks quickly to try to make amends. There is little pause between "Your Grace mistakes" and "only to be brief," which contains medial truncation. The shared verse line between Northumberland and York that follows the line of medial truncation allows York to answer just as quickly, ensuring that another such mistake by Northumberland will not be tolerated. Once again, we have an example of Shakespeare underscoring the dramatic tension of the scene with appropriate rhythms.

USING THE CAESURA

JOE: A **caesura** (pronounced "si-ZHOO-ruh") is a noun that comes from the Latin *caesere* which means "to cut." In Shakespeare's verse, it means "a break or pause within a line."

In the jargon of scansion, *all punctuation marks are referred to as caesuras*. Periods, question marks, exclamation points, and colons are called *strong* or *stopped* caesuras. Commas are *weak* or *light* caesuras. Most semicolons are strong caesuras.

It gets a little more complicated, however, because an actor can take a caesura (pause) anywhere he or she thinks appropriate, whether or not there is punctuation. Conversely, there are sections of dialogue where it makes sense to "barrel through" strong punctuation without taking a pause of any sort. In this discussion, *caesura* will be synonymous with "punctuation." There are three types of caesuras in iambic pentameter:

1. The masculine caesura
2. The epic caesura
3. The lyric caesura

Let's take a closer look at each of them, and then see how the actor can use the caesura onstage.

The Masculine Caesura

JOE: Although it can occur after an anapaest or a spondee, *the masculine caesura occurs most often after an iamb.*[7] It is the most common type of caesura. For example:

          ˘ /
And on | a love | -book pray | for my | success?
          (The Two Gentlemen of Verona, 1, 1, 19)

The masculine caesura in the above line is the question mark after the last foot. Here is another example:

       ˘ /
Reli | giously | provokes. | Be pleas | ed then
          (King John, 2, 1, 246)

The masculine caesura in the above line is the period after the third foot.

The Epic Caesura

JOE: *The epic caesura follows a feminine foot. Because run-on feminine feet are rarely accompanied by punctuation, epic caesuras usually accompany what I call an epic feminine foot. These caesuras normally involve strong punctuation. For example:*

  / ˘ / / ˘ / ˘
Since the | first fa | ther wore it. | This ring | he holds
       (All's Well That Ends Well, 3, 7, 25)

The epic caesura in the above line is the period after the third foot. Now consider this example:

      (˘ /)
˘ / ˘ / ˘   ˘ / ˘
What is it? | Cori | olan | us must | I call thee?
          (Coriolanus, 2, 1, 174)

The above line contains two epic caesuras: the question marks after the first and fifth feet.

The Lyric Caesura

JOE: *The lyric caesura falls between the unstressed and stressed beats of an iamb. For example:*

           ˘
FENTON: That now | I aim | at.
          /   ˘ / ˘
ANNE: Gen | tle Mas | ter Fenton
       (The Merry Wives of Windsor, 3, 3, 18)

The lyric caesura in the above line is the period in the middle of the third foot. Here is another example:

        ˘ /
The tri | al just | and no | ble. All | the clerks
          (Henry VIII, 2, 2, 91)

The lyric caesura in the above line is the period in the middle of the fourth foot.

JOE: The masculine caesura gets its name because it is preceded by a stressed beat. The epic and the lyric caesuras are considered feminine caesuras because they are each preceded by an unstressed beat. The following four lines spoken by the Duke in *Measure for Measure* contain all three types of caesuras:

    I know | you'd fain | be gone. | An of | ficer!
    To pri | son with | her! Shall | we thus | permit
    A blast | ing and | a scand | alous breath | to fall
    On him | so near us? | This needs | must be | a practice.
                                (Measure for Measure, 5, 1, 120–123)

The first line in our excerpt has two masculine caesuras: the period after the third foot and the exclamation point after the fifth foot. The second line has one lyric caesura: the exclamation point that falls in the middle of the third foot. The fourth line has two epic caesuras: the question mark that falls after the second foot and the period after the fifth foot.

The Actor's Use of the Caesura

LIZ: How do the three types of caesuras affect what the actor says? Do they really serve a purpose?

JOE: Yes, they do. The masculine caesura, like the iamb, is a generalist. It usually indicates a full stop. The epic caesura is "joined at the hip," so to speak, with the epic feminine foot and can signify everything an epic foot can signify (such as a beat or focus change, heightened emotion, and so on). The majority of lyric caesuras that are stronger than a comma tend to indicate a full stop. However, because they fall in the middle of a unit of rhythm (an iamb), a sizable minority of lyric caesuras seem to indicate that the speaker should take little or no pause at the punctuation. Let's look at two examples from *Romeo and Juliet*:

    Where is | she? And | how doth | she? And | what says
    My conceal'd lady to our cancell'd love.
                                (Romeo and Juliet, 3, 3, 97–98)

    It helps | not, it | prevails | not. Talk | no more.
                                    (Romeo and Juliet, 3, 3, 60)

Here are two more examples:

    Who cannot want the thought, how monstrous
    It was for Malcolm and for Donalbain
    To kill | their grac | ious fa | ther? Dam | ned fact!
                                    (Macbeth, 3, 6, 10–12)

> Ay, in the temple, in the town, the field,
> You do | me mis | chief! Fie, | Deme | trius!
> *(A Midsummer Night's Dream, 2, 1, 239–240)*

The foregoing examples illustrate that some caesuras can be minimized or omitted, even when punctuation appears in the written dialogue. But the actor also has the option of taking a caesura when no punctuation is present. One technique for pointing up a word is to take a brief caesura before and after the word. In Kenneth Branaugh's film of *Henry V*, the actor portraying the Constable of France used this technique to insult the Dauphin. The Dauphin has been bragging obnoxiously at length about his horse. The Constable replies:

> Indeed, my lord, it is a most absolute and excellent ^ horse. ^
> *(Henry V, 3, 7, 25–26)*

The actor's use of the caesura clearly shows that his feelings for the horse's rider are quite the opposite. Be wary, however, of what I call "Captain Kirk" acting—"Spock, we must (pause) beam down to the planet's (pause) surface." Indulgent pausing is deadly. I guarantee that the actor using these kinds of caesuras will be the only one who thinks them "dramatic."

SAM: You've given us a lot of information but I don't see how I can incorporate it all.

JOE: This is your first exposure to verse work and it is perfectly natural that you may be a little overwhelmed at this point. With a little practice, this will pass. The rules of Shakespeare's verse should be treated much in the same way that you dealt with your multiplication tables in elementary school. That is, memorize them! This can be accomplished in a relatively short period of time. This knowledge can then be put to use in helping shape your performance. Scansion is a relatively objective process and should be utilized immediately, even before learning your lines. This allows you to memorize rhythm patterns simultaneously with words, images, and intents. Remember, these rhythms are flexible and not only permit ample pliancy throughout the rehearsal process for growth and change, but also underscore and support the work as it evolves.

LIZ: Will you give Sam and me some hints on how we should go about scanning a line?

JOE: Of course. The first thing to do is to speak the line aloud in order to find its rhythm. Eventually you will be able to do this silently. Often, this will be enough to scan the line. If the rhythms seem strange or do not seem to conform to an acceptable rhythm, then do the following:

1. Mark off any syllables that *do* seem to flow, and then deal with the dialogue that does not.
2. Expect the possibility of a trochee in the first foot of the line and/or a feminine foot in the last foot of the line.
3. If there is punctuation in the line (especially strong punctuation), several things are possible: The measure before the punctuation could be a feminine foot. The

measure after the punctuation could be a trochee or a single stressed beat (medial truncation).

4. See if there are words that can be expanded or compressed, and experiment with lengthening and shortening them until the rhythm conforms to an acceptable rhythm. One trademark of Shakespeare's rhythmic style is an unusually high percentage of words that must be either expanded or compressed to fit the meter. But remember, if this draws unnecessary attention to the word or renders it incomprehensible, then by all means ignore the meter and pronounce the word in a familiar manner.

5. If a line seems to scan as a series of trochees, it's probably a line with initial truncation.

6. Check to see if any words can be elided. The words *the* and *to* are likely candidates for elision.

7. Are there words that can be contracted? (For example: "You will" — "you'll.") If so, an anapaest may be present.

8. If a line refuses to conform to an acceptable rhythm, it probably belongs to the small percentage of verse that is anomalous. Speak such lines as if they were written in prose. Do not force the line into an acceptable rhythm.

9. Check to be sure that you are not trying to scan a section of prose. A simple way to tell verse from prose is that the first letter of the first word of each line of verse is capitalized. Also, the right-hand margin of verse is usually uneven, because every ten syllables or so a new line must begin. The right-hand margin of prose is usually even.

JOE: You should also do the following:

1. If you have a line that is less than five feet in length, determine if a pause or physical action is appropriate.

2. If you deem that a short line *does* suggest such a pause or physical action, then determine if it occurs before or after the line. If there is strong punctuation in the short line, the pause or action may also occur immediately after the punctuation.

3. If you share a line of verse with another character, you must scan the entire line in order to determine the rhythm of your character's dialogue.

SAM: It'll take me a month to scan one scene!
JOE: No it won't. Shakespeare is very consistent with his rhythms and familiar patterns begin to emerge as you continue to scan. You soon expect the possibility of a trochee in the first foot of a line or sentence, for example. Soon, you will be able to scan almost as quickly as you can read.
LIZ: Do I have to mark all of my lines?
JOE: No, of course not. However, as a novice, you may wish to mark each line until you become a competent scanner. As you become more efficient, you will learn the rhythms as you learn your lines. You may wish to mark particularly turbulent passages or sections of special importance to your character, however.

Always keep in mind that scanning is an acting tool. It is an objective process that assists in the subjective process of crafting a performance.

But that's enough for today. Let's meet here again tomorrow, when we'll explore Shakespeare's rhythmic variations.

SUMMARY

In this session, Joe, Sam, and Liz covered the iamb and each of the variant feet, as well as their rhythmic natures. They also covered the variations on the iambic *line*.

- Iambs "flow," trochees "punch," run-on feminine feet "continue," epic feminine feet "end strongly," spondees "explode," pyrrhics "mince," and anapaests "skip."
- Lines of verse can vary in length from one stressed syllable to seven feet.
- Some lines of verse begin with a single stressed beat. This is called initial truncation.
- Others contain a single stressed beat within the line immediately following punctuation. This is called medial truncation.
- The word *caesura* signifies a pause of varying duration.
- All punctuation marks, whether or not they signify a pause, are also called "caesuras." Exclamation marks, question marks, periods, colons, and most semi-colons are "strong" or "stopped" caesuras. Commas are "weak" or "light" caesuras.
- There are three basic types of caesuras in verse. The masculine caesura follows an iamb. The epic caesura follows an epic feminine foot. The lyric caesura falls between the unstressed and stressed syllables of an iamb.

EXERCISES

SOLO EXERCISE 7.1

Now that you are beginning to understand Shakespeare's variations on the iamb and the iambic line, the best way to reinforce and deepen this understanding is to continue scanning. Regularly scanning short sections of speeches and scenes is an excellent way to develop and hone this important acting skill. Begin by scanning fifteen or twenty lines of verse from plays of different periods of Shakespeare's career. For example, try scanning sections of dialogue from the following plays:

Richard II—penned in 1595

Twelfth Night—penned in 1601

Antony and Cleopatra—penned in 1606

The Tempest—penned in 1611

Are the rhythms rough or smooth? Slow or fast? Heavy or light? Are the rhythms terse? Do they overflow? Are there missing syllables or missing feet? If so, are pauses or physical actions appropriate? Do the rhythms fluctuate? A question to ask after each of these questions is, "Why?" What do the rhythms tell you about the dramatic action? As you gain more confidence in your scanning, attempt larger sections of dialogue.

NOTES

1. I have had many a heated discussion concerning the existence of the dactyl with a professor friend and former colleague who shall remain nameless, called Phil Beck.
2. Some Shakespeare practitioners consider even a line that ends in a comma to be an end-stopped line.
3. "Prose" is writing that contains no formal rhythmic structure. More than twenty percent of Shakespeare's dramatic dialogue is written in prose. Prose is discussed in detail in Chapter 9.
4. Other authors agree. Delbert Spain writes that the epic feminine foot, and the epic caesura that follows, "usually is a very strong break, sometimes with a substantial pause" (*Shakespeare Sounded Soundly*, p. 51). George T. Wright states, "The extra syllable [of the epic feminine foot] is almost always followed by punctuation, and the resumption after the implied pause seems like a new beginning, often restrained, hesitant, or deliberate" (*Shakespeare's Metrical Art*, p. 165).
5. One option for marking unusually strong unstressed beats is to place a grave accent above such syllables. This is often the case with heavy iambs and epic feminine feet. Here are two lines that we scanned earlier with grave accents added:

    \ /   / ˘
    The non | pareil | of this. | O ven | geance, vengeance!
    (Cymbeline, 2, 5, 8)

    / ˘   ˘ / \
    O that | I had | her here, | to tear | her limb-meal!
    (Cymbeline, 2, 5, 8)

    Such markings may serve to help remind the actor that, while unstressed, such syllables carry heavy percussive imagery or emotion.
6. Some Shakespeare scholars and experienced Shakespeare practitioners think that looking for pauses and/or physical actions in Shakespeare's short lines is unsubstantiated. Dakin Matthews, in his book *Shakespeare Spoken Here*, writes, "When Shakespeare has short lines, does that mean some kind of action is necessary to fill out the remaining feet? I have heard that said; again, it's probably too good to be true" (p. 81). Others feel that almost all short lines require a pause or physical action. John Barton, in his book *Playing Shakespeare*, writes, "When there is a short line, we can be pretty sure that he [Shakespeare] is indicating a pause of some sort" (p. 30). I am a centrist on this issue. Pauses or physical actions seem to be indicated in a large enough percentage of short lines that the actor should at least take the time to determine whether one or the other is appropriate. Of course, this is rarely the case with extended dialogue written in short lines.
7. Caesuras that are preceded by a stressed syllable are considered masculine. Because pyrrhic feet can be viewed as light iambs, they can also be followed by a masculine caesura. Although it is rare, a caesura can follow a trochee. Because it is preceded by an unstressed syllable, such a caesura would be considered feminine.

CHAPTER 8

EXPLORING SHAKESPEARE'S RHYTHMS

(The next day, I meet with Liz and Sam again at the coffee shop.)

JOE: So far, we have been looking at each variation in isolation. Let us now explore how the iamb and the pentameter line interact with Shakespeare's rhythmic variations in the dialogue of his plays.

LIZ: Can any generalizations be drawn from his rhythms?

JOE: Yes. Simply put, *Shakespeare's verse rhythms allow the dialogue to move from slow and deliberate to sharp and quick, from smooth and flowing to rough and turbulent and from normal flow (five-foot lines) to "overflow" (six-foot lines and lines containing feminine feet) to "underflow" (short lines).* Of course these rhythmic traits overlap. For example, most rough rhythms tend to move more slowly while most smooth rhythms tend to move more quickly—but even here, Shakespeare mixes it up on occasion, surprising our expectations.

Rhythmic Turbulence

Joe: In his book *Shakespeare Spoken Here,* Dakin Matthews writes that "whenever the poet creates the strongest gap between actual rhythm and metrical expectation, I would define that as *rhythmic turbulence,* and suggest that the poet . . . must be doing it for 'extraordinary effect.' If you find the turbulence in a passage, you may well find the emotional center of a passage. Rhythmic turbulence is thus one of Shakespeare's strongest and most reliable 'stage directions' to the actor" (p. 26). I can think of no better term than **rhythmic turbulence** to describe the rough rhythms of Shakespeare's verse dialogue. Shakespeare often provides characters with turbulent rhythms when the dramatic action of his plays becomes tempestuous or explosive. *Turbulent rhythms disrupt the rhythmic flow of the verse.* This often occurs at times of emotional extremes (moments of anger, rage, defiance, grief, jubilation, passion, victory and so on). The variations on iambic pentameter that cause rhythmic turbulence include trochees, epic feminine feet (and epic caesuras), individual spondees, and ionic phrases, as well as lines containing initial and/or medial truncation. Conversely, measures that go with the flow of the verse include iambs, pyrrhics (that are not part of an ionic phrase), anapaests, and run-on feminine feet. I will underline the turbulent measures in the examples that follow.

Shakespeare often uses the trochee and the epic feminine foot to create rough rhythms in his verse dialogue. Now and then he uses these two types of measures as "bookends" in a sense, to begin and end a line or sentence. Here are two examples from lines that we examined earlier:

/ ˘   ˘ / ˘
<u>Cursed</u> | the heart | that had | the heart | <u>to do it</u>
(Richard III, 1, 2, 15)

Meantime, this deep disgrace in brotherhood
/ ˘   ˘ / ˘
<u>Touches</u> | me deep | er than | you can | <u>imagine</u>.
(Richard, III, 1, 1, 111–112)

Here are some more examples:

/ ˘   ˘ / ˘
<u>Out on</u> | thee seem | ing! I | will write | <u>against it!</u>
(Much Ado about Nothing, 4, 1, 56)

/ ˘   ˘ / ˘
<u>Seize on</u> | him fur | ies; take | him un | <u>to torment!</u>
(Richard III, 1, 4, 57)

/ ˘   ˘ / ˘
<u>Now to</u> | that name | my cour | age prove | <u>my title!</u>
(Antony and Cleopatra, 5, 2, 288)

Even out of context, these lines contain strong imagery. In all five examples the trochee provides a strong rhythmic punch, followed by flowing iambs, which carry the imagery along to end with a dramatic epic feminine foot.

By removing the number of smooth iambs in between, the trochee and epic feminine foot creates even greater rhythmic turbulence. In this example, Macbeth tells his wife that he refuses to return to the room where he just murdered King Duncan:

> I'll go no more.
> I am afraid to think on what I have done;
> / ˘ ˘ / ˘
> Look on't | again, | I dare not.   *(Macbeth, 2, 2, 47–49)*

There is great dramatic tension in this scene, and the rough rhythms of the trochee and epic feminine foot help to underscore the emotion and drama.

Trochees and epic feminine feet are effective in comedy as well. For example:

> HELENA: She was a vixen when she went to school;
> And though she be but little, she is fierce.
> /˘ / ˘ ˘ / ˘
> HERMIA: "Little" | again?! | Nothing | but low | and "little"?!
> *(A Midsummer Night's Dream, 3, 2, 324–326)*

The trochees and epic feminine foot in Hermia's line reflect her anger toward Helena, hopefully to the amusement of the audience.

Shakespeare's most turbulent use of the trochee and epic feminine foot removes the iamb altogether. This creates a very rough, two-measure phrase. In the following example from *Othello*, Othello angrily accuses his wife of infidelity. The rough rhythm underscores his rage:

> / ˘ ˘ / ˘
> OTHELLO: Impu | dent strumpet! |
> DESDEMONA: By heav'n, | you do | me wrong.
> *(Othello, 4, 2, 81)*

In the next example, from *Measure for Measure*, Isabel entreats Angelo to spare her brother's life:

> That I do beg his life, if it be sin,
> / ˘ ˘ / ˘
> Heav'n let | me bear it!   *(Measure for Measure, 2, 4, 70)*

In *Henry V*, the Chorus uses rough rhythms to excite the audience about the action to come:

>   And at his heels
> / ˘
> Leash'd in | like hounds | should fam | ine, sword | and fire
> / ˘ ˘ / ˘
> Crouch for | employment.   *(Henry V, 1, Prol., 6–8)*

In *Macbeth*, Macduff reveals the shocking news of Duncan's murder:

Ring the | alar | um bell! | Murder | and treason!
(Macbeth, 2, 3, 74)

Later in the same play, the murdered Banquo returns to confront his murderer. A frantic Macbeth orders the ghost to be gone:

Avaunt | and quit | my sight. | Let the | earth hide thee!
(Macbeth, 3, 4, 92)

Shakespeare also uses rough rhythms in order to ensure that those syllables will stand out from the ones surrounding it, hence giving them emphasis. He does this for many reasons. Let's look at some examples, beginning with this one:

LADY MACBETH: It was | the owl | that shriek'd, | the fa | tal bellman,
Which gives | the stern'st | good night. | He is | about it:
(Macbeth, 2, 2, 3–4)

The change in rhythm draws attention to Lady Macbeth envisioning the murder of Duncan by her husband. Here's another example:

DESDEMONA: *(To Emilia)* I will | not leave | him now | till Cas | sio
Be call'd to him. | *(To Othello)* How is't | with you, | my Lord?
OTHELLO: Well, my | good lady. | *(Aside)* O, hard | ness to | dissemble!
(Othello, 3, 4, 32–34)

Othello's "Well, my good lady" rhythmically reflects that he is trying too hard to put on a "good face" under the recent knowledge of Desdemona's alleged unfaithfulness. This is revealed in his anguished **aside** (a heartfelt comment, usually addressed to the audience, but sometimes self-directed or addressed to another character onstage), which is extremely turbulent.

Shakespeare loves contrasts of many types, and rhythm is no exception. In order to ensure that percussive variations are emphasized or effective, he almost always precedes and follows these variations with largely regular iambic lines. This is true of the two above examples from *Macbeth* and *Othello*. Here is another example:

DUKE: Good night | to ev | ery one. | And no | ble signior,
If vir | tue no | delight | ed beau | ty lack,
Your son | -in-law | is far | more fair | than black.

SENATOR: Adieu | brave Moor, | use Des | demo | na well.

>   / ˘
> BRABANTIO: Look to | her, Moor, | if thou | hast eyes | to see;
>
> She has | deceiv'd | her fa | ther, and | may thee. *(Exit)*
>
>   / ˘ ˘/ ˘
> OTHELLO: My life | upon | her faith! | Honest | Iago,
>
> My Des | demo | na must | I leave | to thee.
>
> I pri | thee let | thy wife | attend | on her,
>
>   ˘ / ˘
> And bring | them af | ter in | the best | advantage.
>
>   (*Othello*, 1, 3, 288–297)

The trochee/epic combination "Honest Iago" is preceded primarily by six and a half feet of iambs (with the exception of a run-on feminine foot, a possible spondee, and a trochee, which gives a strong initial punch to Brabantio's warning to Othello), and is followed by almost three lines of iambs. The irony of Othello's naivete about Iago's true nature is therefore reinforced rhythmically.

 Of course, Shakespeare doesn't use the two-foot configuration of the trochee and epic feminine foot exclusively to create rhythmic turbulence. We have seen several examples already in which additional trochees or epic feminine feet join the trochee/epic combination. Spondees and ionic phrases are also used to create rhythmic turbulence. In this excerpt from *King Lear,* Lear learns from his eldest daughters that they will not accept even one of his hundred attendant knights:

>   ˘ ˘   ˘ ˘
> If on | ly to | go warm | were gor | geous
>
> Why, na | ture needs | not what | thou gor | geous wear'st,
>
>   ˘ ˘ / /
> Which scarce | ly keeps | thee warm. | But for | true need,—
>
> ˘ / ˘ / ˘ ˘ / ˘ / ˘
> You heavens, | give me | that patience, | patience | I need!
>
>   (*King Lear*, 2, 4, 268–271)

The last line and a half, beginning with the ionic phrase "But for true need," are extremely rough as the enraged and exasperated Lear begs the heavens to give him the patience to bear his situation.

 In the following example, Hamlet comes upon his uncle, Claudius, at prayer. He contemplates killing his uncle then and there in revenge for killing his father:

> / ˘   / ˘ ˘ / ˘
> Now might | I do | it pat, | now he | is praying;
>
>   ˘ / ˘
> And now | I'll do't | —and so | he goes | to heaven;
>
>   / ˘
> And so | am I | reveng'd | —that would | be scann'd.
>
> A vil | lain kills | my fa | ther, and | for that,
>
> / ˘ / / ˘ ˘ / /   ˘ / ˘
> I, his | sole son, | do this | same vil | lain send | to heaven.
> / ˘
> O, this | is hire | and sal | ary, no | revenge.

He took | my fa | ther gros | sly, full | of bread,
With all | his crimes | broad blown, | as flush | as May;
And how | his au | dit stands | who knows | save heaven?
But, in | our cir | cumstance | and course | of thought,
'Tis hea | vy with him. | And am | I then, | reveng'd,
To take | him in | the pur | ging of | his soul,
When he | is fit | and sea | son'd for | his passage?
No.
(/ /)
Up, sword, | and know | thou a | more hor | rid hent.
When he | is drunk | asleep, | or in | his rage.
Or in | th' inces | tuous plea | sure of | his bed;
At gam | ing, swear | ing; or | about | some act
That has | no rel | ish of | salva | tion in't—
Then trip | him, that | his heels | may kick | at heaven,
And that | his soul | may be | as damn'd | and black
As hell, | whereto | it goes. | My mo | ther stays;
This phy | sic but | prolongs | thy sick | ly days.

(Hamlet, 3, 3, 73–95)

The first thirteen lines of this soliloquy, in which Hamlet struggles with whether or not to kill his uncle while he is at prayer, are extremely rough, containing trochees, epic feminine feet, spondees, and an ionic phrase. Beginning in the middle of line eleven, with the sentence that begins—"And am I then, reveng'd"—Shakespeare utilizes smooth iambs and a number of pyrrhic feet to accelerate Hamlet's frantic state before it comes to an abrupt stop with the epic feminine foot "his passage," followed by the fourteenth line that consists of a single stressed beat—the word "No!" Because line fourteen is a short line, a substantial pause may follow. In this way, Shakespeare juxtaposes emotional speed with dramatic silence. After Hamlet has made his fatal decision, he speaks nine more lines in which he rationalizes his choice by promising to execute Claudius while he is engaged in a more appropriate activity. These nine lines are smooth, being completely iambic or pyrrhic except for a possible spondee (which underscores the sheathing of his weapons) and one run-on feminine foot. These rhythms are a clear indication of the torturous conflict within Hamlet (rough rhythms), followed by the relief of choosing procrastination (smooth rhythms). The informed actor can use these rhythms accordingly. Now let's look at a very different type of scene, from *Twelfth Night*:

                      / ᵕ
VIOLA: Madam, | I come | to whet | your gen | tle thoughts   (105)

    On his | behalf. |
                          / ᵕ   ᵕ / ᵕ
OLIVIA: O, by | your leave, | I pray you!   (106)

    I bade | you ne | ver speak | again | of him;   (107)

    But, would | you un | dertake | ano | ther suit,   (108)
    ᵕ ᵕ /
    I had ra | ther hear | you to | soli | cit that   (109)

    Than mu | sic from | the spheres. |
                                    ᵕ / ᵕ
VIOLA: ^ Dear lady—   (110)
          /
OLIVIA: Give | me leave, | beseech | you. I | did send,   (111)
    / ᵕ
    After | the last | enchant | ment you | did here,   (112)
                         /
    A ring | in chase | of you; | so | did I | abuse   (113)

    Myself, | my ser | vant, and | I fear | me you.   (114)

                    (*Twelfth Night*, 3, 1, 105–114)

Here, the rhythms reinforce the romantic comedy of this section. This scene marks the second meeting of Viola (still in disguise as Cesario) and Olivia. Once again, Viola is sent to lavish praise on Olivia in the name of her master, Orsino. Viola begins her message with the punch of a trochee. Olivia scorns Orsino and is now totally smitten with Viola (Cesario). Olivia cuts Viola off in the middle of line 106, finishing the line of verse that Viola has started. Olivia's response starts with a trochee and ends with an epic feminine foot, reflecting her impatience with talk of Orsino. Olivia's next four lines (107–110) are almost completely iambic except for one anapaest, reflecting her clarity of amorous feelings and intent concerning the disguised Viola. Viola may pause (the missing foot, represented by the "^" symbol, after the punctuation in line 110), put off by Olivia's advances. Viola's response begins with an epic feminine foot, as she is about to launch a protestation. Olivia cuts her off beginning with a single strong beat on a line of initial truncation (line 111) as she continues her wooing. Line 113 contains medial truncation, putting strong emphasis on the word *so*. The word in this instance means "because I did such a thing." In other words, Olivia is confessing that her ploy to lure Viola back by means of the ring was injurious to all concerned.

    As a point of interest, line 110 can be scanned a second way, as follows:

    Than mu | sic from | the spheres. |

VIOLA: Dear La | dy—

OLIVIA: Give me leave, beseech you. I did send,

In the above scanning, line 110 is entirely iambic. However, before Viola can finish the line, Olivia interrupts her, preventing her from completing the final iamb. The effect is similar to my first scanning. But with this option, Viola might speak up immediately with "Dear Lady," rather than pausing to gather her thoughts. Both choices are valid.

Rhythmic Pacing

JOE: As I stated earlier, Shakespeare doesn't shift only from smooth to rough, but also from unhurried to swift as we saw in the example from *Hamlet*. Just as he enjoys preceding and following rough rhythms with smooth ones, he also enjoys alternating the **rhythmic pacing** of his syllables—the speed at which the dialogue is spoken.

SAM: Are there types of feet that move faster than others?

JOE: As we now know, a major factor in the speed at which a syllable can travel is its level of stress. The pyrrhic foot is of its nature extremely light and is therefore the fastest moving measure. The spondee is of its nature extremely heavy and is therefore the slowest moving measure. But other types of measures are more varied. The anapaest moves fairly quickly because of its first two light, unstressed syllables and its skipping nature. The stressed syllables of trochees and feminine feet tend to be heavy, but factors such as punctuation and placement in a sentence also help determine their pacing. The iamb is by far the most flexible measure in terms of stress, and Shakespeare takes great advantage of its adaptability. An iamb can be pushed so far in one direction that it becomes a pyrrhic and so far in the other direction that it becomes a spondee. And we also have the wide range of stress levels in between, from a 1–2 iamb to a 4–5 iamb, to use our sliding scale of stress. Let's look at the possible stress levels of an excerpt from *Henry V*:

Thus with imagin'd wing our swift scene flies

1 4   1   1   1   2   2 4   1 1
In mo | tion of | no less | celer | ity

1   2   1   5
Than that | of thought.   *(Henry V, 3, Prol., 1–3)*

In the above lines, the Chorus informs the audience that the play, which has been set in England, will now move to France. Although travel from one country to the other usually takes some time, the play will cover the distance at almost the speed of thought. Because the meaning and imagery of these lines is about velocity, Shakespeare supplies the Chorus not only with smooth rhythms but also with primarily light rhythms—light iambs and pyrrhics—which can be spoken quite rapidly. Even the strongly stressed syllables in the words *motion* and *celerity* as well as the word *thought* contain short, clipped vowel sounds, helping those words to be spoken quickly. In addition, *motion* is a two-syllable word and *celerity* is a four-syllable word. As we now know, multiple-syllable words allow a line to hasten. The single-syllable words in the above lines are small, linking words that contain little imagery and hence can be accelerated.

Conversely, Ophelia's soliloquy in the third act of *Hamlet*, in which she laments the loss of Hamlet's love as well as his apparent descent into madness, although fairly smooth, is slower paced and dirge-like, reflecting her grief. Here are the first two lines of her speech with possible stress levels added:

```
4    2    1 5    1    5    1  3    2    5
O, what | a no | ble mind | is here | o'erthrown!

1    5    1    5    1    5    1    5    4 (5)    5
The cour | tier's, sol | diers, schol | ar's eye, | tongue, sword,
```
(Hamlet, 3, 1, 150–151)

Except for the initial trochee in the first foot of the first line, in which Ophelia may almost wail the word *O*, and a possible spondee in the last foot of the second line, this passage is fairly smooth. But the predominantly heavy iambs move more slowly and deliberately. In addition, the long vowel sound in the word *O*, the half-long vowel sound in *noble*, and the long stressed vowel sound in *o'erthrown* further slow the delivery of the line and reinforce Ophelia's anguish. In the second line, only the vowel sounds in *scholar* and *tongue* are truly short vowel sounds.

In *A Midsummer Night's Dream*, Titania, under a spell, awakes to fall in love with Bottom the Weaver, who has been transformed into a donkey. The enamored Titania woos Bottom, telling him that her fairies will provide him with a life of luxury:

```
1    4    2    5    1 1    1 5    1    3
I'll give | thee fair | ies to | attend | on thee;

1    2    2    4    2    5    1    2    1    5
And they | shall fetch | thee jew | els from | the deep,

1    5    2    3    1    4    1    5    2    5
And sing | while thou | on pres | sed flowers | dost sleep.
```
(A Midsummer Night's Dream, 3, 1, 157–159)

Most of the rhythms here are slow paced, smooth and luxurious, mirroring the imagery and emotion of the lines. The syllables flow, with many strong stresses and some long vowel sounds. The second and third lines are particularly sumptuous. Strongly stressed one-syllable words like *fetch* and *sing* as well as the sensuous vowel sounds in *jewels, deep, flowers,* and *sleep* add to the seductive pacing of the lines. There are even some elongated consonant sounds such as the "n" sounds in *attend* and *sing*.

We also know that Shakespeare supplies some of his verse lines with too few syllables (like the single-beat line "No" in the earlier example from *Hamlet*) as well as too many syllables, which cause such lines to "overflow."

Let's look at a section of dialogue from *The Two Gentlemen of Verona*, in which Shakespeare effectively uses short lines in conjunction with flowing iambic pentameter. In this scene, Julia, in disguise as a page, is sent by her master, Proteus, who formerly pledged his love to Julia, to deliver a love letter and a ring to Silvia, with whom the callous Proteus has fallen in love. The situation here somewhat resembles the Viola—Orsino—Olivia love triangle in Shakespeare's later play, *Twelfth Night*. The short lines are underlined, and possible pauses and/or physical actions are denoted by the "^" symbol:

(*Enter Silvia, attended.*)

JULIA: Gentle | woman, | good day! | I pray | you, be | my mean   *(108)*

   To bring | me where | to speak | with Ma | dam Sil | via.   *(109)*

SILVIA: What would | you with | her, if | that I | be she?   *(110)*

JULIA: If you | be she | I do | entreat | your patience   *(111)*

   To hear | me speak | the mes | sage I | am sent on.   *(112)*

SILVIA: ^ From whom?   *(113)*

JULIA: From my | master, | Sir Prot | eus, | madam.   *(114)*

SILVIA: O, | he sends | you for | a picture?   *(115)*

JULIA: Ay, madam.   *(116)*

SILVIA: Ursu | la, bring | my pic | ture here. ^   *(117)*

   Go give | your mas | ter this: | tell him | from me,   *(118)*

   One Jul | ia, that | his chang | ing thoughts | forget,   *(119)*

   Would bet | ter fit | his cham | ber than | this shadow.   *(120)*

JULIA: Madam, | please you | peruse | this let | ter— ^   *(121)*

   Pardon | me, ma | dam; I | have un | advis'd   *(122)*

   Deli | ver'd you | a pa | per that | I should not: *(123)*

   This is | the let | ter to | your la | dyship.   *(124)*

SILVIA: I pray | thee, let | me look | on that | again.   *(125)*

JULIA: It may | not be; | good ma | dam, par | don me.   *(126)*

SILVIA: There, hold! ^   *(127)*

   I will | not look | upon | your mas | ter's lines: *(128)*

I know | they are stuff'd | with pro | testa | tions   (129)

And full | of new | -found oaths; | which he | will break   (130)

As ea | sily | as I | do tear | his paper.   (131)

(The Two Gentlemen of Verona, 4, 4, 108–131)

In this one excerpt, Shakespeare uses short lines for terse exchanges, dramatic pauses, and physical actions. In order to help with the contrast between full lines of verse and short lines, Shakespeare begins the scene with two six-foot lines (lines 108 and 109). These alexandrines help with Julia's formal introduction to Silvia, the mistress of the house. Because Julia is in disguise as a lowly page, she must treat Silvia as a superior. The first alexandrine splits neatly and equally into two three-foot phrases and the second alexandrine is completely iambic. This helps to reinforce a courtly and formal delivery on Julia's part. Silvia responds in an equally formal manner and the rhythms continue in a flowing manner until the short line "From whom?" (line 113). Silvia may pause before asking this question of Julia, because the message could be either from the banished Valentine, with whom Silvia is in love, or from the duplicitous Proteus. The following short lines (115–117) allow terser exchanges between Julia and Silvia.[1] Line 117 is a four-foot line. The missing fifth foot is the physical action of Silvia's maid, Ursula, retrieving Silvia's picture and giving it to Julia. The lines then flow once more until line 121. The final stressed syllable is missing from this line which signals that Julia, realizing that she is about to hand Silvia an old love letter written to her from Proteus, takes the letter back. The ensuing dialogue is primarily iambic (especially lines 125 and 126) and can move quite quickly. In this way, the dramatic pause that follows Silvia's command, "There, hold!" (line 127), is particularly effective. There is also a physical action that occurs here, although that action is interpretive. Most likely, Silvia takes both letters, examines them, and returns to Julia the mistaken letter. The remainder of the dialogue (lines 128–131) continues to flow strongly and quickly, culminating in Silvia's tearing of Proteus's letter. Lines 124 and 131 are good examples of the fact that physical actions don't always occur on short lines.

Let's move from Shakespeare's use of short lines to his use of overflowing lines. We'll examine a passage from *Hamlet* in which Shakespeare moves from smooth to rough, slow to quick, and flow to overflow:

That it | should come | to this!   (137)

But two | months dead, | nay not | so much, | not two.   (138)

So ex | cellent | a king, | that was | to this   (139)

Hyper | ion to | a satyr, | so lov | ing to | my mother (140)

That he | might not | between | the winds | of heaven   (141)

Visit | her face | too roughly. | Heaven | and earth,   (142)

| /   ᵕ   ᵕ /   ᵕ
Must I | remember? | Why, she | should hang | on him   *(143)*

ᵕ   ᵕ   ᵕ   /
As if | increase | of ap | petite | had grown   *(144)*

        ᵕ   /
By what | it fed on; | and yet | within | a month—   *(145)*

 /   ᵕ   /   ᵕ   /   ᵕ   ᵕ   /   ᵕ
Let me | not think on't! | Frailty, | thy name | is woman! *(146)*

(Hamlet, 1, 2, 137–146)

The rhythms of this speech are an excellent example of contrasts in rhythm, stress, and speed. Hamlet is distressed and enraged at his mother's marriage to his father's brother, Claudius, who is now king in his father's stead. The first two and a half lines contain many strong stresses, especially the phrase "But two months dead" and the ionic phrase "so excellent." This reflects Hamlet's agony about his mother's hasty remarriage. But then the rhythms begin to quicken. The second half of line 139 moves quickly because of many lightly stressed syllables along with terse, strong stresses to contrast the word *king* (Hamlet's deceased father) and the word *this* (referring to Claudius), both of which contain short vowel sounds. Similarly, the first half of line 140 moves rapidly because of light stresses and clipped, strong stresses, contrasting "Hyperion" (Hamlet Senior) and "satyr" (Claudius). The ionic phrase "so loving to" in the second half of line 140 echoes the earlier ionic phrase "so excellent." Beginning with line 140, the verse begins to overflow, underscoring Hamlet's overflow of emotion. Line 140 is a six-foot line with two feminine feet. This line contains fourteen syllables rather than ten. Line 141, which ends in a run-on feminine foot, is smooth but also overflows. In fact, with the exception of line 144, all of the remaining lines in this excerpt overflow. The smooth rhythms of line 141 suddenly become extremely rough with line 142 and the first half of line 143. These lines slow down because of the strong, turbulent stresses. The pace then increases once more, beginning with the second half of line 143. However, by line 146, the rhythms turn even more turbulent. This famous last line has only one iamb in it. The smooth rhythms of the speech are like a car that has lost its brakes while descending a hill. The rough rhythms are like the sandbank that the car must drive into in order to stop.

PHRASING

JOE: With dramatic poetry, the actor is constantly confronted with both lines of verse and complete sentences. Sometimes they coincide, as in the following example:

Then tell me, whither were I best to send him?
(The Two Gentlemen of Verona, 1, 3, 24)

But most often they do not:

As would take in some virtue. O, my master,
Thy mind to her is now as low as were

> <u>Thy fortunes.</u> How? That I should murder her,
>
> *(Cymbeline, 3, 2, 9–11)*

As indicated by the underlined portion above, the complete sentence extends beyond a single line of verse. Phrases and clauses also often begin at the top of a line of verse and end in the last syllable of a line of verse, like these three lines:

> Hadst thou but lov'd him half so well as I,
> Or felt that pain which I did for him once,
> Or nourish'd him as I did with my blood,
>
> *(Henry VI Part 3, 1, 1, 220–222)*

But not always:

> In asking their good loves, <u>but thou wilt frame</u>
> <u>Thyself,</u> forsooth, <u>hereafter theirs,</u> so far
>
> *(Coriolanus, 3, 2, 84–85)*

There are two widely opposite schools of thought concerning the actor's phrasing of Shakespearean words—and I am in disagreement with both. One school insists that there must be a caesura, however brief, at the end of each and every line of verse. The other school insists that the actor should never pause in Shakespeare, even after strong punctuation, other than to catch one's breath briefly at the end of an occasional sentence. However, in my opinion, *Shakespeare's dialogue is first and foremost human speech and must be phrased accordingly.* Let's look at an excerpt from *King Lear:*

> But true it is, from France there comes a power
> Into this scattered kingdom, who already
> Wise in our negligence, have secret feet
> In some of our best ports, and are at point
> To show their open banner. Now to you:
>
> *(King Lear, 3, 1, 30–34)*

The phrasing of the above lines of verse is as follows:

> But true it is ^
> from France there comes a power into this scattered kingdom ^
> who already wise in our negligence ^
> have secret feet in some of our best ports ^
> and are at point to show their open banner. ^
> Now to you: ^

The above caesuras (indicated by the "^" symbol) are of varying lengths, those after the period and colon probably being of the longest duration. Such phrasing does not adversely affect the integrity of the verse line. The two exist simultaneously. To pause at the end of each line of verse in the above example or to plow through the entire piece without a pause of any kind would confuse the listener as well as perplex the speaker. Meaning and imagery must determine phrasing.[2]

Prose, in contrast to verse, presents its own challenges for the actor. We'll take up that subject next time we meet.

Summary

In this chapter, Liz and Sam explored the various rhythms that Shakespeare used in his dramatic verse. Joe explained how rhythmic variations interact with the iamb and the pentameter line.

- Shakespeare uses the iamb and the variations on the iamb and the iambic line to supply variety to his rhythms and to underscore his dramatic action.
- Rhythmic turbulence disrupts the metric flow of the dialogue. Stress levels in such instances are usually strong but rough. This happens most often at times of emotional extremes.
- Variations that can cause turbulence are trochees, epic feminine feet, spondees, and ionic phrases, as well as truncation.
- Shakespeare also uses isolated rough rhythms to ensure that certain measures will be emphasized.
- He almost always alternates between rough and smooth rhythms.
- Shakespeare often uses the varied stress levels of the iamb to increase or decrease the pace of smooth verse.
- The iamb can be pushed to the extreme in one direction, creating the fast-moving pyrrhic foot. It can also be pushed to the opposite extreme, creating the slow-moving spondee.
- Variations that can create smooth rhythms are the iamb, the pyrrhic foot, the anapaest, and the run-on feminine foot.
- Shakespeare also robs certain lines of syllables, thus enabling terse exchanges, signaling physical actions, or providing characters with dramatic silences.
- He gives other lines more syllables than is usual, causing such verse lines to overflow.
- Shakespeare also uses clipped vowel sounds to increase the rate of a word, phrase, or line and long vowel sounds to slow the rate of a word, phrase, or line.
- The phrasing of Shakespeare's words must be determined by meaning and imagery, not by artificially pausing at the end of each line of verse or by removing all pauses from his dialogue.

Exercises

SOLO EXERCISE 8.1

After gaining more confidence in your scansion skills by scanning short sections of Shakespeare's verse dialogue, try scanning entire speeches and scenes. Here are a few suggestions:

Hamlet's soliloquy that begins, "O, what a rogue and peasant slave am I" *(Hamlet, 2, 2, 550–605)*

Helena's soliloquy that begins, "O, were that all!" *(All's Well That Ends Well, 1, 1, 79–98)*

The Chorus's soliloquy that opens *Henry V*

The scene between Brutus and Cassius in *Julius Caesar (4, 3, 1–123)*

The scene between Oberon and Titania in *A Midsummer Night's Dream (2, 1, 60–145)*

The second scene between Olivia and Viola in *Twelfth Night (3, 1, 93–164)*

There are hundreds more speeches and scenes from which to choose. Ask and answer the same questions as in Solo Exercise 7.1. Are the rhythms rough or smooth? Slow or fast? Heavy or light? Are the rhythms terse? Do they overflow? Are there missing syllables or missing feet? If so, are pauses or physical actions appropriate? Do the rhythms fluctuate? What do the rhythms tell you about the dramatic action? Ask why after each of these questions.

NOTES

1. Although I have scanned lines 113–116, it is very possible that these lines are written in prose. Line 114 is particularly problematic. Regardless of whether the lines are prose or verse, the short lines allow brief exchanges between the two characters.
2. Phrasing is discussed in detail in Chapter 11 under the heading "Diagramming the Text."

CHAPTER 9

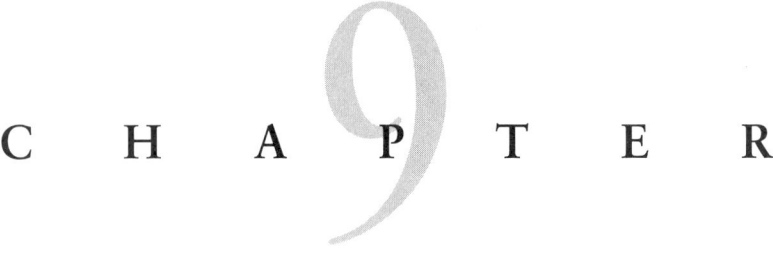

Exploring Shakespeare's Prose

(We three meet again at the coffee shop later that week.)

JOE: Shakespeare didn't write only in verse, as you know. **Prose** is defined as *speech or writing without rhythmic structure. The ordinary form of written or spoken language, without metrical structure.* More than twenty percent of Shakespeare's dramatic dialogue is written in prose.

THE PURPOSES OF PROSE

LIZ: Why did he write in prose?
JOE: Your question does not have a simple, straightforward answer. In the first fourteen plays that Shakespeare wrote, there was a fairly clear distinction between verse dialogue and prose dialogue (Wright, *Shakespeare's Metrical Art*, p. 109). For one thing, *verse was for the highborn and prose was for the lowborn.* For another, *verse was for dramatic dialogue and prose for comedy.* But even in his earliest plays, Shakespeare didn't always stick to the rules. In *The Two Gentlemen of Verona*, the noble Proteus speaks prose with his friend's servant, Speed. Speed, although lowborn, joins Proteus in speaking verse at the beginning of the scene. Here is a portion of that scene, with prose dialogue in bold print:

206

SPEED: Sir Proteus, save you! Saw you my master?
PROTEUS: But now he parted hence, to embark for Milan.
SPEED: Twenty to one then he is shipp'd already,
　And I have play'd the sheep in losing him.
PROTEUS: Indeed, a sheep doth very often stray,
　An if the shepherd be a while away.
SPEED: You conclude that my master is a shepherd, then, and I a sheep?
PROTEUS: I do.
SPEED: Why then, my horns are his horns, whether I wake or sleep.
PROTEUS: A silly answer, and fitting well a sheep.
SPEED: This proves me still a sheep.
PROTEUS: True; and thy master a shepherd.
SPEED: Nay, that I can deny by a circumstance.
PROTEUS: It shall go hard but I'll prove it by another.
SPEED: The shepherd seeks the sheep, and not the sheep the shepherd; but I seek my master, and my master seeks not me: therefore I am no sheep.
PROTEUS: The sheep for fodder follow the shepherd; the shepherd for food follows not the sheep: thou for wages followest thy master; thy master for wages follows not thee: therefore thou art a sheep.
SPEED: Such another proof will make me cry "baa."
　　　　(*The Two Gentlemen of Verona* 1, 1, 70–93)[1]

As I stated, both Proteus, who is highborn, and Speed, who is lowborn, begin the scene in verse. However, beginning with Speed's line "You conclude that my master is a shepherd then, and I a sheep?," both characters switch to prose. On hearing Speed's line, the Elizabethan audience knew that they were about to see and hear a section of verbal wit and wordplay. In other words, the two characters take a break from the storyline to engage in the Elizabethan equivalent of a vaudeville act. Because the section is low comedy, it is written in prose.

If the dialogue is bawdy or of a lower order, it will often be in prose. In this section from *Henry IV Part 1*, Prince Hal and Falstaff discuss picking pockets:

PRINCE: Where shall we take a purse tomorrow, Jack?
FALSTAFF: 'Zounds, where thou wilt, lad, I'll make one, an' I do not, call me villain and baffle me.
PRINCE: I see a good amendment of life in thee, from praying to purse-taking.
FALSTAFF: Why, Hal, 'tis my vocation, Hal, 'tis no sin for a man to labor in his vocation.　　　　(*Henry IV Part 1*, 1, 2, 99–105)

SAM: Does Shakespeare switch from verse to prose and from prose to verse for a specific reason?
JOE: Yes, but I would say for specific *reasons*. Shakespeare may shift from verse to prose, or from prose to verse, in order to signify a change in the speaker's intent, a change in subject matter, tone, or mood, or for some other purpose. Each must be examined on a case-by-case basis.

In *Hamlet,* for instance, Ophelia, under orders from her father Polonius, seeks out Hamlet in order to return love tokens that he gave to her. Hamlet has just discovered from the ghost of his murdered father that Claudius, his father's brother, is responsible for the crime. Hamlet, who is in love with Ophelia, may wish to remove her from harm. Feigning madness, he insults and frightens her, perhaps in order to ensure that she will remain far from him and danger. Another possibility is that Hamlet verbally attacks Ophelia because he feels that she has betrayed him by allying with Polonius and Claudius. Here is the opening section of that scene. Again, the prose dialogue appears in bold print:

HAMLET: —Soft you now!
 The fair Ophelia! Nymph, in thy orisons
 Be all my sins remember'd.
OPHELIA: Good my lord,
 How does your honour for this many a day?
HAMLET: I humbly thank you; well, well, well.
OPHELIA: My lord, I have remembrances of yours,
 That I have longed long to re-deliver;
 I pray you, now receive them.
HAMLET: No, not I;
 I never gave you aught.
OPHELIA: My honour'd lord, you know right well you did;
 And, with them, words of so sweet breath composed
 As made the things more rich: their perfume lost,
 Take these again; for to the noble mind
 Rich gifts wax poor when givers prove unkind.
 There, my lord.
HAMLET: **Ha, ha! are you honest?**
OPHELIA: **My lord?**
HAMLET: **Are you fair?**
OPHELIA: **What means your lordship?**
HAMLET: **That if you be honest and fair, your honesty should admit no discourse to your beauty.**
OPHELIA: **Could beauty, my lord, have better commerce than with honesty?**
HAMLET: **Ay, truly; for the power of beauty will sooner transform honesty from what it is to a bawd than the force of honesty can translate beauty into his likeness: this was sometime a paradox, but now the time gives it proof. I did love you once.**
OPHELIA: **Indeed, my lord, you made me believe so.**
HAMLET: **You should not have believed me; for virtue cannot so inoculate our old stock but we shall relish of it: I loved you not.**
OPHELIA: **I was the more deceived.**

HAMLET: Get thee to a nunnery: why wouldst thou be a breeder
of sinners?   *(Hamlet 3, 1, 87–121)*

Claudius and Polonius hide themselves in order to overhear the exchange between the two lovers. It is clear during the scene that Hamlet discovers that he and Ophelia are being watched because later in the scene he suddenly asks Ophelia, "Where is your father?" However, exactly when he comes to this knowledge is interpretive. The beginning of the scene is composed of formal verse that is polite and courtly. Ophelia agonizes over returning Hamlet's gifts and her verse dialogue is constrained but anguished. Suddenly, the entire tenor of the scene shifts with Hamlet's line "Ha, ha! are you honest?" in which he changes from verse to prose. The dialogue here shifts from polite and controlled to aggressive and hostile. Ophelia joins Hamlet in speaking prose for the remainder of the scene until Ophelia's verse soliloquy after Hamlet's exit. Why this sudden shift? There are several possibilities. First, this may be where Hamlet hears a noise and realizes that they are being watched. If so, it would inform him that Ophelia is even more entangled in this dangerous web than he first suspected. Knowing this, he may shift into "high gear" in order to alienate Ophelia for her own good or he may wish to punish her for her treachery. He would also wish to reinforce his appearance of madness before Polonius and Claudius. A madman would be more likely to speak prose than verse. Another possibility is that Hamlet is moved by Ophelia's verse dialogue, which ends with "Rich gifts wax poor when givers prove unkind." He may have the impulse to kiss her or to reveal his true feelings for her. Realizing that this would be a selfish and dangerous thing to do, he alters his course and pushes strongly to alienate Ophelia for her own well-being.

In *Much Ado about Nothing,* Don Pedro and his followers, Benedick and Claudio, have recently arrived in Messina. Claudio is smitten with Hero, the daughter of Leonato, the governor of Messina. At the beginning of this section of the play, Don Pedro and Claudio have been joking with Benedick about his aversion to marriage. This playful kidding is in prose and continues until Benedick's exit. However, when Don Pedro and Claudio are alone, the dialogue switches to verse. The tone of the scene is more serious in this section, in which Claudio seeks the assistance of his boss in wooing Hero:

DON PEDRO: Well, you will temporize with the hours. In the meantime, good Signior Benedick, repair to Leonato's: commend me to him and tell him I will not fail him at supper; for indeed he hath made great preparation.
BENEDICK: I have almost matter enough in me for such an embassage; and so I commit you—
CLAUDIO: To the tuition of God: From my house, if I had it—
DON PEDRO: The sixth of July: Your loving friend, Benedick.
BENEDICK: Nay, mock not, mock not. The body of your discourse is sometime guarded with fragments, and the guards are but slightly basted on neither: ere you flout old ends any further, examine your conscience: and so I leave you.

[Exit]

CLAUDIO: My liege, your highness now may do me good.
DON PEDRO: My love is thine to teach: teach it but how,
  And thou shalt see how apt it is to learn
  Any hard lesson that may do thee good.
CLAUDIO: Hath Leonato any son, my lord?
DON PEDRO: No child but Hero; she's his only heir.
  Dost thou affect her, Claudio?
CLAUDIO: O, my lord,
  When you went onward on this ended action,
  I look'd upon her with a soldier's eye,
  That liked, but had a rougher task in hand
  Than to drive liking to the name of love:
  But now I am return'd and that war-thoughts
  Have left their places vacant, in their rooms
  Come thronging soft and delicate desires,
  All prompting me how fair young Hero is,
  Saying I lik'd her ere I went to wars.
DON PEDRO: Thou wilt be like a lover presently
  And tire the hearer with a book of words.
  If thou dost love fair Hero, cherish it,
  And I will break with her and with her father,
  And thou shalt have her. Was't not to this end
  That thou began'st to twist so fine a story?
CLAUDIO: How sweetly you do minister to love,
  That know love's grief by his complexion!
            (Much Ado about Nothing 1, 1, 274–313)

The prose dialogue that begins the above excerpt is the tail end of a section in which the three noble soldiers relax, unwind, and have fun with one another. They playfully mock each other concerning women and marriage. It is "guy talk," if you will. When Benedick exits, Claudio knows that he can now approach Don Pedro about a very serious subject, his love for the young maiden, Hero. The tone of the language shifts here. It is the language of a man in love (much like Romeo). It is filled with rich imagery and strong emotion. Don Pedro's language is more down-to-earth, but speaking verse reflects that he is more than willing to help his young protégé achieve his goal of winning Hero.

In *Othello*, Emilia tries to cheer up Desdemona after Othello's brutal display of anger at Desdemona's supposed infidelity. The section begins with both characters speaking in verse. When Emilia's talk turns bawdy she switches to prose. But as Desdemona's need for Emilia increases, Emilia returns to verse in order to be more helpful to her friend and employer:

DESDEMONA: O, these men, these men!
Dost thou in conscience think,—tell me, Emilia,—
That there be women do abuse their husbands
In such gross kind?
EMILIA: There be some such, no question.
DESDEMONA: Wouldst thou do such a deed for all the world?
EMILIA: Why, would not you?
DESDEMONA: No, by this heavenly light!
EMILIA: Nor I neither by this heavenly light;
I might do't as well i' the dark.
DESDEMONA: Wouldst thou do such a deed for all the world?
EMILIA: The world's a huge thing: it is a great price
For a small vice.
DESDEMONA: In troth, I think thou wouldst not.
EMILIA: **In troth, I think I should; and undo't when I had done. Marry, I would not do such a thing for a joint-ring, nor for measures of lawn, nor for gowns, petticoats, nor caps, nor any petty exhibition; but for the whole world,—why, who would not make her husband a cuckold to make him a monarch? I should venture purgatory for't.**
DESDEMONA: Beshrew me, if I would do such a wrong
For the whole world.
EMILIA: **Why the wrong is but a wrong i' the world: and having the world for your labour, tis a wrong in your own world, and you might quickly make it right.**
DESDEMONA: I do not think there is any such woman.
EMILIA: **Yes, a dozen; and as many to the vantage as would store the world they played for.**
But I do think it is their husbands' faults
If wives do fall: say that they slack their duties,
And pour our treasures into foreign laps,
Or else break out in peevish jealousies,
Throwing restraint upon us; or say they strike us,
Or scant our former having in despite;
Why, we have galls, and though we have some grace,
Yet have we some revenge. Let husbands know
Their wives have sense like them: they see and smell
And have their palates both for sweet and sour,
As husbands have. What is it that they do
When they change us for others? Is it sport?
I think it is: and doth affection breed it?

> I think it doth: is't frailty that thus errs?
> It is so too: and have not we affections,
> Desires for sport, and frailty, as men have?
> Then let them use us well: else let them know,
> The ills we do, their ills instruct us so.
>
> DESDEMONA: Good night, good night: heaven me such uses send,
> Not to pick bad from bad, but by bad mend!
>
> *[Exeunt]*
>
> (Othello 4, 3, 60–105)

While Desdemona speaks in verse throughout, Emilia switches from verse to prose and back again. The reason for this is that Emilia's first attempt to bolster Desdemona is an "earthy" one and is therefore in prose. She tells her that infidelity is not necessarily a bad thing. Some women, Emilia included, would "venture purgatory" in order to help their husbands' careers. In this way, Emilia attempts to instill confidence in Desdemona by defending womankind. Emilia knows full well that Desdemona is faithful. But she tells her that women who cheat on their husbands do it for different reasons than do men. While men are selfish, women are unselfish. They don't engage in extramarital affairs for personal pleasure, but rather for the good of their spouses. When Desdemona refuses to believe that such women exist, Emilia switches to verse to make it clear that Desdemona is being abused by Othello and must stand up to her husband. It is a "wake up and smell the coffee" type of speech that Emilia speaks at the end of this scene. The imagery and intention are concentrated, the rhythms formal and structured. Phrases like "and though we have some grace, / Yet have we some revenge" are emotionally loaded and are meant to help Desdemona acquire the emotional strength to stand up for herself when Othello returns.

LIZ: You say that Emilia's last speech is in verse because the imagery and intention are concentrated. Is prose speech incapable of containing strong imagery and intention?

JOE: No. Prose dialogue can contain very strong imagery and intent. *It is a mistake to think of prose dialogue as being somehow inferior to verse.* Particularly in his middle and later plays, Shakespeare's prose can contain strong, poetic imagery. In *Henry V*, King Henry uses both verse and prose. At 3 A.M. on the day of the upcoming battle of Agincourt, in which the French outnumber the British by more than ten to one, King Henry moves about his camp of soldiers in disguise in order to discover the morale of his men. In this excerpt, he approaches a group of men talking around a campfire:

WILLIAMS: We see yonder the beginning of the day, but I think we shall never see the end of it. Who goes there?

KING HENRY V: A friend.

WILLIAMS: Under what captain serve you?

KING HENRY V: Under Sir Thomas Erpingham.

WILLIAMS: A good old commander and a most kind gentleman: I pray you, what thinks he of our estate?

KING HENRY V: Even as men wrecked upon a sand, that look to be washed off the next tide.

BATES: He hath not told his thought to the king?

KING HENRY V: No; nor it is not meet he should. For, though I speak it to you, I think the king is but a man, as I am: the violet smells to him as it doth to me: the element shows to him as it doth to me; all his senses have but human conditions: his ceremonies laid by, in his nakedness he appears but a man; and though his affections are higher mounted than ours, yet, when they stoop, they stoop with the like wing. Therefore when he sees reason of fears, as we do, his fears, out of doubt, be of the same relish as ours are: yet, in reason, no man should possess him with any appearance of fear, lest he, by showing it, should dishearten his army.

(Henry V 4, 1, 90–112)

Henry's speech, which ends this excerpt, is heartfelt and well spoken. He tells his men that the king is a man as they are, and as such, experiences fear and apprehension concerning the upcoming battle. However, it is the responsibility of all men, including the king, to allay their fears and prepare for victory against the French. Shakespeare chooses prose for Henry here because, being in disguise, prose speech helps him to blend in with his men.

Now let's look at a section of a scene from *Twelfth Night*:

OLIVIA: Give us the place alone: we will hear this divinity.
[Exeunt Maria and Attendants] Now, sir, what is your text?

VIOLA: Most sweet lady,—

OLIVIA: A comfortable doctrine, and much may be said of it. Where lies your text?

VIOLA: In Orsino's bosom.

OLIVIA: In his bosom! In what chapter of his bosom?

VIOLA: To answer by the method, in the first of his heart.

OLIVIA: O, I have read it: it is heresy. Have you no more to say?

VIOLA: Good madam, let me see your face.

OLIVIA: Have you any commission from your lord to negotiate with my face? You are now out of your text: but we will draw the curtain and show you the picture. Look you, sir, such a one I was this present: *[Unveiling]* is't not well done?

VIOLA: Excellently done, if God did all.

OLIVIA: 'Tis in grain, sir; 'twill endure wind and weather.

VIOLA: 'Tis beauty truly blent, whose red and white
Nature's own sweet and cunning hand laid on:
Lady, you are the cruelest she alive,
If you will lead these graces to the grave
And leave the world no copy.

OLIVIA: O, sir, I will not be so hard-hearted; I will give out divers schedules of my beauty: it shall be inventoried, and every particle and utensil labelled to my will: as, item, two lips, indifferent red; item, two grey eyes, with lids to them; item, one neck, one chin, and so forth. Were you sent hither to praise me?

VIOLA: I see you what you are, you are too proud;
But, if you were the devil, you are fair.
My lord and master loves you: O, such love
Could be but recompensed, though you were crown'd
The nonpareil of beauty!

OLIVIA: How does he love me?

VIOLA: With adorations, fertile tears,
With groans that thunder love, with sighs of fire.

OLIVIA: Your lord does know my mind; I cannot love him:
Yet I suppose him virtuous, know him noble,
Of great estate, of fresh and stainless youth;
In voices well divulged, free, learn'd and valiant;
And in dimension and the shape of nature
A gracious person: but yet I cannot love him;
He might have took his answer long ago.

VIOLA: If I did love you in my master's flame,
With such a suffering, such a deadly life,
In your denial I would find no sense;
I would not understand it.

OLIVIA: Why, what would you?

VIOLA: Make me a willow cabin at your gate,
And call upon my soul within the house;
Write loyal cantons of contemned love
And sing them loud even in the dead of night;
Halloo your name to the reverberate hills
And make the babbling gossip of the air
Cry out "Olivia!" O, You should not rest
Between the elements of air and earth,
But you should pity me!

OLIVIA: You might do much. What is your parentage?

VIOLA: Above my fortunes, yet my state is well:
I am a gentleman.

OLIVIA: Get you to your lord;
I cannot love him: let him send no more;

> Unless, perchance, you come to me again,
> To tell me how he takes it. Fare you well:
>
> *(Twelfth Night 1, 5, 218–282)*

The first 238 lines of this scene (217 of which are not printed here) are spoken in prose. In this scene, Olivia and Viola meet for the first time. As I explained earlier, Viola is disguised as a young man called Cesario, and is sent to woo Olivia in the name of her master, Orsino. Shakespeare chooses prose for Olivia at the top of the scene because Olivia does not take "Cesario" very seriously and disdains anything and anyone associated with Orsino, whose affections she abhors. Shakespeare chooses prose for Viola because she is nervous and unconfident in her ability to carry out her mission. As the scene progresses, Olivia reveals various aspects of her personality as well as revealing her physical features to Viola. This knowledge gives Viola the confidence she needs to begin pursuing specific ways to woo Olivia for her master, Orsino. She speaks her first words of verse in the scene soon after Olivia removes her veil ("'Tis beauty truly blent, . . . / And leave the world no copy"). Not only is Viola's verse about Olivia's beauty, but it is also elegant, elevated, "classy" language. Although Olivia now begins to be impressed with this "young man," she continues with disdainful prose. However, she is soon won over and Shakespeare has her join Viola in speaking verse. He even chooses to have the two characters share lines of verse on occasion. Although Olivia begins to be smitten with Viola soon after Viola's first words in verse, it is Viola's famous "Make me a willow cabin at your gate" speech that causes Olivia to fall head over heels for "Cesario."

THE ACTOR'S USE OF PROSE

SAM: How should an actor approach working on prose dialogue?
JOE: Much in the same manner as for verse dialogue. The only difference is that, with prose, there are no rhythmic rules to provide the actor with clues to operative words, pacing, dramatic action, and so on.
LIZ: That's quite a handicap, isn't it?
JOE: Not necessarily. I certainly hope that I have made it clear in the previous chapters on verse that it is an invaluable acting tool. However, while not formal, prose dialogue also has very specific rhythms. The actor should discover these rhythms by finding the operative words in prose dialogue, giving such words the strongest emphasis, and working the rhythm of the dialogue around those strong stresses. These stresses will carry the most powerful imagery. The rules on operative words and the structure of prose speeches are the same as those of verse speeches. Moreover, *it is important to ascertain where and why Shakespeare switches from verse to prose and from prose to verse.* Doing so will provide the actor with invaluable information about the nature of the scene and how to act it. As our examples show, these reasons vary and are sometimes interpretive, but the answers can always be found by examining the given circumstances of the scene and play.

And now that we've covered verse and prose in general, you should know about the specific figures of speech and other literary devices that Shakespeare employed. We'll talk about those tomorrow.

SUMMARY

In this chapter, Joe, Sam, and Liz explored the ways that Shakespeare used prose as an effective alternative to verse.

- Prose is writing or speaking that lacks a formal rhythm.
- More than twenty percent of Shakespeare's dramatic dialogue is written in prose.
- Often, the lower classes in Shakespeare's plays (rustic characters, clowns, servants, and commoners) speak prose.
- Sometimes the subject matter of prose is comic, bawdy, or relaxed.
- However, Shakespeare often writes prose that is filled with rich imagery and is spoken by nobility.
- Ascertaining where and why Shakespeare switches from verse to prose or from prose to verse can provide the actor with valuable clues about a scene.

EXERCISES

SOLO EXERCISE 9.1

Begin by reading those plays of Shakespeare in which prose is the rule rather than the exception. Such plays include *The Merry Wives of Windsor* (eighty-seven percent prose) and *Much Ado about Nothing* (seventy-two percent prose). Why do you think Shakespeare chose prose as the predominant form for these plays?

Identify the dialogue in the plays that is spoken in verse. Why do you think he switches from prose to verse in these sections? What does it tell you about the characters? Their situations? Is the imagery of the prose dialogue of a different ilk from the imagery of the verse dialogue? If so, in what way is it different? Are there sections of prose dialogue that are eloquent and rich in imagery? If so, why do you think Shakespeare chose prose to express this imagery?

Now move on to plays in which Shakespeare's characters speak equally in both forms and ask and answer the same questions. Such plays include *As You Like It* (fifty-four percent prose), *Henry IV Part 2* (forty-nine percent prose), and *All's Well That Ends Well* (forty-six percent prose).

NOTES

1. Throughout this chapter, I have ignored the lineation (how lines are ordered in my copy of Shakespeare's Complete Works) of all prose dialogue. Instead, I have used a word-wrapping technique for easier reading.

CHAPTER 10

EXPLORING SHAKESPEARE'S RHETORICAL FIGURES

(We meet at the coffee shop the following morning.)

JOE: Before we begin today, consider this: In his book *Acting Shakespeare,* Bertram Joseph states that "while Shakespeare is a powerful dramatist, he is no less a superb poet. . . . The person who does not respond to his plays fully as poetry is at the same time unable to respond to them fully as drama" (p. 1). He goes on to say that "with Shakespeare . . . character and poetry are so inseparable that a failure to communicate the poetic quality will be accompanied by a failure to penetrate the living depths of the character" (p. 2).

We have examined in depth how Shakespeare's characters use the metrical form of poetry to help express intentions that are strongly rooted in emotion. We have also examined how heightened language is used by Shakespeare in both verse and prose to help communicate imagery and meaning. We will now examine how Shakespeare utilized rhetoric in his dramatic dialogue.

RHETORIC DEFINED

JOE: You'll recall that our definition of the *function* of poetry is "language adapted to stir the imagination and emotions." Our definition of the *form* of poetry is "composition in verse or metrical language: usually also with choice of elevated words and figurative uses." The last part of that definition, "figurative uses," is the subject we will now explore. The figurative use of language is an essential part of Elizabethan rhetoric.

SAM: What exactly is rhetoric?

JOE: The OED defines **rhetoric** (pronounced "RET-uh-rik") as follows: "1. The art of using language so as to persuade or influence others. 2. Speech or writing expressed in terms calculated to persuade. Shakespeare's dialogue cannot be fully grasped by the actor without at least a working knowledge of the playwright's use of rhetoric and rhetorical figures, also known as rhetorical devices. Volumes have been written on the subject, but our aim here is to examine some of the most common figures used during Shakespeare's time."

RHETORICAL FIGURES

LIZ: What are "figures"?

JOE: **Rhetorical figures** or devices are more commonly known as **figures of speech**. The OED defines *figure* as "a form of expression deviating from the normal arrangement or use of words, which are adopted in order to give beauty, variety or force to a composition." Simply put, a figure is "a form of speech artfully varied from common usage" (Corbett and Connors, *Classical Rhetoric for the Modern Student,* p. 379). Further:

> Because figures can render our thoughts vividly concrete, they help us to communicate with our audience clearly and effectively; because they stir emotional responses, they can carry truth, in Wordsworth's phrase, "alive into the heart by passion"; and because they elicit admiration for the eloquence of the speaker, they can exert a powerful ethical appeal. (Corbett and Connors, p. 378)

Shakespeare's characters use rhetorical figures in order to persuade others through logical reasoning, emotional inducement, and by impressing others with their powers of speech. Sister Miriam Joseph, in her book *Rhetoric in Shakespeare's Time,* makes the following point:

> Rhetoric, as Aristotle defines it, is the faculty of observing in any given case the available means of persuasion, and since the orator addresses a popular audience including untrained thinkers, his appeal is threefold: to their reason (logos), to their feelings (pathos), and to their confidence in his character, that is, in his virtue, competence, courtesy, good sense, good will (ethos). (p. 19)

There are two categories of rhetorical figures: *schemes and tropes*. A scheme is defined as "any of the recognized modes of deviating from the ordinary arrangement of words for the sake of effectiveness or beauty of expression." A **trope** is "a figure of speech which consists in the use of a word or phrase in a sense other than that which is proper to it." In other words, schemes have to do with the unconventional *arrangement* of words, while tropes have to do with the unconventional *meaning* of words. *Most of Shakespeare's figures involve balance, repetition (of sounds, words,* *phrases, ideas, and themes), and/or sensory properties.* Scansion is a form of rhetoric. Can either of you tell me which of the two categories it would fall under?

Liz: Wouldn't it be a scheme?

Joe: Yes, because scansion concerns itself with the unconventional *arrangement* of words. Scansion is a rhythmic scheme that artificially arranges the words in a sentence or phrase in order to fit a specific rhythm. Rhyming verse is not only a rhythmic scheme, but also a rhyme scheme that artificially arranges words to create end rhymes (the word "artificial" has positive rather than negative connotations in rhetoric). Because rhetoric is *speech that is calculated to persuade,* all rhetorical figures are purposeful. The utilization of these figures by your character increases your chances of getting what you want from those around you.

Liz: Are figures of speech only found in Shakespeare's verse dialogue?

Joe: No. Although figures appear more often in verse dialogue, rhetorical figures also appear in Shakespeare's prose dialogue.

Sam: Will you give us some examples of figures of speech so that we can better understand what they are and how they are used?

Schemes

Joe: Of course. Let's begin with figures that fall under the category of schemes. A scheme, as we just learned, involves a deviation from the usual arrangement of words. Shakespeare's schemes are divided into schemes of *balance,* schemes of *unusual word order,* schemes of *omission,* and schemes of *repetition* (Burton, Gideon O. *Silva Rhetoricae,* Brigham Young University, 2000; as well as Corbett and Connors, "Classical Rhetoric for the Modern Student"). Let's take a look at these categories.

Schemes of Balance

Joe: Among the schemes of balance, let's look first at parallelism. **Parallelism** is a figure of speech that involves recurring syntactical similarity. In this figure, words, phrases, or clauses are structured similarly. Here are two examples of *parallelism of words:*

>   Cry woe, destruction, ruin and decay: *(Richard II, 3, 2, 102)*

>   Overthrows thy joys, friends, fortune, and thy state
>   *(Richard II, 3, 2, 72)*

Now here are examples of *parallelism of phrases* and *clauses:*

>   I live with bread like you, feel want,
>   Taste grief, need friends; subjected thus,
>   *(Richard II, 3, 2, 175–176)*

The parallel phrases above are underlined (throughout this chapter I'll continue to use underlining to point out the appropriate, words, phrases, or letters under discussion.)

> How some have been depos'd, some slain in war,
> Some haunted by the ghosts they have depos'd,
> Some poison'd by their wives, some sleeping kill'd,
> (*Richard II*, 3, 2, 157–159)
>
> Why should he call her whore? Who keeps her company?
> What place? What time? What form? What likelihood?
> (*Othello*, 4, 2, 137–138)

Another scheme of balance, **isocolon** (pronounced eye-so-CO-lon) is a type of parallelism in which similarly structured elements have the same length of syllables and words. For example:

> Instance, O instance, strong as Pluto's gates, . . .
> Instance, O instance, strong as heav'n itself,
> (*Troilus and Cressida*, 5, 2, 153 &155)

> O'er courtiers' knees, that dream on cour'sies straight;
> O'er lawyers' fingers, who straight dream on fees;
> O'er ladies' lips, who straight on kisses dream,
> (*Romeo and Juliet*, 1, 4, 72–74)

Parallelism, including isocolon, shows that each word, phrase, or clause spoken is of equal importance. It also adds balance, a repeated rhythm and clarity to the dialogue.

On the other hand, **antithesis** is a contrast or opposition of thoughts, usually in two phrases, clauses, or sentences.[1] For example:

> Not that I loved Caesar less, but that I loved Rome more.
> (*Julius Caesar* 3, 2, 21–22)

> And thus the native hue of resolution
> Is sicklied o'er with the pale cast of thought,
> (*Hamlet*, 3, 1, 83–84)

Antithesis establishes a clear, contrasting relationship between two ideas or emotions. In this way complex concepts can be expressed clearly, succinctly, and powerfully.

Schemes of Unusual Word Order

JOE: The next category is schemes of unusual word order. Our first example, **anastrophe** (pronounced "uh-NAS-truh-fee"), is the inversion of natural word order. For example:

> The barge she sat in, like a burnish'd throne,
> Burnt on the water. The poop was beaten gold,
> <u>Purple the sails</u>, and so perfumed that
> > *(Antony and Cleopatra 2, 2, 191–193)*

> Be't as our gods will have't! it only stands
> <u>Our lives upon, to use our strongest hands.</u>
> > *(Antony and Cleopatra, 2, 1, 50–51)*

Anastrophe is used to procure emphasis. The beginning and ending of phrases, lines, and sentences are usually strong positions. In the example above, Enobarbus is describing Cleopatra's magnificent barge. The color of the sails is important because purple connotes royalty as well as a godlike quality. Therefore, "purple" is given special emphasis by inverting the normal word order.

> All causes shall give way. <u>I am in blood</u>
> <u>Stepp'd in so far</u> that, should I wade no more,
> Returning were as tedious as go o'er.   *(Macbeth, 3, 4, 135–137)*

In this example, Macbeth is in the middle of his "killing spree." He has murdered Duncan, has had Banquo murdered and is about to arrange the murder of Macduff's wife and sons. Here, Macbeth says in essence, "I have walked so far into this river of blood, that it would be just as difficult to turn back as it would to continue forward to the opposite bank." By inverting normal word order, Shakespeare places the important words "blood" and "stepped" in strong positions at the end and beginning of lines of verse. "Returning" and its antithesis "go o'er" are likewise in strong positions.

Now let's look at **parenthesis,** which is the insertion of a word or phrase within a sentence that interrupts the normal syntactical flow. For example:

> But what might you think,
> When I had seen this hot love on the wing—
> <u>As I perceiv'd it (I must tell you that)</u>
> <u>Before my daughter told me</u>—what might you,
> Or my dear Majesty your queen here, think,
> If I had play'd the desk or table-book,   *(Hamlet 2, 2, 131–136)*

The parenthesis is underlined. Prior to the above dialogue, Polonius has read excerpts to Claudius and Gertrude from a love letter written by Hamlet to Polonius's daughter, Ophelia. He is appalled at the letter and thinks that it proves that Hamlet is mad. In the above lines, Polonius asks the king and queen in essence, "What would you have thought of me if I pretended not to notice the love between Hamlet and my daughter?" However, Polonius interrupts himself to editorialize on his own comments to the king and queen. He inserts a parenthesis to impress the king and queen with his powers of observation. A more complete paraphrase would be, "What would you have thought of me when I noticed this passionate love affair—*as I recognized the signs, I have to tell you that, even before my daughter told me*—what would you have thought of me, or what would the queen here have thought, if I just stood dumbly by and let the letters continue to be exchanged?"

>Yea, my gravity,
>Wherein—<u>let no man hear me</u>—I take pride,
>Could I, with boot, change for an idle plume,
>Which the air beats for vain. *(Measure for Measure, 2, 4, 9–12)*

The above is a portion of Angelo's soliloquy that we examined in Chapter 4. Here Angelo says that he would gladly exchange his dignified demeanor for indulgent, wanton behavior. The parenthesis, "let no man hear me" reveals that Angelo is both ashamed of his lustful feelings and fearful that his true nature will be discovered.

With parenthesis, "for a brief moment, we hear the author's voice, commenting, editorializing, and, for that reason, the sentence gets an emotional charge that it would otherwise not have" (Corbett and Connors, p. 385).

Schemes of Omission

JOE: **Ellipsis** is the omission of a word or words necessary for complete grammatical construction but understood in the context. For example:

>And he to England <u>shall along with you.</u> *(Hamlet, 3, 3, 4)*

>Are my discourses dull? <u>Barren my wit?</u>
>*(The Comedy of Errors, 1, 2, 91)*

The above examples of ellipses are also examples of anastrophe (unusual word order). And in the words of Corbett and Connors, "Ellipsis can be an artful and arresting means of securing economy of expression" (p. 387).

Asyndeton (pronounced "uh-SIN-duh-ton") is a figure of speech that omits conjunctions between words, phrases, or clauses. For example:

>To appoint myself in this vexation, sully
>The purity and whiteness of my sheets
>Which to preserve is sleep: which being spotted
>Is <u>goads, thorns, nettles, tails of wasps,</u>
>*(The Winter's Tale, 1, 2, 326–329)*

>Upon mine honor,
>Myself, my brother and this grieved count
><u>Did see her, hear her,</u> at that hour last night
>Talk with a ruffian at her chamber-window.
>*(Much Ado about Nothing, 4, 1, 88–91)*

Asyndeton gives a rushed or intense quality to the line. In the first example above, Leontes is obsessed with his wife's supposed infidelity. The figure of asyndeton in this instance is not rushed, but is extremely strong and intense. In the second example, the evil Don John accuses Hero unjustly of infidelity. He uses asyndeton to give a hurried, profound quality to his accusation.

Polysyndeton[2] (pronounced "poly-SIN-duh-ton") is the opposite of asyndeton. In other words, rather than being a scheme of *omission,* polynsyndeton is the insertion of many conjunctions between words or clauses. For example:

> ROSALINE: That same Berowne I'll torture ere I go.
> How I would make him fawn, <u>and</u> beg, <u>and</u> seek,
> O that I knew he were but in by th' week!
> <u>And</u> wait the season, <u>and</u> observe the times,
> <u>And</u> spend his prodigal wits in bootless rhymes,
> <u>And</u> shape his service wholly to my device,
> <u>And</u> make him proud to make me proud that jests!
> *(Love's Labor's Lost, 5, 2, 60–66)*

The effect of polysyndeton is that it slows the rhythm of the line. In the above example it gives special emphasis to the plethora of "tortures" that Rosaline has in store for the hapless Berowne.

Schemes of Repetition

JOE: Among the schemes of repetition, **alliteration** is the repetition of an initial sound, usually a consonant, in two or more words of a phrase or line. This figure helps to tie two or more words into a single image or related images. For example:

> O, what authority and show of truth
> <u>C</u>an <u>c</u>unning sin <u>c</u>over itself withal!
> *(Much Ado about Nothing, 4, 1, 35–36)*

> And grow <u>b</u>ig-<u>b</u>ellied <u>w</u>ith the <u>w</u>anton <u>w</u>ind:
> *(A Midsummer Night's Dream, 2 ,1, 129)*

Another scheme of repetition is **assonance**, the repetition of a sound, usually a vowel or diphthong, within two or more words of a phrase or line. For example:

> No, rather I abjure all r<u>oo</u>fs, and ch<u>oo</u>se
> To wage against the enmity o' th' air, *(King Lear, 2, 4, 208–209)*

> O, r<u>ea</u>son not the n<u>ee</u>d! our basest beggars *(King Lear, 2, 4, 264)*

As you can see from the second example above, it is not unusual for Shakespeare to use both assonance and alliteration in the same line (the beginning 'b' sounds in "basest" and "beggars"). Occasionally, Shakespeare will combine the two figures, using the same alliterative and assonant sound in two or more words.

For example:

> When we have laughed to see the sails conceive
> *(A Midsummer Night's Dream, 2, 1, 128)*

In the above line, the consonant 's' sound is alliterative in "see" and "sails" but assonant in the word "conceive." There is also an assonant "ee" vowel sound in the words "we," "see," and "conceive."

In addition to helping tie images together, the speaker can put a good deal of emotional life into the utterance of alliterative and assonant sounds. For instance, in the example given a little earlier, which begins with "O, what authority and show of truth . . ." the actor playing Claudio can imbue the recurring alliterative "k" sound with the rage and jealousy that he feels toward Hero.

Schemes of repetition can involve not only repeating *sounds*, but *words* as well. For instance, **anaphora** (pronounced "uh-NAF-er-uh") is the repetition of the same word or group of words at or near the beginning of successive clauses, sentences, or lines. Here is an example:

> What must the King do now? Must he submit?
> The King shall do it. Must he be deposed?
> The King shall be contented. Must he lose
> The name of king? A' God's name let it go.
> *(Richard II, 3, 3, 143–146)*

The purpose of all figures of repetition is to reinforce or "drive home" an idea or emotion. With anaphora, not only do the words repeat, but the rhythm repeats as well. This produces a strong emotional effect. In the above example, King Richard attempts to instill guilt and shame into the treacherous Northumberland for his part in helping to overthrow him. Repetition of "must" and "king" reinforces the fact that no one save God has the right to demand anything of the rightful king.

In contrast to anastrophe is **epistrophe** (pronounced "i-PIS-truh-fee"), the repetition of the same word or group of words at the *end* of successive clauses, sentences, or lines. For example:

> Brutus and Caesar: what should be in that "Caesar"?
> *(Julius Caesar, 1, 2, 142)*

> And mine eternal jewel
> Given to the common enemy of man,
> To make them kings—the seeds of Banquo kings!
> *(Macbeth, 3, 1, 67–69)*

In the first example above, from *Julius Caesar*, Cassius uses epistrophe to reinforce the idea that "Caesar" is just a word. Caesar is simply a man as Brutus and Cassius are.

In the second example, from *Macbeth,* Macbeth ponders the prophecy of the three "weird sisters" who said that although Macbeth will be king, it is Banquo's progeny who will inherit the throne. The idea that he will die without an heir and will be succeeded by a long line of kings from Banquo's lineage grows larger and larger in the mind of Macbeth until he decides to murder Banquo in order to stop the prophecy from coming true. With epistrophe, not only are the word and rhythm repeated, but the word is also given special emphasis by being placed at the end of the phrase, clause, or sentence.

Epanalepsis (pronounced "eppa-nuh-LEP-sis") is the same word at or near both the beginning and end of a phrase, clause, or sentence. For example:

> Seems, madam? Nay it is, I know not "seems."
> *(Hamlet, 1, 2, 76)*

> Blood hath bought blood, and blows have answered blows;
> Strength match'd with strength, and power confronted power;
> *(King John, 2, 1, 329–330)*

Because the same word both begins and ends the phrase or line, epanalepsis can convey extremely strong emotion.

A related figure, **anadiplosis** (pronounced "anna-dih-PLOE-sis") occurs when the last word of one clause or sentence is repeated at or near the beginning of the next. For example:

> The love of wicked men converts to fear,
> That fear to hate, and hate turns one or both
> To worthy danger and deserved death.
> *(King Richard II, 5, 1, 66–68)*

Anadiplosis helps to link image to image, which assists with a logical progression of thought.

Climax[3] is the arrangement of words, phrases, or clauses in an order of increasing importance, often in parallel structure and thus a scheme of repetition. For example:

> Richard except, those whom we fight against
> Had rather have us win than him they follow:
> For what is he they follow? Truly, gentlemen,
> A bloody tyrant and a homicide;
> One rais'd in blood, and one in blood establish'd;
> One that made means to come by what he hath,
> And slaughter'd those that were the means to help him;
> A base foul stone, made previous by the foil
> Of England's chair, where he is falsely set;
> One that hath ever been God's enemy.
> *(Richard III, 5, 3, 243–252)*

> This she? No, this is Diomed's Cressida.
> If beauty have a soul, this is not she;
> If souls guide vows, if vows be sanctimonies,
> If sanctimony be the gods' delight,
> If there be rule in unity itself,
> This was not she.   *(Troilus and Cressida, 5, 2, 137–142)*

Climax is one of the most ubiquitous figures in Shakespeare. It permits an incremental build of imagery and emotion.

Antimetabole (pronounced "anti-muh-TAB-oh-lee") reverses the order of repeated words or phrases. For example:

> who mayst see
> Plainly as heaven sees earth and earth sees heaven,
> How I am galled—   *(The Winter's Tale, 1, 2, 314–316)*

In the above example, Leontes attempts to convince his skeptical assistant, Camillo, that his wife is unfaithful. He tells Camillo that his wife's infidelity should be as obvious and as clear to Camillo as the earth views heaven and heaven views the earth. "Antimetabole . . . repeats words in converse order, often thereby sharpening their sense" (Joseph, *Rhetoric in Shakespeare's Time*, p. 305). Often this shift in word order is accompanied by a shift in meaning. In *As You Like It*, Orlando, hungry and desperate, draws his sword on Duke Senior and his men in the forest of Arden and demands food. Duke Senior replies:

> What would you have? Your gentleness shall force
> More than your force move us to gentleness.
>   *(As You Like It, 2, 7, 102–103)*

In the first line, the word "force" means "urge" or "compel." In other words, the Duke tells Orlando, "Gentle behavior on your part will compel us to help you more than threats of violence will cause us to be gentle."

Polyptoton (pronounced "pol-ip-TOE-tun") is a figure that repeats words derived from the same root. For example:

> They would do that
> Which should undo more doing;
>   *(The Winter's Tale, 1, 2, 311–312)*

> The noble Brutus
> Hath told you Caesar was ambitious;
> If it were so, it was a grievous fault,
> And grievously hath Caesar answer'd it;
>   *(Julius Caesar, 3, 2, 77–80)*

>   I am a man
> More <u>sinn'd</u> against than <u>sinning</u>.   *(King Lear, 3, 2, 59–60)*

Whereas polyptoton plays on sound and meaning, **epizeuxis** (pronounced "epi-ZUKE-sis") provides emphasis through the repetition of a single word. For example:

>   O, <u>Lear, Lear, Lear!</u>
> Beat at this gate, that let thy folly in   *(King Lear, 1, 4, 270–271)*

> O <u>blood, blood, blood!</u>   *(Othello, 3, 3, 451)*

Epizeuxis is used most often at times of extreme emotion.

Tropes

JOE: Let's move on to tropes. A trope, as you will recall, involves a deviation from the usual meaning of a word. Most of Shakespeare's tropes can be categorized as either unconventional *reference to one thing as another, puns and wordplay, substitutions, semantic inversions,* or *overstatement* (Burton, Gideon O., *Silva Rhetoricae*).

Reference to One Thing as Another

JOE: A trope that we already talked about in Chapter 2 is **metaphor**,[4] a figure of speech containing an implied comparison, in which a word or phrase ordinarily and primarily used for one thing is applied to another. It is a comparison between two unlike things that does not use the words "like" or "as." For example:

>   throw thine eye
> On yon young boy. I'll tell thee what, my friend,
> <u>He is a very serpent</u> in my way,
> And wheresoe'er this foot of mine doth tread,
> He lies before me.   *(King John, 3, 3, 59–63)*

King John fears that Arthur, the rightful heir to the British throne, will take the crown from him. He uses metaphor to liken the young Arthur to a serpent who must be eliminated. Metaphor can be a strong emotional persuader. In the above example, the connotations of the word "serpent" are used by King John to liken the young Arthur to vermin, which must, by its nature, be eradicated.[5] As we can see by this example, metaphor also often contains physical imagery—sights, sounds, textures, even tastes and smells. Giving an idea or concept a physical reality can help to persuade others.

Now let's examine another example of metaphor. In *Henry V*, King Henry attempts to persuade the governor of the French town of Harfleur to surrender to his forces after a long, costly battle, in order to put a stop to the further bloodshed of French and English alike. Henry tells the governor what will happen if he refuses to surrender:

> The <u>gates of mercy</u> shall be all shut up,   *(Henry V, 3, 3, 10)*

The "gates of mercy" is a metaphor that utilizes sensory imagery. Listening to Henry's words, the governor can actually envision this "gate" being closed on the citizens of Harfleur. Henry can help sway the governor by utilizing these kinds of distinct physical realities.

Another trope that we mentioned briefly in Chapter 2 is **simile**, an explicit comparison using the words "like" or "as." For example:

> These <u>eyes, like lamps</u> whose wasting oil is spent,
> Wax dim, as drawing to their exigent;   *(Henry VI Part 1, 2, 5, 8–9)*

In the above example, Edward Mortimer tells his jailers that he is near death. He likens his eyes to two lamps that are about to burn out. Simile is closely related to metaphor. In our next example, Shakespeare also uses sensory imagery:

> If I must die,
> <u>I will encounter darkness as a bride,</u>
> And hug it in mine arms.   *(Measure for Measure, 3, 1, 82–84)*

In the above excerpt, Claudio reassures his sister Isabella that he is not afraid of his upcoming execution. As this example illustrates, simile and metaphor are not only strong emotional persuaders that contain physical imagery, but they are also extremely efficient. Claudio communicates more in this one sentence than he could with paragraphs of nonrhetorical language. In fact, most rhetorical figures are quite efficient.

Metonymy (pronounced "met-THAN-uh-mee") is the reference to something or someone by one of its attributes. For example:

> So high above his limits swells the rage
> Of Bullingbrook, covering your fearful land
> With hard bright <u>steel</u>, and <u>hearts</u> harder than steel.
> <u>White beards</u> have armed their thin and hairless scalps
> Against thy majesty: *(Richard II, 3, 2, 109–113)*

In the above example, "steel" stands for all of the weaponry that Bullingbrook's armies have in their possession. "Hearts" is used to represent the soldiers themselves, and "white beards" represents the old men who have taken up weapons against Richard. Like metaphor and simile, the sensory imagery of metonymy is an emotional persuader. The sensory imagery used in metonymy often communicates the "emotional essence" of the thing it describes. For example, "white beards" conjures up a stronger image than "old men."

Our next trope is **personification**, or referring to abstractions or inanimate objects as though they had human attributes. For example:

> O beware, my lord, of <u>jealousy</u>!
> It is <u>the green-eyed monster</u> which doth mock
> The meat it feeds on.   *(Othello, 3, 3, 165–167)*

In the above example, Iago speaks of jealousy as if it were a living, breathing beast. Personification is a strong emotional persuader because it gives concrete, animated imagery to inanimate objects, concepts, and emotions.

We examined *apostrophe* in Chapter 4. In an **apostrophe**, the character addresses a dead or absent person, inanimate object, or abstraction, usually with strong emotion. For example:

> O, pardon me, thou bleeding piece of earth,
> That I am meek and gentle with these butchers!
> Thou art the ruins of the noblest man
> That ever lived in the tide of times. *(Julius Caesar, 3, 1, 254–257)*

In the section of dialogue above, Mark Antony addresses the corpse of Julius Caesar immediately following his assassination by Brutus, Cassius, and their fellow conspirators. Mark Antony's address to the murdered Caesar is an impassioned one, in which he vows to avenge the homicide. Later in the same scene, Mark Antony uses apostrophe to sway the crowd:

> For Brutus, as you know, was Caesar's angel.
> Judge, O you gods, how dearly Caesar lov'd him!
> This was the most unkindest cut of all;
>   *(Julius Caesar, 3, 2, 181–183)*

Here, Mark Antony uses apostrophe to convince the crowd that Caesar loved Brutus like a son. In this way, Brutus's part in the assassination is made to seem reprehensible. Apostrophe is closely related to personification and is designed to stir the emotions of the listener.

Puns and Wordplay

JOE: **Puns** are figures that play on words. Two types of puns are *antanaclasis* and *paronomasia*. **Antanaclasis** (pronounced "anta-NACK-luh-sis") is the repetition of a word with two different meanings. For example:

> That lie shall lie so heavy on my sword,
> That it shall render vengeance and revenge
>   *(Richard II, 4, 1, 66–67)*

In the first instance above, "lie" means "to tell a falsehood." In the second instance, "lie" means "to lay down onto."

Whereas antanaclasis repeats a word that has more than one meaning, **paronomasia**, (pronounced "para-noe-MAY-zhuh") involves words that sound alike but that differ in meaning. For example:

> But, for all this, thou shalt have as many dolors for thy daughters
> as thou canst tell in a year.   *(King Lear, 2, 4, 54–55)*

In the above sentence, the Fool's pun on "dolors" (sorrows) and "dollars" is a venomous, prophetic statement aimed at Lear for his foolishness in financially cutting off Cordelia, his only loving daughter, while giving all to the loveless Goneril and Regan. As you can see by these examples, Shakespeare's puns are rarely meant to be funny. They are most often ironic, cutting, or prophetic.

Another type of pun that is used extensively in Shakespeare is the dirty joke pun. This type of pun needs little discussion, as it is as popular today as it was in Shakespeare's time. However, as many of Shakespeare's bawdy puns are antiquated, we must rely on copious footnotes to alert us to their presence. One example of such a pun is found in *Measure for Measure*. Lucio, the "ne'er-do-well with a heart of gold," is maligning Duke Vincentio to a monk (who is actually the duke in disguise):

> The Duke (I say to thee again) would eat mutton on Fridays.
> *(Measure for Measure, 3, 2, 181)*

Here Lucio makes reference to the Roman Catholic practice of avoiding meat on Fridays. In Shakespeare's day, mutton was a slang term for a prostitute.[6]

Another type of wordplay is **onomatopoeia** (pronounced "ONNA-mah-tuh-PEE-yah"). Here, the playwright makes use of words whose sound echoes the sense. For example:

> Now entertain conjecture of a time
> When creeping murmur and the poring dark
> Fills the wide vessel of the universe.
> From camp to camp, through the foul womb of night,
> The hum of either army stilly sounds,
> That the fixed sentinels almost receive
> The secret whispers of each other's watch.
> *(Henry V, 4, Prol., 1–7)*

These are the first lines of a soliloquy spoken by the Chorus describing the English and French camps in the wee hours of the morning, before the battle of Agincourt. The Chorus describes the quiet whispers of the men in both camps. Words like "murmur" and "hum" imitate the sounds of whispering. Shakespeare also provides the Chorus with many "s" and "z" sounds, further echoing the soft whispers of the soldiers. There are also words that, while possibly not true onomatopoeia, have an onomatopoetic effect including "wide" (with its long vowel sound), "creeping," and "whispers." Onomatopoeia provides words with a texture of sound that underscores meaning. Like metaphor and simile, it also helps to create sensory imagery.

Substitution

JOE: Now we turn to tropes that are categorized as substitutions. **Anthimeria** (pronounced "ann-thuh-MER-ee-uh") is the substitution of one part of speech for another, as in a noun used as a verb. For example:

> Lord Angelo <u>dukes</u> it well in his absence; he puts transgression to't.
> *(Measure for Measure, 3, 2, 94)*

In the above excerpt, Lucio uses the noun "duke" as a verb. The reference is a sarcastic one.

> I'll <u>unhair</u> thy head.   *(Antony and Cleopatra, 2, 5, 64)*

> The thunder would not <u>peace</u> at my bidding
> *(King Lear 4, 6, 103)*

As you can see by these examples, anthimeria is a theatrical figure because it surprises the listener. Using a noun as a verb or a verb as a noun is unexpected and can help the speaker drive home a point.

Another form of substitution is **periphrasis** (pronounced "puh-RIFF-ruh-sis"). This trope uses a proper name for qualities associated with that name or uses a descriptive word or phrase for a proper name. For example:

> FALSTAFF: Truly, mine host, I must turn away some of my followers.
> HOST: Discard, bully <u>Hercules</u>, cashier; let them wag; trot, trot.
> FALSTAFF: I sit at ten pounds a week.
> HOST: Thou'rt an <u>emperor</u>—Caesar, Kaiser, and Vizier. I will entertain Bardolph; he shall draw, he shall tap. Said I well, bully <u>Hector</u>?
> FALSTAFF: Do so, good mine host.
> *(The Merry Wives of Windsor, 1, 3, 4–12)*

In the dialogue above, the Host of the Garter Inn compliments the vain Falstaff. By using names like "Hercules," "Caesar," and "Hector" (a valiant Trojan warrior), the Host effectively, efficiently, and dynamically communicates the myriad of qualities associated with these names: bravery, nobility, strength, and so on.

Semantic Inversions

JOE: The next group of tropes involves semantic invesions. Semantics, as you know, has to do with the meaning of words. Our first example is one we touched on in Chapter 2: the **rhetorical question,** a question asked, not for an answer, but for effect or to emphasize a point. For example:

> Did not great Julius bleed for justice' sake?
> What villain touch'd his body, that did stab
> And not for justice? What, shall one of us,
> That struck the foremost man of all this world
> But for supporting robbers, shall we now
> Contaminate our fingers with base bribes?

>   And sell the mighty space of our large honors
>   For so much trash as may be grasped thus?
>
>   *(Julius Caesar, 4, 1, 19–26)*

In the above dialogue, Brutus berates his friend Cassius for taking bribes in order to help fund the war against Mark Antony and Octavius Caesar. Brutus puts four successive rhetorical questions to Cassius in order to make the impassioned point that winning the war by unjust means betrays the justice that they sought by murdering Julius Caesar. Rhetorical questions are often used when the speaker is making an impassioned point. The silent, apparent answers to such questions resound in the mind of the listener, deepening their effect.

Irony is speaking in such a way as to imply the contrary of what one says, often for the purpose of derision, mockery, or jest. For example:

>   Here, under leave of Brutus and the rest
>   (For Brutus is an honorable man,
>   So are they all, all honorable men),
>   Come I to speak in Caesar's funeral.
>   He was my friend, faithful and just to me;
>   But Brutus says he was ambitious,
>   And Brutus is an honorable man.   *(Julius Caesar, 3, 2, 81–87)*

Mark Antony cleverly uses irony by referring to Brutus and his accomplices, who assassinated Caesar, as honorable men. As he continues his speech, praising Caesar and his selfless accomplishments on behalf of Rome, the irony rings more and more strongly.

Oxymoron is the combining of two normally opposite or contradictory terms. For example:

>   Good night, good night! Parting is such sweet sorrow,
>   *(Romeo and Juliet, 2, 2, 184)*

>   Beautiful tyrant! Fiend angelical!
>   Dove-feathered raven! Wolvish ravening lamb!
>   *(Romeo and Juliet, 3, 2, 75–76)*

Like the figure of anthimeria, oxymoron startles the listener because it is unexpected. It is also effective because the two apparently contradictory terms are in fact true and compatible. Juliet speaks both examples above. In the first excerpt, her love for Romeo does indeed make their separation "sweet sorrow." In the second excerpt, the Nurse has just told Juliet that Romeo has been banished for killing Tybalt, Juliet's cousin. Again, her seemingly contradictory statements about Romeo ring true.

Overstatement

JOE: The last trope we will examine is hyperbole. **Hyperbole** (pronounced hie-PUR-bo-lee) is the use of exaggerated terms for emphasis or heightened effect. For example:

> What would he do
> Had he the motive and the cue for passion
> That I have? <u>He would drown the stage with tears,</u>
> *(Hamlet, 2, 2, 560–562)*

Hamlet speaks the above lines after he sees an actor in a traveling company produce real tears onstage. Hamlet asks himself what would happen if the actor had a true cause for passion, as he has. He concludes that the actor would produce a torrent of tears. This exaggeration is used to express Hamlet's strong emotional turmoil as he struggles over whether to avenge the death of his murdered father.

THE ACTOR'S USE OF RHETORICAL FIGURES

SAM: Since we'll be encountering these figures in our acting, do you think we should memorize all their names?

JOE: You certainly don't need to. There were more than two hundred figures used in Shakespeare's time, sixty or seventy of which were used extensively by Renaissance writers. We certainly can't be expected to remember all their names. The definition and nature of each figure as well as why it is used is far more important than its name. Keep in mind that clever speakers utilized these figures long before they were given labels. Also, it is important to understand that all rhetorical figures are merely means to an end, rather than ends in themselves. Just as we actors need to view Shakespeare's dialogue as words chosen by our characters in the moment, so must we view Shakespeare's rhetorical figures as our characters' best means of expressing those words in order to achieve our objectives from those around us. In *Acting Shakespeare*, Bertram Joseph writes that Shakespeare "had been brought up in a living tradition in which it had become second nature for him to express himself by means of figures; they were not his aim, but expression through them was" (p. 22).

LIZ: It will take a good deal of time to become familiar with the figures and their purposes.

JOE: Yes, but it will be time well spent. It will take a good deal less time, however, to retain the fact that *most of Shakespeare's figures involve physical imagery, repetition, and balance.* Physical imagery is used to give concrete form to abstract concepts; remember our example of "the gates of mercy" from *Henry V*. Figures of repetition are used to reinforce and drive home an idea, action, or emotion. Figures of balance are often used to compare and contrast two opposing objects, ideas, or emotions. By keeping these larger rhetorical categories in mind, the individual figures become more easily assimilated. This will enable the actor to interpret Shakespeare's text more effectively—a topic that we'll take up next time we meet.

Summary

In this chapter, Joe, Liz, and Sam explore the various rhetorial devices that Shakespeare employed in his writing.

- Rhetoric is the art of using language to persuade or influence others. Shakespeare's characters use rhetoric extensively in his plays.
- Shakespeare's rhetoric usually manifests itself by means of figures. *Rhetorical figures* (or devices) are more commonly known as *figures of speech*. A figure deviates from the usual arrangement or use of words in order to sway others.
- Figures can persuade through *reason*, through *emotion*, or by *impressing the listener with our powers of speech*.
- There are two types of rhetorical figures: *schemes* and *tropes*. A scheme deviates from the usual *arrangement* of words. A trope deviates from the usual *meaning* of a word.
- Most of Shakespeare's figures involve *balance, repetition* (of sounds, words, phrases, ideas, or themes), and/or *sensory properties*.
- Shakespeare's schemes are divided into categories: schemes of *balance*, schemes of *unusual word order*, schemes of *omission*, and schemes of *repetition*.
- Shakespeare's tropes are also divided into categories: *reference to one thing as another, puns and wordplay, substitutions, semantic inversions,* and *overstatement*.
- Rhetorical language is more efficient than nonrhetorical language.
- Rhetorical figures are a means to an end, not an end in themselves. They are the forms that Shakespeare found best suited for the expression of our characters' desires, emotions, and actions.

Exercises

FOUR BASIC EXERCISES IN RHETORIC

Compliment/Insult. The following four exercises (Couple Exercises 10.1a–10.1d) are designed to give the actor experience at conceiving, processing, and expressing by means of rhetorical figures. Fortunately, we actors do not need to *write* rhetorically, but we do need to *speak* rhetorically. The rhetoric that we will speak, because Shakespeare penned it, is of the highest caliber. Our challenge, instead, is to practice gathering and expressing our thoughts rhetorically, as this is what the characters that inhabit his plays do.

All of these exercises are done between two scene partners. Actors sit comfortably facing one another. *Exercises should be about the character, not about the actor.* In other words, actor A does not compliment or insult actor B. Instead, the character that actor A is portraying compliments or insults the character that actor B is portraying. It is not vital that your use of these figures be of the highest artistic quality. The point of these exercises is to begin to *think and express rhetorically.*

When you feel comfortable exploring the rhetorical qualities of metaphor, repetition, and balance (by means of antithesis), try inventing compliments and insults based on omission, puns, and scrambled word order.

COUPLE EXERCISE 10.1A

Metaphor/Simile. This exercise is designed to help the actor use metaphor and simile effectively. Each actor uses a metaphor or a simile to compliment a *physical trait* of his or her partner. For example: "Your eyes are sparkling emeralds." Next, each partner selects a metaphor or simile to insult a physical trait of his or her partner. For example: "Your hair is like a barbed wire fence."

Now each actor uses a metaphor or simile to compliment a *personality trait* of his or her partner. For example, "Your wit is a sharp knife." Finally, characters exchange insults concerning personality traits. For example: "You are as affectionate as an iceberg."

COUPLE EXERCISE 10.1B

Repetition. This exercise is executed in precisely the same manner as the "Metaphor/Simile" exercise. The difference is that this time the actors' compliments and insults are exchanged using repetition. First try repeating words at the beginning of a sentence or phrase. For example: "Your smile is infectious, your smile is bright, your smile is electric." This also happens to be an example of climax. Now try different forms of repetition:

> Repetition near the beginning and end of a phrase or sentence: ("Your smile makes me smile.")

> Repetition at the ends of phrases: ("Polished to a gloss is your smile, wide as the ocean is your smile, like no other smile is your smile.")

> Repetition at or near the end of one phrase and at the beginning of the next: ("I love your smile, a smile that gives me energy, energy to take on the world, a world that is often frightening, frightening and wonderful.")

You will probably combine rhetorical figures in these exercises. So much the better. And remember, quality doesn't matter. Don't be inhibited from expressing rhetorically.

COUPLE EXERCISE 10.1C

Antithesis. In this variation, the actors compliment and insult their partners' characters antithetically. For example: "Your have the face of an angel, but the heart of a devil."

COUPLE EXERCISE 10.1D

Overstatement. Actors in this exercise use exaggeration to compliment and insult their partners' character. For example: "Your presence dims the sun" or "your talent is the envy of the civilized world."

NOTES

1. Antithesis is perhaps the most important of Shakespeare's figures. It is discussed in more detail in Chapter 11.
2. Polysyndeton cannot truly be categorized as a "scheme of omission." However, because it is so closely related to asyndeton, I am placing it here.
3. Purists believe that the figure of climax must involve at least three consecutive instances of anadiplosis, which you'll recall involves the repetition of the same word at the end of one clause and the beginning of the following clause. I believe that this is too strict a definition. Climax is one of the most important figures in Shakespeare's plays.
4. Metaphor (and its first cousin, simile) round out the list of, in my opinion, the three most important rhetorical figures in Shakespeare. These three figures—*antithesis, climax,* and *metaphor*—are addressed in more detail in Chapter 11.
5. This metaphor may also be an allusion to Genesis 3:14–15. In these verses God curses Satan and Eve—for Eve's sin of eating from the Tree of the Knowledge of Good and Evil, and for Satan's role in this sin. Satan is cursed forever to crawl on his belly, eating dust, while a curse is placed on Eve in which eternal enmity shall exist between Satan's breed (serpents) and Eve's (man) to the effect that man will forever tread upon the head of the serpent and the serpent will forever bite at the heel of man. This allusion makes even more dramatic the enmity between King John and the young Arthur.
6. A valuable resource for uncovering Shakespeare's sexual puns and references is *Shakespeare's Bawdy* by Eric Partridge, published by Macmillan.

CHAPTER 11

Exploring the Text

Passion and Form

(We meet at the coffee shop a week later.)

JOE: Acting Shakespeare is equal parts of passion and form. *Passion* is the truth from the actor's soul, and *form* is the expression of that truth, first on paper, and then through the spoken word. We have been working to a large extent in both arenas.

We have explored ways to connect to the passion of our characters, and the given circumstances in which they find themselves, by means of personalization—including substitution, fantasizing in sensory detail, and trusting our instincts. We now know that we must connect to the desires, problems, and actions or "doings" of our characters. We know that these actions must be outwardly directed as we strive against all odds to achieve our goals. We recognize that we must connect to the emotional life of our characters and, while not indulging in those emotions, use them to motivate our passionate wants and needs. We have discussed "discoveries in the moment" as well as the necessity to put all of our attention on our scene partners, both of which keep us "rooted in the moment."

We have explored the form that this passion takes by investigating clarity of meaning—including multiple definitions, definitions of words that have changed over time, and words whose sounds and rhythms mirror Shakespeare's imagery and meaning. We have also decided that we actors must work from the general to the specific by first choosing objectives for our speeches and scenes and then breaking them into their component parts. We now understand that it is important to make decisions about the transitions that "ignite" our characters from beat to beat, ensuring a dynamic, forward momentum of thought. We have examined Shakespeare's blank verse and rhyming verse and how they relate to the acting process. Moreover, we have inspected Shakespeare's use of prose and rhetorical figures, and we have touched on phrasing and levels of emphasis as well. However, we have not specifically addressed how to marry all of this to the spoken word. After all, the ultimate goal for us as actors is to utter Shakespeare's words onstage in a manner that clearly, efficiently, and powerfully conveys the stories of his plays to a riveted audience.

Liz: Where do we begin?

Joe: That's the same question you asked at the beginning of our work together. Now, however, we are at a different "beginning." After delving into the many aspects of acting Shakespeare, we're ready to work on the speaking of his text.

Operative Words

Joe: Let's begin by determining how to locate the **operative words** in our dialogue. In other words, we must discover which words need to be emphasized over other words in a phrase, sentence, or paragraph in order to be fully understood by the character(s) to whom we are speaking and consequently to the audience as well. These operative or "key" words are those that carry the imagery, meaning, and/or emotion of a passage.

Identifying Operative Words

Joe: Words that carry imagery, meaning, and emotion are most often *nouns* (words denoting a person, place, thing, or quality), *active verbs* (any word expressing action), *adjectives* (words that describe or modify nouns by specifying size, color, number, and so on), and *adverbs* (words that describe verbs, adjectives, and other adverbs, specifying in what manner, when, where, and how much). Let's look at a line of Shakespeare's verse dialogue:

> The <u>crow</u> doth sing as sweetly as the <u>lark</u>
> *(The Merchant of Venice, 5, 1, 102)*

"Crow" and "lark," underlined above, are nouns that contain imagery and meaning. Now take another look at the same line:

> The crow doth <u>sing</u> as <u>sweetly</u> as the lark

"Sing" is a verb of action and "sweetly" is the adverb that specifies "in what manner" the crow sings. Both "sing" and "sweetly" contain imagery and meaning. In this case, the adverb is more important than the verb because it is the *quality* of the singing that is important in this line. As we can see, then, adverbs are treated as part of the verb they modify. Similarly, adjectives are treated as part of the noun they modify. For example:

> Take him and cut him out in <u>little</u> stars,
> *(Romeo and Juliet, 3, 2, 22)*

In Juliet's line above, the adjective "little" modifies the noun "stars." In many cases, adjectives receive slightly less emphasis than the nouns they modify. But this is certainly not always the case. Often adjectives and nouns form a single image where it seems appropriate for each to receive equal emphasis. For example:

> Nor is not mov'd with concord of <u>sweet sounds,</u>
> *(The Merchant of Venice, 5, 1, 84)*

Sometimes the emotion and imagery of the line make it possible for the adjective to receive slightly more emphasis than the noun it modifies. Even if the actor decides to give the noun the primary stress, such adjectives demand a kind of vocal coloring.

SAM: What exactly does that mean?
JOE: Okay, first consider the following passage:

> No sooner had they told this <u>hellish</u> tale,
> But straight they told me they would bind me here
> Unto the body of a <u>dismal</u> yew,
> And leave me to this <u>miserable</u> death.
> And then they call'd me <u>foul</u> adulteress,
> <u>Lascivious</u> Goth, and all the <u>bitterest</u> terms
> That ever ear did hear to such effect;
> *(Titus Andronicus, 2, 3, 105–111)*

The adjectives, underlined above, are emotionally loaded. By **vocal coloring,** I mean using the sound and rhythm of such words to fully express your character's "emotional opinion" of those words. (I will discuss this more fully in a moment.) Meanwhile, active verbs in Shakespeare also often carry strong emotion and imagery, hence deserving strong emphasis. For example:

> I would, while it was <u>smiling</u> in my face,
> Have <u>pluck'd</u> my nipple from his boneless gums,
> And <u>dash'd</u> the brains out, had I so sworn as you
> Have done to this. *(Macbeth, 1, 7, 56–59)*

Verbs like those underlined above also deserve a good deal of vocal coloring. Other operative words are possessive nouns (as in "my *father's* house"), which usually receive as much emphasis as the nouns they possess. For example:

>   By the fire
> That quickens <u>Nilus' slime,</u> I go from hence
>   *(Antony and Cleopatra, 1, 3, 68–69)*

I should mention here that **inoperative words** do not contain strong emotion or imagery. Such words often include negatives *(not, no)*, prepositions *(to, of, for, in)*, conjunctions *(and, but, or, if, when, as, though)*, articles *(a, an, the)*, pronouns *(I, he, she, them, you)*, possessive pronouns *(my, mine, his, hers)*, and verbs of being *(is, are, be)*. For example:

> <u>I will not</u> keep <u>this</u> form <u>upon my</u> head
> <u>When there is</u> such disorder <u>in my</u> wit.
>   *(King John, 3, 4, 101–102)*

The underlined words above contain little or no imagery or emotion. Hence, they are not given emphasis. Such words are important, however, in that they link image to image, showing the relationship between images and demonstrating how words interrelate. They are invaluable in understanding the entire sentence. They must be audible, even though they are not emphasized. However, as I mentioned earlier, many of these types of words sometimes *are* emphasized when involved in a comparison or a contrast or if they qualify or modify something spoken previously. This is an instance of *contextual or rhetorical emphasis.* In other words, the context of the dialogue demands that these usually inoperative words receive a fair degree of stress. You will find that comparison and contrast occurs quite often in Shakespeare. Here is an example from *A Midsummer Night's Dream*:

> DEMETRIUS: <u>Tempt</u> not too much the <u>hatred</u> of my <u>spirit,</u>
>   For I am <u>sick</u> when I do <u>look</u> on thee.
> HELENA: And <u>I</u> am sick when I look <u>not</u> on <u>you.</u>
>   *(A Midsummer Night's Dream, 2, 1, 211–213)*

I have underlined the operative words above. As you can see from Demetrius's lines, nouns and verbs often carry imagery and are therefore operative. However, Helena emphasizes pronouns and negatives in order to contrast Demetrius's words. Later in the play, Helena is upset at the treatment she receives from Hermia, her friend since childhood, whom she thinks is in cahoots with Demetrius and Lysander in slandering her:

> HELENA: And will you <u>rent</u> our <u>ancient love asunder,</u>
>   To <u>join</u> with <u>men</u> in <u>scorning</u> your <u>poor friend?</u> . . .
> HERMIA: I am <u>amazed</u> at your <u>passionate words.</u>
>   I scorn you <u>not</u>; it seems that <u>you</u> scorn <u>me.</u>
>   *(A Midsummer Night's Dream, 3, 2, 215–216 and 220–221)*

Once again, the operative words are underlined. Hermia emphasizes pronouns and negatives in order to contrast Helena's words. Recall that adjectives and adverbs are usually treated as part of the nouns or verbs they modify, and work together to form an image. This is true in the above dialogue. In the first line, the verb "rent" (meaning "rend" or "tear") is modified by the adverb "asunder" ("rent asunder" means "tear apart"). The noun "love" is modified by the adjective "ancient." Now consider this:

> A broken voice, and his whole function suiting
> With forms to his conceit? And all for nothing,
> for Hecuba!
> What's Hecuba to <u>him</u>, or <u>he</u> to Hecuba,
> That he should weep for her?
>
> *(Hamlet, 2, 2, 557–562)*

Here, Hamlet compares and contrasts Hecuba and the Player king. In fact, pronouns are often given emphasis in Shakespeare, as shown in this excerpt:

> NESTOR: Who, Thersites?
> ULYSSES: <u>He</u>.
>
> *(Troilus and Cressida, 2, 3, 92–93)*

As the above example illustrates, the words *he* and *she* can receive emphasis when they mean "man" or "woman" or refer to a particular person:

> I swear to thee, youth, by the white hand of Rosalind, I am that <u>he</u>, that
> unfortunate <u>he.</u>   *(As You Like It, 3, 2, 394–395)*

> Lady, you are the cruelest <u>she</u> alive   *(Twelfth Night, 1, 5, 241)*

Pronouns are often emphasized when uttered in an emotional or emphatic manner:

> Could great men thunder
> As Jove <u>himself</u> does, Jove would never be quiet,
>
> *(Measure for Measure, 2, 2, 110–111)*

Although "great men" and the first utterance of "Jove" receive a good deal of emphasis as nouns that are juxtaposed against each other, "himself" is quite emphatic and may receive even more emphasis than the first vocalization of "Jove." Now in the excerpt below, Othello has just accused his wife Desdemona of being a whore—and when Emilia enters, he turns his wrath upon her, accusing her of being Desdemona's pimp. Notice his use of the pronoun *you:*

> [Enter Emilia.]

> OTHELLO: *[Raising his voice]* <u>You</u>, mistress,
>   That have the office opposite to Saint Peter,
>   And keeps the gate of hell! <u>You, you!</u> Ay, <u>you!</u>
>
> *(Othello, 4, 2, 90–92)*

SAM: How about small words that are not pronouns? You mentioned earlier that small words are often given emphasis in Shakespeare.

JOE: Yes, that's true. Sometimes small words carry enough meaning, imagery, or emotion to warrant emphasis:

> How would you <u>be</u>
> If <u>He,</u> which is the top of judgment, should
> But judge you as you <u>are?</u> O, think on <u>that,</u>
> And mercy then will breathe within your lips,
> Like man new made.   *(Measure for Measure, 2, 2, 75–79)*

In this example, Isabel asks Angelo how he would exist if "He," meaning God, were to judge Angelo in his current condition, that of an imperfect sinner, as is all mankind. She tells him to dwell on what she has just said in order to become merciful. The passage gives a good deal of emphasis to "be," "he," "are," and "that," which are rarely operative. This is an example of contextual or rhetorical emphasis.

Another rule to consider is that *a repeated image is usually not operative.* What *is* operative is the word or words that qualify or modify the image. This is true of the dialogue from *Measure for Measure* that we examined a little earlier:

> Could great men thunder
> As <u>Jove</u> himself does, Jove would never be <u>quiet,</u>
>   *(Measure for Measure, 2, 2, 110–111)*

As we said earlier, the first "Jove" is given a fair amount of emphasis. However, when the word is repeated, although it still receives emphasis, "quiet" receives the *stronger* emphasis because it modifies the second vocalization of "Jove." Here is another example:

> I would I could find in my <u>heart</u> that I had not a <u>hard</u> heart, for
> truly I love none.   *(Much Ado about Nothing, 1, 1, 126–127)*

Benedick speaks the above dialogue. The first time he speaks the image word "heart," it is operative. However, it is the modifier "hard" that receives the primary emphasis when "heart" is repeated. Next we see another example from *The Winter's Tale.* Paulina wishes access to Leontes in order to show him his newborn daughter. Her husband and other lords attempt to prevent her from entering Leontes's chambers:

> LORD: Madam, he hath not <u>slept</u> tonight; commanded
>   None should come at him.
> PAULINA: Not so hot, good sir:
>   I come to <u>bring</u> him sleep. 'Tis such as you,
>   That creep like shadows by him and do sigh
>   At each his needless heavings, such as you
>   Nourish the cause of his awaking: I

>   Do come with words as medicinal as true,
>   Honest as either, to purge him of that humour
>   That <u>presses</u> him from sleep.
>
>   *(The Winter's Tale, 2, 3, 31–39)*

The Lord first mentions the image of sleep: "he hath not *slept* tonight." Because the word has been spoken and emphasized, Paulina then emphasizes the words that qualify it. This rule also applies on occasion to some rhetorical figures that involve repetition. Let's reexamine an example of anaphora that we looked at in our chapter on rhetorical figures. *Anaphora*, as you will recall, is the repetition of the same word or group of words at the beginning of successive clauses, sentences, or lines. The repetitions are underlined:

>   What <u>must</u> the <u>King</u> do now? <u>Must he</u> submit?
>   <u>The King</u> shall do it. <u>Must he</u> be depos'd?
>   <u>The King</u> shall be contented. <u>Must he</u> lose
>   The name of <u>king</u>? A' God's name let it go.
>
>   *(Richard II, 3, 3, 143–146)*

As I stated earlier, King Richard attempts to instill guilt and shame into the treacherous Northumberland for his part in helping to overthrow him. Repetition of "must" and "king" reinforces the fact that no one save God has the right to demand anything of the rightful king. However, these words need special emphasis only the first time they are spoken. Thereafter, the words that modify or qualify them are given the emphasis. Let's look at it again, with the emphasized words underlined:

>   What <u>must the King</u> do now? Must he <u>submit</u>?
>   The King shall <u>do</u> it. Must he be <u>depos'd</u>?
>   The King shall be <u>contented</u>. Must he <u>lose</u>
>   The <u>name</u> of king? A' <u>God's name</u>, let it <u>go</u>!

Although they are not strongly emphasized after their first utterance, the repetition of "must" and "king" are still audible and effective. *The exception to this rule is when an image is repeated for emphasis, or when the image is repeated because it looms ever larger in the imagination of the speaker.* In such cases, the word receives *more* emphasis each time it is repeated. This is particularly true with the figure of epizeuxis (the repetition of a single word for emphasis):

>   O <u>monstrous</u>! <u>monstrous</u>!   *(Othello, 3, 3, 427)*

>   O <u>villain</u>, villain, smiling, damned <u>villain</u>!   *(Hamlet, 1, 5, 106)*

This is also sometimes true of other figures of repetition, including epistrophe. *Epistrophe*, as you'll recall, is the repetition of the same word or group of words at the end of successive clauses, sentences, or lines. For example:

>   Here is your husband, like a mildewed ear,
>   Blasting his wholesome brother. <u>Have you eyes</u>?

> Could you on this fair mountain leave to feed
> And batten on this moor? Ha, have you eyes?
>
> *(Hamlet, 3, 4, 64–67)*

As I said, in cases like those above, the repeated words receive slightly more emphasis each time they are uttered, reinforcing the fact that the image and emotion grow stronger and stronger within the character.

SAM: What about repeated sounds, like alliteration and assonance?

JOE: Alliterative and assonant sounds usually get a little extra vocal attention because they help to tie two or more words into a single image or related images. (*Alliteration* is the repetition of an initial sound in two or more words in a phrase or line. *Assonance* is the repetition of a sound within two or more words in a phrase or line.) Alliterative and assonant sounds also deserve extra stressing because they often reflect the emotion of the image. Therefore, the speaker can put a good deal of emotional life into the utterance of these sounds.

In *The Taming of the Shrew*, Petruchio woos the reluctant, headstrong Katherine. He has just received permission from her father to marry her but does not want an unwilling bride. Toward the end of a rather turbulent first meeting, Petruchio says:

> Now, Kate, I am a husband for your turn,
> For by this light whereby I see thy beauty,
> Thy beauty that doth make me like thee well,
> Thou must be married to no man but me;
>
> *(The Taming of the Shrew, 2, 1, 272-275)*

The repetition of the "m" consonant sound (all in stressed positions) in the last line is sensuous. After all, the sound we make after tasting something sinfully pleasing is often "mmmmmmmm." The alliteration in this line reinforces the fact that Petruchio will marry Kate regardless of her wishes, but perhaps more importantly, the repetition of the sensuous "mmm" sound is used to help woo Kate.

In *Julius Caesar,* Cassius uses both assonance and alliteration to show his disdain for Caesar:

> And this man
> Is now become a god and Cassius is
> A wretched creature, and must bend his body
> If Caesar carelessly but nod on him.
>
> *(Julius Caesar, 1, 2, 115-118)*

Cassius is trying to convince Brutus that Caesar's megalomania has reached proportions that necessitate his removal and that Brutus should join him in his plot to have Caesar killed. He repeats consonant sounds within two words, "wretched" and "creature," which share both an "r" sound and a "ch" sound, helping to link the two words into a single image. These sounds are harsh. The actor playing Cassius can instill the sounds with his disdain for Caesar. It also helps to contrast his sarcastic comparison of Caesar as a "god" and himself as a "wretched creature." Cassius is trying to drive home the idea that Caesar's inflated opinion of himself can only lead to Rome's destruction and therefore he must be assassinated. The actor playing Cassius can also point up the alliterative "b" sounds in "bend" and "body" to reinforce the fact that he must prostrate himself before Caesar.

LIZ: Are there more rules concerning operative words?

JOE: Yes. *Antithetical words and phrases must receive strong and equal emphasis.* (*Antithesis*, you'll remember, is a contrast or opposition of thoughts.) *Antithesis is perhaps the most important rhetorical figure in Shakespeare.* Antithesis is ubiquitous in the dialogue of his characters. They often conceive, process, and express their thoughts, intents, and emotions antithetically. Therefore it is vital for the actor to convey antithetical words and ideas clearly and strongly. For example:

> To be, or not to be; that is the question:
> Whether 'tis nobler in the mind to suffer
> The slings and arrows of outrageous fortune
> Or to take arms against a sea of troubles
> And by opposing, end them.   *(Hamlet, 3, 1, 55–59)*

Hamlet's entire soliloquy is based on an antithesis: Continue to live in emotional turmoil, or commit suicide? "To be" is set against "not to be," and "in the mind to suffer" is set against "take arms." Hamlet asks if he should continue to exist or cease to exist. Should he suffer in silence or take action to *end* his suffering? *Each set of antitheses should receive strong and equal stressing.* Later in the same soliloquy, Hamlet says that it is the fear of what lies in store for us after death that makes us fear suicide:

> the dread of something after death,
> The undiscover'd country, from whose bourn
> No traveler returns, puzzles the will,
> And makes us rather bear those ills we have,
> Than fly to others that we know not of?   *(Hamlet, 3, 1, 77–81)*

In the last two lines of this section, Hamlet has three sets of antitheses. "Bear" is set against "fly," "ills" is set against "others," and "have" is set against "know not of." Again, each image in every set of antitheses must be clearly, strongly, and equally played against its counterpart. Shakespeare loves to point, play, or juxtapose one word or phrase against another in order to clarify meaning and intent, even when such juxtaposition may not be true antithesis. Let's look again at the last two lines from the "To be, or not to be" excerpt:

> Or to take arms against a sea of troubles
> And by opposing, end them.   *(Hamlet, 3, 1, 58–59)*

"Opposing" is set against "end them." This is a cause-and-effect juxtaposition. Here is another example from *Hamlet*:

> Purpose is but the slave to memory,   *(Hamlet, 3, 2, 188)*

Here "purpose" must be balanced with "memory." Of course, more than one rule concerning operative words can apply in one line. Again from *Hamlet*:

> Most necessary 'tis that we forget
> To <u>pay ourselves</u> what <u>to</u> ourselves is <u>debt</u>.
>
> *(Hamlet, 3, 2, 192–193)*

In the above example, "pay" must be balanced with "debt"—and whereas "ourselves" is given emphasis when first uttered, it is "to" that is later given precedence, as it qualifies the second utterance of "ourselves."

In addition, *other words that need special emphasis are those that contain new information.* In *The Winter's Tale,* Lord Antigonus is ordered by King Leontes to leave Leontes's baby daughter in a remote place because he thinks (erroneously) that his former best friend, Polixenes, fathered the child. In Act 3, scene 3, Antigonus, infant in arms, enters a remote place with a Mariner. He asks the Mariner in the first words of the scene:

> Thou art perfect then, our ship hath touch'd upon
> The deserts of <u>Bohemia</u>?   *(The Winter's Tale, 3, 3, 1–2)*

Bohemia is the country ruled by Leontes's ex-friend, Polixenes. This is important new information in the play. Later in the same scene Antigonus says that the baby's mother, Queen Hermione, appeared to him in a dream and told him:

> and for the babe
> Is counted lost forever, <u>Perdita</u>
> I prithee call it.   *(The Winter's Tale, 3, 3, 32–34)*

This is the first time that we hear the child's name. She soon becomes a major character in the story and consequently her name must be strongly emphasized.

You should also give special emphasis to words, phrases, or sentences that state the structure or steps of a story or argument. Let's look at another example from *The Winter's Tale*. Hermione, on trial for her life, has fainted at the news of her son's death and is carried offstage. A short while later, Antigonus's wife Paulina reenters and lambastes Leontes in the following speech:

> What studied torments, tyrant, hast for me?
> What wheels? Racks? Fires? What flaying? Boiling
> In leads or oils? What old or newer torture
> Must I receive, whose every word deserves
> To taste of thy most worst? Thy tyranny
> Together working with thy jealousies,
> Fancies too weak for boys, too green and idle
> For girls of nine, O, think what they have done
> And then run mad indeed, stark mad! For all
> Thy by-gone fooleries were but spices of it.

> That thou betray'dst Polixenes, 'twas nothing;
> That did but show thee, of a fool, inconstant
> And damnable ingrateful: <u>nor was't much,</u>
> <u>Thou wouldst have poison'd good Camillo's honour,</u>
> <u>To have him kill a king:</u> poor trespasses,
> More monstrous standing by: <u>whereof I reckon</u>
> <u>The casting forth to crows thy baby-daughter</u>
> <u>To be or none or little;</u> though a devil
> Would have shed water out of fire ere done't:
> <u>Nor is't directly laid to thee, the death</u>
> <u>Of the young prince,</u> whose honourable thoughts,
> Thoughts high for one so tender, cleft the heart
> That could conceive a gross and foolish sire
> Blemish'd his gracious dam: this is not, no,
> Laid to thy answer: <u>but the last,</u> —O lords,
> When I have said, cry "woe!" <u>the queen, the queen,</u>
> <u>The sweet'st, dear'st creature's dead, and vengeance for't</u>
> <u>Not dropp'd down yet.</u>   *(The Winter's Tale, 3, 2, 175–202)*

The underlined sections are the steps that lead to the ultimate point of the argument: that Leontes is responsible for the death of his wife and that such an act must be revenged. (Although the Queen is in fact, very much alive, Paulina must convince Leontes otherwise.)

Figures of climax also need special attention. Climax, as you now know, is the arrangement of words, phrases, or clauses in an order of increasing importance. Climax is more commonly known as a *build* or a *list*. The actor must give each item in a build or list slightly more emphasis than the preceding item. This reflects that each item increases in importance and imagery. Builds are almost as important to the actor as antithesis. Shakespeare's characters love builds. Here is an example, spoken by Hermione in *The Winter's Tale*:

> for behold me,
> <u>A fellow of the royal bed,</u> which owe
> <u>A moiety of the throne, a great king's daughter,</u>
> <u>The mother to a hopeful prince,</u> here standing
> To prate and talk for life and honor 'fore
> Who please to come and hear.   *(The Winter's Tale, 3, 2, 37–42)*

Hermione uses a build of four to create an image of herself as a royal, privileged, and honorable queen, daughter, mother, wife, and woman. This build of imagery is to shame her husband for making her stand trial in a manner unfit even for a commoner. As shown in the above example, builds have a commonality: They are often smaller images that, put together, form a large image. The actress playing Hermione must increase, slightly, the emphasis of each item on her list.

Marking Operative Words

LIZ: Are all operative words *equally* emphasized?

JOE: No. There are degrees of emphasis, as we mentioned when we worked on scansion. One option for the actor is to mark *the strongest emphasis with a double underline, secondary emphasis with a single underline, and tertiary emphasis with a dotted underline.* Let's look once more at Helena's lines from *A Midsummer Night's Dream:*

> And will you rent our ancient love asunder,
> To join with men in scorning your poor friend?
> *(A Midsummer Night's Dream, 3, 2, 215–216)*

There are four possibly emphasized words in the first line above, and five in the second. Let's try a possible marking:

> And will you rent our ancient love asunder,
> To join with men in scorning your poor friend?

LIZ: Is this the only way to score these two lines of verse?

JOE: No, of course not. The point is *if you give all operative words equal emphasis, it will confuse your scene partner as well as the audience.* Also, some actors give emphasis even to non-image words. Many actors new to Shakespeare feel that every word is precious and refuse to "throw words away."

SAM: What do you mean by "throw words away"?

JOE: It's a figurative expression. It means to soft-pedal certain words, while vocally committing to words that contain meaning, emotion, and imagery. I don't mean that the actor should mumble these non-image words, but instead should allow the rhythms and the sense of the line to dictate the degrees of stress they will receive—which will be considerably less than for words that carry imagery. Ironically, some actors stubbornly emphasize non-image words as well as image words because they want to ensure that their words are fully comprehended, when in reality, this only causes confusion on the part of the listener.

LIZ: It's helpful to know rules about operative words and degrees of emphasis, but how do we do all of this and still sound natural when speaking Shakespeare's words?

SAM: Yes, in doing all this, how do we have it appear as if our characters talk this way in everyday life?

DIAGRAMMING THE TEXT[1]

JOE: In daily conversation, we speak without thinking about *how* we're saying things. Natural tendencies take over. We naturally group words together into images and emphasize important words and images, depending on the ideas we wish to communicate. When we use long sentences, we naturally pause in appropriate places. But, for some reason, when it comes to classical texts—especially Shakespeare—most of our natural instincts seem to fly out the window.

LIZ: Why?

JOE: Maybe it's because the language and imagery in classical plays are almost by definition richer and more heightened. Maybe it's just because they have a lot more words. Diagramming sentences can help solve the problem of trying to sound "natural" when speaking heightened language, by mechanically figuring out what we naturally do when we just talk normally. It takes chunks of Shakespeare's dialogue that may at first glance look intimidating and breaks it up into pieces that we can understand. In short, diagramming can figure out the subject of the sentence—the main idea, the supporting ideas, and where to pause without breaking up images. It also figures out the rhythms and builds that the playwright has written into the text. When diagramming, start big, and work toward the little things.

Step 1: Place Braces ({ }) around Complete Sentences

JOE: Before we diagram a Shakespeare piece, let's try it on a contemporary monologue. Here's a monologue spoken by a marine sergeant whose platoon is facing its last and greatest battle. They are wildly outnumbered, and afraid they will die. One marine, Andy Westerly—who happens to be the cousin of the platoon's sergeant—voices everyone's wish for an influx of reserves to better their odds of survival. The sergeant overhears this wish:

SARGE: Who said that? Andy? Nah, cuz, if our number's up, then the thirty of us are more than enough to be missed and mourned by the good ol' U.S. But if we make it, each of us comes home a bigger hero, and with a bigger share of honor. So for the love of God, don't ask for a single solitary soldier more. *(He pauses, realizing the other men are listening. They want and need to hear more. He begins to talk to all of them.)* You know, I'm not the kind of guy who wants to be a millionaire, and I sure don't care if people hit me up for a buck or two. And it doesn't bother me if people borrow my stuff and don't return it—those are shallow things, and I could care less about 'em. But if it's wrong or shallow to care about what we're taught in basic training—duty, honor, country—then I guess I'm the shallowest guy on earth.

Put braces around the complete sentences. Your diagrammed monologue will look like this:

SARGE: {Who said that?} {Andy?} {Nah, cuz, if our number's up, then the thirty of us are more than enough to be missed and mourned by the good ol' U.S.} {But if we make it, each of us comes home a bigger hero, and with a bigger share of honor.} {So for the love of God, don't ask for a single solitary soldier more.} {You know, I'm not the kind of guy who wants to be a millionaire, and I don't care if people hit me up for a buck or two.} {And it sure doesn't bother me if people borrow my stuff and don't return it—those are shallow things, and I could care less about 'em.} {But if it's wrong or shallow to care about what we're taught in basic training—duty, honor, country—then I guess I'm the shallowest guy on earth.}

By placing braces around each complete sentence, we get an idea of how the character's mind is working: In this case, we see some short, declarative sentences at the beginning of the piece, but by the end, his enthusiasm seems to be flowing along with that last long sentence. That's a good clue to the fact that the sergeant is warming up to his objective of instilling strength and confidence in his troops.

Step 2: Place Angle Brackets (< >) around Images Made of Two or More Words

JOE: When do we take natural pauses in day-to-day speech? What words do we tend to group together? Following are three sentences. Read them out loud to yourself—or better yet to someone else—and notice where you paused (even if it's a tiny pause) and what words you grouped together. Try to read the sentences naturally, as if this were part of a conversation you were having with a friend.

1. A big black dog chased me down the street.
2. I live in a white house with blue trim and a red door.
3. My internship with the customer relations department gave me real-life experience dealing with all kinds of people.

Did you notice that you tend to run together words that make up an image? And that the linking words—like "in a" in the second sentence and "with" in the third sentence—stick pretty close to the images? For instance, you probably read the first sentence like this:

>Abigblackdog chased me down the street.

The second sentence might have sounded like:

>I live inawhitehouse withbluetrimandareddoor.

And the third:

>Myinternship withthecustomerrealtionsdepartment gave me reallifeexperience dealing withallkindsofpeople.

Since we group words together that make up an image in "real life," we have to remember to do it in Shakespeare as well. So, using the sergeant's monologue, place angle brackets around images made up of two or more words, and then read the monologue, making sure you don't pause in the middle of—or otherwise break up—any of the images inside the angle brackets. If you have to pause, do it before or after the image.

SARGE: {Who said that?} {Andy?} {Nah, cuz, if our <number's up,> then <the thirty of us> are more than enough to be missed and mourned by <the good ol' U.S.>} {But if we make it, each of us comes home < a bigger hero,> and with <a

bigger share of honor.>} {So for <the love of God,> don't ask for <a single solitary soldier more.>} {You know, I'm not <the kind of guy who wants to be a millionaire,> and I don't care if people hit me up for <a buck or two.>} {And it sure doesn't bother me if people borrow my stuff and don't return it—those are <shallow things,> and I could care less about 'em.} {But if it's wrong or shallow to care about what we're taught in <basic training>—duty, honor, and country—then I guess I'm <the shallowest guy on earth.>}

SAM: Using the angle brackets makes it a little easier to read.
JOE: Yes. So far, so good, but we've only just begun. There are other ways we naturally group words together.

Step 3: Place Straight Brackets ([ ]) around the Predicate

JOE: Read the following sentences out loud, in a conversational tone.

1. I wish Shakespeare weren't so complicated.
2. Lucy likes people who aren't afraid to try new things.
3. I don't care that you're about to travel on the Space Shuttle.

In the first sentence, you probably put a tiny pause or caesura (remember Chapter 6 and the ^ symbol?) between "wish" and "Shakespeare," or maybe you ran the words "Shakespeare weren't so complicated" together a bit. In the second sentence you probably paused before "people" and grouped together "people who aren't afraid to try new things" or maybe you paused before "aren't" and grouped together "afraid to try new things." In the last sentence, you probably paused after "care" or "that" and grouped "you're about to travel on the Space Shuttle" together. This is because we naturally tend to separate the main subject and verb of a sentence from the rest of the sentence, which is called the *predicate*. (Technically the predicate includes the verb, but for the sake of diagramming, let's pretend it doesn't.) Now this rule isn't set in stone, but it does tend to be true. What's nice about this rule is that it helps us break down the long, complex sentences that Shakespeare often writes into more easily understood—and spoken—ideas.

Another way of figuring out what you should put straight brackets around is to isolate the subject and verb in the sentence, and then ask yourself either "what?" or "who?" or "where?" The answer to that question is what I mean by the predicate. For instance, look at the three sentences we just read:

1. I wish *(what?)* [Shakespeare weren't so complicated].
2. Lucy likes *(who?)* [people who aren't afraid to try new things]. OR
   Lucy likes people who *(what?)* [aren't afraid to try new things].
3. I don't care that *(what?)* [you're about to travel on the Space Shuttle].

Now let's insert the straight brackets into Sarge's monologue. For the sake of clarifying this point, I've added small "whats" and "whos" before the straight brackets. You shouldn't do this in your diagramming.

SARGE: {Who said that?} {Andy?} {Nah, cuz, if our <number's up,> then *(what?)* [<the thirty of us> are more than enough to be missed and mourned by <the good ol' U.S.>]} {But if we make it, each of us comes home *(what?)* [< a bigger hero,> covered in *(what?)* [even greater honor.]]} {So for <the love of God,> don't ask for *(what?)* [<a single solitary soldier more.>]} {You know, I'm not <the kind of guy who *(what?)* [wants to be a millionaire,>] and I don't care if *(what?)* [people hit me up for *(what?)* [<a buck or two.>]]} {And it sure doesn't bother me if *(what?)* [people borrow my stuff and don't return it]—those are <shallow things,> and I could *(what?)* [care less about 'em.]} {But if it's wrong or shallow to *(what?)* [care about what we're taught in <basic training>]—duty, honor, country—then I guess I'm *(what?)* [<the shallowest guy on earth.>]}

LIZ: The way you diagrammed it, you show angle or straight brackets within angle or straight brackets, like where the segeant says, "and with a bigger share of honor" and "I don't care if people hit me up for a buck or two." Is the okay?

JOE: That's more than okay—it actually happens a lot. You can have brackets within brackets, and often will when the sentences and ideas get more complex. Now let's try a couple of examples from Shakespeare. Remember, start with the braces ({ }), then the angle brackets (< >), and finally the straight brackets ([ ]):

> For what offence have I this fortnight been
> A banish'd woman from my Harry's bed?
> Tell me, sweet lord, what is't that takes from thee
> Thy stomach, pleasure, and thy golden sleep?
>
> *(Henry IV Part 1, 2, 3, 38–41)*

Your diagram should look like this:

> {For what offence have I this fortnight been
> [A <banish'd woman> from <my Harry's bed?>]}
> {Tell me, <sweet lord>, what is't that [takes from thee
> [Thy stomach, pleasure, and <thy golden sleep?>]]}

So diagramming tells us the good places to take caesuras without breaking up the images or thought groups. In the example above, you probably could pause after "been," "that," and "thee."

SAM: Would you want to have caesuras in all these places?

JOE: Probably not—that would break up the flow of the speech too much. But if you needed to pause in this section of the monologue (for an intake of breath, for example), you now know where you can and still keep the images intact. Let's try one more example:

> This was your husband. Look you now what follows:
> Here is your husband, like a mildewed ear
> Blasting his wholesome brother. Have you eyes?
>
> *(Hamlet, 3, 4, 63–65)*

Your diagram should look like this:

> {This was <your husband.>} {Look you now what follows:
> Here is [<your husband,> like [<<a mildewed ear>
> Blasting his <wholesome brother>>]]}. {Have you eyes?}

In this case, not only do we have straight brackets within straight brackets, but we also have angle brackets within angle brackets. When brackets start to pile up like this, it usually means something important has just been said, a big emotion has just been expressed, or a big idea has just been completed. In other words, you've earned the right to take a caesura.

Step 4: Circle the Antithesis

JOE: Now let's incorporate some of the information we've already learned into diagramming our text. First, let's add in antithesis, by circling antithetical thoughts and connecting them with a line. That way when it comes time to read the piece, the antithesis should be heard loud and clear. Since we've done so much work on the sergeant's monologue already, let's continue with it. Is there any antithesis in it?

LIZ: Yes—Sarge compares their "number being up" with "making it."

JOE: Great. Circle it and connect it. It should look something like this:

> SARGE: ... {Nah, cuz, if our <(number's up)> then [the <thirty of us> are more than enough to be missed and mourned by <the good ol' U.S.>]} {But if we (make it,) each of us comes home [< a bigger hero,> and with [a bigger share of honor.]]}

Step 5: Underline Alliteration and Assonance

JOE: As I mentioned in Chapter 10, Shakespeare is fond of using clusters of similar sounds either in the beginnings of words (alliteration) or within words (assonance). Since word play was the name of the game in those days and Shakespeare often used alliteration and assonance to help the character make a point or to indicate a certain trait about the character, it makes sense to mark them when we diagram. Most contemporary writers don't rely on assonance and alliteration as much as poets (like Shakespeare), but let's practice on the sergeant's speech anyway, just to get into the habit of underlining assonance and alliteration. Is there any alliteration in Sarge's speech?

SAM: Yes—in two spots. He says, "the thirty of us are more than enough to be missed and mourned by the good ol' U.S." and "for the love of God, don't ask for a single solitary soldier more." Both of those examples are alliterative.

JOE: Excellent. Now underline the repetitive sounds.

> SARGE: ... {Nah, cuz, if our <number's up,> then [the <thirty of us> are <u>more</u> than enough to be <u>missed</u> and <u>mourned</u> by <the good ol' U.S.>]}. . . {So for <the love of God,> <u>don't</u> ask for [<a <u>single</u> <u>solitary</u> soldier more.>]}

Step 6: Mark Run-On Lines with an Arrow

JOE: This is another step that really only works in verse. Very often we get into the habit of stopping at the end of a line of verse, pausing, and then starting fresh at the beginning of the next line. This would be fine if every verse line were a complete idea, but in many cases ideas are carried on for more than one line. If we pause at the end of each line, it defeats all the work we've done trying to keep images together and thoughts clear. Marking thoughts that continue to the next line with an arrow gives you a visual reminder to keep your vocal energy going past the end of the line and on to the next. Here are a few examples. Notice how adding an arrow helps keep the vocal energy flowing forward:

> Deform'd, unfinish'd, sent before my time →
> Into this breathing world scarce half made up,
> And that so lamely and unfashionable →
> That dogs bark at me as I halt by them.
> *(Richard III, 1, 1, 20–24)*

> Kent, Sir, the banish'd Kent, who in disguise →
> Followed his enemy king, and did him service →
> Improper for a slave. *(King Lear, 5, 3, 220–222)*

>   My third comfort
> (Starr'd most unluckily) is from my breast
> (The innocent milk in it most innocent mouth)
> Hal'd out to murder; myself on every post →
> Proclaim'd a strumpet, with immodest hatred →
> The child-bed privilege denied, which 'longs →
> To women of all fashion; lastly hurried →
> Here, to this place, i'th' open air, before →
> I have got strength of limit. Now, my liege,
> Tell me what blessings I have here alive,
> That I should fear to die? Therefore proceed.
> *(The Winter's Tale, 3, 2, 98–108)*

The first three lines in the above dialogue from *The Winter's Tale* are not run-on lines because there must be a brief caesura both before and after the parenthetical phrase in lines two and three.

Step 7: Mark Lists and Builds with Numbers

JOE: Marking the parts of a list or a build (especially if the items in the list are long phrases) not only reminds you to vocally build to the next item in the list, but also helps identify exactly what is part of the list or build. And since each successive item in a Shakespeare list tends to be more important than the last, marking the lists helps build the speech. Sarge has a list in his speech. Let's mark it.

SARGE: You know, I'm not the kind of guy who ① wants to be a millionaire, and I sure don't care if ② people hit me up for a buck or two. And it doesn't bother me if ③ people borrow my stuff and don't return it—those are shallow things, and I could care less about 'em.

Step 8: Put It All Together

JOE: Now that we've learned the steps to diagramming text, let's try it out on the real thing—a monologue from Shakespeare's *Henry V,* Act 4, scene 3. It is the first section of Henry's famous "Saint Crispin's Day" speech. In the opening of the speech, King Henry and his English troops are moments before the climactic battle of Agincourt with the French. They are greatly outnumbered and know it. Henry's cousin Westmoreland wishes aloud that they had more English comrades to fight with them to better their chance of survival. Henry overhears this wish and responds:

> KING HENRY V: What's he that wishes so?
> My cousin Westmoreland? No, my fair cousin:
> If we are mark'd to die, we are enow
> To do our country loss; and if to live,
> The fewer men, the greater share of honour.
> God's will! I pray thee, wish not one man more.
> By Jove, I am not covetous for gold,
> Nor care I who doth feed upon my cost;
> It yearns me not if men my garments wear;
> Such outward things dwell not in my desires:
> But if it be a sin to covet honour,
> I am the most offending soul alive.   *(Henry V, 4, 3, 18–29)*

LIZ: Hey, that sounds a lot like—

JOE: Yes, you're right. The sergeant's speech that we've been working on is just a really bad, contemporary version of this section of the "Crispin's Day" speech. What can I tell you? Shakespeare, I'm not. But at least you're very familiar with the material now. So, let's diagram it, step by step. First, let's put braces around complete sentences:

> {What's he that wishes so?}
> {My cousin Westmoreland?} {No, my fair cousin:
> If we are mark'd to die, we are enow
> To do our country loss; and if to live,
> The fewer men, the greater share of honour.}
> {God's will!} {I pray thee, wish not one man more.}
> {By Jove, I am not covetous for gold,
> Nor care I who doth feed upon my cost;

>   It yearns me not if men my garments wear;
>   Such outward things dwell not in my desires:
>   But if it be a sin to covet honour,
>   I am the most offending soul alive.}

Second, put angle brackets around images made of two or more words:

>   {What's he that wishes so?}
>   {My <cousin Westmoreland?>} {No, <my fair cousin:>
>   If we are mark'd to die, we are enow
>   To do our country loss; and if to live,
>   The <fewer men,> the <greater share of honour.>}
>   {God's will!} {I pray thee, wish not one man more.}
>   {By Jove, I am not covetous for gold,
>   Nor care I who doth feed upon my cost;
>   It yearns me not if men my garments wear;
>   Such <outward things> dwell not in my desires:
>   But if it be a sin to <covet honour,>
>   I am <the most offending soul alive.>}

Next, place straight brackets around the predicate:

>   {What's he that wishes so?}
>   {My <cousin Westmoreland?>} {No, <my fair cousin:>
>   If we are [mark'd to die,] we are [enow
>   To do our country loss;] and if to live,
>   The <fewer men,> the <greater share of honour.>}
>   {God's will!} {I pray thee, wish not [one man more.]}
>   {By Jove, I am not [covetous for gold,]
>   Nor care I who doth [feed upon my cost;]
>   It yearns me not if [men my garments wear;]
>   Such <outward things> dwell not [in my desires:]
>   But if it be [a sin to <covet honour,>]
>   I am [<the most offending soul alive.>]}

Now, circle and connect the antithesis:

>   {{What's he that wishes so?}
>   {My <cousin Westmoreland?>} {No, <my fair cousin:>
>   If we are [mark'd (to die,)] we are [enow
>   To do our country loss;] and if (to live,)
>   The <(fewer men,)> the <(greater share of honour.)>}

Diagramming the Text   **257**

       {God's will!} {I pray thee, wish not [one man more.]}
       {By Jove, I am not [covetous for gold,]
       Nor care I who doth [feed upon my cost;]
       It yearns me not if [men my garments wear;]
       Such <outward things> dwell not [in my desires:]
       But if it be [a sin to <covet honour,>]
       I am [<the most offending soul alive.>]}

Now, underline the alliteration and assonance:

       {What's he that wishes so?}
       {My <cousin Westmoreland?>} {No, <my fair cousin:>
       If we are [mark'd to die,] we are [enow
       To do our country loss;] and if to live,
       The <fewer men,> the <greater share of honour.>}
       {God's will!} {I pray thee, wish not [one man more.]}
       {By Jove, I am not [covetous for gold,]
       Nor care I who doth [feed upon my cost;]
       It yearns me not if [men my garments wear;]
       Such <outward things> dwell not [in my desires:]
       But if it be [a sin to <covet honour,>]
       I am [<the most offending soul alive.>]}

Now mark the run-ons. In this instance there is only one:

       {What's he that wishes so?}
       {My <cousin Westmoreland?>} {No, <my fair cousin:>
       If we are [mark'd to die,] we are [enow →
       To do our country loss;] and if to live,
       The <fewer men,> the <greater share of honour.>}
       {God's will!} {I pray thee, wish not [one man more.]}
       {By Jove, I am not [covetous for gold,]
       Nor care I who doth [feed upon my cost;]
       It yearns me not if [men my garments wear;]

Such <outward things> dwell not [in my desires:]

But if it be [a sin to <covet honour,>]

I am [<the most offending soul alive.>]}

And finally, mark the lists and/or builds:

{What's he that wishes so?}

{My <cousin Westmoreland?>} {No, <my fair cousin:>

If we are [mark'd to (die,)] we are [enow →

To do our country loss;] and if (to live,)

The <(fewer men,)> the <(greater share of honour.)>}

{God's will!} {I pray thee, wish not [one man more.]}

{By Jove, I am not ① [covetous for gold,]

Nor care I who doth ② [feed upon my cost;]

It yearns me not if ③ [men my garments wear;]

Such <outward things> dwell not [in my desires:]

But if it be [a sin to <covet honour,>]

I am [<the most offending soul alive.>]}

And now that we've diagrammed it we are, at last, ready to read it.

SAM: That's a lot of work.

JOE: Yes, but as is the case with scansion and rhetoric, things get easier as you become more and more familiar with the material. Diagramming is a tool for the actor. It is a means to an end and should be set aside when it has served its purpose.

SPEAKING THE TEXT

> Drama presents human beings bound to each other by speech, not merely declaiming but defining themselves through words they speak to and receive from one another. Speech breeds speech, requires it, goads it, desires it—in life as in drama. (Wright, *Shakespeare's Metrical Art*, p. 138)

LIZ: Now that we know how to identify and mark operative words, and how to diagram our text so that the imagery is clear and so that we sound natural—how do we put all of this into the speaking of our characters' words?

JOE: We have been working on *what* to emphasize. Now let's work on *how* to emphasize. Actually, we will be focusing on far more than that. We need to explore the vocal production of all of Shakespeare's dialogue. Let's begin, however, with ways to emphasize syllables, words, and phrases.

SAM: Does emphasis mean that we speak our operative words louder than our inoperative words?

JOE: That's certainly part of it. However, there is more to it than that. There are three basic ways to give emphasis to a syllable, word, or phrase. It may be helpful to think of them as the Three Ps.

The Three Ps: Punch, Pitch, and Pace

JOE: **Punch** is the *amount of vocal force* we give to a syllable, word, or phrase. This involves volume. We do this naturally in English when we use vocal force to emphasize one syllable over another for clarity. For example, the word *honest* is punched on the first syllable. Let's look at a simple sentence from Shakespeare:

> Do you not love me? *(Henry IV Part 1, 2, 3, 96)*

The word *love* contains the imagery and meaning of this sentence, which is a question asked of Hotspur by his wife, Lady Percy. We may mark the sentence like this:

> Do you not <u>love</u> me?

You'll recall that a possible way to mark operative words is to give a double underline to words that receive the strongest stress, a single underline to words that receive secondary stress, and a dotted underline to words that receive tertiary stress. It makes sense to give "love" a strong vocal punch here. So far, so good. But Lady Percy asks another question. The two questions together form a line of verse:

> Do you not love me? Do you not indeed? *(Henry IV Part 1, 2, 3, 96)*

Now what? Well, we have another operative word, "indeed." It's possible that the line may now be marked like this:

> Do you not <u>love</u> me? Do you not <u>indeed</u>?

LIZ: Why does "indeed" receive stronger emphasis than "love"?

JOE: First of all, it is a valid choice to decide that both words receive equally strong stress. However, Lady Percy becomes more emphatic with the second question. She is worried about her husband, who has just told her (in jest) that he does not love her. However, Lady Percy is not sure if he is joking or serious. She is emotionally vulnerable as she asks her husband these two questions, and the second question is even more emotionally loaded than the first. Therefore, the operative word "indeed" would receive slightly more emphasis than the operative word "love."

SAM: Would that mean that "indeed" would get a slightly stronger punch than "love"?

JOE: That is one option. Another option is to use pitch rather than punch. **Pitch** is the *tone of the voice* in speaking. We American actors, particularly, need to develop and use a wider range of pitch in our acting. We need to "play more notes" with our words.

LIZ: So, if I were playing Lady Percy, I could emphasize "love" with vocal force and I could emphasize "indeed" by raising the pitch of my voice.

JOE: Yes.
SAM: But wouldn't you have to also punch the word "indeed" to a certain extent?
JOE: Yes. *The three forms of emphasis are not mutually exclusive.* In other words, Liz could give "love" and "indeed" equal punch, but by raising the pitch of her voice on "indeed," it will receive a little more emphasis.
LIZ: What about the use of pace to give words emphasis?
JOE: **Pace** is the *rate of speed* that we give to a syllable, word, or phrase. In our example, "indeed" has a long "ee" vowel sound that should be used by the actress. Here is another example:

> Do not <u>muse</u> at me my most worthy friends.   *(Macbeth, 3, 4, 84)*

We examined this line earlier as an example of concurrent trochees. The verb "muse" is the principal operative word in the sentence. The word can be lifted out of the sentence with volume, but the primary means of emphasis should come from the lengthening of the long "u" vowel sound in the word. Now let's look at an instance in which a quick pace is used to help provide emphasis:

> A sceptre <u>snatched</u> with an unruly hand   *(King John, 3, 4, 135)*

There are several operative words in this line: "sceptre," "snatched," "unruly," and "hand." When we are presented with multiple operative words in a line or sentence, not only is it unwise to give them all equal emphasis, but it is also unwise to use the same means to provide that emphasis. The rhythm of the verb "snatched" fits what it means. Although the actor must punch the word to give it emphasis, its primary means of emphasis should come from its quick pace. The actor should utter it more tersely than the other words in the line. In this way it will be emphasized in a different manner from the other operative words in the line.

Pace or rate of speech is for more than emphasis, however. *We must often decide what rate of speech best serves the imagery of the text.* In the following dialogue from *Romeo and Juliet*, Juliet admonishes the absent Nurse for taking so long in coming home from her meeting with Romeo:

> Had she affections and warm youthful blood,
> She would be as swift in motion as a ball;
> My words would bandy her to my sweet love,
> And his to me:
> But old folks, many feign as they were dead;
> Unwieldy, slow, heavy and pale as lead.
>   *(Romeo and Juliet, 2, 5, 12–17)*

Juliet's first four lines, which are about the energy of young love, should have a quick pace. However, the last two lines, which are about old age, should have a slower, more deliberate pace. In fact, the short line "And his to me" may signify a substantial caesura, as Juliet shifts into an unhurried rate of speech for her last two lines of verse. Let's look at a longer section of dialogue spoken by Cassius in *Julius Caesar*:

> For once, upon a raw and gusty day,
> The troubl'd Tiber chafing with her shores,
> Caesar said to me "Dar'st thou, Cassius, now
> Leap in with me into this angry flood,
> And swim to yonder point?" Upon the word,
> Accoutred as I was, I plunged in,
> And bade him follow; so indeed he did.
> The torrent roar'd, and we did buffet it
> With lusty sinews, throwing it aside,
> And stemming it with hearts of controversy.
>
> *(Julius Caesar, 1, 2, 100–109)*

This passage is rapid, strong, and vital. Let's contrast it with a passage, which we examined in Chapter 5, spoken by Lady Macbeth in *Macbeth:*

> His two chamberlains
> Will I with wine and wassail so convince,
> That memory, the warder of the brain,
> Shall be a fume, and the receipt of reason
> A limbeck only: when in swinish sleep
> Their drenched natures lie, as in a death,
> What cannot you and I perform upon
> Th' unguarded Duncan?   *(Macbeth, 1, 7, 64–70)*

The imagery here, on the other hand, is like an opiate. It is slow, smooth, and somewhat perverse.

LIZ: Won't a slow rate of speech cause the play to drag?

JOE: Only if the actor is indulgent. A slower rate of speech must sometimes be used to get what you want from your scene partner. For example, Lady Macbeth wants to paint a specific picture for her husband in order to convince him to kill Duncan. Speech rate is relative. Even an unhurried rate of utterance must efficiently move the story forward.

SAM: Are there other ways to give emphasis to a word?

JOE: Yes. *We can give emphasis to a word by framing it with silence.* For instance, in *Othello*, Desdemona seeks Iago's advice about getting back into Othello's good graces. Othello thinks, erroneously, that she is an adultress. I will use the "^" symbol to indicate a possible silence:

> I cannot say ^ "whore." ^
> It abhors me now I speak the word;   *(Othello, 4, 2, 161–162)*

By placing a caesura on either side of "whore," the word is lifted out of the sentence. In *A Midsummer Night's Dream,* Bottom the Weaver gets an inflated ego by the compliments he receives from Titania. He tells her that he is able to make a clever remark from time to time:

> Nay, I can ^ gleek ^ upon occasion.
> *(A Midsummer Night's Dream, 3, 1, 146)*

The word "gleek" means to make a clever jest. The actor playing Bottom can frame the word with caesuras to give it special emphasis, perhaps to impress Titania.

LIZ: This all sounds awfully technical. For instance, getting back to the line that you first cited from *Henry IV Part 1*—I worry that, as Lady Percy, I would be so focused on making sure that I used equal punch on *love* and *indeed,* as well as remembering to change my pitch and elongate the stressed vowel sound on *indeed,* that I would disconnect from my scene partner and the intent of the scene.

JOE: Text work is homework, just as scansion is homework. It should be consciously forgotten once we step onstage during a performance. We must be focused on the other characters onstage with us while in performance of a scene or play. Although we will have worked diligently at crafting our words, this crafting must be malleable enough to allow us to respond to our scene partners based on what they are giving us in the moment. You bring me to an important point. Technical emphasis through punch, pitch, pace, or silence is only half of the equation when we speak Shakespeare's words. The actor must also *image* his operative words. For instance, if I have the line "I am really happy," I must not merely *emphasize* the operative word "happy," but I must *image* it as well, infusing the word with specificity and emotional life. *When you emphasize operative words you provide objective meaning; when you image those words you provide subjective meaning. The two together create a kind of dramatic clarity.*

LIZ: So, if I'm emotionally connected to the imagery of Lady Percy's line, I would want to punch the words *love* and *indeed* because they carry the meaning, imagery, and intent of the line?

JOE: Yes. And your upward pitch change and elongation of the vowel sound in *indeed* will come from a strong emotional connection to the material.

Vocal Coloring

LIZ: You mentioned something earlier called vocal coloring. Does that have something to do with imaging the words as you utter them?

JOE: Yes. There is a kind of texturing or coloring that we give to certain words when we personalize their imagery and intent. You may recall from Chapter 6 that spoken English relies on sound patterns for clarity and force. I want to reiterate a quote about sound patterns from Dakin Matthews's book, *Shakespeare Spoken Here:* "[Sound patterns are] the whole complex of sound qualities—loud, soft, fast and slow, up and down, smooth and rough, strong and weak, pleasant and unpleasant—that inform spoken speech" (p. 11). Vocal coloring uses these sound patterns to express the emotional life of the imagery of a word or phrase. It is difficult to write about but easy to hear. Just listen to someone relating an event that caused either elation or horror. Imagery and emotional life will color or texture many of the words.

Sound Texturing

JOE: This brings me to the following topic: Shakespeare often supplies his dialogue with sound texturing. "**Sound texturing** is a figure of speech (a scheme) in which sound clusters are chosen and arranged to capture the emotional quality of the sense in sound" (Matthews, *Shakespeare Spoken Here,* p. 84). Such dialogue requires a good deal of vocal coloring.

SAM: Will you elaborate on sound texturing?

JOE: Of course. Dakin Matthews puts it best. In *Shakespeare Spoken Here,* he goes on to say that with sound texturing, "The words do not strictly 'sound like' what they describe (that would be onomatopoeia), but somehow they capture its emotional resonance. This, for me, is one of Shakespeare's most frequent and most powerful poetic devices . . . [Sound texturing] is about capturing 'emotional quality in sound'" (pp. 84–85).

You'll recall from Chapter 10 that onomatopoeia is a figure of speech (a trope). *Webster's New World Dictionary* defines it as "the formation of a word by imitating the natural sound associated with the object or action involved." Although Shakespeare's sound texturing is not reliant on onomatopoeia, he sometimes uses this trope to create sound texturing. Let's examine a section of dialogue, which we looked at earlier, spoken by the Chorus in *Henry V:*

> The hum of either army stilly sounds,
> That the fix'd sentinels almost receive
> The secret whispers of each other's watch.
>
> *(Henry V, 4, Chorus 5–7)*

Here the Chorus speaks of the night before the famous battle of Agincourt. The French and English armies whisper quietly around their respective campfires. "Hum" is certainly an example of onomatopoeia. "Whispers," while possibly not true onomatopoeia, certainly has an onomatopoetic effect. In addition, the numerous "s" and "z" sounds as well as the "ch" sounds in "each" and "watch" mirror the sounds of whispering.

We have seen Shakespeare's use of sound texturing when we explored alliteration and assonance (the sensuous repetition of "m" sounds in "Thou shalt be married to no man but me" from *The Taming of the Shrew,* for example). In fact, although we did not give it a label, we have talked about sound texturing as early as Chapter 2, where we discussed the importance of identifying words whose sounds and rhythm underscore meaning and emotion.

Let's look at a simple word: "Dog." Shakespeare uses synonyms for this animal in his plays. These synonyms are used figuratively. Let's examine an earlier section of dialogue spoken by the Chorus in *Henry V:*

> Then should the warlike Harry, like himself,
> Assume the port of Mars, and at his heels
> Leash'd in like hounds, should famine, sword and fire
> Crouch for employment.   *(Henry V, Prol. 5–8)*

The above is from the opening of the play, in which the Chorus is whetting the appetite of the audience for the action to come. Here war is glorified and King Henry is painted as a noble, brave warrior. "Hounds" fits this imagery perfectly. The word suggests a fierce, sleek hunting animal. The open "ow" diphthong and the long, continuant consonant sounds "nnn" and "zzz" fit the emotional imagery of the word. Of course, there is even more sound texturing in this passage. The repetitive "r" sound in "warlike," "Harry," "port," "Mars," "sword," "fire," and "crouch" are harsh and mirror the warning growl of a fighting hound before it attacks. In addition, the long consonant "l" and open "ee" vowel sounds in "heels" and "leash'd" echo the open, vital sounds in the word "hounds."

Compare the word "hounds" with the following synonym in this excerpt from *Coriolanus*:

> You common cry of curs, whose breath I hate
> As reek a' th' rotten fens,   *(Coriolanus, 3, 3,120–121)*

In the above dialogue, the warrior Coriolanus berates his fellow Romans. A cur is quite a different kind of canine from a hound. A cur summons up the image of a dirty, flea-bitten, underfed animal and the sounds echo that image. The "k" and "r" sounds are harsh and abrupt and the vowel sound is short and clipped, quite the opposite of the continuant consonant sounds and open vowel sound in "hounds." Once again, the repetition of the assonant "r" sounds in "cry" and "curs" as well as the alliterative "r" sounds in "reek" and "rotten" are abrupt and confrontational, although uttered under different circumstances than those in *Henry V*. And finally the alliterative "k" sounds in "common," "cry" and "curs" have a similar harsh and abrupt quality.

Of course, such sound texturing will be effective to a certain extent, whether or not the actor consciously utilizes it, but it will be most effective if the actor uses vocal coloring to give the sound texturing specificity and dynamism.

Basically, I'm back to what I said at the beginning of this chapter: *Acting Shakespeare is equal parts of form and passion.* This is a symbiotic relationship. The Shakespearean actor must work with the head as well as the heart. If you master the form without the passion, you will become a masterful, but soulless technician. If you master the passion without marrying it to the form, you will be emotionally connected, but unintelligible. We must work on *balancing* the form and the passion, a delicate but achievable task. So now let's examine how we can use punch, pitch, pace, coloring, and texture when speaking some of Shakespeare's most ubiquitous rhetorical figures.

Vocalizing Antitheses

JOE: As I stated earlier, Shakespeare's characters often conceive, process, and utter their thoughts by means of antithesis. We now know that the words involved in antithesis must be given strong and equal emphasis. Here is an example of antithesis that we have already examined:

> And thus the native hue of resolution
> Is sicklied o'er with the pale cast of thought,
>
> *(Hamlet, 3, 1, 83–84)*

These lines may be marked like this:

> And thus the <u>native</u> <u>hue</u> of <u>resolution</u>
> Is <u>sicklied</u> o'er with the <u>pale</u> <u>cast</u> of <u>thought,</u>

"Native hue" must match "pale cast" in degree of emphasis, and "resolution" must match "thought" in degree of emphasis. This can be done with vocal force as well as pitch. But remember this is only half the task. Because antithetical words involve a contrast or opposition, they often contain not only a good deal of imagery and emotional life, but also *contrasting* imagery and emotional life. We must infuse those words accordingly. "Sicklied" in the lines above should also be strongly colored. In this example, which you will recall is from Hamlet's "To be or not to be" soliloquy in which he contemplates suicide, Hamlet states that it is the fear of the afterlife that prevents us from deciding on suicide as an escape from the pain of life. Because of this fear, Hamlet states, the natural, healthy skin tone of resolve is transformed into the white, sickly pallor of thought. As he does so often, Shakespeare gives us sensory imagery, this time in the form of personification. The contrasting concepts of *resolve* and *thought* are given human faces—one pink-skinned and healthy, the other ghostly white and anemic. The actor portraying Hamlet must texture the words with this contrasting imagery.

Vocalizing Alliteration and Assonance

JOE: Like antithesis, alliteration and assonance are often used when a strong emotional life is present. Here is a section of dialogue that we looked at earlier, with alliteration underlined:

> If that my <u>c</u>ousin <u>k</u>ing be <u>K</u>ing in England,
> It must be granted I am Duke of Lancaster.
> You have a son, Aumerle, my noble cousin,
>
> *(Richard II, 2, 3, 123–125)*

The actor playing Henry Bullingbrook, who speaks these words, must give the alliterative "k" sounds in "cousin" and "king" a little extra stressing. He must also infuse those consonant sounds with the ridicule he has for his cousin, King Richard. As we discovered when we examined this speech in Chapter 4, the dialogue is also an example of antithesis—"cousin king" is played against "noble cousin":

> If that my <u>cousin king</u> be King in England,
> It must be granted I am Duke of Lancaster.
> You have a son, Aumerle, my <u>noble cousin,</u>

The actor portraying Bullingbrook must infuse "cousin king" with a contrasting emotional life and imagery to that of "noble cousin." The word *cousin* in the phrase "cousin king" can contain a vocal coloring appropriate to the secondary meaning "cozen," which we now know means to cheat. The word *noble* should receive an antithetical vocal coloring, signifying the respect that Bullingbrook has for York's son, Aumerle. The actor may also wish to raise the pitch of "noble" or give it a strong punch because it is more important than the utterance of "cousin" in that phrase.

Now let's look at an example of assonance:

>O, reason not the need! *(King Lear, 2, 4, 264)*

Here the long "ee" vowel sounds in "reason" and "need" reflect Lear's anger at his daughters, Goneril and Regan, for dismissing his retinue of a hundred Knights, saying that they were not needed. Because vowels are open sounds, Lear can infuse these assonant "ee" sounds with his anguish. The actor playing Lear should also elongate the vowel sounds, particularly in the word "need."

Vocalizing Builds and Lists

JOE: Builds should be vocalized utilizing *pitch* rather than volume. Here is a simple build:

>Shall we be thus afflicted in his wreaks,
>His fits, his frenzy, and his bitterness?
>*(Titus Andronicus, 4, 4, 11–12)*

Here we have a simple build of four. We know that each element in a list or build must receive slightly more emphasis than the preceding element. If the actor uses volume or punch for emphasis in an extended build, he will be screaming by the end of it. Use pitch instead.

When speaking the words of a build, begin at a "normal" pitch and raise your pitch slightly at the end of each item on the list, allowing your pitch to drop slightly after the last item on the list. This gives the illusion of increasing the pace and volume of the dialogue with the utterance of each article of the build. It also gives the impression that each item is slightly more important than the one before it. Let's examine how this may be accomplished with a more extended build. In the following dialogue from *Richard II*, Henry Bullingbrook lists the wrongs that he feels he has suffered at the hands of Bushy and Green:

>*(Normal pitch)* . . . Whilst you have fed upon my signories,
>*(Raise pitch slightly)* Dispark'd my parks and fell'd my forest woods,
>*(Raise pitch again)* From my own windows torn my household coat,
>*(And again)* Raz'd out my imprese, *(and one more time)* leaving me no sign,
>Save men's opinions and my living blood,
>To show the world I am a gentleman. *(Richard II, 3, 1, 22–27)*

The Four Basic Inflections

JOE: Another function of pitch is to provide different inflections at the ends of images, phrases, and sentences. *Inflection*, you'll recall from Chapter 6, is defined as "any change in tone or pitch of the voice." There are four basic inflections:

1. The *sustained* inflection (→)
2. The *circumflex* inflection (⌒)
3. The *rising* inflection (⤴)
4. The *resolve* inflection (⤵)

Sustained Inflection

JOE: A **sustained inflection** neither rises nor drops in pitch. It keeps the "ball in the air" and is used to indicate that the speaker is in mid-thought, or when a caesura (pause) is either appropriate or necessary due to lack of breath while in the middle of a thought or idea. Sustained inflections are invaluable when speaking unusually long sentences. I will mark the following passage with the symbol "(→)" to indicate that a sustained inflection is possible. This dialogue is spoken by the Earl of Northumberland in *Richard II*:

> Thy thrice noble cousin
> Harry Bullingbrook doth humbly kiss thy hand;
> And by the honourable tomb he swears, (→)
> That stands upon your royal grandsire's bones, (→)
> And by the royalties of both your bloods, (→)
> Currents that spring from one most gracious head, (→)
> And by the buried hand of warlike Gaunt, (→)
> And by the worth and honour of himself, (→)
> Comprising all that may be sworn or said, (→)
> His coming hither hath no further scope (→)
> Than for his lineal royalties (→) and to beg
> Enfranchisement immediate on his knees:
>
> (*Richard II*, 3, 3, 103–114)

Many of the possible sustained inflections in this passage do not demand a substantial pause and some require no pause at all. But the actor playing Northumberland can be confident that if he is in need of a breath, a sustained inflection will ensure that the listener will stay with him, knowing that he is in mid-thought.

If you find a sustained inflection difficult to execute, try stopping yourself in the middle of speaking a sentence. For example, think of saying "I live at 123 Main Street" but say only "I live at . . ." Most likely, your inflection after you say "at" will be sustained.

Circumflex Inflection

JOE: A **circumflex inflection** changes pitch before ending in a sustained inflection. *Circumflex* means "curved" or "bending," indicating that pitch rises and falls or falls and rises before sustaining. A circumflex inflection can be used at any point that a sustained inflection is appropriate. The actor may wish to alternate between the two:

> My father's loss,(→) Like a most royal prince, (⌢↑)
> Restor'd me to my honors;   *(Henry VIII, 2, 1, 113–114)*

Rising Inflection

JOE: A **rising inflection** rises in pitch. It is sometimes used when asking a question. In the example below, I've used the symbol "(—↗)" to denote the rising inflection:

> ANGELO: Your brother cannot live.
> ISABEL: Even so. —Heaven keep your honor!
> ANGELO: Yet may he live awhile, and, it may be
>   As long as you or I. Yet he must die.
> ISABEL: Under your sentence? (—↗)
> ANGELO: Yea.   *(Measure for Measure, 2, 4, 33–38)*

A rising inflection is not appropriate for all questions, however. For instance, a rising inflection at the end of Angelo's question below, spoken earlier in the same scene, would sound odd:

> ANGELO: How now! Who's there?
> SERVANT: One Isabel, a sister, desires access to you.

The rising inflection can also be theatrical in nature and would be appropriate at the end of a line such as:

> Cry, "God for Harry, England and Saint George (—↗)!
>   *(Henry V, 3, 1, 34)*

A veteran actor once advised me, "If your character expires onstage, let his last words take him to heaven on the wings of a rising inflection."

LIZ: Getting back to Angelo's line "Who's there?" . . . If a rising inflection is inappropriate, what inflection would you recommend?

Resolve Inflection

JOE: In cases like that, I'd recommend a **resolve inflection,** because it drops slightly in pitch. It is almost always used to end a thought or action. It would be the inflection at the end of "I live at 123 Main Street (—↘)." Here is an example from Shakespeare's dialogue:

> Vouchsafe to those that have not read the story
> That I may prompt them(⤵).   *(Henry V, 5, Prol., 1–2)*

Many sentences that end in strong punctuation require a resolve inflection.

SAM: But our acting teachers always tell us to never drop off vocally at the end of a line.

JOE: You're confusing a resolve inflection with a *down ending*. A **down ending** occurs when the speaker lacks a clear objective. In such a case the line drops off in every way—volume, pitch, and (most importantly) intent. A resolve inflection should carry intent and should drop in pitch but not in volume. It simply signals a shift between ideas. I have seen many acting students stubbornly use a rising inflection at the end of a thought for fear that doing otherwise would result in the "dreaded down-ending." This results in a group of young actors who seem to be speaking with bad Swedish accents.

Vocalizing Parenthetical Words and Phrases

JOE: Pitch can also be a valuable tool in speaking parenthetical words and phrases.

SAM: Is that anything like a "parenthesis"?

JOE: Yes. A *parenthesis,* as we learned in Chapter 10, is an additional word, phrase, or clause inserted as an explanation or comment within an already complete sentence. *Parenthetical* refers to words interjected as qualifying information or explanation. Parenthetical words can be removed from a sentence without affecting the meaning of the sentence. When speaking lines that contain parenthetical phrases, either raise or lower the pitch of those words and come back to your usual pitch as you exit the parenthetical phrase and return to the main body of the text. Use a sustained or circumflex inflection when leaving and returning to the principal dialogue. In addition, the actor should take a brief caesura both before and after a parenthetical phrase. You may also wish to increase the rate of the parenthetical phrase slightly. This technique can be especially valuable. If you are playing the role of Horatio in *Hamlet,* you may be quite thankful for knowing how to score a speech loaded with parenthetical phrases. For instance, here Horatio speaks to Bernardo and Marcellus:

> <u>Our last king,</u>
> (Whose image even but now appear'd to us,)
> <u>Was,</u> (as you know,) <u>by Fortinbras of Norway,</u>
> (Thereto prick'd on by a most emulate pride,)
> <u>Dared to the combat; in which our valiant Hamlet—</u>
> (For so this side of our known world esteem'd him—)
> <u>Did slay this Fortinbras; who</u> (by a seal'd compact,
> Well ratified by law and heraldry,)
> <u>Did forfeit,</u> (with his life,) <u>all those his lands</u>
> (Which he stood seized of,) <u>to the conqueror:</u>
>   *(Hamlet, 1, 1, 80–89)*

These are only the first ten lines of a twenty-eight-line speech! I have underlined the main thrust of these lines—the "spine" of this section of the speech—and have enclosed parenthetical phrases in parenthesis. This is a very complex speech, full of important information. If the actor playing Horatio does not separate the vital information from the information that qualifies or explains it, the result will be a confused audience as well as a perplexed Bernardo and Marcellus.[2]

For the sake of clarity, let's look at a possible marking of the beginning of Horatio's speech. I will use the caret symbol (^) to indicate a brief caesura and arrow symbols to indicate sustained and circumflex infections. I will also drop the print of the parenthetical phrases to indicate a lower pitch:

Our last king, →^   ^Was, →^
    Whose image even but not appear'd to us,   as you know . . .

Vocalizing Shared Builds and Shared Antitheses

JOE: In Shakespeare you may often find yourself sharing a list or build with another character. For example, here King Lear comes upon his servant (Kent in disguise) in the stocks:

> LEAR: What's he that hath so much thy place mistook
>   To set thee here?
> KENT: It is both he and she,
>   Your son and daughter.
> LEAR: No.
> KENT: Yes.
> LEAR: No, I say.
> KENT: I say yea.
> LEAR: No, no, they would not.
> KENT: Yes, they have.
> LEAR: By Jupiter, I swear no.
> KENT: By Juno, I swear ay.
>
>   (*King Lear*, 2, 4, 12–22)

Lear and Kent must "top" each other throughout this exchange. The energy of each line must be greater than the one before or the entire build will collapse. This can be done with volume and pitch but most importantly it will be the emotional life of the characters that will ensure the increase of vocal energy. In the following example, Richard III attempts to convince Queen Elizabeth that he would be the ideal husband for her daughter. Elizabeth questions his sincerity:

> QUEEN ELIZABETH: If something thou wouldst swear to be believ'd,
>   Swear then by something that thou hast not wrong'd.
> RICHARD: Then by myself—

QUEEN ELIZABETH:	Thyself is self-misus'd.
RICHARD: Now by the world—	
QUEEN ELIZABETH:	'Tis full of thy foul wrongs.
RICHARD: My father's death—	
QUEEN ELIZABETH:	Thy life hath it dishonor'd.
RICHARD: Why then, by God—	
QUEEN ELIZABETH:	God's wrong is most of all.

(Richard III, 4, 4, 372–377)

Again, it is vital for Elizabeth and Richard to continually top one another throughout this shared build. The shared verse lines further intensify the build. The concept of "topping your partner" also applies with shared antitheses (our examples from *King Lear* and *Richard III* also contain shared antitheses). Here is a simple example of shared antithesis from *King Lear*.

> GONERIL: Pray you let us hit together; if our father carry authority with such disposition as he bears, this last surrender of his will but offend us.
> REGAN: We shall further think of it.
> GONERIL: We must do something and i' th' heat.
> *(King Lear, 1, 1, 303–398)*

The above dialogue concludes the tempestuous first scene of the play. Sisters Goneril and Regan discuss their father's volatile behavior. Goneril warns her sister that they may be the next victims of their father's wrath unless they take steps to prevent it. While Regan must emphasize "think" strongly, Goneril must emphasize "do" even more strongly. There are many such shared antitheses between Lady Anne and Richard in *Richard III*. For example:

> ANNE: O wonderful, when devils tell the truth!
> RICHARD: More wonderful, when angels are so angry.
> *(Richard III, 1, 2, 73–74)*

Anne must pronounce "wonderful," "devils," and "truth" strongly and specifically, but Richard must vocally top her with "more wonderful," "angels," and "angry." Many sections of Shakespeare's scenes require that characters continually top one another vocally. Here is a larger section of dialogue from the same scene:

> RICHARD: Say that I slew them not?
> ANNE: Then say they were not slain.
> But dead they are, and, devilish slave, by thee.
> RICHARD: I did not kill your husband.
> ANNE: Why then he is alive.

RICHARD: Nay, he is dead, and slain by Edward's hands.
ANNE: In thy foul throat thou liest! Queen Margaret saw
    Thy murd'rous falchion smoking in his blood;
    The which thou once didst bend against her breast,
    But that thy brothers beat aside the point.
RICHARD: I was provoked by her sland'rous tongue,
    That laid their guilt upon my guiltless shoulders.
ANNE: Thou wast provoked by thy bloody mind
    That never dreamt on aught but butcheries.
(Richard III, 1, 2, 89–100)

Richard and Anne top one another throughout this entire section. There are several shared antitheses in the scene, but even dialogue that is not antithetical must build in energy throughout the scene.

Modulating Shakespeare's Builds

SAM: Do all of Shakespeare's scenes and speeches build in energy?
JOE: No, at least not in the way that you mean. Let's look at a portion of the famous "O, what a rogue and peasant slave am I" speech spoken by Hamlet:

    for it cannot be
But I am pigeon-liver'd, and lack gall
To make oppression bitter, or ere this
I should have fatted all the region kites
With this slave's offal! Bloody, bawdy villain!
Remorseless, treacherous, lecherous, kindless villain!
O, vengeance!
Why, what an ass am I! This is most brave,
That I, the son of a dear father murdered,
Prompted to my revenge by heaven and hell,
Must like a whore unpack my heart with words,
And fall a-cursing like a very drab,
A scullion. Fie upon't, foh!
About, my brain! Hum—I have heard
That guilty creatures sitting at a play
Have by the very cunning of the scene
Been struck so to the soul, that presently
They have proclaim'd their malefactions:
For murder, though it have no tongue, will speak
With most miraculous organ. I'll have these players
Play something like the murder of my father

> Before mine uncle. I'll observe his looks,
> I'll tent him to the quick. If he but blench,
> I know my course. *(Hamlet 2, 2, 576–599)*

In this speech, Hamlet berates himself for his inability to take action to revenge his father's murder at the hands of his uncle Claudius, Hamlet's father's brother. Finally, he comes up with a plan that involves a troop of traveling actors.

The first section printed above contains strong emotion as Hamlet curses his uncle. Hamlet's self-loathing combined with his growing hatred for Claudius builds until it explodes with "O, vengeance!" To further build the energy of the speech from this point is impossible and makes no sense. Instead, the energy modulates with the next beat that begins "Why, what an ass am I!" Explosive anger transforms into a more contained, seething sarcasm as he rebukes himself for his inaction. This second section builds in intensity until the line "About, my brain!" A possible paraphrase for this line might be "Get to work, brain!" At this point there is another modulation of energy. Beginning with "Hum —" Hamlet gets a brainstorm. He has finally thought of a plan of action. As he vocalizes his plan in this third section of dialogue, the energy is calmer but much more focused.

So, as you can see, while energy never drops off in a speech or scene, energy certainly modulates or "morphs," if you will, into different types of energy.

SAM: I see.

What Is Elevated Language?

JOE: This brings me to my final point for this meeting. We have been discussing Shakespeare's use of elevated language for some time now without explicitly defining it. We know that elevated language is one of the elements of his dramatic verse dialogue. He also uses elevated language in his prose dialogue from time to time.

LIZ: My first impression of elevated language is "fancy" language. You know, using words that most people would have to look up in a dictionary.

JOE: You mean using a word like "vicissitude" rather than the simple word "change," for instance?

LIZ: Yes. But that isn't true, is it?

JOE: No, it isn't. I think that *elevated* language is actually *concentrated* language. We have seen this with Shakespeare's use of sound texturing. In fact, we have even seen this as far back as Chapter 2 when we uncovered the meaning of your speeches from *Romeo and Juliet*. **Elevated language** takes advantage of every aspect of the spoken word—literal definitions, figurative definitions, sensory definitions, multiple definitions as well as sound and rhythm to persuade and stir the emotions of the listener. We have examined many examples of Shakespeare's use of this kind of language during our work together. Another aspect of elevated language is its use of the connotation of words and phrases.

SAM: How do you mean?

JOE: Words and phrases have denotative and connotative meanings. **Denotative meaning** is the objective, dictionary meaning of a word or phrase. **Connotative meaning** is the associations and overtones of a word or phrase. For example, the denotative, explicit meaning of "mother" is a "female parent." But the word also connotes "love," "safety," "comfort," and so on. Connotative meaning tends to work on the emotions rather than the intellect of the listener. Therefore, connotative meanings are better "persuaders" than denotative meanings.

LIZ: This information is going to help for our workshop production of *Romeo and Juliet*.

JOE: Yes, by now you've built up a pretty good basis for taking on your roles as Romeo and Juliet. But there are still a few things that we haven't covered yet. Let's meet again tomorrow.

SUMMARY

In this chapter, Joe showed Sam and Liz how to identify operative words and phrases in Shakespeare's text, how to diagram the text so as to discover word patterns and rhythms, and how to use vocalization to convey the meaning and emotion of the text to fellow actors as well as to the audience.

- Acting Shakespeare is equal parts of passion and form. Passion is the truth from the actor's soul and form is the expression of that truth—first on paper, and then through the spoken word.
- The first step in text work is to locate the operative words in Shakespeare's dialogue. Operative or "key" words are those that carry the imagery, meaning, and emotion of the sentence.
- Operative words most often include nouns, possessive nouns, active verbs, adjectives, and adverbs.
- Words that are usually inoperative include negatives, prepositions, conjunctions, articles, pronouns, possessive pronouns, and verbs of being.
- Words that are usually inoperative can become operative if they are part of a contrast or comparison or other contextual emphasis, or when they carry strong emotion.
- Image words that are repeated are usually not operative. What *is* operative is the word or words that qualify or modify the image.
- The exception to this rule is when an image is repeated for emphasis, or when the image is repeated because it looms ever larger in the imagination of the speaker. In such cases, the word receives more emphasis each time it is repeated.
- Alliterative and assonant sounds usually get a little extra vocal attention because they help to tie two or more words into a single image or related images. Instances of alliteration and assonance also deserve extra stressing because they often reflect the emotion of the image.
- Antithetical words and phrases must receive strong and equal emphasis.
- Words that are juxtaposed against one another, even if not true antithesis, must also be given strong and equal emphasis.

- Words that contain new information need special emphasis.
- Words, phrases, or sentences that state the structure or steps of a story or argument need special emphasis.
- Figures of climax (also known as a "list" or a "build") need special attention regarding emphasis.
- There are degrees of emphasis. A possible system of scoring operative words is to mark the strongest emphasis with a double underline, secondary emphasis with a single underline, and tertiary emphasis with a dotted underline.
- An actor must also commit to "throwing away" inoperative words. As vital as it is for an actor to commit to his operative words, it is just as vital that he give no emphasis to words that contain little or no imagery or emotion. Emphasizing non-image words together with operative words will confuse fellow actors onstage as well as the audience.
- Diagramming helps the actor to group words together into images, helps reveal important words and images, and in long sentences, helps the actor to know where to pause in appropriate places. It also takes sections of Shakespeare's dialogue that may at first glance look intimidating, and breaks it up into pieces that are easier to understand.
- Diagramming can reveal the subject of the sentence—the main idea and supporting ideas—and indicates where to take caesuras without breaking up images or thought groups.
- It also reveals the rhythms and builds that the playwright has written into the text.
- When diagramming, start big, and work toward the little things.
- First, place braces ({ }) around complete sentences. This helps us get an idea of the overall rhythm of the piece as well as how the character's mind is working.
- Second, place angle brackets (< >) around images made of two or more words. Since we group words together that make up an image in "real life," we have to remember to do it in Shakespeare.
- Third, place straight brackets ([ ]) around the predicate to separate the main subject and verb from the rest of the sentence. This helps us break down the long, complex sentences that Shakespeare often writes into more easily understood—and spoken—ideas.
- Fourth, circle the antithesis. This way, when it comes time to read the piece, the antithesis should be heard loud and clear.
- Fifth, underline alliteration and assonance. It makes sense to mark them when we diagram because word play was the name of the game in Shakespeare's day, and he often used alliteration and assonance to help the character make a point, reinforce emotion or indicate a certain trait about the character.
- Sixth, mark run-on lines with an arrow. (This really only works in verse.) Marking thoughts that continue to the next line with an arrow gives you a visual reminder to keep your vocal energy going past the end of the line and on to the next.
- Seventh, mark lists and builds with numbers. Marking the parts of a list or a build (especially if the items in the list are long phrases) not only reminds you to vocally build to the next item, but also helps identify exactly what is part of the list or

build. And since each successive item in a Shakespearean list tends to be more important than the last, marking the lists helps build the speech.
- There are three basic ways to give emphasis to a syllable, word, or phrase: punch, pitch, and pace. Punch refers to the amount of "vocal force" (volume) that we use. Pitch refers to the tone of the voice, and involves raising (or sometimes lowering) our intonation in order to impart emphasis. Pace refers to the speed with which we speak a sound, syllable, word, or phrase, with emphasis provided by shortening or elongating the sound(s).
- The actor can also emphasize a word by framing it with silence, placing a small caesura on either side of the word.
- There is a kind of vocal coloring that we give to certain words when we personalize their imagery and intent. Vocal coloring occurs when we use sound patterns to express the emotional life of the imagery of a word or phrase.
- Shakespeare often supplies his dialogue with sound texturing. Sound texturing is a figure of speech (a scheme) in which sound clusters are chosen and arranged to capture the emotional quality of the sense in sound. Sound texturing requires a good deal of vocal coloring.
- Antithetical words must be equally emphasized through vocal force, pitch change, rate change, or a combination of these.
- Alliteration and assonance need special vocal attention and extra stressing. Consonant sounds are usually punched, while dipthong and vowel sounds use pace to elongate the sound. Sound texturing is often needed as well.
- When speaking the words of a build or list, the actor should employ pitch rather than volume.
- The four basic vocal inflections are the sustained inflection, the circumflex inflection, the rising inflection, and the resolve inflection. These inflections are used at the end of a phrase, clause, or sentence.
- When speaking lines that contain parenthetical phrases, either raise or lower the pitch of those words and come back to your usual pitch as you exit the parenthetical phrase and return to the main body of the text.
- When sharing a build with another character, increase the energy of each exchange through volume, pitch, or both. The energy of each line must be greater than the one before or the entire build will collapse. This is also true of shared antithesis.
- Shakespeare often modulated the energy of his speeches and scenes rather than continually building it. While energy never drops off in a speech or scene, energy certainly modulates or "morphs" into different types of energy.
- We now know that Shakespeare used elevated language in his plays. Elevated language takes advantage of every aspect of the spoken word—literal definitions, figurative definitions sensory definitions, multiple definitions as well as sound and rhythm to persuade and stir the emotions of the listener.
- Elevated language is also reliant on connotative meaning. Connotative meaning is the associations and overtones of a word or phrase as opposed to the literal, denotative meaning of a word or phrase. Connotative meaning tends to work on the emotions rather than the intellect of the listener and is therefore a better "persuader" than denotative meaning.

EXERCISES

In addition to the exercises that follow, the rhetoric exercises at the end of Chapter 10 are valuable text exercises.

COUPLE (OR GROUP) EXERCISE 11.1

Singing the Scene. Rehearsing a scene as if it were an opera or a musical can be helpful for several reasons. First, it can inject fun into a scene that has temporarily lost its spontaneity. Second, it is an excellent way to improve pitch and rate variation. The actor may feel free to explore pitches previously unvisited after having sung the dialogue. This is true of rate as well. We are more open to a slower or increased pace when we are singing. Third, singing engages the right hemisphere of the brain, the brain's creative center, while speaking engages the analytical side of the brain. Therefore singing the lines may reveal aspects of the scene that would otherwise remain undiscovered.

COUPLE EXERCISE 11.2

Telegram. Two scene partners sit comfortably across from one another. The premise is that the dialogue of the scene is the contents of a telegram being sent to the other person, and each has a limited amount of money to spend. Hence, only certain words can be spoken—and yet these words must still convey the meaning and intent of the dialogue. (This exercise should be done only after the actors have memorized their lines and have a degree of understanding of the scene.) The actors should relay only those words that contain imagery and intent and to which they have a physical connection. Each puts total concentration on the other and attempts to connect with his partner. Let's use the following dialogue as an example:

> BENEDICK: Lady Beatrice, have you wept all this while?
>
> BEATRICE: Yea, and I will weep a while longer.
>
> BENEDICK: I will not desire that.
>
> BEATRICE: You have no reason, I do it freely.
>
> BENEDICK: Surely I do believe your fair cousin is wronged.
>
> BEATRICE: Ah, how much might the man deserve of me that would right her!
>
> BENEDICK: Is there any way to show such friendship?
>
> BEATRICE: A very even way, but no such friend.
>
> BENEDICK: May a man do it?
>
> BEATRICE: It is a man's office, but not yours.
>
> *(Much Ado about Nothing, 4, 1, 255–266)*

The dialogue above is the first beat of a scene between Benedick and Beatrice. Benedick's friend, Claudio, has just jilted Beatrice's cousin, Hero, at the altar. Hero fainted after being accused of infidelity by her fiancé. She has been escorted from the chapel, leaving Benedick and Beatrice alone. The "Telegram" exercise for the scene may go something like this:

> BENEDICK: Beatrice, wept while?
> BEATRICE: Yea, weep longer.
> BENEDICK: not desire.
> BEATRICE: no reason, freely.
> BENEDICK: believe fair cousin wronged.
> BEATRICE: Ah, man deserve right her!
> BENEDICK: way show friendship?
> BEATRICE: very even way, no friend.
> BENEDICK: man do it?
> BEATRICE: man's office, not yours.

The exercise can be even sparser if the scene partners leave out negatives, non-image pronouns, and small words, as well as repeated words. For example:

> BENEDICK: wept while?
> BEATRICE: Yea, longer.
> BENEDICK: desire.
> BEATRICE: reason, freely.
> BENEDICK: fair cousin wronged.
> BEATRICE: Ah, man deserve right!
> BENEDICK: way show friendship?
> BEATRICE: very even, friend.
> BENEDICK: man?
> BEATRICE: office, yours.

This sparer version contains less literal sense than the first, but the actors must think of the literal sense as they utter the above words. This exercise is an excellent way to discover the essential image words of your dialogue. It can reveal which words must be strongly imaged and emphasized, as well as which words must be "given away" or "thrown away."

Variation: Actors go through the scene voicing only consonant sounds. Then repeat using only vowel and dipthong sounds. Think of communicating both the literal and emotional sense of the scene.

COUPLE EXERCISE 11.3

Getting to the End of the Line. English is a language that tends to put primary emphasis on the predicate rather than the subject. For example:

> I woke <u>up</u>
>
> I woke up <u>late</u>
>
> I woke up late on <u>Sunday</u>

This exercise is designed to help you get to the end of a line with vocal power and intent. It is especially useful for long, involved sentences. A partner or friend must help.

You speak the first short phrase of the line. Your partner repeats the phrase and adds "what?" after it. You then speak the first and second phrases and your partner continues to add "what?" until the line is completed. This will become clear after this example from *Twelfth Night*:

> ACTOR: If <u>music</u> . . .
> PARTNER: If music *what?*
> ACTOR: If music be the <u>food</u> . . .
> PARTNER: If music be the food *what?*
> ACTOR: If music be the food of <u>love</u> . . .
> PARTNER: If music be the food of love *what?*
> ACTOR: If music be the food of love, play <u>on</u> . . .
> PARTNER: If music be the food of love, play on *what?*
> ACTOR: If music be the food of love, play on give me <u>excess</u> of it.

With each utterance of your partner's question "what?" you will be reminded that to answer the question clearly, you must give the strongest emphasis to the image word at the end of the phrase or line. This can help prevent an image word from being muttered or dropped in intensity, particularly with a long sentence like the one above.

GROUP EXERCISE 11.1
Circle of Imagery. This exercise requires at least four or five actors. Actors lie on their backs on the floor in a circle with heads to the center of the circle, eyes closed. Actor A selects a word from a scene or monologue that he is having trouble connecting with or imaging fully. The others should be familiar with the meaning and sense of the word within the context of the scene. The actor speaks the word, and then, proceeding clockwise, each person in the circle says aloud the first image that the word triggers. This is repeated until the circle returns to actor A, who then says the word again, using any imagery from his fellow actors that he found useful to help him speak the word more fully. The cycle continues as long as is useful. Then actor B chooses a word, and so on. If an actor cannot come up with an image, he or she simply says "Pass" and the exercise proceeds to the next person. Responses need not be confined to a single word. For example, let's say that an actor portraying Olivia in a scene from *Twelfth Night* is having trouble imaging and uttering "cypress" in the following dialogue:

> To one of your receiving
> Enough is shown; a <u>cypress</u>, not a bosom,
> Hides my heart. So let me hear you speak.
> *(Twelfth Night, 3, 2, 120–122)*

In the above dialogue, Olivia lays her heart open to Viola, who is in disguise as Cesario. "Cypress" is a transparent black fabric, here used figuratively. Olivia means that she is displaying her love openly and vulnerably to this young "man," even though doing so may invite rejection. With actor A playing Olivia, the exercise might go something like this:

> ACTOR A: Cypress.
> ACTOR B: Fragile.
> ACTOR C: Delicate.
> ACTOR D: Easily shattered.
> ACTOR E: Overflowing with passion.
> ACTOR F: Please love me.
> ACTOR A: Cypress.

Actor A would use any of the utterances of her peers to help her infuse "cypress" with a stronger, more specific emotional life and intent. This exercise reminds you that a fellow actor may hit on an image for your problem word that you find helpful and had not thought of.

NOTES

1. I am deeply indebted to Professor Judith Moreland, a friend and valued colleague, for contributing to this chapter by penning (brilliantly) the section on diagramming the text. Both Judy and I wish to thank Professor Nancy Houfek, our former voice and text instructor at the American Conservatory Theatre, who introduced us both to text diagramming, and Lynne Soffer, who continued and refined the diagramming tradition at ACT.
2. I want to thank my good friend and former colleague Professor Jerry McGonigle for his recommendation of, and assistance on, Horatio's speech.

CHAPTER 12

POTPOURRI

(We meet the next day.)

JOE: Now I want to briefly cover a potpourri of items about acting Shakespeare that we haven't covered yet, as well as a few that I think need reiteration.

ASIDES

JOE: I first want to discuss Shakespeare's use of *asides*. Most often, an **aside** is a truthful comment, personal in nature, that is either addressed to the audience or self-directed. Let's look at a section we examined earlier:

>DESDEMONA: How is't with you, my lord?
>OTHELLO: Well, my good lady. *[Aside]* O, hardness to dissemble! —
>How do you, Desdemona?
>DESDEMONA: Well, my good lord.
>   *(Othello, 3, 4, 33–35)*

As you will recall, Othello is in mental anguish over Desdemona's supposed infidelity. He covers it up and pretends that all is well. His aside is an emotional outburst about how difficult it is for him to put on a happy front. It is a convention of Elizabethan theatre that no one onstage can hear the character speak an aside. Therefore, the actor needn't mumble the words of an aside. *Asides are most often emotionally laden* and the actor should allow his character to express the words fully and strongly. The other characters onstage do not "freeze" during an aside (unless it is a director's production concept). In the above example, Desdemona can keep her focus on Othello until he finishes the aside and follows it with his question to her, or she can shift her focus to another character or a physical action for a brief moment, but she shouldn't stand immobile, as if time has stopped. I have seen directors purposely freeze actors during asides in comedies, but it was for a comic effect. For longer asides (some of them can be several lines long), the other characters onstage can carry on with their physical life in the scene, oblivious to the words of the aside.

In *Twelfth Night*, Olivia delivers an aside that is a passionate comment concerning Viola, in disguise as Cesario:

> OLIVIA: Stay!
>   I prithee tell me what thou think'st of me.
> VIOLA: That you do think you are not what you are.
> OLIVIA: If I think so, I think the same of you.
> VIOLA: Then think you right: I am not what I am.
> OLIVIA: I would you were as I would have you be.
> VIOLA: Would it be better, madam, than I am?
>   I wish it might, for now I am your fool.
> OLIVIA: *[Aside]* O, what a deal of scorn looks beautiful
>   In the contempt and anger of his lip!
>   A murd'rous guilt shows not itself more soon
>   Than love that would seem hid: love's night is noon. —
>   Cesario, by the roses of the spring,
>   By maidhood, honor, truth, and every thing,
>   I love thee so, that maugre all thy pride,
>   Nor wit nor reason can my passion hide.
>   *(Twelfth Night, 3, 1, 137–152)*

Olivia's passionate aside, which is an exclamation of her attraction to Cesario, motivates her subsequent overt confession of love to Cesario "himself." The actress playing Olivia can direct her aside to the audience or to herself. Most Shakespeare editions signal the end of an aside with a dash ("—"), as in the excerpt from *Twelfth Night* above and in our earlier example from *Othello*.

Occasionally, an aside will be directed to another character onstage. In such cases, it is a convention that the other onstage characters do not overhear the conversation. Here is an example from *Titus Andronicus:*

> TAMARA: But on my mine honor dare I undertake
>   For good Lord Titus' innocence in all,
>   Whose fury not dissembled speaks his griefs.

>   Lose not so noble a friend on vain suppose,
>   Nor with sour looks afflict his gentle heart.
>   *[Aside to Saturninus.]* My lord, be ruled by me, be won at last,
>   Dissemble all your griefs and discontents.
>   You are but newly planted on the throne;
>   Lest then the people, and patricians too,
>   Upon a just survey take Titus' part,
>   And so supplant you for ingratitude,
>   Which Rome reputes to be a heinous sin,
>   Yield all entreats; and then let me alone,
>   I'll find a way to massacre them all,
>   *(Titus Andronicus, 1, 1, 436–450)*

Queen Tamara of the Goths, recently married to Saturninus, newly made emperor of Rome, publicly advises her new husband to make amends with Titus Andronicus, Rome's foremost general, with whom he has had a falling out. Her aside to her husband reveals that her public statement is a lie and that she plans to help Saturninus destroy Titus and his family. I have printed the first nine lines of Tamara's fourteen-line aside to Saturninus. There are many major and minor characters onstage at the time. It is an Elizabethan convention that they are oblivious to Tamara's words to the emperor.

Asides addressed to another character may or may not be truthful, but asides that are self-directed or audience-directed are always truthful and heartfelt.

STAGE DIRECTIONS

JOE: Shakespeare often provides stage directions in his dialogue. Many of Shakespeare's stage directions are printed out: "Exit, pursued by a bear," for instance (my personal favorite from *The Winter's Tale*). But *much of Shakespeare's physical directions to the actor are buried in his dialogue.* For example:

> PETRUCHIO: Nay, hear you Kate. In sooth <u>you scape not so.</u>
> KATHERINE: I chafe you if I tarry. <u>Let me go.</u>
>   *(The Taming of the Shrew, 2, 1, 240–241)*

In this scene, the fiery Katherine is trying to dampen the advances of her suitor, Petruchio. She tries to leave him, as indicated by Petruchio's underlined dialogue, but, as we can tell from Katherine's dialogue that I've underlined, Petruchio restrains her. He most likely restrains her physically but he could also block her exit. Two former students, who presented this scene in class, decided that Petruchio had locked the exit door. The actress portraying Katherine grabbed the door knob in order to thrust the door open to make her escape, and finding it locked, turned to Petruchio and exclaimed, "Let me go." My point is this: Although sometimes the physical action is interpretive, the actor should always look to the dialogue for Shakespeare's stage directions.

Language Peculiarities

"Thou" and "You"

JOE: The next item on my list is *language peculiarities*. I want to begin with the differences between the words *thou* and *you*. I briefly touched on this earlier, but it deserves a more detailed examination. Many languages today have both a formal and informal word for *you*. This was true of English in Shakespeare's day but has since fallen out of use.

SAM: It's too bad. I like saying it in *Romeo and Juliet*.

JOE: Many actors agree with you. The words *thee*, *thou*, and *thine* sound somewhat special, elevated, and romantic today because we no longer use them. However, in Shakespeare's time, *thou* was the informal form of *you*. One would address one's superiors as "you" and inferiors as "thou." Friends, equals, and lovers would often address one another as "thou" unless circumstances caused an emotional distance, in which case "you" could be used to reinforce that distance. One can also flatter an equal with "you." Consider the underlined words in the following excerpts:

> SILVIUS: Say that you love me not, but say not so
> In bitterness.   *(As You Like It, 3, 5, 2–3)*

> PHEBE: I would not be thy executioner;
> I fly thee for I would not injure thee.   *(As You Like It, 3, 5, 9–10)*

Although equals, Silvius adores Phebe and uses the formal "you," while Phebe the informal uses "thy" and "thee." Below, Celia uses the familiar form when addressing her cousin and best friend:

> CELIA: O my poor Rosalind, whither wilt thou go?
>   *(As You Like It, 1, 3, 90)*

Compare that with the following exchange between Orlando and his servant:

> ORLANDO: Why, whither, Adam wouldst thou have me go?
> ADAM: No matter whither, so you come not here.
>   *(As You Like It, 2, 3, 29–30)*

Here, Orlando addresses his servant with the familiar "thou," while Adam uses the formal "you" to address his young master.

The Royal "We"

JOE: Another language distinction in Shakespeare's time was the use of the **royal "we."** Kings and queens in Shakespeare's plays often refer to themselves in the plural. They may say "we" rather than "I," "us" rather than "me," "our" rather than "my," and "ourself" (not "ourselves") rather than "myself." In *Richard II*, King Richard often refers to himself in the plural. Here he addresses the treacherous Earl of Northumberland:

> We are amazed; and thus long have we stood
> To watch the fearful bending of thy knee,
> Because we thought ourself thy lawful king;
> And if we be, how dare thy joints forget
> To pay their awful duty to our presence?
> If we be not, show us the hand of God
> That hath dismiss'd us from our stewardship;
> For well we know no hand of blood and bone
> Can grip the sacred handle of our scepter,
> Unless he do profane, steal, or usurp. (*Richard II*, 3, 3, 72–81)

You'll also notice that because he is an inferior, Richard addresses Northumberland with "thy."

Frequently Mispronounced Words

JOE: Although I stressed the use of a pronunciation dictionary at the beginning of this book, I want to go over several of the most frequently mispronounced words in Shakespeare's plays:

- The past tense of the verb "bid" is "bade"—pronounced "bad" (as in the opposite of "good"). It does not rhyme with "made."
- "Err" (the verb meaning "to make a mistake"), rhymes with "fur." It is not pronounced "air."
- "E'er" (a contraction of "ever") and "ere" (meaning "before") are pronounced identically—like the word "air."
- The word "sirrah" is accented on the first syllable, not the second.
- "Signor" is most often stressed on the first syllable.
- The name "Viola" (pronounced "VYE-oh-luh"), is accented on the first syllable. It is not a musical instrument.
- "Troth" can be pronounced two ways, rhyming with either "oath" or "sloth."
- The word "doth" has the vowel of "puff," not the vowel of "off." Thus, it is pronounced "duth."
- "Gaol" is an archaic spelling of "jail." Similarly, "murther" is an archaic spelling of "murder." And "accompt" is an archaic spelling of "account." The actor may use the modern, familiar pronunciations of these words.
- "Ay" (meaning "yes") is pronounced "eye."
- "Aye" (meaning "forever") is pronounced like the first letter of the alphabet: "a."

- "A" is a mutilation of the pronoun "he" and is pronounced "uh."
- Many proper names are often mispronounced. For example *Gloucester* (should be pronounced "GLAW-ster"), *Worcester* ("WOO-ster"), and *Berkley* ("BAR-klee").

History of the Period

JOE: When acting Shakespeare or the plays of any other Elizabethan playwright, it is essential to have a working understanding of the history of England during the late sixteenth and early seventeenth centuries. Knowledge of the time and place in which Shakespeare wrote is essential when working on his plays, regardless of the production concept. Specific information concerning social issues, religion, economics, politics, and daily life is invaluable for the actor and director. While there are many books on the subject, I would like to recommend two. Both are inexpensive paperbacks.

In keeping with the spirit of the title *Shakespeare without Fear,* my first recommendation is *Shakespeare Alive!,* by Joseph Papp and Elizabeth Kirkland. It is a user-friendly, easy-to-read, comprehensible, and concise treatment of life in Shakespeare's England (especially London). It also explores the life of the theatregoer and theatre participant during Shakespeare's time.

The Elizabethan World Picture, by E. M. W. Tillyard, is a more scholarly work and is now considered somewhat of a classic. It is of special importance to actors because it gives a detailed description of the Elizabethan mind set. How English men and women of the sixteenth and early seventeenth centuries saw their world and their place in it is of vital importance when considering objectives, motivations, and personalizations. I recommend reading both books, rather than one or the other.

Elizabethan Philosophy

JOE: Although both *The Elizabethan World Picture* and *Shakespeare Alive* contain detailed information concerning the philosophy and belief system of the average Englishman during Shakespeare's time, I feel it may be helpful here to briefly cover some of the salient aspects of Elizabethan views, as they often play an implicit role in Shakespeare's writing.

Great Chain of Being

JOE: Elizabethans believed in a **Great Chain of Being,** which reflected their strong sense of order and hierarchy. This chain or ladder linked all things from stones all the way up to God. Lowest on the totem pole were inanimate objects. Next came plants and trees, followed by the lowest forms of animal life, such as insects. Next came animals, followed by man, angels, and then God. There was a hierarchy within each class as well. For example, the eagle was the highest form of bird; the lion was the highest form of animal; and the king, queen, or emperor was the highest form of man. The king or queen ruled by God's consent and was answerable only to God, not to the people—although it was a monarch's solemn duty to care for his or her subjects.

The Four Elements and the Four Humors

JOE: The Renaissance Englishman believed that the planet and the entire universe were made up of **four elements**—*earth, water, air,* and *fire*—and that these elements had a hierarchy. Those elements that tended to rise to heaven (air and fire) were considered higher than those that tended to sink (earth and water). Thus, earth was the basest of the elements, followed by water, air, and finally fire.

Renaissance Englishmen also believed that every human contained **four humors**—*blood* (or *sanguine*), *phlegm, choler,* and *melancholy*. These humors determined the health or sickness of the individual. When all four humors were balanced in the body, the individual was healthy and happy. However, if one of the four humors was predominant, then the individual would take on the traits of that particular humor.

Each humor had a corresponding element. Furthermore, each element and humor was associated with a condition—either *moist* or *dry,* and either *cold* or *hot*. All of these things combined gave each humor its predominant trait, as follows:

1. *Blood*—the element of *air,* the condition of *moist* and *hot*. People who are predominantly blood (or sanguine) have the traits of warmth, passion, amorousness, joy, and affection. Othello, at the top of the play, can be said to be predominantly blood.
2. *Phlegm*—the element of *water,* the condition of *moist* and *cold*. People who are predominantly phlegm are impassive, apathetic, and dull. Sir Andrew Aguecheek in *Twelfth Night* can be said to be phlegmatic.
3. *Choler*—the element of *fire,* the condition of *dry* and *hot*. People who are predominantly choler are quick-tempered, impatient, and stubborn. Choleric characters may include Hotspur in *Henry IV Part 1,* and Cassius in *Julius Caesar.*
4. *Melancholy*—the element of *earth,* the condition of *dry* and *cold*. People who are predominantly melancholy are pensive, depressed, and indecisive. Melancholic characters may include Hamlet, and Jacques in *As You Like It.*

Characters who have all four humors in balance may include Henry V, and Portia in *The Merchant of Venice.*

Even a primarily positive humor like blood can go awry under certain circumstances. Othello, who is primarily sanguine, begins the play by showing the traits of friendliness, amorousness, and generosity. However, Iago quickly pushes his traits to jealousy and overwhelming, uncontrolled passion. Of course, no character can be reduced to a simple formula based on the four humors. However, Shakespeare makes frequent reference to the humors, and Elizabethans often viewed his characters accordingly.

Folios and Quartos

If you continue to act and study Shakespeare, it is inevitable that you will hear mention of the quartos and folios of his plays, particularly the famous First Folio. **The First Folio** is a collection of thirty-six of Shakespeare's extant plays, eighteen of which were published for the first time in the collection. It was published in 1623, seven years after Shakespeare's death. The publishers apparently worked in close collaboration with members of the King's Men, the acting company of which Shakespeare was a member and co-owner, in bringing the collection to fruition. Shakespeare acted as well as wrote plays for the company. Two of his oldest colleagues, John Heminge and Henry Condell, signed the preface to the collection. While eighteen of the plays appeared for the first time in the First Folio, the other eighteen plays had been published earlier in quarto form. The **quarto** versions of Shakespeare's plays were individual editions rather than collections. Quartos get their name because the large sheets of paper on which they were printed were folded twice, into quarters (hence "quarto"). Folio paper was folded only once. The First Folio is often represented with the symbol "F1." There are four folios of Shakespeare's plays but the first is by far the most important and prominent. Quarto versions of his plays are often represented with the symbol "Q1" for the first quarto of a particular play, "Q2" for the second, and so on. Two more plays were attributed to Shakespeare since the publication of the First Folio; *Pericles*, co-authored with one or more unknown playwrights, and *The Two Noble Kinsmen*, co-authored with John Fletcher.

Shakespeare's Sonnets

Shakespeare wrote poems as well as plays. He wrote at least three long poems—*Venus and Adonis, The Rape of Lucrece,* and *The Phoenix and the Turtle*—as well as 154 sonnets. A **sonnet** is a fourteen-line poem, written in verse, which deals with a single theme or idea. The format for a sonnet is three quatrains followed by a rhyming couplet. A quatrain consists of four lines of verse written in alternating rhyming couplets (line one rhyming with line three and line two rhyming with line four). The first 126 sonnets seem to be written to a male friend of Shakespeare, probably young, handsome, immoral, and of noble birth. Sonnets 127–152 seem to involve a mysterious "Dark Lady," apparently Shakespeare's mistress. She was evidently sensual, alluring, and unfaithful. The final two sonnets are translations from the Greek. Here is sonnet 127, the first whose subject is the mysterious "dark lady of the sonnets":

> In the old age black was not counted fair
> Or if it were it bore not beauty's name;

But now is black beauty's successive heir,
And beauty slander'd with a bastard shame,
For since each hand hath put on nature's power,
Fairing the foul with art's false borrow'd face,
Sweet beauty hath no name, no holy bower,
But is profan'd, if not lives in disgrace.
Therefore my mistress' eyes are raven black,
Her eyes so suited, and they mourners seem
At such who, not born fair, no beauty lack,
Sland'ring creation with a false esteem:
Yet so they mourn, becoming of their woe,
That every tongue says beauty should look so.

If you are interested in learning more about Shakespeare's sonnets, I want to recommend an excellent book on the subject: *The Art of Shakespeare's Sonnets* by Helen Vendler and published by The Bellknap Press of Harvard University Press.

SOUND AND RHYTHM: A REMINDER

JOE: I have talked a good deal about sound and rhythm in Shakespeare. But I want to reinforce as much as possible the importance of using specifically, both when acting in his plays. He was deliberate in his choice of the sound and rhythm of his words. For example, the word *wide* has a long vowel that gives the word a certain width. The word *smooth* is a smooth word! The consonant sounds and especially the "oo" vowel sound fit the meaning of the word. The verb *pluck* has a quick, sudden rhythm, and the consonants and short vowel sound are abrupt and terse. They are the perfect sensory expression of the action that they represent.

In fact, if Shakespeare could not find a word that he was satisfied with, he made one up! For instance, the first time the word "assassination" appears in the English language is in *Macbeth*.

Shakespeare loves to layer *sensory* understanding under *cognitive* understanding. But we must play these sounds and rhythms the way that a musician plays a musical score. Actors often give a "sameness" to Shakespeare's rhythm: Consonants become muddy, short vowels are slightly elongated, and long vowels are slightly shortened until both have a boring uniformity. Don't fall into that trap. Make a conscious effort to use the sensory properties of the language. Use the sounds and rhythms that Shakespeare has provided to affect your partner and the audience viscerally. The emotional life and longings of Shakespeare's characters are often so heightened that they need every property of the spoken word to express their imagery. Embrace, savor, relish, and use every aspect of the spoken word—sound, sense, and rhythm.

Act on the Word

JOE: When acting Shakespeare, be sure to *act on the word!* I have seen many actors put their emotional response into a sigh or other sound before they speak, thus robbing the lines of energy and specificity. If you feel this happening to you, take your instinctive emotional connection and *put it into the words.* Always remember that in Shakespeare, the text is the source and the words are the action.

Also, I have often heard it said that the actor should seldom pause when acting Shakespeare. I think we now see that this is untrue. We have explored short lines that seem to indicate silences, and we've learned that pauses, however brief, are most often indicated after punctuation in both verse and prose. However, Shakespeare's characters pause far less often than characters of most other genres. Always remember that Shakespeare's characters spend much more time *speaking* their thoughts than *thinking* their thoughts.

Subtext in Shakespeare

JOE: I have also often heard it said that there is little room for subtext when acting Shakespeare. This can be a confusing and misleading notion.

LIZ: What do you mean by *subtext?*

JOE: **Subtext** is the full meaning beneath our character's words. Shakespeare's *text* must always "float" on our character's *subtext.*

SAM: Can you give us an example?

JOE: Let's take a simple, one-word text: the line "Hello." Uttering a simple hello can be motivated by a myriad of subtexts. I may pass a colleague in the hall who has recently "stabbed me in the back." Feeling guilty, he may give me a friendly greeting. I may respond with an icy "Hello" as I pass him without making eye contact. Or, I may glimpse a dear friend whom I haven't seen in years walking down the street. I run up to him excitedly, hug him in my arms, and exclaim "Hello!" I think you begin to get my point. The subtext of our character's lines is acquired and deepened by an understanding of and connection to the given circumstances of the play. Questions that arise from holes in the given circumstances must be filled in with imaginary circumstances. Subtext gives the text specificity and life.

SAM: So why would anyone say that there is little room for subtext in Shakespeare?

JOE: I think that it is a question of semantics. Some people think of subtext as a deep, hidden meaning behind the text. In other words, characters often say one thing and mean another. Numerous plays written since the works of Henrik Ibsen, as well as many teleplays and screenplays, contain such subtext. A character may *say* "Your clock is five minutes fast" while *thinking* "Why don't you love me?" This rarely happens in Shakespeare. Shakespeare's characters almost always say what they mean and mean what they say. If a character is lying, he or she will usually say so in a soliloquy or in an aside. If a character is about to deceive another character, like Iago does in most of his scenes with Othello, the audience is usually made aware of it. Therefore, the Shakespearean actor must often *dare to be obvious*. For instance, when Othello says to Iago, "Villain, be sure thou prove my love a whore!" he *means* "Villain, be sure thou prove my love a whore!" When Olivia confesses her love to Viola/Cesario in *Twelfth Night*, Viola responds by saying "I pity you," and she *means* just that.

However, there is more to subtext than whether or not meaning and text coincide. For example, Viola's line "I pity you" comes at a time in the play in which the disguised Viola finally becomes aware of the simpatico that she has with Olivia. Just as Olivia's love for "Cesario" is unrequited, so too is Viola's love for Orsino. Instead of merely *sympathizing* with Olivia, Viola now *empathizes* with her. She understands Olivia's pain with her head, heart, gut, and soul because it parallels her own. Viola also comprehends Olivia's situation more implicitly because ironically, she is herself the object of Olivia's unrequited love. Hence, Viola's "I pity you" is spoken "woman to woman" and "sister to sister." When the actress portraying Viola comes to a full, imaginative understanding of these circumstances, her line will be infused with specificity and emotional life. This is what provides the subtext on which floats the text "I pity you."

SAM: So subtext is more than just the meaning behind the lines, right?

JOE: Yes. Subtext involves not only meaning, but also thought, intent, and emotion, all of which are derived from detailed and imaginative attention to given and imaginary circumstances.

LIZ: Do Shakespeare's characters *always* say what they mean and mean what they say?

JOE: Certainly not. As I have just pointed out, Shakespeare's characters sometimes lie and deceive. In addition, there are many occasions in which the exact meaning of Shakespeare's lines is somewhat veiled. For example, let's look at an earlier section of dialogue from a scene from *Othello* that we first examined in Chapter 9. In this scene, which takes place in Desdemona's bedroom, Emilia attempts to soothe Desdemona after Othello struck her in a jealous rage before a large company of people:

> EMILIA: I have laid those sheets you bade me on the bed.
> DESDEMONA: All's one. Good faith, how foolish are our minds!
> If I do die before thee, prithee shroud me
> In one of these same sheets.
> EMILIA: Come, come; you talk.
> (*Othello*, 4, 3, 22–25)

In the previous scene, just after Othello's abusive behavior to his wife, Desdemona made a request of Emilia:

> Prithee tonight
> Lay on my bed my wedding sheets—remember;
> (*Othello*, 4, 2, 104–105)

In Shakespeare's time, wedding sheets were used only twice: on one's wedding night and to wrap one's body in before entombment. Therefore, Emilia's seemingly simple, banal line, "I have laid those sheets you bade me on the bed," is loaded with subtext. Beneath the spoken words, Emilia may be thinking and asking "Why in the world did you ask for your wedding sheets?! Are you contemplating suicide? Are you giving up and refusing to fight back? Othello is abusing you and you must stand up to him. You're scaring me with this macabre behavior!" and so on. In fact, it seems that Desdemona understands at least some of Emilia's subtext because she replies "Good faith, how foolish are our minds! / If I do die before thee, prithee shroud me / In one of these same sheets." What is Desdemona's subtext here? Why does she say "Good faith, how foolish are our minds!?" Is she foreseeing her own death? Has she decided to let Othello's will be done? If so, is she then ensuring that Emilia will make proper funeral arrangements for her? Or is Desdemona purposely shocking Emilia so that Emilia will help her come up with a plan to confront Othello upon his return?

LIZ: What are the answers to all of those questions?

JOE: That's up to the director and actors of the particular production. Like any great playwright, Shakespeare provides a skeleton with his text, to which the actors and director provide flesh. Shakespeare often leaves vital questions unanswered. He gives us tantalizing clues, but the questions remain both fascinating and frustrating.

SAM: How can we be sure that we are coming up with the right answers?

JOE: Remember that there is no right or wrong, only valid and invalid. The answers are always in the text, but they will not always be the same answers for every actor, director, and production. That's why every production of *Hamlet* will be unique, for instance, *Hamlet* is full of unanswered questions. That's one of the reasons why so many articles and books have been written on the play; it is not only one of the greatest plays ever written, but it is also one of the most enigmatic. For instance, what is Hamlet's relationship with his mother, Gertrude? He often seems jealous of her relationship with Claudius in the way that a lover would be jealous. Does he have an oedipal complex? If so, what is his relationship with Ophelia? It is a strange relationship to be sure. Ophelia is a woman-child. She is a "daddy's girl," seemingly incapable of making a decision on her own. She seems to be firmly under the thumb or her father, Polonius, who is far from an ideal patriarch. Does Hamlet honestly love her? How close are Ophelia and Hamlet? After all, Hamlet has spent much of his time away from Elsinore. What is Hamlet trying to accomplish in the "Get thee to a nunnery" scene? Does he want to scare her away so that she will be unharmed when he finally seeks his revenge on Claudius? Or does he feel betrayed by her when he realizes that Claudius and Polonius are overhearing them? If so, his behavior toward her would be considered abusive and violent. Hamlet seethes whenever Gertrude and Claudius are affectionate with one another. He responds this way even before he talks to the ghost of his father. Is this because Gertrude and Hamlet Sr. were not affectionate and Hamlet isn't used to seeing his mother in love? If so, was the marriage of Gertrude and Hamlet Sr. a political, loveless one? Could Gertrude and Claudius have been in love all along and did they continue to have a clandestine relationship after Gertrude married Claudius's brother? Why did Claudius murder his brother? Was it blind ambition? Was it for love of Gertrude? We know that Hamlet Sr. was a brave, warrior king—but was he a *good* king? Was his country solvent or was he running Denmark into the ground, emptying the country's coffers to pay for endless wars? If this was the case, did Claudius feel that Hamlet Sr. had to be removed in order to save Denmark? Hamlet is apparently much loved by the people of Denmark. Why? Not only is it questionable that Hamlet loves (or loved) Ophelia, it seems that he is incapable of loving *anyone*. He seems to love the *image* of his dead father, but he shows no remorse after mistakenly killing Polonius or for sending Rosencrantz and Guildenstern to their deaths or for hounding Ophelia to madness and suicide, and his parting words to his dead mother are "Wretched queen, adieu!"

SAM: Okay—my mind is spinning!

JOE: You see my point. All of these questions and many more must be answered. As long as the answers are specific and true to character, relationship, and plot, they will go a long way to ensuring an exciting, well-told story. The late Constantin Stanislavski, the great Russian acting teacher and former director of the Moscow Art Theatre, once said, "Spectators come to the theatre to hear the subtext. They can read the text at home."

This wraps up the bulk of our work together, but I want to leave you with a few words about auditioning, scene work suggestions, and a few recommended Shakespeare Web sites.

SUMMARY

In this chapter Joe provided Liz and Sam with a potpourri of information about Shakespeare and his time—covering Shakespeare's dramatic devices, some historical background, and Elizabethan philosophy. Joe then explained how Shakespearean actors can apply these varied tools to their roles.

- Shakespeare's characters sometimes speak in asides. An aside is a truthful comment, personal in nature, either addressed to the audience or self-directed. Occasionally, an aside will be directed to another character.
- While some of Shakespeare's stage directions are printed in the text, much of Shakespeare's physical directions to the actor are buried in his dialogue.
- In Shakespeare's time, the word *you* was formal and the word *thou* was informal. One would address one's superiors as "you" and inferiors and equals as "thou."
- Another language distinction in Shakespeare's time was the use of the royal "we." Kings and queens in Shakespeare's plays often refer to themselves in the plural.
- When acting Shakespeare or the plays of any other Elizabethan playwright, it is essential to have a working understanding of the history of the period.
- Elizabethans believed in a Great Chain of Being, which reflected their strong sense of order and hierarchy. This chain or ladder linked all life from stones all the way up to God.
- Sixteenth and early seventeenth century Englishmen believed that the planet and the entire universe were made up of four elements—*earth, water, air,* and *fire*. Associated with these elements were four humors found in every individual—*blood* (or *sanguine*), *phlegm, choler,* and *melancholy*—which determined the health or

sickness of the individual. Each element and humor was considered either *moist* or *dry*, and either *cold* or *hot*.
- Shakespeare's plays were first presented in quarto and folio form. Quartos were individual editions of his plays. Approximately half of his plays appeared in quarto form. The First Folio of Shakespeare is a collection of thirty-six of his plays.
- In addition to plays, Shakespeare wrote long poems and 154 sonnets. A sonnet is a verse poem that is fourteen lines in length and deals with a single theme or idea.
- When acting Shakespeare, use the sounds and rhythms that he has provided to affect your partner and the audience viscerally. The emotional life and longings of Shakespeare's characters are often so heightened that they need every aspect of the spoken word—sound, sense, and rhythm—to express their imagery.
- When acting Shakespeare, be sure to *act on the word!*
- Subtext is the full meaning beneath our character's words. Subtext also involves thought, intent, and emotion, all of which are derived from detailed and imaginative attention to given and imaginary circumstances. Subtext gives the text specificity and life.
- Shakespeare's characters almost always say what they mean and mean what they say. If a character is lying or deceiving another character, the audience is made aware of it, usually by means of a soliloquy or an aside. However, sometimes the exact meaning of Shakespeare's lines is more veiled than usual.
- Shakespeare provides a skeleton with his text, to which the actors and director provide flesh. Shakespeare often leaves vital questions unanswered.
- The answers are always in the text, but they will not always be the same answers for every actor, director, and production. Remember that there is no right or wrong, only valid and invalid.
- As long as the answers are specific and true to character, relationship, and plot, they will go a long way to ensuring an exciting, well-told story.

Appendix: Getting the Part, Finding the Scene, Getting Online

(Following are some suggestions for auditioning, as well as other acting exercises and resources.)

Auditioning

Joe: I would like to take some time to talk to you about the dreaded "A" word—auditioning.
Liz: It seems that all actors hate to audition. Is there a way to actually enjoy it?
Joe: There are actors who enjoy auditioning—although, unfortunately, they are probably in the minority. This need not be the case. Auditioning can be a very gratifying experience. It is a chance to show off your talent, range, and high level of craftmanship as an artist. But it is understandable to be nervous about auditioning,

because so much may depend on the outcome. There are some simple rules to keep in mind, which should go a long way in at least lessening the pain of auditioning.

LIZ: So how do we go about selecting an audition piece?

SAM: I was wondering that, too. And how can we get it ready for presentation?

Choosing a Piece

JOE: The first rule is also the Boy Scout motto: *"Be prepared."* Your audition pieces should be fully researched and rehearsed. You should have several backup audition pieces ready as well, just in case. This will instill you with confidence. You may find it helpful to look through the catalogues of play publishers in order to find audition pieces. The catalogues of *Samuel French, Dramatists Play Service, Broadway Play Publishing, faber and faber* and other play publishers, contain detailed synopses of their plays. Another rule is to *choose pieces that you enjoy*. By working methodically, you will slowly but surely make the speeches your own. This can only add to your enjoyment in presenting them. Another good guideline is that *once you find a piece that you enjoy, be certain it is right for you*. Of course, I certainly don't mean that you should limit yourself by only choosing material that fits into a narrow range of your personality. On the other hand, however, it would be unwise for either of you two actors to choose a character that is sixty years old, or a character that despairs of being overweight when you are thin. Know your strengths and play to them.

Additionally, most audition situations require the actor to *prepare two contrasting pieces*. Your second piece should not only be one that you enjoy, but should also be the antithesis of your first piece. For example, if your first piece is dramatic, your second piece should be comic. A classical piece should usually be paired with a contemporary piece.[1] If you are auditioning for a Shakespeare festival or a classical theatre, both of your selections should be classical. However, you can choose one verse piece and one prose piece, as well as contrasting a well-spoken character with a rustic one. If your first character is shy, awkward, and soft-spoken, your second character should be confident, dexterous, and outspoken. In this way you show the director two extremes and he/she will assume that you can play characters between those extremes with equal skill.

I would also advise *choosing pieces that are like mini one-act plays*. In other words, select a piece with a clear beginning, middle, and end. It should make sense outside the context of the play. I have often seen actors choose a monologue that worked wonderfully in a production, but fell flat as an audition piece because it needed the context of the play to be effective.

Another piece of advice is to *always leave them wanting more*. To this end, I advise choosing selections that are between ninety seconds and two minutes in length, unless otherwise requested by the director or producers. Never present a monologue that is under one minute or over three minutes in length. An audition piece under one minute is too short to show your auditors what you are capable of. Conversely, I have seen many an actor lose the attention of his audience by adding a minute or so to what could have been an effective audition.

Furthermore, *avoid choosing a character from the play for which you are auditioning unless otherwise requested.* It is wise, however, to choose a similar character from another play. For example, Liz might choose a speech spoken by Miranda in *The Tempest* or Viola in *Twelfth Night* if she had to audition for the role of Juliet. If Sam had to audition for the role of Romeo, he might choose a speech spoken by Ferdinand in *The Tempest* or Sebastian in *Twelfth Night*. You may also consider choosing a different Elizabethan playwright when auditioning for Shakespeare. Shakespeare had many talented contemporaries, including Ben Jonson and Christopher Marlowe. Another option is to piece together a monologue from several smaller speeches. Actors often complain about Shakespeare speeches that are overdone as audition pieces. A way to avoid this is to find a scene in which your character does most of the talking. Then see if you can remove the other characters' lines in such a way that your character's words follow a clear and logical progression.

Another good idea is to select dialogue spoken by a minor character in a major play as an audition piece. For instance, rather than choosing a speech spoken by Macbeth, Sam may consider choosing dialogue spoken by Malcolm or Macduff. While these characters are not minor, they are certainly secondary to Macbeth. Rather than choosing a speech spoken by Isabella in *Measure for Measure*, Liz may choose dialogue spoken by Mariana. Another option is to choose a piece spoken by a major character in a minor play. Sam may choose a speech spoken by Timon from *Timon of Athens* and Liz may choose a speech spoken by Marina (a much overlooked ingenue role) from *Pericles*.

Preparing Your Piece

JOE: Once you select your audition piece, you'll need to do some preparation. *Creating an environment in your imagination for each audition piece is essential.* Having a strong, specific "sense of place," as it is often called, will stimulate you and free you of tension. For example, Liz would want to create, in her mind's eye, a specific balcony for herself as well as what surrounds it if she were auditioning with her Juliet speech. This entails all of the senses. If Juliet's balcony overlooks a forested area, Liz must not only decide what the trees look like but also how they smell. Is there a breeze? If so, do the trees rustle? Is there moonlight? Is it full? Waxing? Waning? What is the balcony railing made of? What does it feel like? I think you get my point. Because you have an unlimited budget for your imaginary "scenic design," you may choose anything that you feel serves your character and situation. The environment needn't be Elizabethan. Until actors research what life was like in Elizabethan England, they often have cliché mind pictures of generic arbors, castles, and so on. Feel free to use any settings you are familiar with. For instance, if Sam were to audition with his Romeo speech, it may help him to use the environment of the party he told us about when we first started, where he met his "ideal woman," as a substitution for the Capulet party. Thus, he would not have to invent an environment, but rather could recall a space that he had actually experienced. Actors who fail to surround themselves with an imaginary environment will be stuck instead with an unfamiliar, cold audition space.

Moreover, it is a good idea to *have your pieces coached,* preferably by an acting teacher whom you respect. If this isn't possible, it should be a theatre artist whom you trust and in whom you have confidence. On the other hand, *avoid seeking too many opinions on your work.* This can cause confusion and frustration. Too many cooks definitely spoil the broth in these cases.

The Audition Process

SAM: That's good advice, but I'm still a little unclear about the procedure from the time you arrive at the audition until the time you leave.

JOE: Let's start even further back than that. Make sure that you get a good night's sleep before the audition. Eat well and sensibly and do a full physical and vocal warm-up. Dress appropriately—comfortably but respectfully. In other words, don't wear torn jeans and dirty sneakers. On the other hand, I have seen actors dress as if they just came from an elegant cocktail party, which is also unadvisable. Your clothes should not be in competition with your acting. That is, avoid loud colors or wild prints as well as clothing with printed material on it. Your outfit should be somewhat neutral and work equally well for both characters if you will be presenting two pieces.

Get to the audition early. Bring several pictures and resumés with you. You never know when you will need more than one. If you know some or all of the other actors at the audition, by all means say hello and wish them well, but don't waste your time in counterproductive social chatter. You are not at a party—you are there to do the best job possible, in hopes of being cast in the production. If you are unfamiliar with the audition space, ask the stage manager if it is possible to enter the space briefly in order to become familiar with the vocal and physical limitations of the room. Before your audition, find a place where you can focus on your material. Spend some time with the characters you will be portraying in the audition. Go over your lines, intentions, motivations, transitions, and so on.

When you are called into the audition space, take a deep, cleansing breath and focus on the fact that those who are about to watch your audition are looking forward to your presentation. *They want to like you.* Also, focus on the fact that you are about to present fully prepared and rehearsed pieces that you enjoy. This may allow you to actually have fun. When you enter the space, *be present.* In other words, turn off your inner voice, which will probably be screaming with sensory overload. Don't focus on your monologues at this point. Look the auditors in the eye and listen and respond to what is being said to you. Say hello, make eye contact, and pay attention to any instructions that you are given. Set up your space, if necessary—that is, find a chair or bench if you'll be using one and set it where it is needed—*before* you announce your pieces. Put your imaginary "scene partner"— the person or persons that you are addressing in your monologues—on the back wall of the space, slightly above and between the heads of the auditors. Find a spot that you can return to when you break eye contact during your speech. Say your name in a clear, positive manner. Then announce your monologues in the order you'll be presenting them. All you need say is the name of the character and the name of the play. You don't need to say the name of the playwright or give a synopsis of the story line surrounding your monologue. For instance, let's say that Sam was presenting a Hotspur speech in addition to his Romeo speech. He would say something like—"Hi, my name is Sam Smith, and the pieces I will be presenting today are Romeo from *Romeo and Juliet* and Hotspur from *Henry the Fourth Part One*."

Never use those auditioning you as the focus of your pieces unless requested to do so. This makes auditors nervous. They feel put on the spot and can have a difficult time evaluating your work.

Let your imaginary partner start the monologue for you. In other words, put your attention on the stimulus that makes your character begin to speak. This allows you to *react* rather than *act* at the start of your pieces. In Sam's case, it may be that Juliet's laugh is what gets his attention. Or he may notice her smile or the way she tosses back her long, beautiful hair. Sam would then find his spot on the back wall, put his attention on the stimulus that causes him to speak, and then begin his monologue.

When you finish your first selection, take a second or so to let the intention of your last word "land." Then go to neutral for a few seconds, shift gears into your next character, find the stimulus that begins your speech, and start your second selection. When you finish your audition, go to neutral—that is, return to being your good old personable self, look your auditors in the eye, and thank them. Then exit in an orderly manner, saying a friendly goodbye.

After you leave the building, jot down in a notebook your assessment of how the audition went for you—what went well, what you would change next time, and so forth. Then forget it! Do something fun. Go to lunch with a friend or catch a movie.

Acting Exercises: Recommended Scenes

JOE: Even when you're not auditioning, you'll want to hone your classical acting skills. Therefore, I'd like to give you a list of two-person scenes from Shakespeare's plays that I find most useful. The actor should not think of such work as a "performance" but rather as a sophisticated acting exercise. The result, then, is not a finished performance (if there is such a thing), but an incremental growth in your skills as a Shakespearean actor.

When working on a scene in class, focus primarily on those skill areas that you wish to improve. Of course there are basic questions that the actor must answer and address when working on any scene—What do I want? What do I do to get it? and so on—but beyond that, you should focus on one or two things that are most important for your growth at the time. For example, you may want to work on using the sounds of Shakespeare's words more specifically in order to achieve your objective. If you are presenting the scene more than once, listen to what your instructor or director feels you should work on in order to improve it, and then focus on those aspects of the work in your subsequent rehearsals. And finally, remember that when you present the scene, forget about all notes, comments, and insecurities. Your only job at that point is to trust your partner, put your attention on your partner, listen, respond, and—I'll say it again—have fun!

The scenes that I am recommending are those that I think work best as "practice" for acting Shakespeare. I have included any soliloquies that occur immediately before and after scenes. It is obviously the decision of the actors whether to include them in their presentations. Some scenes include one or two additional characters that have few or no lines. I suggest asking your peers to assist you by playing these small roles. However, be sure to rehearse with them as much as possible before presenting the scene. Even characters with no lines in the scene can greatly influence your character's behavior. Hence, adding them to the mix at the last minute is a bad idea.[2]

Scenes for Two Women

ALL'S WELL THAT ENDS WELL	Helena, Countess—Act 1, scene 3, line 128
	Helena, Widow—Act 3, scene 7 (entire scene)
AS YOU LIKE IT	Rosalind, Celia—Act 3, scene 2, line 163
HENRY V	Katherine, Alice—Act 3, scene 4 (entire scene) in French
THE MERCHANT OF VENICE	Portia, Nerissa—Act 1, scene 2 (entire scene)
THE MERRY WIVES OF WINDSOR	Mistress Page, Mistress Ford—Act 2, scene 1, line 1
OTHELLO	Desdemona, Emilia—Act 4, scene 3, line 11
ROMEO AND JULIET	Juliet, Nurse—Act 2, scene 5 (entire scene)
	Juliet, Nurse—Act 3, scene 2 (entire scene)
	Juliet, Lady Capulet—Act 3, scene 5, line 64
TWELFTH NIGHT	Viola, Olivia—Act 1, scene 5, line 165
	Viola, Olivia—Act 3, scene 1, line 93
THE TWO GENTLEMEN OF VERONA	Julia, Lucetta—Act 1, scene 2 (entire scene)
	Julia, Silvia—Act 4, scene 4, line 90

Scenes for Two Men

AS YOU LIKE IT	Orlando, Adam—Act 2, scene 3 (entire scene)
THE COMEDY OF ERRORS	Antipholus of S., Dromio of E.—Act 1, scene 2, line 33
	Antipholus of S., Dromio of S.—Act 2, scene 2, line 1
CORIOLANUS	Coriolanus, Aufidius—Act 4, scene 5, line 50
CYMBELINE	Posthumus, Iachimo—Act 2, scene 4, line 26
HENRY IV PART 1	Falstaff, Prince Hal—Act 1, scene 2, line 1
HENRY IV PART 2	King Henry IV, Prince Hal—Act 4, scene 5, line 88
HENRY VI PART 3	King Henry VI, Richard—Act 5, scene 6 (entire scene)
JULIUS CAESAR	Brutus, Cassius—Act 1, scene 2, line 25
	Brutus, Cassius—Act 4, scene 3, line 1

KING JOHN	Hubert, Arthur—Act 4, scene 1, line 8
	Hubert, King John—Act 4, scene 2, line 181
KING LEAR	Edmund, Gloucester—Act 1, scene 2, line 1
	Edgar, Gloucester—Act 4, scene 6, line 1
LOVE'S LABOR'S LOST	Armado, Moth—Act 1, scene 2, line 1
MACBETH	Malcolm, Macduff—Act 4, scene 3, line 1
MEASURE FOR MEASURE	Duke, Lucio—Act 3, scene 2, line 86
THE MERRY WIVES OF WINDSOR	Falstaff, Ford—Act 2, scene 2, line 154
	Falstaff, Ford—Act 3, scene 4, line 60
OTHELLO	Iago, Roderigo—Act 4, scene 2, line 172
	Iago, Cassio—Act 2, scene 3, line 259
	Iago, Othello—Act 3, scene 3, line 90
	Iago, Othello—Act 3, scene 3, line 321
ROMEO AND JULIET	Romeo, Friar—Act 2, scene 3, line 1
	Romeo, Friar—Act 3, scene 3, line 1
THE TEMPEST	Antonio, Sebastian—Act 2, scene 1, line 199
TIMON OF ATHENS	Timon, Flavius—Act 2, scene 2, line 124
	Timon, Flavius—Act 4, scene 3, line 458
TROILUS AND CRESSIDA	Troilus, Pandarus—Act 1, scene 1, line 1
THE TWO GENTLEMEN OF VERONA	Valentine, Duke—Act 3, scene 1, line 51
THE WINTER'S TALE	Leontes, Camillo—Act 1, scene 2, line 212
	Camillo, Polixenes—Act 1, scene 2, line 351
	Clown, Autolycus—Act 4, scene 3, line 32

Scenes for One Woman and One Man

ALL'S WELL THAT ENDS WELL	Bertram, Diana—Act 4, scene 2 (entire scene)
ANTONY AND CLEOPATRA	Antony, Cleopatra—Act 1, scene 3, line 13
	Cleopatra, Messenger—Act 2, scene 5, line 23
AS YOU LIKE IT	Orlando, Rosalind—Act 3, scene 2, line 297
	Orlando, Rosalind—Act 4, scene 1, line 38
THE COMEDY OF ERRORS	Luciana, Antipholus of S.—Act 3, scene 2, line 1
CYMBELINE	Imogen, Cloten—Act 2, scene 3, line 86
	Imogen, Iachimo—Act 1, scene 6 (entire scene)
	Imogen, Pisanio—Act 3, scene 2 (entire scene)
HAMLET	Hamlet, Ophelia—Act 3, scene 1, line 55
	Hamlet, Gertrude—Act 3, scene 4, line 8
HENRY IV PART 1	Hotspur, Lady Percy—Act 2, scene 3 (entire scene)
HENRY VI PART 1	Suffolk, Margaret—Act 5, scene 3, line 45
JULIUS CAESAR	Portia, Brutus—Act 2, scene 1, line 233
MACBETH	Macbeth, Lady Macbeth—Act 1, scene 7 (entire scene)
	Macbeth, Lady Macbeth—Act 2, scene 2 entire scene)

	Macbeth, Lady Macbeth—Act 3, scene 2 (entire scene)
MEASURE FOR MEASURE	Isabella, Angelo—Act 2, scene 2, line 25
	Isabella, Angelo—Act 2, scene 4 (entire scene)
	Isabella, Claudio—Act 3, scene 1, line 54
THE MERCHANT OF VENICE	Portia, Bassanio—Act 3, scene 2, line 1
A MIDSUMMER NIGHT'S DREAM	Helena, Demetrius—Act 2, scene 1, line 188
MUCH ADO ABOUT NOTHING	Beatrice, Benedick—Act 4, scene 1, line 255
	Beatrice, Benedick—Act 5, scene 2, line 26
OTHELLO	Desdemona, Othello—Act 3, scene 3, line 41
	Desdemona, Othello—Act 3, scene 4, line 33
	Desdemona, Othello—Act 4, scene 2, line 24
	Desdemona, Othello—Act 5, scene 2, line 1
RICHARD III	Richard, Lady Anne—Act 1, scene 2, line 33
	Richard, Queen Elizabeth—Act 4, scene 4, line 197
ROMEO AND JULIET	Romeo, Juliet—Act 2, scene 2 (entire scene)
	Romeo, Juliet—Act 3, scene 5, line 1
THE TAMING OF THE SHREW	Katherine, Petruchio—Act 2, scene 1, line 169
THE TEMPEST	Miranda, Ferdinand—Act 3, scene 1 (entire scene)
TROILUS AND CRESSIDA	Troilus, Cressida—Act 3, scene 2, line 60

SHAKESPEARE ON THE WEB

JOE: The Internet has a wealth of information on Shakespeare and all things Shakespearean. Here are some good Web sites:

Mr. William Shakespeare and the Internet
http://daphne.palomar.edu/shakespeare/
Great site with lots of links to other great sites.

The Collected Works of Shakespeare
http://www.gh.cs.su.oz.au/~matty/Shakespeare/Shakespeare.html
Contains a Shakespeare search engine.

Shakespeare and Elizabethan Links
http://www.elizreview.com/links.htm
Links to general Renaissance and Shakespeare studies, Shakespeare authorship, Shakespeare onstage, literary resources, Renaissance music, Shakespeare films, and more.

Voice of the Shuttle English Literature Page
http://vos.ucsb.edu/shuttle/english.html

Voice of the Shuttle is a fabulous site from the University of California, Santa Barbara. The English Literature page has a section on Renaissance and seventeenth century literature, including Shakespeare.

The Arden Shakespeare on the Internet
http://www.ardenshakespeare.com/main/welcome.html
Web site of the popular *Arden Shakespeare,* which publishes highly regarded editions of the plays.

Surfing with the Bard
http://www.ulen.com/shakespeare/
A Shakespeare classroom on the Internet.

Shakespeare Online: Your Ultimate Shakespeare Resource
http://www.shakespeare-online.com/shakespeare-online.html
A new, comprehensive Shakespeare site.

There are other Shakespeare and Shakespeare-related Web sites, and more are coming online all the time. Web sites tend to be very generous in providing links to other sites. Starting with the sites suggested above will lead you to a great many others.

SUMMARY

In this appendix, Joe gives Sam and Liz a few pointers about auditioning, suggestions for Shakespeare practice scenes, and recommendations for Shakespearen Web sites.

- Your audition pieces should be fully researched and rehearsed. You should have several backup audition pieces ready as well, just in case.
- Choose audition pieces that you enjoy and that are right for you.
- Most audition situations require the actor to prepare two contrasting pieces. Your second piece should be the antithesis of your first piece.
- Your audition pieces should have a clear beginning, middle, and end.
- Your monologues should be between ninety seconds and two minutes in length. Never present a monologue that is under one minute or over three minutes in length.
- Try to avoid using an audition speech from the play for which you are auditioning.
- If auditioning for a Shakespeare festival or classical theatre company, consider choosing one piece from a play by one of Shakespeare's contemporaries.
- Create a strong environment in your mind's eye for each of your pieces.
- Have your pieces coached by a theatre professional whom you respect.
- The Internet offers many Web sites with valuable information about Shakespeare and his works.

EXERCISES

SOLO EXERCISE A.1
This is an ongoing exercise. At a time when you have no auditions on the horizon, find a Shakespeare piece that excites you and fits you like a glove. Work on this audition piece until it is in good enough shape to be coached. After you feel comfortable with your audition piece, find an antithetical piece that you also enjoy. Only look for new audition monologues when you have no auditions forthcoming. Continue until you have at least eight pieces: four contemporary and four classical, of which four are serious and four are comic. Continue to work on your pieces weekly so that you will be ready for any audition, no matter how late the notice. Remember the adage: Luck occurs when opportunity meets preparation.

GROUP EXERCISE A.1
Form an audition group. Get together with several responsible actor friends and meet weekly, biweekly, or monthly to work and critique one another's audition pieces. Being part of such a group is beneficial for several reasons, such as advice, support, discipline, and routine. You may also wish to form a "cold reading" group, in which you would read Shakespearean scenes with little or no preparation. Reading scenes in this way sharpens your acting and vocal skills and challenges you to commit to strong, specific choices quickly and efficiently, while responding honestly to your partner even with script in hand.

NOTES

1. A "classical" audition piece is loosely defined as material from a play between the time of Greek theatre and the end of the eighteenth century. This includes Greek and Roman theatre, Elizabethan and Jacobean theatre, Restoration theatre, and Georgian theatre. Plays by Molière or Marivaux and theatre of the Spanish Golden Age are also acceptable. Most theatre companies consider plays by Ibsen, Shaw, Brecht, Chekhov, Strindberg, and others as Contemporary Classical theatre. A more contemporary audition piece is usually from a play written since the 1920s (even though Shaw lived until 1950). The early plays of Eugene O'Neill seem to signify the beginning of the American Contemporary period.
2. All line numbers refer to where scenes begin. Line numbers are taken from the *Riverside Shakespeare*.

GLOSSARY

accent: a prominence given to one syllable in a word or phrase, over the adjacent syllables.
action: what your character does in order to try to get what he wants. To *act* is to *do*.
alexandrine: a line of verse consisting of six consecutive iambs (also known iambic hexameter).
alliteration: a figure of speech characterized by repetition of an initial sound, usually a consonant, in two or more words of a phrase or line. For example, "Can cunning sin cover itself withal!"
allusion: an indirect reference.
alternating rhyme: see *cross rhyme*.
amphibrach: see *feminine foot*.
anadiplosis: a figure of speech characterized by the repetition of the last word of one clause or sentence at or near the beginning of the next. For example, "Eyes without feeling, feeling without sight."
anapaest: in scansion, a unit that consists of two unstressed syllables followed by a stressed syllable. The first two unstressed syllables are spoken more quickly than the final stressed syllable. For example, "it is gone," "I am mad," and "my intent."
anaphora: a figure of speech characterized by repetition of the same word or group of words at the beginning of successive clauses, sentences, or lines. For example, "Our discontented counties do revolt; /Our people quarrel with obedience,"
anastrophe: a figure of speech characterized by the inversion of natural word order. For example, "It only stands / Our lives upon, to use our strongest hands."
antanaclasis: a type of pun that involves the repetition of a word with two different meanings. For example, "Your argument is sound, nothing but sound."
anthimeria: a figure of speech characterized by the substitution of one part of speech for another, as in a noun used as a verb. For example, "Lord Angelo dukes it well in his absence."
antimetabole: a figure of speech that reverses the order of repeated words or phrases. For example, "Plainly as heaven sees earth and earth sees heaven."
antithesis: a figure of speech characterized by a contrast or opposition of thoughts, usually in two phrases, clauses, or sentences. For example, "Wherein I am false, I am honest: not true to be true."
apostrophe: a figure of speech in which a character addresses an absent or dead person, inanimate object, or abstraction, usually with strong emotion. For example, "Thou, Nature art my goddess . . ."
aside: most often, a truthful, heartfelt comment, personal in nature, either addressed to the audience or self-directed. Occasionally, an aside will be directed to another onstage character.
"as if": use of a person, place, event, or thing from the actor's life (or to which the actor can strongly relate) that parallels that of the actor's character.

assonance: a figure of speech characterized by repetition of a sound, usually a vowel or diphthong, within two or more words of a phrase or line. For example, "No, rather I abjure all roofs, and choose...."

asyndeton: a figure of speech characterized by the omission of conjunctions between words, phrases, or clauses. For example: "Did see her, hear her, at that hour last night."

beat (in acting): a specific unit of thought or action.

beat (in scansion): a syllable of verse dialogue.

blank verse: language that does not rhyme, written in iambic pentameter or an accepted variation thereof.

caesura: a break or pause within a line of verse.

circumflex inflection: a vocal inflection that changes pitch before ending in a sustained inflection. *Circumflex* means "curved" or "bending," indicating that pitch rises and falls or falls and rises before sustaining. A circumflex inflection can be used at any time that a sustained inflection is appropriate.

climax: a figure of speech characterized by the arrangement of words, phrases, or clauses in an order of increasing importance, often in parallel structure. Also known as a *build* or a *list*.

compression: in scansion, the removal of one or more unstressed syllables from certain words in verse dialogue in order to fit an acceptable rhythm.

connotative meaning: the associations and overtones of a word or phrase.

context: the parts of a sentence, paragraph, discourse, or other construction immediately next to or surrounding a specified word or passage and determining its exact meaning.

contraction: making two words into one by eliminating certain sounds or letters.

convention: a customary practice, rule, or method.

cross rhyme: a rhyme pattern comprising at least four lines of verse in which the final syllables of lines one and three rhyme, and the final syllables of lines two and four rhyme. Also known as *alternating rhyme*.

dactyl: a three-syllable unit consisting of a stressed syllable followed by two unstressed syllables. The two unstressed syllables are spoken more quickly than the first stressed syllable. For example, "universe," "argument," and "terminal."

denotative meaning: the objective, dictionary definition of a word or phrase.

down ending: a vocal inflection that occurs when the speaker lacks a clear objective. In such a case the line drops off in every way—volume, pitch, and (most importantly) intent. A down ending should not be confused with a *resolve inflection*.

drama: a composition in prose or verse, adapted to be acted upon a stage, in which a story is related by means of dialogue and action; a play.

dramatic poetry: verse language of a higher order that is in dialogue form and is used to tell the story of a play through the words of the characters in that play.

elevated language: concentrated language that takes advantage of every aspect of the spoken word—literal definitions, figurative definitions, sensory definitions, multiple definitions as well as sound and rhythm to persuade and stir the emotions of the listener.

elision: the omission, assimilation, or slurring over of a vowel, syllable, or other element in pronunciation; often used in poetry to preserve meter, as when a word that ends with a vowel immediately precedes a word beginning with a vowel. For example, "th' artist."

ellipsis: the omission from a sentence of one or more words that would be needed to complete the grammatical construction or to fully express the sense.

emotional life: an honest connection to the primary emotion of one's character at a particular point in a play.

endow: to enrich or furnish with any "gift," quality, or power of mind or body; to invest (imaginatively) with a quality.

end-stopped line: a line of verse that ends with strong punctuation.

enjambment: see *run-on line*.

epanalepsis: a figure of speech in which the same word occurs at or near both the beginning and end of a phrase, clause, or sentence. For example, "<u>Blood</u> hath bought <u>blood</u>, and <u>blows</u> have answered <u>blows</u>."

epistrophe: a figure of speech characterized by repetition of the same word or group of words at the end of successive clauses, sentences, or lines. For example, "To make them <u>kings</u>—the seeds of Banquo <u>kings</u>!"

epizeuxis: a figure of speech characterized by the repetition of a single word for emphasis. For example: "O, <u>Lear, Lear, Lear</u>!"

expansion: in scansion, the addition of one or more unstressed syllables to certain words in verse language in order to fit an acceptable rhythm.

feminine foot: in scansion, a three-syllable unit consisting of an unstressed syllable, followed by a stressed syllable, followed by another unstressed syllable. Words that have this rhythm include "rehearsal," involvement," and "seclusion." Also known as an *amphibrach*.

figure of speech: a form of expression deviating from the normal arrangement or use of words, which is adopted in order to give beauty, variety, or force to a composition. Also known as a *rhetorical figure* or *rhetorical device*.

First Folio: a collection of thirty-six of Shakespeare's extant plays, eighteen of which were published for the first time in the collection.

foot: in scansion, a synonym for an iamb or one of its variant units, including the trochee, anapaest, amphibrach, spondee, and pyrrhic. Also called a *measure*.

form of poetry: literary form comprising a composition in verse or metrical language, usually also with elevated words and figurative uses, and with a syntactical order differing more or less from ordinary speech or prose writing.

four elements: the four components that Elizabethans believed made up the planet and the entire universe: earth, water, air, and fire.

four humors: the four qualities that Elizabethans believed were present in every human being (and that determined the health or sickness of the individual): blood (or sanguine), phlegm, choler, and melancholy.

fourth wall: term that began with the advent of the proscenium stage, originally referring to the space occupied by the audience. Because only three of the four walls of the theatre consisted of the set, actors needed to use their imaginations to complete the environment in their mind's eye, transforming the space occupied by the audience into the "fourth wall" of their set. Today, with the proliferation of thrust and arena stages, actors must often use their detailed imaginations to fill in two, three, and even all four walls.

function of poetry: the expression or embodiment of beautiful or elevated thought, imagination, or feeling, using language adapted to stir the imagination and emotions.

genre: kind; sort; style. There are many genres of theatre. Shakespeare's plays are of the genre of Elizabethan drama or Renaissance drama.

given circumstances: everything that the playwright has written about your character's past, present, and expected future. The given circumstances of the *play* are all of the facts that the playwright provides in the dialogue of the characters.

gloss: a note of comment or explanation accompanying a text, as in a footnote or marginal note.

Great Chain of Being: a reflection of the Elizabethan's strong sense of order and hierarchy. This chain or ladder linked all things from stones all the way up to God.

hyperbole: a figure of speech characterized by the use of exaggerated terms for emphasis or heightened effect. For example, "Will all great Neptune's ocean wash this blood /Clean from my hand?"

iamb: a two-syllable unit that consists of an unstressed syllable followed by a stressed syllable. The iamb is the cornerstone of Shakespeare's verse form.

iambic pentameter: a line of verse consisting of five consecutive iambs.

imaginary circumstances: those circumstances invented by the actor to help make a fuller connection with the written material of the play.

inflection: any change in tone or pitch of the voice.

initial truncation: a line of verse in which the first measure consists of a single stressed syllable. For example: "Ay, what else? And but I be deceiv'd."

inoperative words: words that do not contain strong emotion or imagery—often including negatives, prepositions, conjunctions, articles, pronouns, possessive pronouns, and verbs of being.

ionic (or ionic phrase): in scansion, a two-measure configuration consisting of a pyrrhic followed by a spondee or a spondee followed by a pyrrhic. Examples include "in the strong wind" and "rich widower."

IPA: acronym for the *International Phonetic Alphabet*. The IPA provides a symbol for every vowel, diphthong, and consonant in the English language as well as other languages.

irony: a figure of speech characterized by speaking in such a way as to imply the contrary of what one says, often for the purpose of derision, mockery, or jest. For example, "For Brutus is an honorable man, /So are they all, all honorable men."

isocolon: a figure of speech comprising a type of parallelism in which similarly structured elements have the same length of syllables and words. For example, "Was ever woman in this humor wooed? /Was ever woman in this humor won?"

measure: in scansion, a synonym for an iamb or one of its variant units, including the trochee, anapaest, amphibrach, spondee, and pyrrhic. Also called a *foot*.

medial truncation: a line of verse in which a single stressed syllable occurs within the line, after punctuation. For example: "And so all yours. O, these naughty times."

metaphor: a figure of speech containing an implied comparison, in which a word or phrase ordinarily and primarily used of one thing is applied to another; a comparison between two unlike things that does not use the words *like* or *as*. For example, "Life's but a walking shadow, a poor player . . ."

meter: any specific form of poetic rhythm, its kind being determined by the character and number of syllables of which it consists.

metonymy: a figure of speech characterized by the reference to something or someone by one of its attributes. For example, "With hard, bright steel, and hearts harder than steel."

monologue: any speech spoken by a character in a play. For our purposes in this book, it refers specifically to speeches that are directed to a character or characters who are onstage with the speaker and who are also listening intently to what is being said to them. This is to differentiate such speeches from *soliloquies*, in which the actor is alone onstage.

motivation: that which "moves" or induces a person to act in a certain way.

objective: something aimed at or striven for. In order for a soliloquy to be effective, for example, the actor must have an objective—a reason or need to speak the words.

obstacle: anything that gets in the way or hinders; an impediment, obstruction, or hindrance. Actors must determine what obstacles are hindering their characters from getting what they want.

OED: acronym for the *Oxford English Dictionary*. The OED defines nearly every word ever used in the English language as well as how definitions of a word have changed over time.

onomatopoeia: a figure of speech characterized by the use of words whose sound echoes the sense. For example, "hum", "murmur", "twinkle"

operative words: "key" words that carry the imagery, meaning, and/or the emotion of a passage. In Shakespeare's dialogue, these words must be emphasized over other words in a phrase, clause, sentence, and/or paragraph. Operative words often include nouns, possessive nouns, verbs of action, adjectives and adverbs.

oxymoron: a figure of speech characterized by the combining of two normally opposite or contradictory terms. For example, "Beautiful tyrant! Fiend angelical!"
pace: when speaking, the rate of speed given to a sound, syllable, word, or phrase.
parallelism: a figure of speech that entails recurring syntactical similarity. In this figure, words, phrases, or clauses are structured similarly. For example, "What place? What time? What form? What likelihood?"
paraphrase: from a Greek word meaning "to tell the same thing in other words," (noun) an expression in other words, usually fuller and clearer, of the sense of any passage or text; (verb) to express the meaning of a word, phrase, passage, or work by using other words, usually with the object of fuller and clearer exposition.
parenthesis: a figure of speech characterized by the insertion of a word or phrase within a sentence that interrupts the normal syntactical flow. For example, "My gravity, /Wherein (let no man hear me) I take pride, Could I, with boot, change for an idle plume,"
paronomasia: a type of pun that involves words that sound alike but that differ in meaning. For example, "In the reproof of chance/ Lies the true proof of men."
periphrasis: a figure of speech characterized by the use of a proper name for qualities associated with that name or the use of a descriptive word or phrase for a proper name. For example, "Discard, bully Hercules, cashier;"
personalize: to apply to a particular person, especially to oneself. To render personal.
personification: a figure of speech that involves referring to abstractions or inanimate objects as though they had human attributes.
pitch: the tone of the voice in speaking.
poetry: the art or work of the poet.
polyptoton: a figure of speech characterized by the repetition of words that are derived from the same root. For example, "More sinned against than sinning."
polysyndeton: a figure of speech characterized by the use of many conjunctions between clauses. For example, "How I would make him fawn, and beg, and seek, / And wait the season."
prose: speech or writing without rhythmic structure.
pun: figures that play on words. Two types of puns are *antanaclasis* and *paronomasia*.
punch: when speaking, the amount of "vocal force" given to a sound, syllable, word, or phrase.
pyrrhic: in scansion, a two-syllable unit in which both syllables are very lightly stressed. For example, "in the," "it is."
quarto: roughly half of Shakespeare's plays were first published in quarto form; so called because the large sheets of paper on which they were printed were folded twice, into quarters. Quartos are individual plays rather than collections.
resolve inflection: a vocal inflection that drops slightly in pitch. It is almost always used to end a thought or action.
rhetoric: the art of using language so as to persuade or influence others; speech or writing expressed in terms calculated to persuade.
rhetorical figure: a form of expression deviating from the normal arrangement or use of words, which is adopted in order to give beauty, variety, or force to a composition. Also known as a *rhetorical device* or *figure of speech*.
rhetorical question: a figure of speech that is a question asked, not for an answer, but for effect or to emphasize a point.
rhyming couplet: two successive lines of verse whose final syllables rhyme.
rhyming verse: language that rhymes, written in iambic pentameter or an accepted variation thereof. Also called *rhymed verse*.
rhythm: The recurrence or repetition of stress, beat, sound, accent, motion, and so forth, usually occurring in a regular or harmonious pattern or manner.

rhythmic pacing: the speed at which the dialogue is spoken. Lightly stressed syllables tend to move more quickly, while heavily stressed syllables tend to move more slowly. Shakespeare would often alternate the rhythmic pacing of his verse dialogue.

rhythmic turbulence: a gap between actual rhythm and metrical expectation, such as when Shakespeare's verse rhythms become heavy and rough rather than smooth. This occurs most often at times of emotional intensity.

rising inflection: a vocal inflection that rises in pitch.

royal "we": the plural term by which kings and queens in Shakespeare's plays often refer to themselves. They may say "we" rather than "I," "us" rather than "me," "our" rather than "my," and "ourself" (not "ourselves") rather than "myself."

run-on line: a line of verse that ends without punctuation or occasionally with weak punctuation (at most a comma). Also called *enjambment* or an *enjambed line*.

scansion: the identification and analysis of stress patterns in poetry. *Scansion* is a noun. The verb is *to scan*.

scheme: in rhetoric, one of two categories of rhetorical figures (the other being *tropes*). Schemes have to do with the unconventional *arrangement* of words in a sentence or phrase.

shared line: a line of verse dialogue that is shared by two or more characters. In such cases, there is rarely a significant pause between speakers.

simile: a figure of speech characterized by an explicit comparison using the words *like* or *as*. For example, "I see you stand like greyhounds in the slips,"

soliloquy: an act or instance of talking to oneself; lines in a drama in which a character reveals his thoughts to the audience, but not to the other characters, by speaking as if to himself.

sonnet: a fourteen-line poem, written in verse, which deals with a single theme or idea.

sound patterns: all the sound qualities—loud and soft, fast and slow, up and down, smooth and rough, strong and weak, pleasant and unpleasant—that characterize spoken speech.

sound texturing: a figure of speech (a scheme) in which sound clusters are chosen and arranged to capture the emotional quality of the sense in sound.

spondee: in scansion, a two-syllable unit in which both syllables are strongly stressed. For example, "downtown" and "time out."

stress: the relative loudness or force of vocal utterance; to lay the stress or emphasis on, to emphasize a word or phrase in speaking.

substitute: to put in place of; a person, event, place, or thing serving or used in place of another.

subtext: the full meaning beneath a character's words. Subtext involves thought, intent, and emotion, all of which are derived from detailed and imaginative attention to given and imaginary circumstances.

sustained inflection: a vocal inflection that neither rises nor drops in pitch. It keeps the "ball in the air" and is used when the speaker is in mid-thought or when a caesura (pause) is either appropriate or necessary for an intake of breath in the middle of a thought or action.

syntax: the arrangement of words (in their appropriate forms) that shows their connection and relation in a sentence.

trochee: in scansion, the rhythmic opposite of the iamb. It is a two-syllable unit that consists of a stressed syllable followed by an unstressed syllable. Words that have this rhythm include "table," "lettuce," and "paper."

trope: in rhetoric, one of two categories of rhetorical figures (the other being *schemes*). Tropes have to do with the unconventional *meaning* of words.

verse: language or literary work written or spoken in meter; poetry, especially with reference to metrical form.

vocal coloring: use of sound patterns to express your character's "emotional opinion" of a word or phrase.

BIBLIOGRAPHY

The Arden Shakespeare. Edited by Richard Proudfoot, et al. London and New York: Methuen, 1997.

Barton, John. *Playing Shakespeare.* London and New York: Methuen, 1984.

Brubaker, E. S. *Shakespeare Aloud.* Privately published, 1977.

Burton, Gideon O. "Silva Rhetoricae." Brigham Young University, 2000 (Online at http://humanities.byu.edu/rhetoric/silva.htm)

Corbett, Edward P. J., and Connors, Robert J. *Classical Rhetoric for the Modern Student.* New York and Oxford: Oxford University Press, 1999.

Jones, Daniel. *Everyman's English Pronouncing Dictionary.* Extensively revised and edited by A. C. Gimson. London and Melbourne: Dent, 1986.

Joseph, Bertram. *Acting Shakespeare.* New York and London: Methuen, 1960.

Joseph, Sister Miriam. *Rhetoric in Shakespeare's Time.* New York: Harcourt Brace, 1967.

Kenyon, John Samuel, and Knott, Thomas Albert. *A Pronouncing Dictionary of American English.* Springfield, Mass.: Merriam-Webster, 1953.

Kökeritz, Helge. *Shakespeare's Names: A Pronouncing Dictionary.* New Haven: Yale University Press, 1966.

Matthews, Dakin. *Shakespeare Spoken Here.* Los Angeles: Andak, 1976.

The New Folger Library Shakespeare. Edited by Barbara A. Mowat and Paul Werstine. New York: Washington Square Press, 1992.

New Swan Shakespeare. Edited by Bernard Lott. Essex: Longman, 1986.

A New Variorum Edition of Shakespeare. Edited by H. H. Furness. New York: Dover Publications, 1963.

Onions, C. T. *A Shakespeare Glossary.* Oxford: Oxford University Press, 1986.

Oxford University, *The Compact Edition of the Oxford English Dictionary,* 2 vols. Oxford: Oxford University Press, 1988.

Papp, Joseph, and Kirkland, Elizabeth. *Shakespeare Alive!* New York: Bantam, 1988.

Partridge, Eric. *Shakespeare's Bawdy,* rev. ed. London: Macmillan, 1955.

The Riverside Shakespeare, 2nd ed. Edited by G. Blakemore Evans. Boston: Houghton Mifflin, 1997.

Schmidt, Alexander. *Shakespeare Lexicon and Quotation Dictionary,* 3rd ed. Revised and enlarged by Gregor Sarrazin. New York: Dover Publications, 1971.

Shakespeare: The Complete Works. Edited by G. B. Harrison. Fort Worth: Harcourt Brace, 1980.

Sipe, Dorothy L. *Shakespeare's Metrics.* New Haven: Yale University Press, 1968.

Spain, Delbert. *Shakespeare Sounded Soundly.* Santa Barbara: Capra Press, 1988.

Tillyard, E. M. W. *The Elizabethan World Picture.* New York: Vintage, 1967.

Vendler, Helen. *The Art of Shakespeare's Sonnets.* Cambridge, MA, and London: The Bellknap Press of Harvard University Press, 1997.

Webster's New World Dictionary, 2nd college ed. Edited by David B. Guralnik. New York: Simon and Schuster, 1984.

Wright, George T. *Shakespeare's Metrical Art.* Berkeley, Los Angeles, and Oxford: University of California Press, 1988.

SUGGESTIONS FOR FURTHER READING

Books on Acting

An Actor Prepares by Constantin Stanislavski, Published by Theatre Arts Books

Acting: The First Six Lessons by Richard Boleslavsky, Published by Theatre Arts Books

Respect for Acting by Uta Hagen, Published by Macmillan

Acting is Believing: A Basic Method by Charles McGaw and Larry D. Clark, Published by Harcourt College Publishers

The Craftsmen of Dionysus by Jerome Rockwood, Published by Applause Books

An Actor Performs by Mel Shapiro, Published by Harcourt College Publishers

Books on Acting Shakespeare

Playing Shakespeare by John Barton, Published by Methuen (Rent the companion videos as well).

Acting Shakespeare by Bertram Joseph, Published by Methuen

Shakespeare Spoken Here by Dakin Matthews, Published by Andak Theatrical Services (While not strictly an acting book, it is an invaluable resource for the actor).

Books on Voice, Speech, and Text

Voice and the Actor by Cicely Berry, Published by Macmillan

The Actor and His Text by Cicely Berry, Published by Scribners

Speak With Distinction by Edith Skinner, Published by Applause Books

Freeing Shakespeare's Voice by Kristin Linklater, Published by Theatre Communications Group

Freeing the Natural Voice by Kristin Linklater, Published by Drama Book Publishers

Books on Scansion and Rhetoric

Shakespeare's Metrical Art by George T. Wright, Published by University of California Press

Shakespeare Aloud by E.S. Brubaker, Published by the Author

Classical Rhetoric for the Modern Student by Edward P.J. Corbett and Robert J. Connors, Published by Oxford University Press

Books on English History

Shakespeare Alive! By Joseph Papp and Elizabeth Kirkland, Published by Bantam Books

The Elizabethan World Picture by E.M.W. Tillyard, Published by Vintage Books

A World Lit Only By Fire: The Medieval Mind and the Renaissance: Portrait of an Age by William Manchester and published by Little Brown

Understanding Shakespeare's England: a companion for the American reader by Jo McMurtry and published by Archon Books

Shakespeare Companion Texts

Shakespeare A to Z: The Essential Reference to His Plays, His Poems, His Life, His Times and More Charles Boyce, David Allen White, Published by Laurel

The Friendly Shakespeare: A Thoroughly Painless Guide to the Bard by Norrie Epstein, Published by Penguin Books

Shakespeare's Bawdy by Eric Partridge, Published by Routeledge

A Shakespeare Companion by F.E. Halliday, Published by Penguin (a Shakespeare encylopedia).

Shakespeare: The Invention of the Human by Harold Bloom, Published by Riverhead Books (A wonderful collection of insightful essays on Shakespeare's plays by a brilliant scholar).

ADDITIONAL INDIVIDUAL EDITIONS OF SHAKESPEARE'S PLAYS

In addition to those mentioned in Chapter 1, I would also like to recommend:

The New Cambridge Shakespeare, Published by Cambridge University Press (Excellent, but a bit pricey.)

The New Variorum Shakespeare, Published by Dover Publications

(Also excellent, but unfortunately out of print. Look for copies in used bookstores. They're easy to spot because of their oversized paperback format and yellow or orange covers, complete with a picture of Shakespeare.)

riverside Shakespear

Lexicon - Two voluine dictionary

The First Folio - written in Shakespears hand writing

Half.com
Half price books